LIGHTS OF CREATION & TRANSCENDENCE

David Birnbaum / Mesorah Matrix Series

www.MesorahMatrix.com

MESORAH MATRIX
VOLUME 3

BIRKAT
KOHANIM

David Birnbaum / Mesorah Matrix Series

LIGHTS OF CREATION & TRANSCENDENCE

EXPLORING HIGHER DIMENSIONS

Editors

David
Birnbaum & Cohen
Martin S.

Associate Editor: **Saul J. Berman**

New Paradigm Matrix®

Published by NEW PARADIGM MATRIX

COPYRIGHT © 2016
NEW PARADIGM MATRIX FOUNDATION

Library of Congress Cataloging-in-Publication Data

Birnbaum, David.

Birkat Kohanim / David Birnbaum and Martin S. Cohen.

ISBN 978-0-9961995-1-3

1. Birkat Kohanim.   2. Jewish Spiritual.   I. Title.

21st CENTURY PUBLISHING

New Paradigm Matrix
att: David Birnbaum
Tower 49
Twelve E. 49th St.,
11th Floor,
New York, NY 10017

www.NewParadigmMatrix.com

Direct contact to Editor-in-Chief

David.Birnbaum.NY@gmail.com

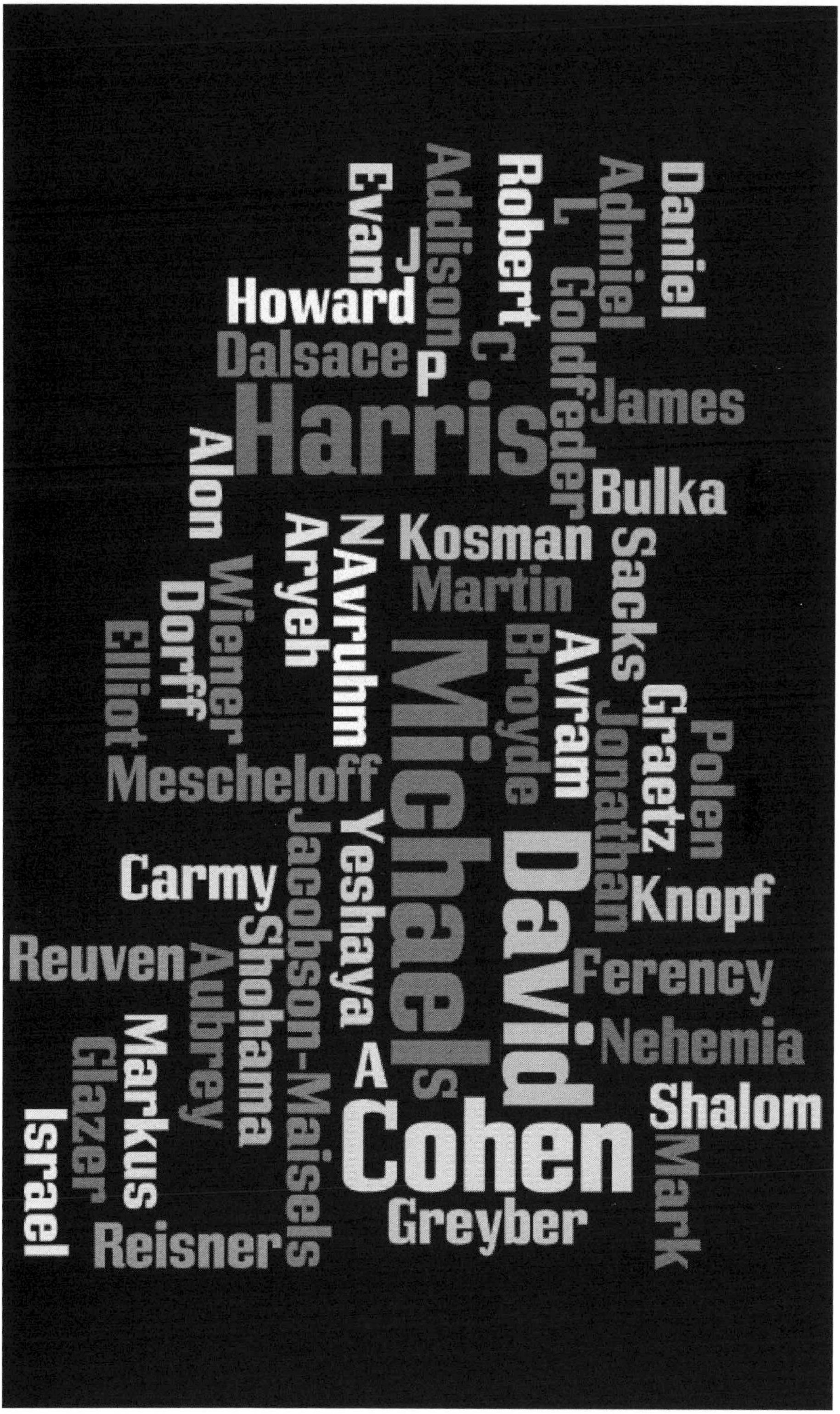

Daniel
Admiel
L
Goldfeder
James
Robert
C
Addison
P
J
Evan
Howard
Dalsace
Harris
A
Alon
Bulka
Kosman
N
Avruhm
Aryeh
Sacks
Martin
Michael
Avram
Broyde
Jonathan
Graetz
Polen
Wiener
Dorff
Elliot
Mescheloff
Yeshaya
Jacobson-Maisels
Carmy
Shohama
Reuven
A
Aubrey
Markus
Glazer
Israel
David
Knopf
Ferency
Nehemia
Shalom
Mark
S
A
Cohen
Greyber
Reisner

Birkat Kohanim

The Priestly Blessing

David Birnbaum and Martin S. Cohen

Editors

NEW PARADIGM MATRIX

www.NewParadigmMatrix.com

David Birnbaum & Martin S. Cohen

Birkat Kohanim

The Priestly Blessing

with essays by

Howard Avruhm Addison, Michael J. Broyde & Mark Goldfeder,
Reuven P. Bulka, Shalom Carmy, Aryeh Cohen, Martin S. Cohen,
Yeshaya Dalsace, Elliot N. Dorff, Alon C. Ferency, Aubrey L. Glazer,
Michael Graetz, Daniel Greyber, Robert A. Harris, James Jacobson-Maisels,
Michael Knopf, Admiel Kosman, David Mescheloff,
Nehemia Polen, Avram Israel Reisner, Jonathan Sacks,
and Shohama Harris Wiener & David Evan Markus

Saul J. Berman
Associate Editor

New Paradigm Matrix Publishing
New York
2016

21st CENTURY PUBLISHING

From the Editor-in-Chief

May 10, 2016

It is a privilege to be serving as Editor-in-Chief of this unique
10-theme series. I am honored to be working with world-class
editors Benjamin Blech, Martin S. Cohen, Saul J. Berman, and
Shalom Carmy.

It is our hope and prayer that the series be a catalyst for intellectual
and spiritual expansion – as well as a unifying force both for our
people as well as for individuals of good will globally.

Sincerely,

David Birnbaum

דוד אריה בן אברהם יעקב הלוי   אייר 2 5776

Mesorah Matrix series

jewish thought & spirituality

10-theme

10-volume

200+ original essays

150+ global thought leaders

a decade-long unified endeavor

genre: *applied scholarship*

www.MesorahMatrix.com

New Paradigm Matrix™

21st CENTURY PUBLISHING

Mesorah Matrix series

A POTENTIALLY ICONIC LEGACY SERIES
FOR THE 21ST CENTURY

10-VOLUME SERIES……200+ ESSAYS……A GLOBAL EFFORT

150+ ESSAYISTS….SPANNING THE WORLD'S TOP JEWISH THOUGHT LEADERS

A DYNAMIC CONTEMPORARY GLOBE-SPANING ENDEAVOR AND COLLECTION

ESSAYISTS COVER A VERY WIDE SPECTRUM OF JUDAISM:

THE COMPLETE SERIES TO DATE IS AVAILABLE ON-LINE GRATIS
IN FLIP-BOOK FORM……AND DOWNLOAD-ABLE GRATIS
+
AVAILABLE IN SOFTCOVER VIA AMAZON
+
AVAILABLE IN E-BOOK FORM VIA VARIOUS MODALITIES

A UNIQUE STUDY AND REFERENCE TOOL FOR CLERGY, ACADEMICS, STUDENTS & LAY INTELLIGENSIA

A STELLAR CORE COURSE OF STUDY – WHETHER FOR ONE SEMESTER OR MULTI-YEAR

AND... AS AN UNINTENDED CONSEQUENCE, THE SERIES HAS
BROKEN DOWN BARRIERS - AND SERVED AS A FORCE-MULTIPLIER –
IN UNIFYING THE JEWISH PEOPLE

IN DEPTH & BREADTH……SCOPE & SPECTRUM
A LANDMARK SERIES
UNIQUE ACROSS THE 3,500+ YEAR SPAN OF JEWISH HISTORY

a unique, timeless and potentially multi-semester

Contemporary Jewish Thought

Course Text

a *sui generis* series • all original essays • broad spectrum authorship

a potentially iconic Jewish resource

Am ha-Sefer

This New Paradigm Matrix work
is available via multiple modalities:

amazon: www.AmazonX1000.com

eBooks: www.eReader1000.com

online: www.MesorahMatrix.com

contact: NPM1000@yahoo.com

The ten volumes of the Mesorah Matrix series amount to a contemporary encyclopedia of the best of traditional and new creative thinking on the central issues of Jewish Spirituality for the 21st century. People grappling with the place of truth, personal virtues and social values in their lives, will find multiple essays which challenge them to grow intellectually and spiritually in their Jewish identity. The ideas are all deeply rooted in Jewish texts in ways that enlighten the early texts and brighten the path into the future of the Jewish People.

- Rabbi Saul Berman
  Yeshiva University
  Chanukah, 2018

About the Editors

Martin S. Cohen has been a Senior Editor of the inter-denominational Mesorah Matrix series since 2012.

From 2000-2014, he served as Chairman of the Editorial Board of the quarterly journal *Conservative Judaism*, which was published under the joint auspices of the Jewish Theological Seminary and the Rabbinical Assembly.

Rabbi Cohen also served as the senior editor of *The Observant Life*, a landmark compendium of Jewish law and custom published by the Rabbinical Assembly in 2012.

His weekly blog can be viewed at www.TheRuminativeRabbi.blogspot.com. He has served as rabbi of the Shelter Rock Jewish Center in Roslyn, New York, since 2002.

Rabbi Cohen was educated at the City University of New York and at the Jewish Theological Seminary, where he was ordained a rabbi and received his Ph.D. in Ancient Judaism. He is the recipient of fellowships at the Hebrew University in Jerusalem in 1983 and Harvard University in 1993.

Martin Cohen has taught at Hunter College, the Jewish Theological Seminary, the Institute for Jewish Studies of the University of Heidelberg, as well as at the University of British Columbia and the Vancouver School of Theology.

His published works include *The Boy on the Door on the Ox* (2008) and *Our Haven and Our Strength: A Translation and Commentary on the Book of Psalms* (2004), as well as four novels and four books of essays.

Rabbi Cohen is currently writing a translation and commentary on the Torah and the Five Megillot.

MARTIN S. COHEN MAJOR WORKS

As Senior Editor

Mesorah Matrix series 2012 - present

Conservative Judaism 2000 - 2014

The Observant Life 2012

As Author (Non-Fiction)

Travels on the Private Zodiac: Reflections on Jewish Life, Ritual and Spirituality (1995)

In Pursuit of Wholeness: The Search for Spiritual Integrity in a Delusional World (1996)

Travels on the Road Not Taken: Towards a Bible-Based Theology of Jewish Spirituality (1997)

Sefer Ha-ikarim Li-z'maneinu (2000)

Our Haven and Our Strength: The Book of Psalms (2004)

Siddur Tzur Yisrael (2005)

Zot Nechamati for the House of Mourning (2006)

Riding the River of Peace (2007)

The Boy on the Door on the Ox (2008)

As Author (Fiction)

The Truth About Marvin Kalish (1992)

Light from Dead Stars (1996)

The Sword of Goliath (1998)

Heads You Lose (2002)

About the Editors

David Birnbaum is a philosophical writer, historical chronicler and *conceptual theorist*. His first work *God and Evil* (KTAV, 1988) is considered by many to be a breakthrough *modern day classic* in the field of theodicy. See God-And-Evil.com.

Editor-in-Chief Birnbaum is known globally as "the architect of Potentialism Theory" – a unified philosophy/cosmology/metaphysics. The paradigm-challenging theory (see ParadigmChallenge.com) is delineated in Birnbaum's 3-volume *Summa Metaphysica* series (1988, 2005, 2014). See Philosophy1000.com.

A riposte to *Summa Theologica* of (St.) Thomas Aquinas, the Birnbaum treatise challenges both the mainstream Western philosophy of Aristotelianism and the well propped-up British/atheistic cosmology of Randomness. See Potentialism Theory.com.

The focus of 150+ reviews/articles, Summa Metaphysica has been an assigned Course Text at over 15 institutions of higher learning globally. See SummaCoverage.com.

Summa Metaphysica was the focus of an international academic conference on Science & Religion in April 16-19 2012 (see Conference1000.com). The work has been very widely covered globally. See RewindSumma.com.

David Birnbaum is the Editor-in-Chief of the *Mesorah Matrix* series on Jewish thought and spirituality. The *sui generis* series spans 10-volumes and 10 themes. The entire series is comprised of 200+ specially commissioned original pieces from 150-180 global Jewish thought leader essayists. See Mesorah1000.com.

In the history realm, David Birnbaum is the author/chronicler of the 2-volume *The Crucifixion – of the Jews*, and of the 7-volume *Jews, Church & Civilization*. His Crucifixion series, in particular, traces a direct trajectory from the Canonical Gospels in the First Century to Auschwitz in the Twentieth. See History1000.com.

David Birnbaum has served on the faculty of the New School for Social Research in Manhattan. He is a graduate of Yeshiva University High School (Manhattan), CCNY (City College of New York) and Harvard. His commentary blog is www.ManhattanObserver.com.

DAVID BIRNBAUM MAJOR WORKS

As Author

4-volume *Summa Metaphysica** (www.philosophy1000.com)

2-volume *The Crucifixion* (www.crucifixion1000.com)

7-volume *Jews, Church & Civilization* (www.civilization1000.com)

As Editor-in-Chief

10-volume *Mesorah Matrix* (www.mesorah1000.com)

As Conceptualizer

3-volume *Summa Spinoffs* (www.Spinoffs1000.com)

8-volume *Potentialism Theory* via Graphic-Narrative
(www.TheoryGraphics1000.com)

As Commentator

www.ManhattanObserver.com

YouTube channels

Summa Metaphysica

Mesorah Matrix

*

Summa I: Religious Man / God and Evil
Summa II: Spiritual Man / God and Good
Summa III: Secular Man / The Transcendent Dynamic
Summa IV: Quantum Man / Morphed Cosmic Order

DAVID BIRNBAUM MAJOR WORKS

Summa Metaphysica series

presenting new paradigm
Potentialism Theory
a universal, unified, seamless & fully-integrated
overarching philosophy

www.SummaMetaphysica.com

Summa I:
Religious Man: God and Evil: focus: *theodicy & eternal origins* [1988]**

Summa II:
Spiritual Man: God and Good: focus: *metaphysics & teleology* [2005]

Summa III:
Secular Man: The Transcendent Dynamic: focus: *cosmology & evolution* [2014]

Summa IV:
Quantum Man: Morphed Cosmic Order: focus: *quantum-potential* [2020]

see also secondary site PotentialismTheory.com

see also: RewindSumma.com 222+ panel Scroll-Down tour

YouTube Channel: Summa Metaphysica

see also Supplement: Articles on Summa
(only online - on www.SummaMetaphysica.com)

** see also: www.GodOfPotential.com

** see special YouTube channel: www.UnifyingScienceSpirituality.com

www.BirnbaumAcademic.com

www.David1000.com

www.Major1000.com

Birkat Kohanim

The Priestly Blessing
(Numbers 6:22-27)

וַיְדַבֵּר יְיָ אֶל־מֹשֶׁה לֵּאמֹר:

דַּבֵּר אֶל־אַהֲרֹן וְאֶל־בָּנָיו לֵאמֹר

כֹּה תְבָרֲכוּ אֶת־בְּנֵי יִשְׂרָאֵל אָמוֹר לָהֶם:

יְבָרֶכְךָ יְיָ וְיִשְׁמְרֶךָ:

יָאֵר יְיָ ׀ פָּנָיו אֵלֶיךָ וִיחֻנֶּךָּ:

יִשָּׂא יְיָ ׀ פָּנָיו אֵלֶיךָ וְיָשֵׂם לְךָ שָׁלוֹם:

וְשָׂמוּ אֶת־שְׁמִי עַל־בְּנֵי יִשְׂרָאֵל וַאֲנִי אֲבָרֲכֵם:

²²The Eternal spoke to Moses saying:
²³"Speak to Aaron and to his sons saying,
'Thus shall you bless the Israelites. Say to them,
²⁴May the Eternal bless you and guard you.
²⁵May the Eternal cast the light of His face upon you and be gracious to you.
²⁶May the Eternal lift His face up in your direction and set peace upon you.'
²⁷And so shall they set My name upon the Israelites so that I Myself bless them."

Birkat Kohanim

TABLE OF CONTENTS

where human beings are free agents but are constrained, by the laws of nature, by the freedom of others, by God's freedom, by the self-limitation that is the substance of free choice, and by one's own personality.

A Priestly Blessing of Love and the Question of Pure Consciousness in Judaism
AUBREY L. GLAZER

This essay explores precisely that subtle shift in our awareness from the "thinking I"—that bold declaration of modernity within Rene Descartes' *cogito ergo sum,* "I think therefore I am"—which creates our perception of reality as moderns, to a pure consciousness of love, which permeates the entire constitution of self and universe. The author argues that Judaism provides avenues for glimpsing such transformation of consciousness through liturgical moments like the Priestly Blessing.

What's In a Blessing?
Rashi and the Priestly Benediction of Numbers 6:22–27
ROBERT A. HARRIS

Rashi offers one of the foundational Jewish treatments of this prominent biblical passage. While not thinking of "blessing" in the abstract, Rashi roots his understanding primarily in ancient rabbinic midrash and presents that meaning in a clear-flowing and lucid prose. Moreover, in a departure from age-old rabbinic modalities of conveying meaning, Rashi casts his learning in what was for European Jewry a completely new genre of literature: the line-by-line commentary.

Birkat Kohanim in the *S'fat Emet*
NEHEMIA POLEN

As understood by the S'fat Emet, Rabbi Yehudah Aryeh Leib Alter (1847–1905), the Priestly Blessing does not promise a good in the sense of an advantage or commodity, whether material or spiritual. The Priestly Blessing is more solicitation than transmission. Since all that is offered is a mode of perception, the blesser cannot convey what he or she does not already have. Even more arrestingly, the blesser cannot bestow what the receiver does not already have, within, waiting to be awakened and cultivated.

Preface

Martin S. Cohen

Given the prominence of prayer in traditional Jewish life, it is surprising to note how few prayers the Torah actually ordains be recited by the pious as part of their ongoing effort to foster a relationship with the Divine. Indeed, some of the most famous of all Jewish prayers that do have their origin in Scripture are not presented as liturgical texts in that context at all. (The Shema, for example, the confession of faith par excellence which rabbinic tradition ordains be recited twice daily, appears in the Bible as part of a larger literary unit with no indication that it is intended to be featured prominently in the prayer lives of the faithful.) Other prayer texts are presented *in situ* as features of an ongoing narrative—for example, the prayer of Damesek Eliezer that he find a wife for his master's son (Genesis 24:12–14) or Moses' prayer that Miriam be healed of her skin disease (Numbers 12:13)—have not come to be a part of the fixed Jewish liturgical tradition. And still others, like the prayer ordained for recitation by farmers presenting their first fruits at the sanctuary (Deuteronomy 26:3–10), are presented as liturgical texts to be recited on a specific occasion, but with no hint that they may licitly be recited in circumstances other than the ones specifically ordained by Scripture.

In its own category, however, is the text found at Numbers 6:24–27 and specifically not part of any ongoing narrative. There, Scripture presents God as instructing Moses formally to inform his brother Aaron and the latter's sons that, in blessing the Israelites, they may not use words of their own devising but must use the specific formula provided. Perhaps this is meant as an after-the-fact response to the story presented at Leviticus 9:22 in which Aaron, following the elaborate investiture ceremony of his sons as priests, is depicted as offering a blessing of his own devising. That text reads laconically that "Aaron then raised his hand toward the people and blessed them," but without giving the text of his apparently off-the-cuff effort. Are we to understand, then, that God—eager to prevent any more extemporized prayer on the part of a priesthood that is intended to be highly regulated—is responding to Aaron's spontaneous blessing with a clear statement that future efforts to bless the people meaningfully and substantively must henceforth use a pre-ordained formula? Certainly, one *could* read the text that way!

But no amount of careful scriptural study would lead any reader to imagine how this text, the recitation of which is unambiguously presented in Numbers specifically as a priestly prerogative, would eventually become a hallmark of Jewish liturgical usage regularly recited in non-priestly contexts by Jews other than the descendants of Aaron, both as part of synagogue worship and in other contexts as well. And yet the fifteen words of the so-called Priestly Blessing, called Birkat Kohanim in Hebrew, have indeed become one of the most often-cited and recited Jewish prayer formularies, its use not restricted even in the most punctiliously observant circles to Aaron's priestly descendants.

The volume you are holding in your hands presents the efforts of twenty-three authors to explicate this enigmatic text. They are different in many ways, our authors, but they are united in terms of the estimation in which they hold the ancient idea that the ideal way to delve into Jewishness itself is through the informed, creative, and intellectually rigorous study of its most sacred texts. As you will see, they take many different approaches to the text of Birkat Kohanim. Some focus their thinking on the text as a feature of later liturgy, while others work primarily on the text as part of the biblical heritage of Israel. Still others choose to analyze the text primarily through a rabbinic lens, taking later rabbinic approaches as the basis for their interpretive efforts. Taken all together, these essays will provide readers with a window into a text that, although it could hardly be more brief in terms of its word-count, has evolved into one of the truly foundational texts of Jewish liturgy—and, indeed, of Jewish life. And that, surely, will be its own reward for all who wish to understand Judaism on its own merits, and through the contemplation of its most basic texts.

Unless otherwise indicated, all translations here are the authors' own work; biblical translations referencing "NJPS" refer to the complete translation of Scripture published under the title *Tanakh: The Holy Scriptures* by the Jewish Publication Society in Philadelphia in 1985.

I am grateful to all of our authors for their willingness to participate in this project. And, of course, I am equally grateful to David Birnbaum and Benjamin Blech, the other senior editors of the Mesorah Matrix series, and to Saul J. Berman, our associate editor. And, of course, I am grateful to you, our readers, as well; it is your enthusiasm for this project, and particularly your willingness to support our effort to revitalize the essay as a premiere vehicle of sophisticated, thoughtful Jewish expression, that has encouraged us in our efforts and given us the confidence to persevere with this landmark project. I am grateful to you all.

In closing, I wish to acknowledge the men and women of the Shelter Rock Jewish Center in Roslyn, New York, whom I am privileged to serve as their spiritual leader. Understanding that part and parcel of my sense of what it means for me personally to be a rabbi is writing (as well as editing and publishing the work of others), my congregants have come to accept these complicated book projects I keep taking on as part of who I am and what I do. For their solicitude and their support, I feel deeply beholden and very, very grateful.

Martin S. Cohen
Roslyn, New York
June 19, 2015 / 2 Tammuz 5775

Abbreviations

A.T. - *Arbaah Turim*

B. - Babylonian Talmud

M. - Mishnah

M.T. - *Mishneh Torah*

T. - Tosefta

Y. - Yerushalmi

A Note from the Editors

Every effort has been made to retain a good level of consistency between the essays that appear here in terms of the translation and transliteration of Hebrew. Many of our decisions have, needs be, been arbitrary, but we have done our best to create a book that will be as accessible to newcomers to the study of Judaism as it is inspiring to cognoscenti. The four-letter name of God, left unpronounced by pious Jews as a sign of reverence, is mostly rendered in this volume as "the Eternal" or "the Eternal One." Other divine names are either transliterated or translated to create in English something akin to the way the text reads in Hebrew. All translations are their authors' unless otherwise indicated.

Essays

The Priestly Blessings: Protection, Grace, and Peace

Jonathan Sacks

In Jerusalem, looking down on Israel's Parliament, the Knesset, is a magnificent building: the Israel Museum. It houses an extraordinary array of exhibits, drawn from almost every age, place, and culture. There are items from the entire history and geography of the Diaspora. There is a large collection of idols and graven images from ancient Canaan, reminding us in the most vivid way of what our ancestors broke away from. But in many ways the most remarkable exhibit is not a work of art, nor is it a piece of exquisite workmanship. It is a tiny fragment of silver foil containing a mere fifteen words.

What makes it special is that it is the oldest surviving fragment of biblical literature, some 2700 years old. It comes from the era of the First Temple, built by King Solomon. It is so old that it is not written in the Hebrew alphabet as we recognize it today, which dates from the Babylonian Exile, but rather in the ancient Semitic script, the first alphabet known to humanity.

What is it that has survived twenty-seven centuries, half the history of civilization? By a wonderful stroke of fate, it contains perhaps the oldest liturgical formula still in regular use: the Priestly Blessings set out in the Torah portion called *Naso* in the Book of Numbers. Why someone wrote them down on this piece of foil, it is impossible to say, though it is likely that it was used as what is called in Hebrew a *kamei·a*—a good luck charm, an amulet that brings blessing to its bearer. I find it intensely moving that these words, first said so long ago, still stay with us in this physical form as well as in our prayers.

The Torah sets out the blessings in a simple passage found at Numbers 6:23–27:

The Eternal said to Moses, "Tell Aaron and his sons, 'This is how you are to bless the Israelites. Say to them:

> The Eternal bless you and keep you;
> the Eternal make His face shine upon you and be gracious to you;
> the Eternal turn His face toward you and give you peace.'
So they will put My name on the Israelites, and I will bless them."

The literary structure is precise. In the original Hebrew, the first line has three words; the second, five; and the third, seven. (As I have pointed out elsewhere, these prime numbers have special significance throughout the Mosaic books: three-, five- and seven-fold repetitions always signify a key word).[1] Equally precisely, the first has fifteen (3×5) letters, the second has twenty (4×5) letters, and the third has twenty-five (5×5) letters.

What is the meaning of these blessings?

"The Eternal bless you and keep you." Blessing in the Mosaic books always means material blessing:

So if you faithfully obey the commands I am giving you today—to love the Eternal your God and to serve Him with all your heart and with all your soul—then I will send rain in your land in its season, both autumn and spring rains, so that you may gather in your grain, new wine, and oil. I will provide grass in the fields for your cattle, and you will eat and be satisfied. (Deuteronomy 11:13–15)

Against the idea basic to many other faith systems—which embrace poverty, asceticism, or other forms of self-denial—in Judaism, the world as God's creation is fundamentally good. Religion is neither otherworldly nor anti-worldly. It is precisely in the physical world that God's blessings are to be found.

But material blessings can sometimes dull our sensitivities toward God. The great irony is that when we have most to thank God for, often we express our thanks the least vigorously. We tend to remember God in times of crisis rather than in eras of prosperity and peace:

> When you have eaten and are satisfied, praise the Eternal your God for the good land He has given you. Be careful that you do not forget the Eternal your God, failing to observe His commands, His laws, and His decrees that I am giving you this day. Otherwise, when you eat and are satisfied, when you build fine houses and settle down, and when your herds and flocks grow large and your silver and gold increase and all you have is multiplied, then your heart will become proud and you will forget the Eternal your God, who brought you out of Egypt, out of the land of slavery....You may say to yourself, "My power and the strength of my hands have produced this wealth for me." (Deuteronomy 8:10–17)

More than any other factor, it is this danger that has led to the decline and fall of civilizations. In the early, pioneering years, people are lifted by a collective vision and energy. But as they become affluent, they begin to lose the very qualities that made earlier generations great. They become less motivated by ideals than by the pursuit of pleasure. They think less of others, more of themselves. They begin to be deaf and blind to those in need. They become, in a word, decadent. What happens to nations happens also to individuals and families.

Hence the first blessing, "May the Eternal keep you," means: May God protect you from the blessing turning into a curse.

The second blessing says, "May the Eternal make His face shine upon you and be gracious to you." The word "grace" has such strong Christian associations that we sometimes forget its centrality to Judaism. What is "grace"?

Judaism is a religion of intellect: of study, questioning, ideas, argument, and the life of the mind. The historian Paul Johnson described Rabbinic Judaism as an "ancient and highly efficient social machine for the production of intellectuals."[2] Yet the Book of Proverbs says:

> Let kindness and truth not leave you. Bind them around your throat; inscribe them on the tablet of your heart. Then you will find grace and good intellect in the eyes of the Eternal and humankind. (Proverbs 3:3-4)

Grace (*hein*) takes precedence over good intellect (*seikhel tov*).

In Kaddish D'rabbanan, the prayer we say after studying a rabbinic text, we pray for spiritual leaders who have "grace, lovingkindness, and compassion." Once again, the power of intellect is secondary to the personal qualities of sensitivity and graciousness. Grace is that quality which sees the best in others and seeks the best for others. It is a combination of gentleness and generosity.

The second priestly blessing is that God may "make His face shine on you," meaning: may God's presence be evident in you. May God leave a visible trace of the Divine Being on the face you show to others. How is that presence to be recognized? Not in severity, remoteness, or austerity, but rather in the gentle smile that speaks to what Lincoln in 1861 called, in the concluding words of his First Inaugural Address, "the better angels of our nature." That is grace.

"May the Eternal turn His face toward you and give you peace." To make peace in the world we must be at peace with ourselves. To be at peace with ourselves we must know that we are unconditionally valued. That does not often happen. People value us for what we can give to them. That is conditional value, what the sages called "love that is dependent on a cause" (Pirkei Avot 5:16). God values us unconditionally. We are here because the Almighty wanted us to be. Our very existence testifies to divine love. Unlike others, God never gives up on us. God rejects no one and never loses faith, however many times we fail. When we fall, God lifts us—believing in us more than we believe in ourselves.

You are in a crowd. In the distance you see someone you recognize. This person is well known. You met him once, briefly. Did you make an impression on him? Does he remember you? Does he know who you are? Briefly your eyes touch. From the distance, he smiles at you. Yes, he remembers you; he knows who you are, he is pleased you are here, and by his eye contact and his smile he communicates these things to you. You are relieved, lifted. You are at peace with yourself. You are not merely an anonymous face in a crowd. Your basic worth has in some way been affirmed. That, in human terms, is the meaning of "May the Eternal turn His face toward you and give you peace."

We speak of "seeking recognition." It is a telling phrase. Even more than power or wealth or success or fame, we long for what we believe these things will give us: standing in the eyes of others, respect, esteem, honor, worth. We can dedicate a lifetime to this search, but it is not a good one. People do not confer respect for the right reasons. They follow politicians who pander to their worst instincts. They feel the charisma of pure power. They flatter the wealthy. They are like moths to the flame of fame.

The recognition that counts is our reflection in the eyes of God. God loves us for what we are and what we could become. God loves the good in us, not the successful or persuasive or charismatic. God, knowing us from within, ignores the image we try to project. God's is the voice within us that says, "With Me, you do not have to pretend. I know you. I knew you before you were born. I know you because

I made you, and I made you because I need you—or more precisely, because the world needs you. There is a task only you can do. Now, therefore, be strong and do it. You need not seek praise; you shall not be deflected by criticism; for I will be with you every step of the way. When you feel most alone, that is when I will be closest." That is making eye-contact with God. It is the meaning of the third blessing: "May the Eternal turn His face toward you and give you peace."

The most profound element of the blessing, however, lies in the concluding sentence: "So they will put my name on the Israelites, and I will bless them."

In the ancient world, magi, oracles, and religious virtuosi were held to have the power of blessing. They were able to invoke supernatural forces. This is the meaning of what Balak, king of Moab, says to the pagan prophet Balaam:

> A people has come out of Egypt; they cover the face of the land and have settled next to me. Now come and put a curse on these people, because they are too powerful for me. Perhaps then I will be able to defeat them and drive them out of the country. For I know that those you bless are blessed, and those you curse are cursed. (Numbers 22:5–6)

The biblical story of Balaam is a satire on this idea. Balaam's contemporaries, and perhaps he himself, believed that blessing or curse lay within the power of the holy person. Nothing arouses the ridicule of the Bible more than self-importance. Balaam is made to see that his own donkey has greater powers of spiritual insight than he does. It is not the person who has power over God; it is God who has the power to reveal the Divine Self to the person—and if God so chooses, that gift can be given to a donkey rather than to an esteemed religious figure. Holiness is not (though it is often confused with) self-importance. True holiness is transparency to the Divine.

This is the meaning of "So they will put My name on the Israelites, and I will bless them." It is not the priests who bless the people, but God. In themselves, they have no power. They are intermediaries, channels through which God's blessing flows. An ancient midrash says:[3]

> The house of Israel said to the blessed Holy One: "Ruler of the universe, You order the priests to bless us? We need only Your blessing. Look down from Your holy habitation and bless Your people." The blessed Holy One replied to them, "Though I ordered the priests to bless you, I will stand together with them and bless you."

It is not the priests who bless the people. Rather, it is through them that God blesses the people.

Finally, why was it the priests who were chosen to be vehicles of God's blessing? One reason is self-evident: the entire being of the priests was within the precincts of the holy; they were the intermediaries between the people and God. But there is another reason offered by the commentators. Apparently prosaic, it has nonetheless profound wisdom.

The priests had no share in the land. Unlike the rest of Israelites, they had no fields or farms, no businesses, no source of income through the work of their hands. Instead, they were dependent on the gifts of the people. The Israelites gave them a portion of the harvest called *t'rumah*, and they received other statutory gifts as well. So when the Israelites prospered as a whole, the priests benefitted. They had a direct interest in the prosperity of the nation. More than anyone else, the priests were dependent on the welfare of others. They were able to bless the people with a full heart, because if others were favored, they would they be as well.

This may seem like an appeal to self-interest precisely where it does not belong, in the sphere of the holy, the sacrosanct, the Temple. Yet the genius of Judaism is that it is not predicated on superhuman virtue. It is not addressed to angels or saints, but to human beings in all our fallibility. Though its ideals are surpassingly high, its psychology is realistic throughout.

It was Adam Smith in his masterwork, *The Wealth of Nations*, who pointed out that self-interest, when properly channelled, leads to the welfare of all. Smith himself sensed that there was something religious about this, and he gave it a quasi-religious name. He called it the "invisible hand," which was as near as he could come to speaking about divine providence—the mysterious yet benign way in which, though each of us may be concerned about our own narrow welfare, we are part of something larger than ourselves in ways we cannot always understand.[4] Our separate strands are part of a larger pattern.

The great Spanish poet and philosopher Yehudah Halevi noted that almost all our prayers are in the plural.[5] We do not pray that God should give *me* something; we pray that God should give *us* something: "Bless us, O our Father, all of us together." There is a spirit of community written into the liturgy. We do not ask our God to listen to the prayers of individuals, but rather to those of the Jewish people as a whole. When Moses prayed on behalf of the people, he was answered. When he prayed for himself—to be allowed to enter the Promised Land—he was not.

Halevi adds that there is nothing mystical in this idea. He explains it with the following analogy. Imagine, he said, trying to defend your house against enemies. There are two ways of doing so. One is to build a wall around the house. The other is to combine with neighbors and build a wall around the town. The former is more expensive and offers less protection. To act with others for everyone is easier and more secure.

So it is, he said, with prayer: if we pray only by ourselves for ourselves, then we rely on our own merits, about which we can never be certain. But when we pray together with the whole community, we combine our merits with theirs. Prayer is like a protective wall, and praying together is more powerful and effective. We do not need superhuman piety—merely enlightened self-interest—to realize that our destinies are interconnected. When we are blessed, we are blessed together. Prayer is community made articulate, when we delete the first-person singular and substitute the first-person plural.

Protection, grace, peace: these are God's blessings, communicated by the priests. We are what we pray for. If you seek to understand a people, look at its prayers. The Jewish people did not ask for wealth or power. They did not hunger after empire. They had no desire to conquer or convert the world. They asked for protection, the right to live true to themselves without fear; for grace, the ability to be an agent for good in others; and peace, that fullness of being in which each of us brings our individual gifts to the common good. That is all our ancestors prayed for, and it is still all we need.

NOTES

[1] See my *Covenant and Conversation: A Weekly Reading of the Jewish Bible* (Jerusalem: Maggid Books, 2009), p. 51.

[2] Paul Johnson, *A History of the Jews* (New York: Harper & Row, 1988), pp. 340–341.

[3] Bemidbar Rabbah 11:2.

[4] Adam Smith, *The Wealth of Nations, Part Two* (New York: P. F. Collier, 1902), p. 160.

[5] See *Kuzari* III 17.

Why the Priestly Blessing Is Not Redundant: Three Relationships with God, Three Distinct Blessings

Elliot N. Dorff

It is presented by the Torah as a blessing created by God: "The Eternal spoke to Moses, saying: Speak to Aaron and his sons, saying, 'Thus shall you bless the people of Israel'" (Numbers 6:22–23). Known as the Priestly Blessing, it is the most widely used blessing among Jews to this day. It is part of the regular daily morning service. In some congregations, on some occasions, it is still the descendants of Aaron, the *kohanim*, who stand in front of the congregation, raise their hands, and recite the Priestly Blessing before the congregation (a practice known in Jewish-American English as dukhening); in others, the person leading services recites it throughout the year. It is with this blessing that parents regularly bless their children on Friday night before reciting Kiddush, the blessing over wine to sanctify the Sabbath. In many congregations, it is also said at weddings and bar- and bat-mitzvah services.

What, though, do the words mean? Unfortunately, this is not clear. What does come through seems repetitious, and the order of the phrases seems to lack all rhyme or reason. Some of the ambiguities are reflected in the variety of ways it is translated in Jewish translations of the Bible and in Jewish prayerbooks, as delineated below. Furthermore, especially at life-cycle events, rabbis and others tend to expand on the words to make the blessing say much more than its words denote. What they add may be beautiful, and maybe even implied in the words themselves, but these expansions add to the confusion of what the blessing actually says.

Here are the three verses, as variously rendered in some translations of the Torah (listed in chronological order):

Original JPS translation (1917):[1]
The LORD bless thee, and keep thee;
The LORD make His face to shine upon thee, and be gracious unto thee;
The LORD lift up His countenance upon thee, and give thee peace.

New JPS translation (1962):[2]
The LORD bless you and keep you!
The LORD deal kindly and graciously with you![3]
The LORD bestow His favor upon you and grant you peace![4]

Everett Fox (1995):[6]
May YHWH bless you and keep you!
May YHWH shine his face upon you and favor you!
May YHWH lift up his face toward you and grant you *shalom*!

Richard Elliott Friedman (2001):[7]
May YHWH bless you and watch over you.
May YHWH make His face shine to you and be gracious to you.
May YHWH raise His face to you and give you peace.

Because the Priestly Blessing is used in the morning service, Jewish prayerbooks translate it as well. In prayer one would expect clarity, even if that comes at the expense of accuracy of translation, but one does not get as much poetic license—and as much intelligibility—as one might expect. The following prayerbook translations are arranged in chronological order of publication:

Morris Silverman, *Sabbath and Festival Prayerbook* (1945):[8]
May the Lord bless thee and keep thee;
May the Lord make His countenance to shine upon thee
and be gracious unto thee;
May the Lord turn His countenance unto thee and give thee peace.

Joseph Hertz, *Daily Prayer Book* (1948, rpt. 1963):[9]
May the Lord bless thee and keep thee;
May the Lord make His face to shine upon thee and be
gracious unto thee;
May the Lord turn His face unto thee and give thee peace.

Philip Birnbaum, *Daily Prayer Book* (1949):[10]
May the Lord bless you and protect you;
May the Lord countenance you and be gracious to you;
May the Lord favor you and grant you peace.

Ben Zion Bokser, *The Prayer Book* (1957):[11]
May the Lord bless you and keep you.
May the Lord cause His Presence to shine upon you and be
gracious unto you.
May the Lord turn with favor unto you and give you peace.

Chaim Stern, *Gates of Prayer* (1975):[12]
The Lord bless you and keep you.
The Lord look kindly upon you and be gracious to you.
The Lord bestow His favor upon you and give you peace.

Nosson Scherman and Meri Zlotowitz, *The Complete Artscroll Siddur* (1984):[13]
May HASHEM bless you and safeguard you.

May HASHEM illuminate His countenance for you and be gracious to you.

May HASHEM turn His countenance to you and establish peace for you.

Jules Harlow, *Siddur Sim Shalom* (1985):[14]
May the Lord bless you and guard you.
May the Lord show you favor and be gracious to you.
May the Lord show you kindness and grant you peace.

Richard N. Levy, *On Wings of Awe* (1985):[15]
May God bless you and protect you.
May the light of God's countenance favor you with enlightenment and grace.
May God's countenance be raised up to you that you may find peace.

In summary, the variations in all these translations are as follows:

May the Eternal [or: God, the Lord, Adonai, YHWH, or HASHEM] bless you and keep [or protect or guard or safeguard] you.

May the Eternal [or: God, the Lord, Adonai, YHWH, or HASHEM] make His face [or: cause the divine Presence] to shine upon [or: lift up His countenance upon, or deal kindly with, or look kindly upon] you [or: show you favor] and be gracious unto you [or: show you favor, or favor you with enlightenment and grace].

May the Eternal [or: God, the Lord, Adonai, YHWH, or HASHEM] favor [or: turn His countenance, or turn His face

upon, or turn with favor unto] you [or: show you kindness]
and grant you *shalom*, peace [or: establish peace for you].
When used in the repetition of the Amidah prayer during Shaḥarit
(the morning service) and Musaf (the additional Amidah that is
recited on Sabbaths and other special days), after each of the three
sentences of blessing the congregation responds with, "So, indeed,
may it be God's will" (or, in some versions of the liturgy, with "Amen"
before or in place of that response). In the Torah, however, there is no
record of a response on the part of the people being blessed.

The blessing consists of three Hebrew sentences—presumably
three separate blessings. The use of similar words or phrases in
several places, though, makes it sound as if it is only one blessing
that is being reiterated. If, on the other hand, they are indeed three
separate blessings, how are they related to each other?

I do not believe that the three lines are repetitive at all, and I think
that there is a very clear order among them. I want to suggest that each
addresses a different situation and is appropriate to its particular context.

The first line speaks of general circumstances. It says: in the
normal times of the relationship between you and God, *may God bless
you* (that is, may God give you all the good things in life—whether
material, intellectual, emotional, communal, or spiritual) *and keep you*
from the bad.

When relations between you and God are especially good, the
second blessing then ensues: *May God smile on you*—which is the
meaning, I believe, behind the concept of the light of God's face
shining upon the blessed individual. And that, in turn, may be the
emotional preparation for the second part of this clause, *and be gracious
to you*—meaning that when God smiles on you, God is prepared to
give you beyond what you deserve.[16] The first clause of this second
blessing may also, though, carry another emotional meaning: that
when the relationship between you and God is good, then *may God*

smile on you—that is, may God be willing to express good feelings toward you so that both you and God can share them. The second blessing, in any case, asks God to be unjustifiably generous to you, both materially and emotionally, when you and God are on good terms.

The third blessing, on the other hand, speaks to a time when you have offended God: in such a case, may God not turn the back of the divine neck (or the divine back itself) to you or otherwise hide God's face from you and punish you by cutting you off from all communication—much as parents do when they send naughty children to their rooms. Instead, *may God turn the divine face toward you*—or, more simply, *may God face you*, taking you back in an act of forgiveness and favor, and *may God make peace with you*, despite your transgressions. In biblical Hebrew, when God is angry with us, God "hides the divine face" from us[17] and thereby cuts off communication with us as an act of punishment.[18] At Jeremiah 23:39, the prophet quotes God as saying, as an expression of divine anger, that "I will cast you away from My face." Conversely, "to lift up one's face" means to face someone in compassion and to grant a favor or show partiality beyond what justice demands or even allows.[19] What the third blessing is really saying is that when you offend God in some way, may God nevertheless show favor to you by not cutting you off but rather turning toward you (i.e., facing you) and making peace with you.

To capture the original intent of this biblical prayer and simultaneously to see its significance, I would translate it this way:

> May the Eternal give you all the good things in life and keep you from the bad.
> [When your relationship with God is especially good,] may the Eternal smile on you and give you beyond what you deserve.

[On the other hand, when you are estranged from God,] may the Eternal face you and make peace with you.

When understood this way, the Priestly Blessing articulates important aspects of the Jewish conception of the relationship between God and us. It also has much to teach us about our own human relationships.

First of all, God is in an abiding and caring relationship with us. The Jewish conception of God is not only as a creative force in nature (such a belief is called "deism"); God is personal, interacting with us on an ongoing basis. (This belief is labelled "theism.") Most of the Founding Fathers of the United States—Washington, Franklin, Jefferson, Madison, and others—were deists, not theists. And, indeed, deism was very popular in the eighteenth century, when it was seen as being more consistent with science—or, at least, easier to justify while maintaining a scientific point of view. After all, if God has a personality and will, then God could presumably interfere with the order of nature at will, undermining the laws of science by creating breaches in those laws (or "miracles"). On the other hand, if God is the force that created nature in the first place and continues to operate in creating new plants, animals, and people, then science and religion are devoted to understanding the same thing, albeit in different ways and with different purposes.[20] Hence, in writing the Declaration of Independence, Jefferson specifically says, "We hold these truths to be self-evident, that all men are created equal, that they are endowed by their Creator [rather than "by God"] with certain unalienable rights…" Jefferson's language suggests clearly that he did not want anyone to think that he or any of the other enlightened signatories of the Declaration were simpletons.

On the other hand, the authors of the biblical texts, the ancient and medieval rabbis, and virtually all Jewish thinkers through the twentieth century (with the exception of Spinoza in the seventeenth century and Mordecai Kaplan in the twentieth) affirmed a form of theism. They did so because they experienced God in personal ways: as caring for us, interacting with us, loving us, commanding us, getting angry with us on occasion, forgiving us, and (in this passage) ordering the descendants of Aaron to bless us in God's name. (A deistic God, as a force, could presumably bless us by creating the world in a particular way that supports us, but such a God could not love us, care for us, or command anyone to do anything, such as commanding Aaron's descendants to bless us.) A theistic God can also be a much more potent model for us, and indeed *imitatio Dei*, emulating God, is what we are supposed to do: "And the Eternal spoke to Moses, saying, 'Speak to the whole Israelite community, and say to them, "You shall be holy, for I the Eternal, your God, am holy"'" (Leviticus 19:1–2).

This ancient text speaks directly to this point:

Rabbi Ḥama, son of Rabbi Ḥanina, said: What is the meaning of the verse, "Follow the Eternal your God" (Deuteronomy 13:5)? Is it possible for a mortal to follow God's Presence? After all, the Torah says, "For the Eternal your God is a consuming fire" (Deuteronomy 4:24). Rather, the verse means to teach us that we should follow the attributes of the blessed Holy One. As God clothes the naked...you should clothe the naked; as the blessed Holy One visited the sick...so too you should visit the sick. The blessed Holy One comforted those who mourned... you too should comfort those who mourn. The blessed Holy One buried the dead...you should also bury the dead.[21]

The perspective articulated in this passage reflects a theistic conception of God, and Jewish tradition did not have trouble justifying this kind of spiritual worldview with science because the rabbis maintained that even though God has the power to interfere with the laws of nature, by and large God chooses not to do so, and thus *olam k'minhago noheig*, "the world goes according to its custom."[22]

Second: God, as understood in the Priestly Blessing, has a sense of justice. God can therefore be angered by our transgressions and can—and will—punish us for them. At the same time, God's justice is not blind or automatic; it is tempered with compassion, born out of the love the Eternal has for us. In this way, God is much like a parent—a metaphor for God used often in the Bible and in Jewish liturgy.[23] Conversely, God's balancing of justice with compassion is a model for human parents—and to know when to punish and when to forgive is indeed a godly trait.

Third: God's relationships with us range the spectrum from unusually close and warm to angry and judgmental. Most of the time God and we are on an even keel, where God assures us of the good things in life and keeps us from the bad. Sometimes, though, things are wonderful between us, and then we get and give beyond what either party normally deserves. And sometimes we hurt each other, and then the important thing is to remember that the relationship is too important to let it founder because of this offense, that both God and we must take the initiative to find ways to face each other and to forgive. The third line of the Priestly Blessing speaks only of God's willingness to repair the relationship in that way, because the priests are offering a blessing to the people that God be willing to reconcile with us, presuming that we always want to reconcile with God; but after the Holocaust, at least some Jews think that we need to face God and make peace with God just as much as we hope that God will do the same for us.

The divine–human relationship, as portrayed in this prayer, is thus an important model for our own relationships with each other. The mark of a good relationship is not that everything is always fine, much less that everything is always ideal. It is rather the ability to live through the highs and lows of life, as well as the even planes that make up most of it—knowing all the while how to support each other in the everyday (the first blessing); how to be especially and undeservedly generous to each other, emotionally and materially, during the hopefully many moments of good feeling (the second blessing); and how to take the responsibility of seeking reconciliation when the relationship falters (the third blessing). That is the substance of good human relations, and it is equally the essence of a close and good relationship with God. On the human level and in the divine–human encounter, "So, indeed, may it be God's will!"

NOTES

[1] Alexander Harkavy, *Holy Scriptures* (Philadelphia: Jewish Publication Society of America, 1917), p. 227; also Joseph Hertz, *Pentateuch and Haftorahs* (London: Soncino Press, 1936, 1960), pp. 595–596. [2] *The Torah* (Philadelphia: Jewish Publication Society, 1962), p. 256; also used in Gunther Plaut, *The Torah* (New York: Union of American Hebrew Congregations, 1974), p. 1064, and Jacob Milgrom, *The JPS Torah Commentary: Numbers* (Philadelphia: Jewish Publication Society, 1990), pp. 51–52.

[3] JPS includes the following footnote here: "Others: 'make his face to shine upon thee and be gracious to thee.'"

[4] JPS includes the following footnote here: "Others: 'lift up His countenance.'"

[5] JPS includes the following footnote here: "Or 'friendship.'"

[6] Everett Fox, *The Five Books of Moses* (New York: Schocken, 1995), p. 687.

[7] Richard Elliott Friedman, *Commentary on the Torah* (San Francisco: HarperSanFrancisco, 2001), pp. 445–446.

[8] New York: Rabbinical Assembly and United Synagogue of America, p. 100.

[9] New York: Bloch Publishing Company, New York: Bloch Publishing Company, p.155. Note that this follows the translation in the 1917 JPS translation and in Hertz *Penateuch and Haftorahs*, quoted above.

[10] New York: Hebrew Publishing Company, p. 96.

[11] New York: Hebrew Publishing Company, p. 522.

[12] New York: Central Conference of American Rabbis, p. 522.

[13] Brooklyn, New York: Mesorah Productions, p. 117.

[14] New York: Rabbinical Assembly and United Synagogue of America, p. 121. Note that in the subsequent edition of *Siddur Sim Shalom for Shabbat and Festivals* (1998), "the Lord" was changed to "Adonai."

[15] Washington, DC: B'nai Brith Hillel Foundation, p. 227.

[16] See Genesis 6:8 and B. Sanhedrin 108a for this usage of *ḥein*.

[17] Deuteronomy 31:17–18; 32:20; Isaiah 8:17, 54:8, 64:6; Jeremiah 33:5; Psalms 13:2; 27:9; 30:8.

[18] Amos 8:11–12; Micah 3:4, 6–7; Jeremiah 18:18, 23:29–40; Ezekiel 7:26.

[19] With regard to human beings this usage occurs in, among other places, Genesis 32:20 (21 in some versions), Leviticus 19:15, 1 Samuel 25:35, 2 Kings 3:14, Proverbs 18:5, and Job 32:21. With regard to God, Deuteronomy 10:17 specifically asserts that God "will not show favor [literally, "will not lift His face"] or take a bribe," and that tenet is repeated using the same phrase in Job 34:19 and in Malachi 1:8–9; but in Genesis 19:21 God grants such an unearned favor (again, using the same phrase) to Lot, who, after fleeing Sodom, begs not to be forced to run to the hills but rather to be allowed to settle in another town on the plain. The partiality that God ultimately shows to Job is expressed by this phrase as well (Job 42:8).

[20] David Hume's sarcastic analysis of religious claims to miracles in his "Of Miracles," the tenth section of his 1748 work, *An Enquiry Concerning Human Understanding*, is one articulate expression of this eighteenth-century view.

[21] B. Sotah 14a.

[22] B. Avodah Zarah 54b.

[23] E.g., Deuteronomy 32:19–20; Isaiah 1:2; Job 31:18. The prayer Avinu Malkeinu, "Our Father, Our King," in the High Holy Day *maḥzor* is an example of the use of this theme in the liturgy, and the same phrase is used in the Ahavah Rabbah prayer just before the Shema in the daily morning liturgy.

The Wonderfully Enigmatic Priestly Blessing: A Conduit to *Ahavat Yisrael*

Reuven P. Bulka

Glaring Difficulties

The injunction obligating the *kohanim* (priests; singular, *kohen)* to generate blessing on all Israel is found in the Book of Numbers (6:22–27). I use the word "generate" deliberately, since it is not the *kohen* or the *kohanim* who bless Israel; it is God who blesses Israel. But the blessing is generated by the *kohen* or *kohanim*, as is stated clearly: "They [the *kohanim*] shall place My [God's] name on the Children of Israel, and I will bless them" (Numbers 6:27).

It is as if the *kohanim* press God's button, so to say, whereupon God then commences to bless Israel. The difficulty in this exercise is beyond obvious. It screams out for explanation. Why does God need to have the divine button pushed? If God wants to bless Israel, if Israel needs and/or deserves God's blessing, why does not God simply go and do just that—bless Israel?

Rabbi Aaron Halevi of Barcelona (1235–c.1290), in his classic work, *Sefer Ha-ḥinnukh,* addresses this very question. After introducing the obligation incumbent on the *kohanim* to bless the Israelites every day, he states:

> Do not say that if God desires for the Israelites to be blessed,
> then let God command the divine blessing to be with them,

and there would thus be no need for the blessing of the *kohanim* at all. For I have already told you many times that it is by the power of the worthiness of our acts that blessing is bestowed upon us. For God's hand, blessed is God, is open to every person who asks, when that person is worthy and ready for receiving the good. Therefore, because God chose us from among the nations and desires that we merit God's goodness, God forewarned and commanded us to arrange our actions and establish our worthiness through God's commands, to be deserving of that good. God also commanded us, in God's great goodness, that we should ask God for the blessing, and that we ask for it via the pure ministering servants—as all this will be a merit to our spirits, and because of that, we will merit attaining God's goodness.[1]

This explains, to some extent, why the blessing must be requested. I say "to some extent," because making ourselves worthy should be sufficient for attaining blessing, but according to the explanation in *Sefer Ha-ḥinnukh*, it is not sufficient. We still must entreat. And it certainly leaves unresolved the question of why it is the *kohanim* who must do the entreating for us. Why can we not do this directly? The idea that we need third-party intervention does not seem logical, and even seems to get in the way of our direct relationship with God.

This is not the only glaring difficulty related to the Priestly Blessing. Another complexity, this one textual, concerns the famous real estate matter: location. Quite a bit earlier in the Torah, in the Book of Leviticus, we are told, for the very first time, about Aaron pronouncing blessing on the people: "Aaron raised his hands toward the nation and blessed them..." (9:22). It would seem that right there, precisely at the juncture of Aaron pronouncing blessing, we should be introduced to the eternal obligation of the *kohanim* to bless Israel. Another, even more logical spot would be a bit later on in the narrative, where an entire array of obligations resting on the *kohanim* is introduced (Leviticus 21:1–22:25). Instead, the obligation of blessing is introduced much later, in the Book of Numbers—following two less-than-exhilarating rituals, one involving the *sotah*[2] and the other involving the nazirite.[3] Naḥmanides (1194–1270), in his comment on Numbers 6:23, suggests that the earlier blessing by the priests (in Leviticus) was specific to the consecration of the Tabernacle, for that day only. Here, in Numbers, the obligation is for future generations of *kohanim*, instructing that they must forever bless the Israelites. The distinction is duly noted, but the question concerning the textual location of Birkat *Kohanim* within the Torah still remains.

An Odd Preamble

The Priestly Blessing is itself preceded by a somewhat odd preamble:

> The Eternal spoke unto Moses, saying: "Speak unto Aaron and his sons, saying: 'Thus shall you bless the Children of Israel, saying unto them...'" (Numbers 6:22–23).

These last words, "saying unto them," seem redundant, as it is in the very nature of bestowing a blessing on anyone or on any group that there is a verbal address to them, either directly or indirectly. Rashi, in his comment to Numbers 6:23, cites *Midrash Tanḥuma* and suggests that these words, which are not only redundant but also written using an unusual infinitive form (*amor*, instead of the more usual *leimor*), mean that the blessing must not be pronounced hurriedly or hastily, but instead must be pronounced devoutly and with a full heart.[4] Earlier in his commentary to this verse, Rashi explains that the unusual form of the verb is used to specifically teach that the entirety of the people Israel must hear the blessing.[5] If we put the two explanations together, we are introduced to an interesting notion: namely, that the entire community of Israel must hear the heartfelt, genuine, sincere blessing pronounced by the *kohanim*.

It seems as if the community needs to hear the words of blessing, and that it needs to hear them from its religious functionaries, its leaders. All need to hear the blessing, and all need to hear the genuineness—dare we say, the love—in the blessing. To which we ask: why? Why is this so important that it is one of the 613 commandments? What exactly is gained by fulfilling this *mitzvah*?

What Do the Words Mean?

To further explore these issues, we will try to work through the threefold blessing itself (Numbers 6:24–26). It reads as follows:

> (24) May the Eternal bless you and safeguard you.
> (25) May the Eternal shine the divine countenance upon you and be gracious to you.
> (26) May the Eternal bestow favor upon you and grant you tranquility.

At first glance, this is quite a nice blessing. At second glance, it remains a nice blessing, but a bit puzzling. The words are nice but appear somewhat repetitive, and their meanings are not clear. Many commentators have addressed these concerns, and have come up with interesting explanations.

The first of the three blessings within the blessing is: *May the Eternal bless you and safeguard you.* Simple enough. But if God "blesses," is not "safeguard" implied? Consider being blessed with a brand-new car, only to have that car totaled the next day in a crash that you manage to survive. You were blessed with a car, but you barely had it for a day. Is this a blessing, or a tease, or worse? Or consider a case of a person who purchases a winning lottery ticket, but the next day is told by a doctor that a fatal illness has crept into his or her body. The person has money, but no time to enjoy it. Is that a blessing?

A blessing without a safeguard to preserve the blessing hardly qualifies as a blessing. We understand that a true blessing, certainly a divine blessing, is a lasting blessing. What, then, is added by the "safeguard" that is not contained in the notion of "bless" itself?

The second of the blessings is: *May the Eternal shine the divine countenance upon you and be gracious to you.* What exactly happens when God "shines" upon us? Is it something like getting a tan, a godly tan? Is something tangible transmitted via God's "rays"? Is it transformational? And is not the fact that God shines upon us a distinct manifestation of grace? Yet here the grace seems to be an added feature, above and beyond the shining of the divine countenance.

The third of the blessings is: *May the Eternal bestow favor upon you and grant you tranquility.* As if the first two of the blessings are not sufficient bestowal of favor! And if we are already the beneficiaries of God's favor, does not "tranquility" already inhere in that favor?

There are, of course, other questions that can and should be asked about the meaning of these blessings, but we will stop the asking at this point, and address the questions already posed.

Rashi-nale: The First Blessing

We will attempt to more fully understand the words of blessing mainly through the lens of the great commentator, Rashi.

On the first blessing, *May the Eternal bless you and safeguard you*, Rashi addresses our concern head-on, even though he does not specifically mention our question (namely: "if God 'blesses,' is not 'safeguard' implied?"). He states that the blessing referred to is a material one—that one's possessions increase, and that they be safeguarded from thieves:

> *And safeguard you*—that thieves not attack you to take away your property. For a mortal who gives a present to an employee cannot protect the employee from everyone, and if a band of robbers attack and grab it from the employee, what benefit is gained from this gift? But the blessed Holy One is at once the Giver and the One who safeguards.

It would seem as if Rashi is not at all concerned with our question. He clearly agrees that a gift without a safeguard is wanting, and that God's gifts are by definition safeguarded. We come back to our question. Why is Rashi not bothered by the apparent redundancy, including "safeguard" even though it would seem to be implied in "bless"? Rashi's explanation seems to simply enunciate a self-evident theological principle concerning God's largesse. There is no redundancy because a basic principle is being established, that God's gifts are safeguarded. But that principle is too self-evident to warrant a spelling out. We must be missing something.

I propose a subtext that may adequately explain this quandary. If God bestows blessing, why would God allow thieves to steal that very blessing? Perhaps because the person receiving the blessing is not worthy of it, does not appreciate it, and may misuse the newfound wealth only for narcissistic endeavors, refusing to share it with others. Such a person has transformed the blessing into a curse. The blessing, thus understood, could then be read as follows: *May the Eternal bless you with bounty, and may you be worthy of that bounty being preserved for you through your using the bounty to share the blessing.*

That is the subtext that is suggested by Rashi's explanation. It is not a statement of obvious theological principle. Instead, it is a twofold blessing: that one be worthy of receiving the blessing, and also worthy of maintaining that very blessing.

Rashi-nale: The Second Blessing

We move now to the second blessing: *May the Eternal shine the divine countenance upon you and be gracious to you.* Here again, we call on Rashi. To explain what is meant by shining the divine countenance, Rashi states: "May God show you a smiling countenance, a beaming countenance." If the person materially blessed indeed becomes worthy of having that blessing maintained, this makes God happy. God is delighted with the blessing "investment"; the returns are just what God desires.

What happens when God "shines" on the blessed person? What, if anything, changes? The person receives God's grace, says the verse. But the person already has the blessing, and God's smile. Again, Rashi seems to simply state the obvious: "May God grant you favor." What is the value added here? Perhaps it is that the person, who has used the blessing wisely and responsibly, is now given the blessing of permanence, the gift of grace—or more literally, the gift of becoming a kind person, beyond just having done kind things.

Thus understood, the blessing is for a progression from *doing* to *being.* It is a blessing that the good that you do becomes you, defines you, and guarantees that this is the way you will remain your entire life: as a receiver of blessing who uses the blessing kindly, and who then receives the ultimate transformational blessing of becoming a kind, gracious person.

Rashi-nale: The Third Blessing

We move now to the third blessing: *May the Eternal bestow favor upon you and grant you tranquility.* In the light of our explanation so far, this blessing makes no sense at all. The person has already been blessed with bounty, as well as with the even greater blessing of being transformed into an everlastingly kind person. Is this not more than enough? Is there more "favor" that needs to be bestowed? Listen here to the astounding words of Rashi, explaining what bestowing favor means: "May God conquer (or: suppress) God's anger." Where does this idea come from? Why would God be angry at a person who has so nicely translated the material blessing extended by God?

These words of Rashi suggest a somewhat unconventional understanding of the blessing. We recognize from the outset that blessings are tricky: they can bring out the best in us, or they can bring out the beast in us. We can take the blessing and grow with it, or we can take the blessing and become possessed by it, becoming mean, self-absorbed, and overly protective of the newfound wealth—in which case, the blessing then becomes an imprecation. The first verse expresses the hope that we use the blessing in a blessed manner. If we do, then the consequence will hopefully be that we become blessed persons, as per the second verse of the threefold blessing.

But if we fail, then the third blessing kicks in. Should we use the blessing in a mean-spirited way, God will definitely be angry. If that is how things unfold, then the blessing expressed is that God conquer, or suppress, the anger that we would deserve; the blessing is that rather than dealing harshly with those ingrates, God instead grant them tranquility or calm, so that the wealth does not destroy them. In other words, it is a blessing to those undeserving of God's blessing of bounty—a blessing of quantity and quality—that they should have at least a life of quality. The material blessing may backfire, but hopefully there is something left in reserve.

The Textual Location Issue

Admittedly, this is not the standard understanding of this Priestly Blessing. But it offers an insight that expands the blessing's profundity, and simultaneously helps address some of the remaining issues we raised. We mentioned earlier that the blessing was to be bestowed upon all Israel. All Israel had to hear the blessing—both those who deserve it and those who do not. They are, all together, part of the community.

The idea that the undeserving are also part of the blessing derives from the textual location issue. Where in the biblical text is the Priestly Blessing introduced? Right after the laws concerning the *sotah* and the nazirite.[6]

The *sotah* text (Numbers 5:11–31) deals with the ugliness of a marriage invaded by jealousy instead of appreciation, by accusations of infidelity instead of faithfulness, by suspicion instead of trust. The *kohen* sees this unfolding before his very eyes. He sees what the absence of true love can engender and he sees an unfolding crisis of value distortion in the community as he administers the ritual that will, hopefully, establish the truth and restore the marriage.

This is followed by the nazirite regulations (Numbers 6:1–21). Why would a person resolve to abstain from wine (among other abstentions)? One view in the Talmud considers it sinful to vow to abstain from what is permitted.[7] No one doubts the sincerity of the nazirite, but making a vow to abstain quite likely manifests a struggle with control, perhaps a wrestling with addiction, an addiction resulting from alcohol abuse. Someone who takes substance abuse challenges seriously is to be lauded, but the fact that abuse has become an issue is itself lamentable. The intervention of the *kohen* comes at the conclusion of the period of abstinence—and sometimes earlier, if the period of abstention is compromised because the nazirite breached a condition of the regulations incumbent on himself or herself.

The *kohen* thus sees people who, in different ways, are out of control: the *sotah* and the nazirite. He sees the warts; he knows the failings of the people. And the people know that the *kohanim* know this about them. So, how do the *kohanim* really feel about their flock, about their people? Are they disappointed? Are they fed up? Are they repulsed? Or are they compassionate, understanding, forgiving? By obligating the *kohanim* to bless the people, God is telling them that they must be compassionate. They cannot simply rush the blessing; it must be heartfelt. The people need to hear the blessing—and they need to hear the sincerity, the genuineness, the true emotive wish that emanates from the *kohanim*.

When they are able to hear this, the people can then actually hear the voice of God saying that, in spite of everything, all is not lost. The people are still worthy of blessing. They are still loved, below and above.

The Blessing of Love

This analysis paves the way for a wonderful observation concerning the blessing (*b'rakhah*) that the *kohanim* recite prior to fulfilling their obligation to bless all Israel. The blessing reads as follows: "Blessed are You, Lord our God, Ruler of the universe, who has sanctified us with the holiness of Aaron and has commanded us to bless God's people with love." The *b'rakhah* closely follows the standard formula recited immediately prior to fulfilling a precept, a *mitzvah*. The text is almost what one would expect, but with the notable exception of the last word: *b'ahavah* ("with love"). For no other commandment does the blessing conclude in this way. Why here?

From what we have presented above, the "job" of the *kohanim* in fulfilling their benedictional duty is to convey to the entire community that they are loved by God. It is a love blessing. The word *b'ahavah* added to the blessing is not an add-on feature, but rather speaks to the very core of the *mitzvah* itself: to bless the people with love, to convey the reality that they are loved. Perhaps the last word of the Priestly Blessing, that the people be blessed with "tranquility," is more accurately a blessing for love, love being the most profound generator of tranquility.

One more point. The discerning reader will notice a significant divergence in the body of the blessing, from the wording of the standard blessing recited before performing a *mitzvah*. Normally, when reciting such a blessing, we say: "Blessed are You, Lord our God, Ruler of the universe, who has sanctified us *with the divine commandments*, and…." But here, prior to the Priestly Blessing, the words are: "…who has sanctified us *with the holiness of Aaron*, and…." That is quite a change, unprecedented in the litany of blessings. What is the significance of this change in wording?

There is clearly a message in this. What exactly is meant by "the holiness of Aaron?" To answer this question, we turn to the most eloquent description of Aaron, offered by the sage Hillel: "Be among the disciples of Aaron, loving peace and pursuing peace, loving humankind and bringing them near to the Torah" (Pirkei Avot 1:12). In other words, the core characteristic of Aaron is that he is a person full of love for everyone, who spreads peace (tranquility) throughout the community. The holiness of Aaron inheres in his embracing love of everyone.

These words "who has sanctified us *with the holiness of Aaron*" are uttered by the *kohanim* as they prepare for generating blessing for the people. They are reminded in advance that this benedictory expression is all about love, *Aaronic love*, with which they—as *kohanim*—have been bequeathed, and which they must share with the community. Through the legacy of Aaron, they must bless the community with love: with the express hope and prayer that the community will become suffused with love.

If the most holy of the community, the *kohanim*, can find it in their hearts to bless the entirety of the Israelite community that they be filled with love, even though they know so many whose behavior is less than scintillating, even unholy…then that leaves God with no choice but to endorse that blessing. This must therefore be seen as the heavenly plea to all of Israel to be concerned for each other, to bless each other despite all their imperfections, to express and live their love of everyone. Once we do that, we are indeed blessed!

The Bottom Line

In a word, the *mitzvah* fulfillment of Birkat Kohanim is a concretization, on the loftiest level, of *ahavat yisrael*, loving all Israel, completely and unconditionally. That we have to work hard to get beyond the superficial to uncover the true essence, the great truth of the Priestly Blessing, is itself a reminder that we should do the same with every member of the community: get behind the superficial to see the good in everyone.

NOTES

[1] *Sefer Ha-ḥinnukh*, ed. Ḥayyim Dov Chavel (New York: Shulsinger Bros., 1952), *mitzvah* #367, p. 468. The traditional attribution of *Sefer Ha-ḥinnukh* to Rabbi Aaron of Barcelona has been questioned in recent years. See further Israel Ta-Shma, *"Meḥabb'ro Ha-amitti shel Sefer Ha-ḥinnukh,"* in *Kiryat Sefer* 55 (1980), pp. 787–790.

[2] See Numbers 5:11–31. A *sotah* is a married woman suspected of adultery who undergoes a harrowing ritual intended to establish the truth regarding the suspicion, and which is overseen by a *kohen*. The ritual was abolished by Rabbi Yoḥanan ben Zakkai in the first century C.E.

[3] See Numbers 6:1–21. A nazirite is a person, male or female, who vows to abstain from wine and grape products for a period of time (usually but not always for thirty days) and who afterwards, with the guidance of a *kohen*, engages in various penitential rituals to facilitate return to non-nazirite status.

[4] See Rashi's first comment to Numbers 6:23, s.v. *amor*, and *Midrash Tanḥuma* to Numbers, *parashat Naso* §10. This work is a collection of midrashic homilies on the Pentateuch named for Rabbi Tanḥuma, its presumed author and editor.

[5] See Rashi's second comment to Numbers 6:23, s.v. *amor lahem*. Rashi, as Rabbi Shlomo Yitzaki (1040–1105) is universally known, is by common consent the greatest and most authoritative of all Jewish medieval biblical commentators.

[6] Regarding the *sotah*, see note 2 above. Regarding the nazirite, see note 3 above.

[7] B. Nedarim 10a, commenting on Numbers 6:11.

"And Give You Peace"

Aryeh Cohen

I

The famous Priestly Benediction, presented in Scripture at Numbers 6:22–27, ends with the prayer that God give the Israelites peace (6:26). But the peace so referenced, a peace that "is given" by God, is a peace that is not on the same ontological plane as the quotidian. It is, by definition, a peace that is *of God*. It is God who *gives* the peace. What, then, is this peace? It has something to do, seemingly, with God's "countenance," with God's *face*—the very same face about which it is written, "You shall not be able to see My face, for no human can see Me and live" (Exodus 33:20). And, indeed, that is part of the scriptural context as well: the full verse referenced above begins with the prayer that God "lift up" the divine face *and* grant peace to you. And these words too are deeply meaningful: the face that is "raised up" or "lifted up" to you, in the previous line of the Priestly Blessing (6:25), holds a promise that belies the mortal encounter with the face of God, the encounter that will inevitably lead to death. It is an encounter with the face of God beyond death—not after death, necessarily, but in a place that itself is beyond death…a day perhaps that is "neither day nor night" (Zechariah 14:7), a day that is not part of the mundane accounting of our lives, a day that will only be experienced beyond the place where death holds sway.

The peace given after the countenance is beheld—or, at the least, promised after that face, *the* face, the encounter with *that face*, is promised—is not a peace of this world. It is a peace of "and the wolf shall dwell with the lamb, the leopard lie down with the kid; the calf, the beast of prey, and the fatling together, with a little boy to herd them" (Isaiah 11:6). It is an "on that day" peace: "On that day there shall be one Eternal God possessed of one name" (Zechariah 14:9)…"On that day, men shall fling away the idols of silver and the idols of gold that they made for worshipping" (Isaiah 2:20)…"On that day the Eternal will punish, with God's great, cruel, mighty sword, Leviathan the Elusive Serpent—Leviathan the Twisting Serpent; God will slay the Dragon of the sea…And on that day, a great ram's horn shall be sounded; and the strayed who are in the land of Assyria and the expelled who are in the land of Egypt shall come and worship the Eternal on the holy mount, in Jerusalem" (Isaiah 27:1, 13).

The peace that God will *give* is not a peace that might even be included in an accounting of the world. It is a peace that is a divine gift, a reordering of the world. It is not a *telos* in any known way. It is not the end of history, for in this telling history exists on a different plane. It is beyond the end of history, of a time when the world is reformed in a different ontological model so that the inevitable cycles of war and peace—the Pax Hellena, the Pax Romana, even a Pax Judea—are no longer of any relevance. This is not a peace of victors or vanquished, but something of a different order. It is an Edenic peace, in an Eden refined before and beyond human foibles and sinfulness. It is a peace guaranteed by, and given only by, God.

The divine giving is also a modality that exists in a different ontological context. It is a giving with no expectation of reciprocity. The only reflection of this peace of the end of days (or "on that day") in the human realm is meditation upon this peace.

The complement, or corollary, of the divinely unilateral status of this peace is that it is unachievable. This peace, which is a gift of heaven, is not the end result of human action. There is no war that can be fought that will bring this peace. There is no mystical incantation, no set of righteous actions, that will transform the world from its current mundane existence to the pacific existence of divine peace. This peace, then, while granted in a dream and longed for in blessing, is a vision but is not visionary. There is no path to follow whose ending is this land. Humanity is only given the option to wait through the hardships and the wars, the quotidian and the fantastic, until the arrival of "that day"—whose date and time is determined beyond the grasp of mortals. People plan and God laughs. God's laughter will some day be the eternal joy of lasting peace. There is, however, no mortal way to traverse from here to there.

II

Oseh shalom bi-m'romav hu ya·aseh shalom.
The One who makes peace in the heavens shall make peace.

These words, which conclude every version of the Kaddish and have their scriptural roots in the opening to the twenty-fifty chapter of Job, are portentous in their own right, implying the existence of a second order of peace: the peace that God "makes." This peace is the opposite of evil or "woe" and the equal of light: "I form light and create darkness, I make peace (*shalom*) and create woe—I the Eternal do all these things" (Isaiah 45:7). God is the author of this peace, its creator, its founder. This is a peace that is perhaps of the warp and woof of the world from the moment that heaven and earth, day and night, light and darkness were created. According to some rabbinic traditions, it is only because God made peace that the world was able to be created: peace between the upper waters and the lower waters, peace between the sun and the moon, and peace among the angels.[1]

This type of peace is a peace that lacks open hostility: "And what was the peace that God established in heaven? God did not call ten angels 'Gabriel,' ten others 'Michael,' ten 'Uriel,' ten 'Raphael,' as is the wont of humans; for if God had done thus, then when God called one—all ten would come and they would be jealous of each other…"[2] It is a peace that allows the world to exist. It is of course, only one of the possibilities for existence. War, strife, and enmity are all still live options. The movement from war to peace is like the movement from night to day, from dark to light. There is a natural cycle:

> Dominion and dread are God's;
> He imposes peace in God's own heights.
> Can God's troops be numbered?
> On whom does God's light not shine? (Job 25:2–3)

In this understanding, spoken by Job's friend Bildad, God can impose peace because "dominion and dread are God's." It is because God has innumerable troops and is everywhere. This is something like a divine Pax Romana, a heavenly "mutually assured destruction" standoff—save for the fact that there is only one side. God's intimidating power will overwhelm the power of nations. God's sword will deliver swift justice and the world will be brought to a state of peace. Peace will reign, albeit in a context of fear and trembling.

This peace will come as the end of history, and not as a process of peace-making that is *of* history. There will have been no reconciliation among the peoples of the world. Nation will not take up sword against nation, but not because they have come to a place of meeting and understanding. Rather, it will be God who imposes peace, who takes their weapons, and who installs a regime of fear. The fear of God's power will still the machinery of war. And this will be the end of history and the beginning of the end of days.

This peace is still not a peace that is woven by peacemakers, but is rather imposed by the Peacemaker. It is not a peace in which people turn to their neighbors or enemies and say: "You too are made in the image of God. What is it that we gain by our enmity?" It is, rather, a peace in which people stream to the mountain of God and worship God's awesome power. God will be the world's only superpower, and the world will have peace, as repeatedly in biblical times, "for forty years"…and maybe more.

There is, though, no path that we can choose to travel, to get from here to there. There is no promise that if we lay down our arms we will transcend an understanding of existence that is drenched in death and violent clashes. The world of this peace is a monarchical world in which earthly kings are displaced by God as Sovereign. Yet, the reign of God partakes no less of the power of arms than the reign of earthly kings. God's "arms" are just so much more powerful.

This concept of peace has thus moved peace from the heavenly realm into the earthly sphere. It is on the ground that God makes peace, among the peoples of the world. God does not force the transcending of time and space in order to gift peace. And we have here a glimpse of the possibility of an *imitatio Dei*. Just as God makes peace, so too should we make peace. Yet, at this point, this peace would be too terrible to consider. It would be the peace of the powerful.

There is no change of consciousness in this new order; there is only a change of ruler.

III

Hillel used to say: Count yourselves among the students of Aaron. Be one who loves peace and pursues peace (*oheiv shalom v'rodeif shalom*). Be one who loves people and brings them near to the Torah.[3]

Ḥizkiyah used to say: Great is peace, for in regard to every commandment in the Torah it is written: "when you see…" (Exodus 23:5), "when you encounter…" (Exodus 23:4), "when a bird's nest chances to be before you…" (Deuteronomy 22:6), "when you build…" (Deuteronomy 22:8)—when the possibility for fulfilling a commandment arises, you must act accordingly. However, in regard to peace, what is written? "Seek peace (*shalom*) and pursue it" (Psalm 34:15). Seek it in your place, and pursue it in another place.[4]

What does it mean to pursue peace? The sages[5] relate that when Aaron, the High Priest, Moses' brother, would hear that two people were fighting, he would go to one of them and say: "I was sent here by your friend so-and-so, who is so very sorry about what he did." Immediately, the person Aaron was talking to would think, "Why should such a great and righteous man like Aaron need to come to me to apologize for my friend? It is actually I who must apologize." Aaron would then go to the other person and tell him the same thing. The two people, who earlier in the day had been entangled in an embittered squabble, would set out for each other to apologize— each thinking that the other had already done so. They would meet halfway and would embrace and live in peace.

Aaron is thus considered, in the rabbinic tradition, an exemplar of one who "pursues peace." Aaron's peace is the peace of amity over honesty. It is more important that "we all get along" than that we tell or know the truth. An ancient midrash states this explicitly: "Great is peace, for we find that the Torah speaks falsely in order to make peace between Abraham and Sarah."[6] When Sarah laughs at the thought of giving birth, it is reported that the cause of her mirth was that her husband, Abraham, was old (Genesis 18:12). However, when God relates this story as told to Abraham in the next verse, the cause of Sarah's laughter is reported as her own advanced age (18:13).

This peace effected by Aaron, however, is a peace on a razor's edge. The underlying relationship of enmity can spring up at any moment if Aaron's ruse comes to light. If, when the two men are done hugging, and are sitting down to coffee, one says to the other: "I am so glad that you sent Aaron to me to apologize; I really should have done so first"—the other then might just reply, "Yes, you should have; actually, I thought you did. Why would I apologize?!" The whole peaceful edifice, so carefully crafted by Aaron, might then fall apart.

Rabbi Ishmael claimed that peace was great, "for we find that the blessed Holy One ceded God's own name, which was written in holiness, that it might be erased in the water, in order to make peace between a man and his wife."[7] The reference here is to the ritual for the suspected adulteress (Numbers 5:11–31). When the spirit of jealousy comes upon a man and he suspects his wife of adultery, he brings her to the Tabernacle (later, the Temple in Jerusalem), where she undergoes a humiliating ritual "test." If she fails the test, she dies; if she passes, she is considered exonerated and she will be fruitful. Part of the test, the part that may assure her death, includes making a potion consisting of dirt from the floor of the Tabernacle, mixed in water, with ink from a writ of curses that includes the name of God. The writ is placed in the water and the ink washes off and is assimilated into the potion. The woman is then made to drink the "bitter besetting water." Thus the name of God is ceded for peace between husband and wife. Although the spirit of jealousy might not have claimed a victim on the day that the husband first suspects his wife of infidelity, it still hovered overhead, ready to be summoned at the whim of the husband. The marriage is thus only spuriously helped by the ritual (which includes the effacement of God's name): can there ever be certainty about a deed that nobody saw not happen? Will an insanely jealous husband (one who is possessed by the spirit of jealousy) ever be certain or satisfied? Is there a chance that the relationship will be peaceful from here on out? If this is the model of peace, have we not set the bar rather low?

If peace came into the world at creation, if peace was created with the world (or as part of the world), then enmity came along not much later. When Cain raised his hand to strike Abel, by acting upon his jealousy, he destroyed the peace and invented violence. Is there no way to not be violent, to live non-violently—that is also a way of truth and respect?

The sages urge us also in this direction, using this time as their example Moses, the humblest person on earth: "There is no one humbler than one who pursues peace. Think for yourself: how might one pursue peace if one is not humble? Howbeit? If a person curses another, the peacemaker replies: 'Peace be upon you.' If a person fights with the peacemaker, the peacemaker holds his tongue."[8] Humility. Peace might begin with lessening one's own ego in the world.

IV

The last chapter of the Mishnah tractate Avot, known as *Kinyan Torah* or "Acquisition of Torah," lists forty-eight manners (*d'varim*) by which the Torah is acquired. It is not completely clear what is meant by "acquiring Torah." I will take it to mean the spiritual or moral practices that one must undertake in order to be able to be a link in the chain of tradition, which is listed in the first *mishnah* of Avot: "Moses received the Torah at Sinai and handed it down to Joshua; Joshua, to the Elders; the Elders, to the Men of the Great Assembly…" The list extends to and includes the sages of the Mishnah.

Somewhere down in the middle of the list is "one who carries the yoke with one's fellow" (*nosei b'ol im haveiro*). The late nineteenth-century rabbi and master of the *Musar* tradition, Simḥah Zissel Ziv, also known as the Alter of Kelm, raised up this specific mode of acquisition of Torah and gave it pride of place. For him, the way to acquiring Torah passed through radical empathy. For the Alter of Kelm, radical empathy consists of envisioning oneself *as* the person in distress, feeling that person's suffering, and from that position working to alleviate that suffering. For Reb Simḥah Zissel, the paradigmatic case of this manner of radical empathy is Moses himself. Simḥah Zissel is bothered by Moses' seeming brazenness when he speaks to God after leaving Pharaoh's palace after their first meeting, when he challenges God saying: "O Eternal, why did You bring harm upon this people? Why did You send me? Ever since I came to Pharaoh to speak in Your name, he has dealt worse with this people; and still You have not delivered Your people" (Exodus 5:22–23). The Alter of Kelm wonders how Moses was allowed to get away with this manner of addressing God.

To answer this question, Rabbi Simḥah quotes Rashi, "[Moses] used his eyes and heart to suffer over them," and then expands this idea: "[Moses] so accustomed himself [to their sufferings] by way of imagination, to the point he felt their pain as if he himself was suffering it. So he carried their yoke with them even to a greater extent than his own pain.…Thus he was able to say: 'Why did You bring harm upon this people?'"[9] Rabbi Simḥah seems to be saying that Moses did not *actually* suffer that which the Israelites suffered, since he had been brought up in the Pharaoh's house. He had never been a slave, and he had no firsthand experience of the suffering of the Israelites. Yet he practiced empathy, by way of visualizing and imagining their pain, so that ultimately he was able to actually *feel* their pain enough to challenge God.

This brazen act of bringing the Israelites' pain to God in a defiant manner was a great sin. According to Shemot Rabbah: "At that moment the Attribute of Judgment wished to strike Moses. The blessed Holy One said: 'Leave him be, for he only said this for the honor of Israel.'"[10] This statement of the midrash, for Simḥah Zissel, backs up the point made by Rashi that Moses used his eyes and heart to suffer over the Israelites—that is, he understood intellectually (with his eyes), and he felt their pain as if it was his own pain (in his heart). Thus the practice of "one who carries the yoke with one's fellow," the path of radical empathy, is a practice of understanding and experiencing the pain of another person, *to the point that one suffers that pain oneself.*

Is this then the way of peace? If I feel your pain so intensely, how could I then harm you? Would it not bring about peace if we all practiced this type of radical empathy? There would be no outsiders. No person would ever suffer by themselves, as long as others were around. The possibility of attacking another would dissipate, in the experience of the pain that the other would suffer. There is perhaps hope along this way.

The midrash relates that God's appearance in a burning bush that was not consumed, in order to commission Moses to redeem Israel, was symbolic of God's promise to be with Israel in all their troubles—that God would also suffer the Exile and its tribulations. The radical empathy symbolized by Moses and demanded by Avot is an example of *imitatio Dei*, of acting as God would.

V

What, then, are the demands of peace?

Moses was not an uncomplicated person. While the midrash above, following the Torah, understands Moses as the most humble person, this humility was also infused with, or periodically marked by, violent outbursts. The Torah relates Moses' fateful encounter with an Egyptian taskmaster whom he beat to death for striking an Israelite. When Moses came down from Sinai with the tablets containing the Decalogue and saw the Israelites dancing round the golden calf, he smashed the tablets. The Babylonian Talmud relates that God approved of this act.[11]

Moses, in any event, was only God's agent with regard to Pharaoh. While Moses threatened Pharaoh, warned Pharaoh, and "pulled the trigger" on Pharaoh's punishments, it was ultimately God who landed the blows. God laid Pharaoh low and ultimately killed off most of Pharaoh's people and his army, and laid his country waste.

God did not allow the angels to sing praise while the Egyptians were drowning. But God did indeed drown the Egyptians, and the Israelites sung praise—with Miriam leading the women, and Moses leading the men.

God rewarded Pinḥas' homicidal zealotry with a "covenant of peace" (Numbers 25:12). What manner of peace is that? It is the peace of the ceasefire, the peace of tense disarmament, the peace that is based on war and that will cycle again into war. Forty years of peace. Forty years of war. Almost no one who left Egypt entered Canaan alive, including Moses, Aaron, and Miriam.

What, then, of peace?

Aharon Shmuel Tamares, an Eastern European rabbi who died in 1931, claimed that opposition to violence was one of the fundamental pillars of belief. In fact, in the introduction to the Decalogue, God says just that, according to Tamares:

> The "God of Israel"—that is, the aspect of divinity in which God was revealed before our people on Mount Sinai…this aspect is: the good traits of the blessed Holy One, the trait of righteousness and fairness, and that the archetype of all these divine traits is to hate crass violence (*ko·aḥ ha-egrof*).[12]

When God wiped out the Egyptians, God intentionally did this alone, without help. "I and no other," as we read on the night of the *seder* in the words of the midrash in the Haggadah. God did not empower the Israelites to seek violent revenge against the Egyptians. Rather,

> the blessed Holy One could have given Israel the power to avenge themselves upon the Egyptians; however, the blessed Holy One did not want to show them the way to use violence. For even if in the present moment it was to

defend themselves from the evil ones, it is in this way [i.e., the use of violence] that violence spreads in the world, and from defenders they will ultimately become pursuers.[13]

Tamares' overreaching claim that the Exodus was a realized eschatological moment beclouds the moral acuity of his aspirational vision. The demand of God's own use of violence was that humans should not use violence. Divine violence is separated from human violence in a Maimonidean dichotomy. The violence that God deploys is not such that might be compared to the violence of humans. Even the concept itself is used merely in an analogical way, as the divide between divine and human action is so absolute as to necessitate scare quotes around the term "divine action."

Yet, Tamares also says that when the force of violence is unleashed in the world it is indiscriminate, and so the Israelites had to seal themselves in their houses in order for them not to be tainted by it. This is how he explains the talmudic dictum attributed to Rav Joseph: "Once God gave permission to the Destroyer to destroy, the Destroyer does not distinguish between righteous and evil."[14] Tamares expands this to mean that if God had allowed the Israelites to let loose their own power of destruction, if God had empowered the Israelites to wreak justified revenge on the Egyptians, then their destructive, violent powers would not have distinguished between good and evil—"and they would have eventually turned from being defenders to being oppressors."[15]

VI

Said Resh Lakish: One who raises his hand to his fellow, even if he has not hit him, is called evil, as it says: "And he said to the evil one, 'Why will you strike your fellow?'"

(Exodus 2:13). It does not say "Why have you struck," but rather "Why will you strike"—even though he has not yet struck he is called evil.[16]

It is almost a cliché that Judaism is not a pacifist religion. The Talmud expands on the biblical law of the thief who comes in the night (Exodus 22:1), saying: "If one comes to kill you, kill him first."[17] (This is Rashi's connection,[18] theorizing that the reason that one is allowed to kill a thief who tunnels into the house at night is because he presents a clear danger: since the thief obviously knows that at night people will be home and he presents himself as ready to steal at all costs.) Moreover, preemptive killing is permitted in the case of a person who is pursuing another to kill him or her. In that case, a third party is permitted under certain circumstances to intervene with necessary force, and even kill the pursuer in order to save the life of the would-be victim.[19]

How then do we get from here to there—if "here" rabbinic tradition allows for violence and "there" Tamares demands radical pacifism?

Resh Lakish, in the passage quoted above, sees that the dividing line between good and evil rests on the matter of intention. One is judged to be evil based on whether one *wants* to hit another, and not just on one's actions. The actual deployment of violence is not necessary to be judged evil, only the *intent* to deploy violence. Violence itself, then, is obviously evil. The actual act of raising one's hand and striking another violates the bounds of the permissible.

Is there a way of inferring from Resh Lakish's declaration that even the intent to do violence is evil? On the one hand, Resh Lakish asserts that even the intent to act violently is evil; on the other hand, the Talmud seems to authorize such violence when it will result in saving an innocent life. What, then, are we to conclude about the permissibility of violence or the imperative of pacifism? One way of resolving this tension would be to draw a distinction between self-defense and other cases: "If one comes to kill you, kill him first." In a case where my life is in danger, I must obviously be able to defend myself. What then of the case of the pursuer? My life is not in danger when I see one person running after another with homicidal intent. Yet, I am authorized, there too, to use violent means to stop them.

VII

The "self-defense" objection to nonviolence is in many ways the path of least resistance. Self-defense usually breaks into the discussion of nonviolence in the manner of a challenge: "But what about self-defense?" This is played as a trump and not offered as a move in the dialogue. It seems obvious that one is permitted, even obligated, to defend oneself, to save oneself from harm. This is more than an obligation; it is a natural drive. A person's first instinct is self-preservation. Is that not obvious?

It seems that no, it is not completely obvious to the Jewish tradition. There are three prohibitions for which one is obligated to give up one's life rather than to transgress them: idolatry, impermissible sexual relations, and murder. Let us leave to the side the complicated demands of the jealous God of monotheism and the obsessive purity of sexual mores. Why murder? If I am told to kill you or else I should be killed, why should I not kill you? Is your blood redder than mine? Is your continued existence more important, more pressing, more vital than mine is?

To be clear, it would never even enter my mind to kill you unless there was a gun to my head. However, now that there is a gun to my head—all other things being equal, does my drive to self-preservation not have a voice? And yet, the demand of the law is clear

Rabbi Yoḥanan said in the name of Rabbi Simeon ben Yehotzadak: By a majority vote, it was resolved in the upper chamber of the house of Nitza in Lydda: In regard to every law of the Torah, if a person is commanded: "Transgress and be not killed," one should transgress and not be killed—excepting idolatry, impermissible sexual practices, and murder.[20]

Two out of the three of these demands for martyrdom—the demand that one forfeit one's life rather than worship idols or engage in forbidden sexual practices—are contested. In each, a biblical grounding is sought and presented. However, the demand that one allow oneself to be killed rather than murder another is based purely in s'vara, in argument rather than biblical precept:

And from where do we know [the prohibition concerning] the murderer himself? It is common sense. It is as the one who came before Rabbah and said to him, "The governor of my town has ordered me, 'Go and kill so and so; if not, I will kill you.'" He said to him, "He should kill you and you should not kill; who would say that your blood is redder? Perhaps his blood is redder."[21]

Turning the question around ("who is to say that your blood is redder," rather than "who is to say *his* blood is redder") essentially answers the question for Rabbah. If you are to actively take someone else's life, then you have to be able to articulate an argument that shows that your life *is* more important than that of the other person. In order for you to claim the right to tip the balance in your favor, when you are on one side and another person is on the other, you have to have a substantial—or even overriding—reason. The instinct of self-preservation is not enough.

VIII

Violence is by nature instrumental; like all means, it always stands in need of guidance and justification through the end it pursues. And what needs justification through something else cannot be the essence of anything. The end of war is peace; but to the question, And what is the end of peace?, there is no answer. Peace is an absolute, even though in recorded history the periods of warfare have nearly always outlasted the periods of peace.[22]

The moral consciousness can sustain the mocking gaze of the political man only if the certitude of peace dominates the evidence of war. Such a certitude is not obtained by a simple play of antitheses. The peace of empires issued from war rests on war. It does not restore to the alienated beings their lost identity. For that a primordial and original relation with being is needed.[23]

What of war? Even if we might have led ourselves down the primrose path to the seemingly solid garden wall of *aporia*, of *undecidability*, about the question of personal self-defense, does the same pertain to the idea of war? Is war analogous to a conflict between individuals, where one side might claim self-defense while the other is the aggressor and thereby loses all legitimacy? Do we always voice the psalmist's stark plaint: "I am for peace...they are for war" (Psalm 120:7)?

The cycles of war and peace do not lead to peace. The history of the world is based on these cycles of war and peace. The biblical recording of the rhythm of forty years of peace and then forty years of war could be the template for this history—though the periods of war were far greater and the periods of relative peace far shorter.

Is there any justification for war? Arendt, in her 1969 essay "Reflections on Violence," writes that all violence harbors within itself an element of arbitrariness; nowhere does Fortuna, good or ill luck, play a more important role in human affairs than on the battlefield; and this intrusion of the "Random Event" cannot be eliminated by game theories but only by the certainty of mutual destruction. It seems symbolic of this all pervading unpredictability that those engaged in the perfection of the means of destruction have finally brought about a level of technical development where their aim, namely warfare, is on the point of disappearing altogether.[24]

Almost fifty years later, the role that unpredictability plays is not diminished. With the end of the Cold War, with the end of the threat of mutually assured destruction, Arendt's optimism that war will put itself out of business seems almost quaint. In our age of ongoing genocides in Sudan and Congo and Syria, with the threat that nuclear weapons might get into the hands of non-state actors, with the abilities of the superpowers to destroy the world many times over, it is hard to abide the thought that war could ever be justified. The basic fact of war, as Arendt states clearly, is that "violence harbors within itself an element of arbitrariness." The means of war almost always, almost certainly, will overwhelm whatever ends seem to justify the violence. Along the way, those who will be killed will not entirely— or even, at times, largely—be those who are ostensibly being attacked.

The definition of modern warfare is the unleashing of violence that will very soon be uncontrollable. Embarking on a war means embarking on a course during which it is guaranteed that innocent people will be murdered. Until World War II, it was correct to assume that most of the casualties in war were combatants. Nevertheless, this supposition still requires one to justify the massive homicides of innocent people incidental to military operations, and to justify the killing of enemy combatants as being distinct from other forms of homicide. Be that as it may, from World War II until the present, the ratio of civilian to military casualties is somewhere between 7:1 and 9:1. That is, between seventy and ninety percent of the deaths in contemporary wars are civilian deaths.[25] It is important to appreciate the impact of this fact: when a state mobilizes its army to fight an offensive or defensive war, it is preparing to murder innocents and incidentally to kill combatants.

How then can we hear the intoning of the Priestly Benediction, and the solemn invoking of the final phrase "and give you peace"— putting all our hopes in God that God grant us what we are not willing to exert effort to do for ourselves, and not join in Isaiah's full-throated condemnation?

> Hear the word of the Eternal,
> you chieftains of Sodom;
> give ear to our God's instruction,
> you folk of Gomorrah!
> "What need have I of all your sacrifices?"
> says the Eternal.
> "I am sated with burnt offerings of rams,
> and suet of fatlings,
> and blood of bulls;
> and I have no delight
> in lambs and he-goats.
> That you come to appear before Me—
> who asked that of you?
> Trample My courts no more;
> bringing oblations is futile,
> incense is offensive to Me.
> New Moon and Sabbath,
> proclaiming of solemnities,
> assemblies with iniquity,
> I cannot abide.
> Your New Moons and fixed seasons
> fill Me with loathing;
> they are become a burden to Me,

I cannot endure them.
And when you lift up your hands,
I will turn My eyes away from you;
though you pray at length,
I will not listen.
Your hands are stained with crime—
wash yourselves clean;
put your evil doings
away from My sight.
Cease to do evil;
learn to do good.
Devote yourselves to justice;
aid the wronged.
Uphold the rights of the orphan;
defend the cause of the widow.[26]

As people of faith, as Jews who walk in the path of the covenant of Sinai, the only path forward is to demand, as a first step, that Judaism and all other religions bless war no more. There is no war that is just. Every war is an exercise in mass murder.

We must learn peace. It is not enough to "learn war no more." We must learn peace. This perhaps is what is hinted at by the psalmist:

Come, my children, listen to me; I will teach you what it is to fear the Eternal....
Shun evil and do good, seek peace and pursue it. (Psalm 34:12, 15)

We must not only celebrate peace, bless each other with peace, and pray for peace. We must actively seek peace. We cannot do that through evil means. "Shun evil and do good." What is the good? "Seek peace and pursue it." The path is not easy. However, we should be investing as much time, energy, life, and treasure in that pursuit as we have already in the pursuit of war and killing. We must first reorient ourselves away from the instinctual violent and martial reaction to any and every situation. We must begin to learn nonviolence.[27] Our government must have nonviolence as the option of first choice when conflict starts brewing, and not wait for a shooting war.

To seek peace and pursue it, in an age in which we can easily destroy the whole planet with the stockpile of weapons currently available, is not only good and just. It is the only way to preserve the species—and all other species. Rabbi Tamares' insight is even more valuable today than it was a century ago. Violence only ever begets violence. Violence never begets peace. Only peace begets peace.

NOTES

[1] Cf. the midrash of Rabbi Shimon bar Yoḥai preserved at Vayikra Rabbah *9:9.*

[2] *Avot D'rabbi Natan 12:5.*

[3] M. Avot 1:12.

[4] *Derekh Eretz Zuta* 11.

[5] *Kallah Rabbati* 3b.

[6] Sifrei Bemidbar §42, commenting on Numbers 6:26.

[7] *Derekh Eretz Zuta,* chap. 11.

[8] *Kallah Rabbati* 3b. See Numbers 12:3 for the description of Moses as humble.

[9] Simḥah Zissel Ziv, *Sefer Ḥokhmah U-musar (*ed. New York, 5717 [1956/1957]), p. 3. The quote from Rashi is taken from his Torah commentary to Exodus 2:11, s.v. *va-yar b'sivlotam.*

[10] Shemot Rabbah 5.

[11] B. Yevamot 62a, Bava Batra 14b, and Menaḥot 99b.

[12] Aharon Shmuel Tamares, *Sefer Musar Ha-torah V'ha-yahadut* (Vilna: P. Garber, 5672 [1911/1912]), p. 126.

[13] Ibid., p. 44.

[14] B. Bava Kamma 60.

[15] Tamares, *Sefer Musar Ha-torah,* p. 44.

[16] B. Sanhedrin 48b.

[17] B. Berakhot 58a.

[18] Rashi to Exodus 22:1, s.v. *ein lo damim.*

[19] B. Sanhedrin 73a.

[20] B Sanhedrin 74a.

[21] Ibid.

[22] Hannah Arendt, *On Violence* (Orlando, Austin, New York, San Diego and London: Harcourt, 1970), p. 51.

[23] Emmanuel Levinas, *Totality and Infinity* (1969; rpt. Dordrecht [Netherlands]: Kluwer Academic Publishers, 1991), p. 22.

[24] Hannah Arendt, *On Violence,* p. 4. The version published in *On Violence* was an expansion of the original essay as it appeared in the *Journal of International Affairs* (Winter, 1969), pp. 1–35, and the *New York Review of Books* 12/4 (February 27, 1969), pp. 19–31.

[25] Valerie Epps, "Civilian Casualties in Modern Warfare: The Death of the Collateral Damage Rule," in *Legal Studies Research Paper Series,* Research Paper No. 11–39 (September 16, 2011), and see especially the studies cited in nn. 53–63 on pp. 18–20.

[26] Isaiah 1:10–17, based largely on the NJPS translation.

[27] It is worthwhile mentioning that someone has researched whether armed resistance actually works in overthrowing tyrannies. The conclusion is that nonviolent revolutions succeed far more often than violent revolutions. Erica

Chenoweth and Maria J. Stephan co-authored a book, *Why Civil Resistance Works: The Strategic Logic of Nonviolent Conflict* (New York: Columbia University Press, 2011), which studied 323 violent and nonviolent conflicts between 1900 and 2006. Professor Chenoweth, a domestic terrorism expert by training, started out as a sceptic of nonviolent resistance. However, the facts changed her mind. Chenoweth and Stephan found that "nonviolent resistance campaigns were nearly twice as likely to achieve full or partial success as their violent counterparts." See *Why Civil Resistance Works*, p. 7. This includes the finding that 60% of nonviolent campaigns for regime change succeed while less than 30% of violent campaigns to overthrow regimes succeed.

Divine Encounter: The Priestly Blessing

Avram Israel Reisner

May the LORD bless you and guard you.
May the LORD light up His face to you and grant grace to you.
May the LORD lift up His face to you and give you peace.
—Numbers 6:24–26[1]

The Priestly Blessing is usually discussed in terms of the blessings of protection, grace, and peace that it offers. But it is God's Presence, God's face, that occupies a central place in the blessing formula and requires our more focused attention.

God's Presence

We are far removed, in our modern world, from the intimacy and immediacy of the divine encounter described in the Torah and recognized by some of our sages. The midrash famously says that at the Sea of Reeds, when Moses sang, "This is my God—I extol Him" (Exodus 15:2),[2] God was present and visible to the whole people.[3] The Haggadah insists on this when interpreting Deuteronomy 26:8, "and the LORD brought us out from Egypt, with a strong hand and with an outstretched arm, and with great terror and with signs and with portents," in an interpretation that many later more buttoned-up commentators could not abide:

And the LORD brought us out from Egypt—not by an angel,
not by a seraph, not by an emissary. Rather, the blessed
Holy One, personally and alone, as it says: "And I will cross
through the land of Egypt on this night, and I will strike
down every firstborn in the land of Egypt from man to
beast, and from all the gods of Egypt I will exact retributions.
I am the LORD" (Exodus 12:12).
I will cross through the land of Egypt—I, and not an angel.
I will strike down every firstborn—I, and not a seraph.
From all the gods of Egypt I will exact retribution—I, and not
an emissary.
I am the LORD—I am the one and no other...
And with great terror (mora gadol)—this refers to the
appearance of God's Presence, as it says: "Or has God tried
to take Him a nation from within a nation...with a strong
hand and an outstretched arm, and with great terrors, like
all that the LORD your God did for you in Egypt before
your eyes" (Deuteronomy 4:34).[4]

But this is far from an aberration of rabbinic thinking. The Torah,
read plainly, assumes a physical presence of God leading the people
through the desert. It is God who is described by name as leading
the people in a pillar of fire and of cloud (Exodus 13:21) and it is
God's own glory that offers the people comfort and encouragement
when they hesitate (Exodus 16:10).[5] Later, the cloud that God's
glory inhabits settles on the Tabernacle (Exodus 40:34) and as God's
Presence in that cloud travels, so too do the people of Israel. Thus
it should be no surprise, when the Ark is lifted to proceed on their
journey, that Moses says "Rise, O LORD" and when it rests, he says
"Come back, O LORD" (Numbers 10:35–36). While these two verses
standing alone might be taken as metaphors, the Bible is clear that

God's residence in the Tabernacle and appearance specifically upon the Ark (Exodus 25:22) is a real spatial phenomenon.

The Torah at several points is surprisingly candid, indicating that a real physical manifestation of God may interact with humans. This is most obvious in Exodus 24. After receiving the Ten Commandments but before ascending onto Mount Sinai for forty days to receive the tablets and whatever other material was transmitted at that time, Moses and the people sacrificed and feasted in celebration.[7] That event is described, in part, thus:

> And Moses went up, and with him Aaron, Nadab and Abihu, and seventy of the elders of Israel. And they saw the God of Israel, and beneath His feet was like a fashioning of sapphire pavement and like the very heavens for pureness. But against the elect of the Israelites He did not send forth His hand, and they beheld God and ate and drank. (Exodus 24:9–11)

It is again clear upon a plain reading of Exodus 33:

> And so, when Moses would come to the Tent, the pillar of cloud would come down and stand at the entrance of the Tent and speak with Moses. And all the people would see the pillar of cloud standing at the entrance of the Tent....And the LORD would speak to Moses face to face, as a man speaks to his fellow....And He said, "My Presence shall go, and I will grant you rest." And he said to Him, "If Your Presence does not go, do not take us up from here. And how, then, will it be known that I have found favor in Your eyes, I and Your people? Will it not be by Your going with us...? And he said, "Show me, pray, Your glory." And He said, "I shall make all My goodness pass in front of you....You shall not be able to see My face, for no human can see Me and live." And the

LORD said, "Look, there is a place with Me....And so, when My glory passes over, I shall put you in the cleft of the crag and shield you with My palm until I have passed over. And I shall take away My palm and you will see My back, but My face will not be seen." (Exodus 33:9–11 and 14–23)

To be sure, later theological readings would seek to interpret these as spectral visions, a product of excitement, "in a vision" as it were—but nothing about this biblical text suggests that this was not a physical seeing of some divine image.

Thus, when the Torah says, "And they shall make Me a sanctuary, [10] that I may abide in their midst" (Exodus 25:8), or when it speaks of choosing a place "in which to make His name dwell" (Deuteronomy 12:11), ancient Israel understood that God frequented that place.[11] The sages second that image by insisting that prior to the time of Solomon's Temple, God's Presence resided only in those places where the Tabernacle resided:

> When Rav Dimi came [to Babylonia from Israel], he reported: In [only] three places [in Israel] did God's Presence [i.e., the Shekhinah] rest upon Israel: at Shiloh, at Nob and Gibeon, and at the permanent Temple.[12]

Though this image had long since lost its physical understanding by the time of the sages of classical antiquity, it is maintained in *midrashim* that speak of God's leaving the divine home at the Temple to go with God's children into exile.[13] But it is within the matrix of that spiritual understanding that it is necessary to seek the power and lasting vitality of the Priestly Blessing.[14]

God's Blessing

The Torah makes clear that the Priestly Blessing is not to be seen as a blessing by the priests about God's protection, but rather as a blessing by God through the medium of the priests. The language of the Torah is plain: "And they shall set My name over the Israelites, and I shall bless them" (Numbers 6:27).[15] Thus Sifrei Bemidbar §43:

> So that Israel should not say, "Our blessings are dependent on the priests," therefore it says: "I [Myself] shall bless them." So that the priests should not say, "We bless Israel," therefore it says: "I [Myself] shall bless them"—I will bless My people Israel.[16]

That same idea appears in an amoraic reflection in Talmud Yerushalmi:

> So that you should not say, "That man is an adulterer, a murderer, and he blesses us?"— [therefore] God says, "Who blesses you? Is it not I who blesses you? As it says: "And they shall set My name over the Israelites, and I shall bless them."[17]

Ramban, among the commentaries, seems clearly to have this in mind, when in his commentary to "and I shall bless them" he simply cites Isaiah 52:6: "I, the One who promised, am now at hand."[18]

Not all *midrashim* take this approach,[19] but it is this immediate connection to the Divine that best explains the extraordinary hold that the Priestly Blessing has held over the generations, even those generations who would deny such an interpretation.

God's Name

We have discussed the words of the Priestly Blessing, but not the end of its scriptural setting. These too are significant indicators of the Bible's meaning: "And they shall set My name over the Israelites" (Numbers 6:27). What is meant by this phrase? What precisely is happening?

The other instances of "setting God's name" in the biblical text are all of a piece, in the writings of the Deuteronomist, and all refer to God's choice of the site of the Temple in Jerusalem. The first such reference is Deuteronomy 12:5, where reference is made to "the place that the LORD your God will choose of all your tribes to set His name there (*la-sum sh'mo*), to make it dwell (*l'shikhno*)." The internal explanation serves to define the term: "to set His name" = "to make it dwell."[20] And there is external synony here as well, for in verse 11 "the place God chooses" is described as "the place that the LORD your God will choose in which to make His name dwell (*l'shakkein sh'mo*)," and then in verse 21 again as "the place...that the LORD your God will choose to set His name (*la-sum sh'mo*)." Thus the two terms serve identically throughout the books of Deuteronomy, Kings, and Chronicles. While the passage in Numbers is in some ways anomalous, the weight of this usage is suggestive.[21]   God's name is equivalent to God's Presence. God's indwelling Presence was understood to inhabit the Temple, and that was the intent of the building of the Temple. Here, in the Priestly Blessing, the further claim is made that God's Presence is to rest upon every member of the people of Israel, transferred through the Priestly Blessing.

This somewhat audacious claim is supported by a vestige of this early understanding alive among the classical sages. Mishnah Sotah 7:6 rules that the explicit divine name may be used only in the Temple precincts. This ruling is explained in a tannaitic text on B. Sotah 38a by way of a direct comparison between God's Presence during the Priestly Blessing and at the Temple:

"Thus shall you bless the Israelites" (Numbers 6:23). Does this mean the explicit name (*sheim ha-m'forash*) or just its alternative? The Torah teaches: "And they shall set My name over the Israelites" (Numbers 6:27)—that is, the name specific to Me. Might you do so even throughout the country? It is written of this case, "And they shall set My name (*v'samu et sh'mi*)" and of that case, "to set His name there (*la-sum et sh'mo sham*)" (Deuteronomy 12:5). Just as that refers to the House of [God's] Choosing, so here it refers [only] to the House of [God's] Choosing.Rabbi Josiah says: This is unnecessary. It says, "in every place where I cause My name to be mentioned I will come to you [and bless you]" (Exodus 20:21). Every place? Rather, this verse is disordered. "In every place where I will come to you and bless you, there will I cause My name to be mentioned." Where will I come to you and bless you? In the House of [My] Choosing. That is where I will cause My name to be mentioned: in the House of [My] Choosing.[22]

The implication must be that, whereas outside the Temple precincts the Priestly Blessing is performed in a sub-optimal way, without a real connection to the Divine, that connection is alive and real at the Temple itself.[23]

At B. Yoma 39b, a story is told of the death of Simeon the Righteous. To mark that occasion, the text tells us that "his brother priests refrained from blessing with the name"—that is, they did not use the explicit divine name that was generally used in the Temple.[24] This Simeon the Righteous has been identified for us in Pirkei Avot 1:2 as "one of the remnants of the Great Assembly" and is identified there by the commentator Obadiah of Bertinoro (c.1445–1515) as "the High Priest who followed Ezra." There remains some uncertainty about the identity and date of this figure, but by all accounts he was a pre-Hasmonean High Priest.[25] Nothing about the story guarantees its historicity nor, if it happened, that dispensing with the use of God's explicit name was other than an immediate and short-term gesture of mourning. But the commentary of the Tosafot on B. Sotah 38a, s.v. *harei*, states that the priests refrained, from that day forward, from using the divine name. Noting that the language of the Sifrei, "in every place that I will come to you," means "I, Myself, that is a place of divine manifestation (*gillui sh'khinah*)...specifically the House of [God's] Choosing," Tosafot goes on to explain that "it seems that that is the reason the priests refrained from using the explicit divine name after the death of Simeon the Righteous...because they no longer merited divine manifestation." If Tosafot is right about the meaning of this story, and the context in Yoma suggests that that is the case, then it appears to reflect a tannaitic awareness of a historic shift from a sense of God's real residence at the Temple and consequent real presence at the Priestly Blessing at the Temple (at the very time that a lesser form of Priestly Blessing was being given regularly throughout the countryside), to a lesser state where even in the Temple in its latter days God's Presence was no longer felt. That time when God's Presence was truly present in the Temple is reputed to be far in the legendary past. It is as if to say, "We do not know divine manifestation, although we are still serving at the Temple—but the ancients did."

But another source, perhaps a more reliable one, while it casts doubt on this historic reconstruction, yet confirms the gradual loss of the speaking of God's explicit name during the Priestly Blessing— consequently distancing the observers from the sense of God's real Presence. *Sifrei Zuta* 6:27 recounts the following:

> "And they shall set My name (*v'samu et sh'mi*)" (Numbers 6:27)—the name that is specific to Me. This teaches that they blessed with the explicit divine name. Might you do so even throughout the country? Therefore it says, "And they shall set My name (*v'samu et sh'mi*)," and there it says "to set His name there (*la-sum et sh'mo sham*)" (Deuteronomy 12:5). Just as that refers to the Temple, so here it refers [only] to the Temple.

When impious [priests] grew in number, they would [only] consign it to the pious priests. Said Rabbi Tarfon: It happened that I was standing with my brethren priests in line, I listened carefully to the High Priest, and I heard him saying it during the melody of his brethren priests.

Rabbi Tarfon does not say here when this might have happened, that the public declaration of God's explicit name was no longer performed, but was consigned to select pious priests. From that moment on, with the divine name no longer pronounced during the Priestly Blessing at the Temple, the reality of God's Presence surely receded. But Rabbi Tarfon was a young priest when the Temple was destroyed in 70 C.E., so if he heard the high priest utter the explicit divine name, even *sotto voce*, there was somehow still a vestige of the notion of God's Presence even then. But whatever the chronological story behind the loss of the use of God's explicit name during the Priestly Blessing, while it yet continued, it was reflective of the strong sense that God's Presence was real, was present, and had a hand in the transfer of the blessing onto the people of Israel.[26]

The Priestly Blessing

If we have correctly identified the original weight of the Priestly Blessing, it is appropriate to rethink its message in that context.

The Priestly Blessing is comprised of three strophes of increasing length and complexity—three Hebrew words in the first, five in the second and seven in the third—which comprise Numbers 6:24–26. A close literal translation is that offered by Robert Alter:

May the LORD bless you and guard you.
May the LORD light up His face to you and grant grace to you
May the LORD lift up His face to you and give you peace.

The first strophe carries the essential meaning and message of a blessing: that God should bless and guard. Nothing extraneous. The language is clear and to the point. It is not at all surprising that this text finds itself in use in the oldest example of a biblical text found by archaeologists, dated to the seventh century B.C.E.—on apparent amulets of silver, found in a burial cave at Ketef Hinnom in Jerusalem.[27] But it should be noted that the full text did not appear on either amulet that was found. The Priestly Blessing as recorded in the Torah has six clauses, which may be conveniently numbered as such: (1) bless, (2) guard, (3) light His face, (4) grant grace, (5) lift His face, and (6) give peace. One amulet had only clauses 1–3, being cut off at that point, and the other contained clauses 1–3 and 6, but clearly did not have clauses 4 and 5. This raises speculation about whether the biblical version is an expansion on a shorter earlier text, or whether, alternatively, the first amulet may have had the full text of the biblical Priestly Blessing and the second is simply a conscious contraction thereof or a simple scribal omission due to accidentally skipping from the first occurrence of the word "face" to the subsequent occurrence of the same word. There is no obvious way to resolve the question. The neat numerical word structure (plus the similar pyramid of 15–20–25 letters) recommends the Masoretic text as the original, but this is certainly not dispositive. The full Masoretic text clearly lay behind the Dead Sea Scroll text, 1QS 2:2–4, which has the priests saying:

May He bless you with all good and guard you from all evil. And may He light up your heart with good judgment and grace you with infinite knowledge.[28]
And may He raise His kindly face to you for everlasting peace.[28]

But that is several centuries later than the amulets.

Yet the line of thinking developed here may yield a strong indication that the full Masoretic text was the original form of the Priestly Blessing. The first line of three represents a basic blessing: positive blessing and defense against harm, as represented clearly by the Dead Sea Scroll version. The second strophe differs, in that it contemplates God's own specific acknowledgment of the individual being blessed, whereas the first clause might have been referring to something delegated to an angel or might otherwise represent the distance of upper management. It is the second strophe that insists on God's personal involvement, God's facing toward you, albeit at a distance, and indicating personal regard for or toward you (note the dual meaning of the English term "regard," which is particularly apropos). The third clause is the one that strikes one initially as problematic, for it is unclear what it adds. Indeed, that might, *prima facie*, be an argument for the shortened version of the second Ketef Hinnom amulet mentioned above.

Baruch Levine, in his Anchor Bible volume on Numbers 1–20, walks squarely into this problem of redundancy when, in his notes, he speaks of *ya·eir* as "the request of God that he look upon his people favorably," and of *yissa* as "the request of God that he pay attention to his people, that he look upon them favorably."[29] Levine favors the notion that the shorter version of the Ketef Hinnom text may have been the original and the Masoretic version a "fattened" version. He suggests that there are really only two primary blessings here: those of the first strophe, to bless and to protect. The Ketef Hinnom short version expanded "bless" with *ya·eir*, "to look with favor upon, be well disposed toward," and expanded "guard" with *sim shalom*, a form of protection. The Masoretic text, in this view, doubled the instantiations of blessing and protection, offering both *ya·eir*, "to look with favor," and *yahon*, "to grant grace" as the playing out of blessing, and *yissa panim*, here understood as to "show concern for," and of course shalom as the explication of protection.[30]

But now we are in a position to suggest a different sense of the third strophe, which is specific to and necessary for the Priestly Blessing as we have understood it. The first and second strophes present God at a distance. The meaning of the third strophe, operatively the essence of the Priestly Blessing, is that God should carry God's Presence through the medium of the priests, to the individual being blessed, closing the distance between them—so that God's divine Presence might reside with the one who is blessed and thereby assure him or her of peace.[31] Thus, Numbers 6:27, *v'samu et sh'mi* ("they shall set My name") is indeed similar in meaning to Deuteronomy 12:5, *la-sum et sh'mo sham* ("to set His name there"). It is a late text, to be sure, but is it a wonder that after the Priestly Blessing the congregation says: "Powerful in heaven, residing in might, You are peace and Your name is peace"? For this strophe is precisely intended to convey that God's Presence will close the distance between the Divine Presence and the individual, and place God's own name (*shalom*) upon the congregation.[32]

If this is indeed the intent of the Priestly Blessing—as I think it is—then the three-strophe form, and the third strophe in particular, is substantively necessary. Furthermore, this accounts for the strange power of the Priestly Blessing across the ages. For it is not by chance that, long since the priests ceased speaking the Priestly Blessing in the Temple, long since they ceased to use God's explicit name, Jews have adopted the Priestly Blessing to bless their children on Friday night and rabbis regularly choose it for blessing marrying couples under the *ḥuppah*.

A well known hasidic story tells of the Baal Shem Tov:

When the great Rabbi Israel Baal Shem Tov saw misfortune threatening the Jews, it was his custom to go into a certain part of the forest to meditate. There he would light a fire, say a special prayer, and the miracle would be accomplished and the misfortune averted. Later when his disciple, the celebrated Maggid of Mezritch, had occasion, for the same reason, to intercede with heaven, he would go to the same place in the forest and say: "Master of the Universe, listen! I do not know how to light the fire, but I am still able to say the prayer." And again the miracle would be accomplished. Still later, Rabbi Moshe Leib of Sasov, in order to save his people once more, would go into the forest and say: I do not know how to light the fire, I do not know the prayer, but I know the place and this must be sufficient." It was sufficient, and the miracle was accomplished. Then it fell to Rabbi Israel of Ryzhyn to overcome misfortune. Sitting in his armchair, his head in his hands, he spoke to God: "I am unable to light the fire, and I do not know the prayer, and I cannot even find the place in the forest. All I can do is tell the story, and this must be sufficient." And it was sufficient.[33]

That, in a nutshell, is the story of the Priestly Blessing which once brought God's Presence, really; then brought it only metaphorically, though we still recited God's name explicitly; then, using only a pale imitation of God's name, the tradition carries forward; a pale imitation of itself, but treasured nonetheless.[34]

In Ruth 2:4 Boaz greets his field hands, saying: "The LORD be with you," and they responded "the LORD bless you." This may have been only a nicety, but it spoke the truth of the essence of the Priestly Blessing; that God being with you was the essence of blessing. And it is not in the world of ancient Israel alone that that was the regnant concept of blessing. Indeed, the same language of blessing upon greeting or departure can be found in virtually any language: God be with you (later, "goodbye"), Adieu ("with God"), Vaya con Dios ("go with God"). These expressions become immeasurably richer when we begin to understand that the notion that God might reside with us and travel with us, when we are most in need of God's protection...that that was at its heart, in its inception, not just a turn of phrase, but the real thing.

We are unable to rekindle the fire of our ancestors' burning faith. But at least we can tell the story.

NOTES

[1] The Priestly Blessing is here presented in the translation of Robert Alter, *The Five Books of Moses* (New York: W. W. Norton, 2004), p. 714. English translations from the Torah throughout this article, unless otherwise noted, are likewise from Alter's translation. Translations from the Prophets and Writings will be those of the new JPS translation (Philadelphia: Jewish Publication Society, 1985). Translations of rabbinic texts are the author's own.

[2] Alter's translation. Other translations have "honor," "praise," or "glorify." The new JPS translation, however, differs, translating "I will enshrine Him," understanding the unusual verbal form *anveihu* as derived from the common noun *naveh*, meaning a place, rather than the more standard view that it is a secondary verbal form based upon *na·eh*, "lovely." Compare Exodus 15:17. (The "new JPS translation" of the Torah was originally published by the Jewish Publication Society in 1962, and subsequently reprinted in 1985 in *The Tanakh: The Holy Scriptures —Torah, Nevi'im, Ketuvim*; and again in 1999 as part of *The JPS Hebrew-English Tanakh*.)

[3] See B. Sotah 30b: "Rabbi Yosi the Galilean expounded: When Israel came up out of the [Reed] Sea, they sought to offer song. How was that? Every toddler on their mother's lap, every infant suckling at their mother's breast—when they saw the Divine Presence, every toddler craned their neck, every infant spit the teat out of their mouth and said, 'This is my God; I honor Him.'" Other versions of this midrash are found at Y. Sotah 5:4, 20c, and T. Sotah 6:2.

[4] The Hebrew of the midrash, *u-v'mora gadol—zeh gillui sh'khinah*, seems to hide a pun interpreting *mora*, "terror," as *mareh*, "appearance." This interpretation is seconded by the attached verse that speaks of God's *mora* being displayed visibly. This is the standard Ashkenazic text of the Haggadah. See the extended discussion by Ernst Daniel Goldschmidt who, based on Genizah documents, discusses what he calls "the most ancient Haggadah that is in our hands" (*Haggadah Shel Pesaḥ: M'koroteha V'toldoteha B'meshekh Ha-dorot* (Jerusalem: Mossad Bialik, 1981), pp. 30ff.; the quote appears on p. 73. It is noteworthy that though the midrash to these central verses of the Haggadah is much briefer there, it includes the first two lines above, without the prooftext and elaboration, making the point that it was God acting personally in Egypt.

[5] It is true, however, that the pillar of cloud that stands between Israel and Pharaoh's army is described as a messenger of God in Exodus 14:19. Noting the discrepancy, Alter comments, "The introduction of an agent of the deity here is either an explanation in the original narrative of what God's presence before the people actually meant or an interpolation of later tradition in order to mitigate anthropomorphism" (p. 393).

[6] After the revelation began, wherein God spoke directly to the people but which the people truncated (Exodus 20:16), Moses went up to God to receive the rest

of the revelation (Exodus 20:18). This was not yet the whole of the Torah, for the receipt of which Moses would ascend Mount Sinai again for forty days. The extent of God's verbal revelation may have been the Ten Commandments, or perhaps only the first two commandments; see the baraita of the School of Rabbi Yishmael on B. Horayot 8a and the way that it is understood by Rav Hamnuna on B. Makkot 24a–b. See also Shemot Rabbah 33:7, Shir Hashirim Rabbah 1.2.2, *Tanhuma, Vayeilekh* §2, and *Pirkei D'rabbi Eliezer*, chap. 41. Less clear is a possible reference in Sifrei Bemidbar §112. Moses would later write the full content of that revelation (Exodus 24:3) *before* ascending the mountain for forty days. The chronological presentation in the Torah suggests that the extent of the full revelation that Moses committed to writing at that point might have included the laws of *parashat Mishpatim*. It is not, however, possible to state that with certainty.

[7] The dominant tradition has it that the whole of the Five Books of Moses was transmitted verbatim at that time, but the biblical narrative itself does not support that assertion.

[8] The Hebrew here is particularly opaque, and interpretations differ vastly. The Hebrew is but four words: *panai yeileikhu va-hanihoti lakh.* Alter here, and NJPS and others, interpret it as having positive import—namely, that God will in some way assure Israel's well-being. But it is possible that this was a negative, as in verses 33:2–3. Indeed, from Moses' response ("If Your Presence does not go") it seems that he saw this as negative; thus, one could interpret as follows: "God said, 'My Presence will go away (*panai yeileikhu*); it will leave you (*va-hanihoti lakh*).' Moses replied, 'If Your Presence does not go with us, then leave us here—for how would we then go forward?'" (Note that in this interpretation, the same Hebrew root, *hei-lamed-kaf*, is understood to have two radically differing meanings: "go" and "leave".) In his notes Alter comes close to, but does not actually adopt, this possibility, presumably because he sees God's position as having progressed from what it was earlier in the chapter. He writes: "The Hebrew is altogether cryptic…Presumably, what God is telling Moses is that He will indeed go before the people…and thus lighten Moses' burden, 'grant you rest'…But God, scarcely willing to concede that He Himself will lead the people, words the response so laconically…that Moses is by no means sure what God means, and so he goes on to say, 'If Your Presence does not go up….'" Everett Fox attempts to solve this by casting God's statement as an interrogative: "If My Presence were to go (with you), would I cause you to rest easy?" See his *The Five Books of Moses* (New York: Schocken, 1995), p. 452.

[9] Thus, for instance, the commentary of Abraham ibn Ezra to Exodus 24:10 (both his short and long commentaries), and more extensively in his long commentary to Exodus 33:21.

[10] The translation here departs from Alter's translation. The Hebrew term is *mikdash*, which standardly refers to the Temple and is anachronistic here in the

context of the desert. Thus Alter translates "Tabernacle," though that is nowhere a translation of *mikdash*, but rather of *mishkan*. Surprisingly, Alter does not note the implied emendation in his notes, but compounds the question by seeming to take *mishkan* as the given (Masoretic) text. He writes: "Tabernacle—the Hebrew *mishkan* literally means 'abode'..." I see no indication of the existence of such a variant.

[11] The God of Israel was known as resident in Jerusalem, an expression used regularly by the prophets and in Psalms—see, for example, Isaiah 8:18; Joel 4:17, 21; and Psalm 135:21. It might be noted that the appurtenances of the Tabernacle described in the Torah are the Ark, a table, and a lamp (the menorah). These can be seen as the basic furnishings of an apartment. No chair? "God of Hosts, enthroned on the cherubim" (2 Samuel 6:2). Where is the bed? "See, the guardian of Israel neither slumbers nor sleeps" (Psalm 121:4).
In his recent book *The Bodies of God and the World of Ancient Israel* (New York: Cambridge University Press, 2009), Benjamin Sommer argues that in the J and E sources, given "the absence of any statements telling us that these many verses are mere figures of speech...the ancients who talk about God's body really do think that God has a body." Of the P source, he concludes that the notion was of a lustrous presence rather than a physical corpus, but that "a central theme of priestly tradition—perhaps the central theme of priestly tradition—is the desire of the transcendent God to become immanent on the earth this God has created"—to wit, in the Temple in Jerusalem. Expressly, however, he finds that the D school separated between God (who resides in heaven) and God's name—contrary to other scholars, who understand the *sheim* "as YHWH's cultic presence in the Jerusalem temple" (see pp. 64–68). My inclination is toward those other scholars (B. Janowski, "Ich will in euer Mitte wohnen," in *Jahrbuch für Biblische Theologie* 2 [1987], and S. Dean McBride, "Deuteronomic Name Theology," doctoral dissertation Harvard University, 1969), as will be clear in the continuation. The crux of Sommer's argument is from the prayer of Solomon, reported in 1 Kings 8 and 2 Chronicles 6, which does, indeed, insistently attach to every reference to God's receiving prayer given at the Temple, that God will listen "in Your heavenly abode / in heaven" (verses 30, 32, 34, 36, 39, 43, 45, 49). But that very insistence and the awkwardness thereof suggests to me that these words each time could easily be a gloss, or the whole lengthy prayer an addition, since the opening succinct prayer reads otherwise: "The LORD has chosen to abide in a thick cloud. I have now built for You a stately house, a place where You may dwell forever" (1 Kings 8:12–13).
Be this as it may, the Priestly Benediction is clearly a P text and the palpable sense of God's Presence described here is a feature of the earlier sources. And whatever the Deuteronomists may have intended, as Sommer recognizes, "the theological intuition found in JE and elsewhere did not simply disappear" (p. 79).
[12] B. Zevaḥim 118b. This text clearly counts Nob and Gibeon as one place. An

alternative text reads "four places," in which case they might be counted separately. Alternatively, they might be counted as one and Gilgal, the first stopping-place of the Tabernacle in the days of the conquest under Joshua, might be intended for inclusion. A fuller list of the stations of the Tabernacle appears later on this page of Talmud: "The days of the Tabernacle in the wilderness were forty years less one. The days of the Tabernacle at Gilgal were fourteen [years], seven of conquest and seven of division; at Nob and Gibeon, fifty-seven. There were left to Shiloh three hundred seventy, less one." A similar list is found in Y. Megillah 1:12 at the end (72d).

[13] *Avot D'rabbi Natan*, version A, chap. 34, ed. Solomon Schechter (New York: Feldheim, 1967), p. 52a. See also B. Rosh Hashanah 31a. These *midrashim* are akin to the vision of Ezekiel in Ezekiel 10.

[14] All this is alluded to by David Noel Freedman in an article focusing on a close reading of the wording to the priestly blessing, "The Aaronic Benediction (Num. 6:24–26)," in *Journal of Biblical Literature* 74 (1955), pp. 35–47. On page 40 there, he writes: "The Aaronic Benediction seems to reflect the experience of Moses, and to express the hope that the worshipper may have a share in it, and see the refulgent glory of God's face....The conclusion is that the Aaronic Benediction is a product of that early period in Israel's history when the people went up to present themselves to Yahweh and to 'see His face.'"

[15] My translation. Alter, recognizing the implication that it is God who is presenting the blessing, translates with the emphatic "I Myself shall bless them." Though that translation is consistent with the argument being made here, the Hebrew (*va-ani avar'kheim*) need not be translated emphatically. Therefore, in the interest of transparency I have opted to avoid the emphatic translation and let the argument being made here stand on its own merits.

[16] A more elaborate version of this midrashic idea is found in Bemidbar Rabbah 11:2: "When the blessed Holy One told Aaron and his sons, 'Thus shall you bless...' (Numbers 6:23), Israel said to the blessed Holy One, 'Master of the Universe, you tell the priests to bless us—but we are in need only of Your blessings, to be blessed from Your mouth!'...Said the blessed Holy One to them, 'Even though I told the priests to bless you, I will be standing with them and blessing you. That is why the priests spread their hands, so as to say, 'the blessed Holy One is standing behind us.' And that is why it says (Song of Songs 2:9–10), 'gazing through the window'—between the shoulders of the priests; 'peering through the lattice'—between the fingers of the priests; 'my beloved spoke thus to me'—'and I [Myself] shall bless them' (Numbers 6:27)."

[17] Y. Gittin 5:9, 47b. It is noteworthy, in this regard, that Rabbi Joshua ben Levi's well-known dictum, that even an iron wall cannot interpose between God and Israel (whose original context I cannot determine), was cited by the *g'mara* on B. Sotah 38b to justify the notion that the Priestly Blessing reaches beyond the synagogue's walls; and it appears as well in that very context in Y. Gittin here, in

the name of Rabbi Ḥiyya bar Ba.

[18] I have capitalized "One," as the reference is clearly to God.

[19] See *Sifrei Zuta* 6:27 and *Tanḥuma, Lekh L'kha* §4 (ed. Buber §5). In response to the question "What if the priests refuse to give the blessing?" the text of the *Sifrei Zuta* reads: *ani avar'kheim min ha-shamayim,* "I will bless them from heaven"—asserting that God is not present. But the words "from heaven" are suspect in my eyes, as the parallel text in Sifrei Bemidbar §43 does not have them. Regarding the *Tanḥuma* text, see note 26 below. And see in this regard also Rabbi Akiva's dictum preserved at B. Ḥullin 49a.

[20] The NJPS translation here, understanding these terms as synonyms, reverses the order for the sake of the flow: "the site that the LORD your God will choose…as His habitation, to establish His name there."

[21] "To set His name" appears in Deuteronomy 12:5, 21; 14:24; 1 Kings 9:3; 11:36; 14:21; 2 Kings 21:4, 7; 2 Chronicles 6:20; 12:13; 33:7. "To cause His name to dwell" appears in Deuteronomy 12:11; 14:23; 16:2, 6, 11; 26:2; Jeremiah 7:12, and Nehemiah 1:9. A third synonym, "that His name might abide" (*lihyot sh'mo*), appears only in Kings and Chronicles (at 1 Kings 8:16, 29; 2 Kings 23:27 and 2 Chronicles 6:5–6). At a later date, to be sure, there was a hesitation about making the claim that God was actually resident at the Temple, and more cautious language crept in. See Jeremiah chapter 7 (and elsewhere), which speaks of the House "which bears My name (*nikra sh'mi alav*).

[22] This text appears also in Sifrei Bemidbar §39, with some variation that includes stripping out the specifics of the word comparison that is nonetheless at the heart of the first teaching. The second verse interpreted as an alternative, Exodus 20:21 is presented here in the NJPS version. Alter translates somewhat awkwardly here, and numbers the verse 20:24, which is not in accordance with the Masoretic text. Rashi connects this to the discussion of all the holy spaces from the time of the desert until the Temple which we noted before, commenting, *s.v. m'suras hu*: "Reversed—'in every place where I will come to you'—at the Tabernacle in the desert and at Shiloh and at the permanent Temple." The Sifrei version of the second teaching is more stark. Instead of speaking in the language of the Torah in reordering the verse, "in every place where I will come to you," the text of Sifrei uses rabbinic language: "In every place where I appear to you (*she-ani niglah alekha*)"—a difference that Tosafot, there, mines (see below).

This second verse is explicated *in situ* in Mekhilta D'rabbi Ishmael, *Ba-ḥodesh (Yitro)* §11, and Mekhilta D'rabbi Shimon bar Yoḥai (*Yitro*), to prove both that the explicit divine name is reserved for the Tabernacle, and that the Priestly Blessing is nonetheless to be performed throughout the country. Both texts, once dealing with terrain outside the Temple and no longer dealing with the real phenomenon of divine contact, continue to conclude that another read of this verse is that God even rests on a single person, a teaching that appears in

Pirkei Avot 3:6 and in B. Berakhot 6a.

[23] This *mishnah* also notes a difference in the how the *kohanim* held their hands in the Temple and outside it—above their heads at the Temple, but only to their shoulders outside the Temple—probably also because the priests at the Temple were understood to be channeling the Divine Presence, whereas those outside were not. That distinction arises as well from the dictum of Rabbi Judah bar Naḥmani on B. Ḥagigah 16a; see below, note 26.

[24] The story is of tannaitic provenance, but does not appear in any authentic tannaitic collection. A similar *baraita* appears in Y. Yoma 5:2, 42c, but the detail about the Priestly Blessing appears only here. This is brought as part of a series of tannaitic texts about the weakening of the Temple service upon the death of Simeon the Righteous. One of those appears in T. Sotah 13:7. The impression is left that this is an authentic collection of tannaitic texts.

[25] See Uriel Rappaport's article on "Simeon the Just" in *Encyclopedia Judaica*, 2nd ed. (Detroit: Macmillan Reference USA, 2007), vol. 18, p. 602.

[26] Yeḥiel Epstein felt this. In his *Arukh Ha-shulḥan, Oraḥ Ḥayyim* 128:8, he explains that the Priestly Blessing requires a *minyan* (i.e., a prayer quorum of ten) despite not technically being a *davar she-bi-k'dushah* (a liturgical matter of holiness), "because it says, 'I shall bless them,' whereupon it demands the descent of God's spirit, and the descent of God's spirit only takes place among ten." It is the subtext of the dictum of Rabbi Judah bar Naḥmani on B. Ḥagigah 16a that one who peers at the *kohanim* in the Temple during the Priestly Blessing will be blinded (by God's unassimilable glory), which Rashi explains (*s.v. u-m'var'khin et ha-am*) is because "God's Presence rests on the tips of their fingers." This thesis was presented briefly by Jacob Spiegel in two recensions of an article: the first, entitled *"Birkat Kohanim V'gillui Shekhinah,"* which appeared in a weekly sheet published at Kibbutz Sdei Eliyahu on May 15, 1999, around *parashat Naso*; and the second published in his book, *Pitḥei T'fillah U-mo·eid* (Elkanah, Israel: Mikhlelet Orot, 2010), pp. 38–40, under the title *"Gillui Shekhinah B'eit Birkat Kohanim."* I am disappointed by a discussion about the Priestly Blessing by Yochanan Muffs in chapter 17 of his *The Personhood of God* (Woodstock, VT: Jewish Lights 2005), pp. 151–156, which utilizes exclusively later *midrashim* from the *Tanḥuma* and discusses Birkat Kohanim focusing only on the relationship between the priests and the people during that rite.

[27] Gabriel Barkay et al., "The Challenges of Ketef Hinnom," in *Near Eastern Archaeology* 66:4 (2003), pp. 162–171, and cf. Gabriel Barkay et al., "The Amulets from Ketef Hinnom," in *Bulletin of the American Schools of Oriental Research* 334 (2004), pp. 41–71.

[28] The Hebrew text can be viewed at http://dss.collections.imj.org.il/community, for comparison to the biblical text. The translation is my own, seeking to bear the closest resemblance possible word for word with Alter's translation of the Masoretic text.

[29] Baruch A. Levine, *The Anchor Bible: Numbers 1–20* (New York: Doubleday,

1993), pp. 227–228.

[30] Ibid, p. 240. Menaḥem Haran also takes the position that the blessings are duplicative in his article, *"Birkat Kohanim Mi-ketef Hinnom,"* included as chapter 31 in his collection *Mikra V'olamo* (Jerusalem: Magnes Press, 2009), pp. 421–432, as do Chaim Cohen, in his "The Biblical Priestly Blessing (Num. 6:24-26) in Light of Akkadian Parallels," in *Tel Aviv* 20:2 (1993), pp. 228–238, and others, though in differing ways. Haran's essay originally appeared in *Cathedra* 52 (1989), pp. 77–89.

[31] This is a literal reading of *yissa panav*. As does Levine, Haran and Cohen each take this as an idiom meaning "to favor," essentially the same as that which is found in the previous strophe. Cohen finds two parallels to this usage in the Bible from which to extrapolate, and several Akkadian sources. All the Akkadian sources refer to turning the face or lifting the head without the word *el*, indicating changed attitude but not movement through space, as is indicated by the biblical phrase. And one of the two biblical references—Psalm 4:7 (*n'sa aleinu or panekha,* "cast upon us the light of Your countenance"), translated by Cohen as "pay special attention to us in a joyful way"—uses *al* and not *el* and speaks not of carrying God's face but only of the radiance thereof. Only Deuteronomy 28:50 is apposite, reading *asher lo yissa panim l'zakein v'na·ar lo yaḥon* ("who does not show honor to an elder or favor to a youth"). But the Priestly Blessing is much older than this passage in Deuteronomy, as noted by Freedman (above, note 14), and the later idiom is not an indication of what might have been a very literal use in the earlier material.

[32] This prayer, standard in prayerbooks, has its origin as a prayer to be said at the time of the Priestly Blessing that is mentioned by a 5–6th c. *amora* on B. Berakhot 55b.

[33] This version of the story is the one popularized by Elie Wiesel as the epilogue to his early novel *The Gates of the Forest* (New York: Holt, Rinehart, and Winston, 1966). In *Major Trends in Jewish Mysticism* (1941; rpt. New York: Schocken, 1961), pp. 349–350, Gershom Scholem reports that this story was told to him by S. Y. Agnon, in different words; perhaps that was the proximate source of Elie Wiesel's retelling of the story. The story appears in a collection of folktales by Howard Schwartz, *Leaves from the Garden of Eden* (Oxford: Oxford University Press, 2009), p. 355, #90 (though Schwartz reports that the popular story has significantly different details than the original from which it stems). The original Hebrew text is found in *K'nesset Yisrael* by Reuben Zak (ed. Warsaw, 1906), p. 12a. It is noteworthy that in that Hebrew original the prayer is not a prayer, but the more mystical *yiḥudim v'kavvanot* (not easily translated, these are mystical meditations on the mysteries of God), and it is they, not the forest and the flame, that are lost over time. The loss of the mystical component makes this story all the more relevant to the case being made here.

[34] In an article in *Tarbiz* 62:2 (1992–93), pp. 179–223 (*"T'fillat Sh'moneh*

Esreih"), Ezra Fleischer speculates on the presence of Birkat Kohanim in the Amidah. The sages normally looked to downplay the role of the *kohanim*, so it seems unusual that the prayer was given such prominence, even more so its reenactment. Without taking the speculation further, he posits that there must have been pressure from the *kohanim* or from the people to include it. What we have written here may be seen as support for just such extraordinary import associated with the Priestly Blessing.

From Paternal Prerogative to Priestly Obligation: The Genealogy of Birkat Kohanim

Shalom Carmy

I will address two questions, both of them fundamental for an understanding of the Priestly Blessing. First: what is a blessing? And then: what is the role of the priestly line of Aaron in conveying God's blessing? These questions are deserving of our attention, not only for an accurate understanding of the biblical record but also for its contemporary appropriation.

Blessing Like Prayer

The Hebrew word *b'rakhah*, "blessing," is familiar, but its meaning is mysterious. Religious Jews bless God hundreds of times a day. Every one of the standard prayers prescribed by the Talmud—be it praise, petition, or thanksgiving—begins with the words *barukh atah ha-Shem*, as does every appropriation of nourishment and many performances of divine commandments. The common English translation, "Blessed are You, O God" (which conforms to the views of such mystical writers as Rabbi Ḥayyim of Volozhin, in early nineteenth-century "Jewish Lithuania,") implies that human beings are conferring a blessing on the deity, as it were—whatever that might mean, just as blessing another human being would be an attempt to bestow a blessing on the recipient.[1]

Rationalists like the fifteenth-century Spanish philosopher Rabbi Joseph Albo take pains to avoid suggesting that God is in any way enhanced by human blessing.[2] They parse the word *barukh* as an adjective describing God rather than a performance in which God is blessed. Thus, we humans do not confer blessing on God: God is not the object of our blessings, but we rather refer to God as the source of blessing. But in either the rationalist or mystical interpretation, the act of blessing is a ubiquitous feature of the lives of religious individuals, even though both practitioners and outsiders often fail to consider the exact meaning of the practice. In Birkat Kohanim, the subject of this essay, the object of the blessing is human—and so the problem of blessing God need not detain us further.

Of course, we are concerned with serious, meaningful invocations of blessing. The unthinking secular recourse to the phrase "God bless you," which waxes and wanes with the frequency of upper respiratory infections and allergies and often closes the speeches of politicians, is not helpful here. That usage has become a reflexive rather than reflective routine.

So when we begin to reflect on what it means for one human being to bless another, or to bless God, where do we start? What features of religious language occupy a related semantic field and may thus shed light on the meaning of blessing? The most natural move, for most of us, is to assimilate blessing to petitionary prayer. Both blessing and prayer express a wish for the flourishing of those we bless or those we pray for. Neither prayer nor blessing can be reduced simply to the desire to fulfill our wish. I may wish for something to happen without taking the trouble to petition the One in whose power it is to grant my wish, and without performing the act of calling down a blessing. Wish fulfillment differs from both prayer and blessing, just as wishing—which often means no more than preferring a particular state of affairs but doing nothing to make it happen—differs from action.

Yet despite the significant points of similarity between prayer and blessing, it would be wrong to treat them as interchangeable. Prayer is addressed to God. Petitionary prayer includes reflection on the nature of our legitimate needs, in order to request that God satisfy them.[3] Prayer on behalf of others subsumes their needs under our own needs, thus enabling us to stand in their place before God in the act of petition. But in prayer one takes that desire, and presents it to God as a request of the Divine. In blessing, by contrast, although I am calling upon God I do not always address God in the second person. The formula of Birkat Kohanim ("May God bless you and preserve you…") refers to God in the third person. The act of blessing presupposes that the person uttering the blessing has the capacity to invite divine blessing, but it does not entail speaking to God as "You."

This becomes evident when one considers the Sim Shalom blessing in the Amidah, which immediately follows the Priestly Benediction when it is recited in the synagogue. The body of Sim Shalom is a prayer: it is the conclusion of the Amidah and it is a request addressed to God, as we ask the Divine to bestow the blessing of peace upon the people Israel. The body of Sim Shalom is not formulated as a blessing but rather as an entreaty for the effectiveness of the Priestly Blessing, recited a moment before in the reader's public repetition, and implicit in the individual's private recitation. Only at the end of Sim Shalom, as with the other sections of the Amidah, is the prayer concluded and sealed, so to speak, when we bless God, who is the source of the blessing of peace.

Thus the equation of blessing and prayer, however suggestive, is inadequate.

Blessing Like Prophecy

Another model for blessing is prophecy. Think of the famous blessings in the Torah, such as Isaac and Jacob blessing their children, and Moses blessing the tribes of Israel. They seem to be predicated on the disposition of the patriarch conferring the blessing in that he initiates the blessing as he might initiate a prayerful petition; in that respect these blessings are like prayer. At the same time, they are not petitions addressed to God but are rather destinies assigned to the recipients, as if the giver of the blessing was possessed of a vision of future and his proclamation of that future helps to bring it into being. Thus we think of Isaac, Jacob, and Moses as exercising something like a prophetic capacity in these actions. Their wish is not simply translated into petition, as it would be in prayer, but into prediction.

Isaac's blessings (Genesis 27) illustrate the prophetic nature of blessing because he is, at first, under the impression that he is blessing Esau. He is unaware, until after the first blessing of Jacob, which of his sons he was blessing. If blessing is interpreted as prayer, then Isaac's subjective state should be determinative: it should matter that he intended to bless Esau and not Jacob. Instead, when he discovers Jacob's deception, he affirms the blessings—as if, once uttered, they cannot be retracted. This implies an objective status to the blessing: the efficacy of the blessing is, to some degree, independent of the desire or intention of the person bestowing it.

What is blessing, then, if it is not exactly like prayer and not exactly like prophecy? Like many religious concepts—indeed, like many ubiquitous human concepts and institutions—blessing defies clear-cut, transparent definition. In place of definition, we have pointed to two types of religious act—prayer and prophecy—with which blessing has affinities. Blessing is a distinct religious mode and is therefore not reducible to any other religious category. Nonetheless, keeping prayer and prophecy in mind may be helpful, as these ideas are more readily accessible to us, I think. We understand what petition means, and if we have a religious life we know the experience of petitioning God. We also know what it means for a person to grasp the intentions of another, and thus to "channel" their plan, so to speak—even if the experience of classical prophecy is unavailable to us.

The Biblical Account of Blessing Is Not Static

The two analogies we explored, that I have gleaned from the medieval interpretations, are pertinent to blessing without temporal qualification. Now I want to complicate the picture. Discerning that blessing is similar to prayer or prophecy, in certain respects, does not mean that the relationship between prayer and the other two ideas is always the same or that it is invariant over time. I want to propose that blessing is more like prophecy in some parts of the Bible and is more like prayer in other parts. I hope to explain why this is the case, and to show the relevance of this point to the Priestly Blessing prescribed in the Torah.

In the Book of Genesis, blessings are conferred by human beings and are generally delivered by fathers to their sons. In one case, the priest Melchizedek blesses Abraham on his victorious return from battle (Genesis 14:18). Noah blesses his children, as do Isaac and Jacob. The blessings are quite specific, as the patriarch sets down the destiny of each one of his progeny. As is the case with prophecy, the blessing states God's intention and, by putting the divine intentions into externally expressed words, makes those intentions irrevocable. Individuation of blessings does not come without discrimination and even criticism. While blessing Shem and Japheth, Noah curses Ham's line (Genesis 9). Isaac's blessing gives Jacob preference; his blessing of Esau assigns him a different and inferior role (Genesis 27). Jacob takes Reuben, Simon, and Levi to task (Genesis 49).

This kind of blessing is more like prophecy than it is like prayer. To be sure, insofar as petitionary prayer emerges from our dialogue with God about our genuine needs, there is a sense in which prayer, too, if it is not mere velleity, recognizes the contours of reality, because prayer is more than mere wish fulfillment. When we pray on behalf of a child of limited abilities, we pray, realistically, that she or he have the opportunity to make the most of those abilities, hold a job, enjoy family life, and so forth; we do not ask God to arrange for him or her to receive the Nobel Prize. A person with what medical science regards as a terminal illness may wish for total cure, but when speaking to God honestly he or she prays for a meaningful remission, for the fortitude to tolerate the treatment, to enjoy the next bar mitzvah or the wedding of a child. To that extent, when parents pray for their children and bless them, they may judge their character and attainments accurately and pray accordingly. All the same, Jacob's judgment of his sons—which are explicitly described as the particular blessings given to each one—have more of the flavor of prophecy about them than of prayer on the sons' behalf. If we knew only these biblical blessings, our theory of blessing would give it much more in common with prophecy than with prayer.

A very different picture emerges in the other books of the Torah and in the later biblical books. To begin with, the blessings there are not pronounced by fathers but by leaders—and there is none of the criticism and discrimination that we have seen in the Genesis blessing stories. When Moses and Aaron bless the people at the inauguration of the Tabernacle (Leviticus 9:22–23), they do not discriminate among the people. The formula of Birkat Kohanim recited today is prescribed in Numbers 6:24–26 and it speaks in general terms of divine blessing, preservation, and the disclosure of God's benign countenance and peace. This normative blessing does not mark Israel's destiny in detail, let alone single out individuals. The same is true of Solomon's blessing of the people when he inaugurates the Temple (1 Kings 8). The only exception, that harks back to the patriarchal model of Genesis, is Moses' valedictory blessing (Deuteronomy 33) which, like Jacob's (Genesis 49), reviews the nation tribe by tribe. But even here, although each tribe gets an individualized blessing,[4] none is subjected to direct condemnation. In a word, blessing outside of Genesis— including the halakhically prescribed text of Birkat Kohanim—is much more like prayer than it is like prophecy.

What explains the change between the ancient particularized blessing of the father and the later routine language mandated by the *halakhah* and reflected in the blessings of the post-patriarchal period?

Transition in the Hierarchy of the Cult

According to the Talmud, the sacrificial cult was initially conducted by the firstborn.[5] Later the firstborn lost their privilege, and the tribe of Levi was chosen for spiritual leadership. When did this change occur? According to one talmudic view, it took place before the revelation at Sinai, and therefore the Aaronide priests officiated at the covenant ceremony conjoined to Moses' ascent to Mount Sinai, which is described in Exodus 24:5.[6] The other talmudic view, adopted by many commentators, holds that the firstborn served at that time.[7] A different opinion, held by the Italian Bible commentator Rabbi Ovadiah Seforno (c. 1475–1550), extends this position. He held that the change occurred after the sin of the golden calf, when the Levites stood against the transgressors. In his judgment this transition is a cause for regret and repentance: were it not for sin, the firstborn and not the Levites would have collected the tithes and other benefices now given to the Levites.[8] Why is this a great misfortune? Presumably because the dominance of the firstborn ensures a priesthood distributed uniformly throughout the population of Israel: each family, in effect, would be graced by a spiritual leader. In the aftermath of the sin, that leadership became the property of one tribe alone.[9]

Unlike the sacrificial cult and other priestly prerogatives, the movement of normative blessing from patriarch to priest is not mentioned in the Bible or major commentators, as the institution of Birkat Kohanim by the priests did not uproot what came before; it did not prevent non-priests from bestowing their blessings as they saw fit. Nevertheless, Aaron's initiative in blessing the people as a whole, in which he was joined by Moses, transformed the act of blessing from the function of the *pater familias* to an act no longer anchored in the spiritual economy of the family. In the Book of Numbers, with the law prescribing Birkat Kohanim, that free act becomes a commandment upon Aaron and his descendants to recite the verses of Birkat Kohanim.

Once the blessing becomes a formula, once the blessing is no longer tailored by the father or the leader of the clan to the particularities of his children and their situation, it becomes more like prayer than like prophecy. Once it becomes an obligation, it becomes a routine. From the perspective of religious spontaneity this is a loss, a consequence of the development that replaced the hierarchy of the family leader, the firstborn, with the chosen clan. In the process, the content of the blessing becomes more stable. The priest must bring an undifferentiated benevolence to the work of blessing. He does not attend to the specific needs of individuals and it is not his business, as the conveyor of the blessing, to meditate on and beseech God about their particular destinies and aspirations.

As noted, Seforno and other early modern writers saw the move from the family priesthood to the priesthood of Aaron's clan as a tragic consequence of sin, which induced God to assign religious leadership to a separate group. Whatever we may say about the priesthood in general, the import of shifting the blessing from patriarch to priest is complex. It is not self-evident that this particular change is for the worse. The individual retains the prerogative of blessing others, in whatever language he or she prefers. Yet the phrasing of the "official" halakhically sanctioned blessing bestowed by the *kohen* is now precisely set down. It does not permit individual creativity or the exercise of individual judgment. The priest becomes the vessel for a scripted divine blessing. And this routinized formula molds the experience of blessing outside the framework of Birkat Kohanim.

This change, from a more personal and fateful experience of blessing to a less differentiated, more predictable blessing may not be entirely a change for the worse.

Conclusion

I suspect that many average Jews attending a prayer service at which Birkat Kohanim is recited are not well prepared for the ritual, and I hope that the approach set for here will help them. First, many enter the synagogue with little sense of the structure of the service and the distinctive nature of its constituent parts. This is obviously not the place to review the structure of the Jewish prayer service, but suffice it here to note that Birkat Kohanim is recited, as noted above, in the course of the repetition of the Musaf prayer on holidays, between the penultimate blessing (that of thanksgiving) and the last one (that of peace). In the daily Amidah it is reflected, but not performed, in the transition between these two benedictions. In Israel, Birkat Kohanim is recited on a daily basis.[10] As noted, the act of blessing is not identical with that of praying or wishing. For that reason, the individual reciting or receiving the blessing, who wishes to comprehend the act in which the congregation is engaged, must appreciate the difference between blessing and petition. The fact that the Priestly Blessing prescribed sounds very much like petitionary prayer makes this point particularly prone to confusion.

The exclusive liturgical recitation of the blessing by the priestly descendants of Aaron is another stumbling-block for many contemporaries. It does not make sense to us that the gift or power of blessing be reserved for one lineage rather than being an option for each and every individual, as it was for the paradigmatic figures of the patriarchs in Genesis or for Moses before his death. Of course, the election of Aaron is rooted in biblical history and presented in Scripture as reflective of divine will. Indeed, one of the Torah's commandments is specifically that Aaron's descendants serve as the priests of Israel (cf. Exodus 28:1). The legitimacy of the law, however, is not equivalent to its appropriation as an experience. Here it is necessary to remember that the halakhic ritual, the commandment of Birkat Kohanim, is significantly different in content from the custom-made blessings bestowed by the patriarchs upon their offspring. It is general in content, and administered with an even-tempered joyful benevolence that does not distinguish the individual merits and shortcomings of the recipient or the distinctive attitudes of the conferrer of the blessing. This evolution is part of the transition from the pre-golden-calf era to its aftermath, as Seforno observed. I believe it may also, at the same time, mark the transformation of Israel from a group of families under the leadership of the family elders to a nation bound together at Sinai in the service of God. That experience of national unity is thus integral to our experience of the Birkat Kohanim.

NOTES

[1] *Nefesh Ha-ḥayyim* 2:2 (ed. Brooklyn, 1972), pp. 47–48. In the Jewish world, "Lita" comprised Belarus, Lithuania, Latvia, and the northeastern part of Poland.

[2] *Sefer Ha-ikkarim* 2:26. Readers may wish to consult the English translation by Isaac Husik published as *Book of Principles* (Philadelphia: Jewish Publication Society, 1946).

[3] See my essay "Destiny, Freedom, and the Logic of Petition" in *Tradition* 24:2 (1989), pp. 17–37, which builds on the work of my revered teacher Rabbi Joseph Soloveitchik; see especially his "Redemption, Prayer, Talmud Torah" in *Tradition* 17:2 (1978), pp. 55–72 and "Without Intelligence, Whence Prayer" in *Tradition* 37:1 (2003), pp. 1–26. Regarding the phenomenology of prayer for others, I draw on Rabbi Abraham Isaac Kook, *Olat Re'iyah* I (Jerusalem: Mossad Harav Kook, 1939), p. 26.

[4] Simon, in my opinion, is subsumed under Judah for reasons beyond the scope of this essay.

[5] Cf. B. Zevaḥim 115b.

[6] Ibid.

[7] See, for example, Rashi to Exodus 24:5.

[8] See his commentary to Deuteronomy 26:13.

[9] Compare the discussion in the Spinoza's *Theological-Political Tractate*, ch. 17. I suspect that Spinoza borrowed the insight from Seforno, over a century earlier, or that both thinkers drew on previous writers.

[10] See, for the Amidah and the Shema in general, Rabbi Joseph Soloveitchik, *Worship of the Heart* ed. Shalom Carmy (Hoboken, NJ: KTAV, 2003) and my essays in his tradition cited above in note 3.

August in Light

Martin S. Cohen

Our Torah is a book of riddles and puzzles, each one subtly designed to reveal a secret to the reader that might otherwise remain hidden. Sometimes these conundrums are presented as almost unnoticeable fissures in the narrative surface, other times as slight inconsistencies in this or that detail of ritual law. But there are also riddles present in the text that are not hidden at all, but are fully visible for students of Scripture to notice and then to solve…if they can. In some ways, these often present the greater challenges, precisely for being easy to discover yet paradoxically difficult to solve—somewhat in the way that truly great mystery writers leave all the most important clues out in the open for astute readers either to notice or blithely to skip past without pausing long enough to notice their potential importance.

The fourth *aliyah* of the Torah portion called *Naso*, corresponding to Numbers 5:11–6:27, is a very long one that covers the laws of the wife suspected by her husband of infidelity and, at roughly equal length, the law of the renunciant (a kind of self-obligated ascetic often called a "nazirite" in English, the latter term an attempt to anglicize the Hebrew term *nazir*).[1] This material is completely independent of the biblical narrative in which it is embedded; various midrashic attempts to justify the juxtaposition of these passages and their position in the larger context notwithstanding, there is nothing in the unfolding of the narrative itself that suggests a reason for the inclusion of these particular passages at this specific

·

stage of the story of Israel's journey from slavery in Egypt to the edge of the Promised Land.[2] And then, immediately after setting forth these legal passages and before returning to the narrative of the dedication of the wilderness sanctuary (and without any indication to the reader that something of momentous importance is about to follow), the Torah pauses and in just forty-one words sets in place one of the great foundation stones of biblical theology by identifying specifically the choicest of God's blessings.

The text is briefly put, but simple enough to follow. Moses, who has until now served as the Israelites' highest-ranking religious leader, is about to be permanently replaced in that role by his brother Aaron, who is to assume the role of High Priest and who will serve in that office for the rest of his life: Moses will retain a life-long right to enter the Holiest of Holy Places at will, but Aaron and his sons are the ones who will henceforth function as the priests of Israel.[3] And so, reasonably, just before Moses undertakes the final acts that will inaugurate the wilderness sanctuary for use, God stops him and instructs him to convey to Aaron and his sons that they are henceforth to bless the people using a specific fifteen-word formulary, which Scripture then proceeds to cite in full.

Questions about the passage abound. Are the priests *only* to use these words to convey God's blessings to the people or may they also use others? Does the text mean to ordain the use of those words of blessing as a regularly-recurring ritual—perhaps one connected with the daily *tamid* offerings, or one formally to be undertaken weekly, monthly, or annually—or merely as one intended to recur from time to time, perhaps at the priests' own volition? May non-priests recite these words of blessing or would that be the liturgical equivalent of non-priests usurping the priestly prerogative solely to serve at the altar? Must Aaron and his two surviving sons recite the blessing together or may one of them speak its fifteen words alone?

To none of these questions does Scripture suggest even a tentative answer. Nor is it made explicit what the relationship of this passage is to one earlier in the pentateuchal narrative in which Aaron, in the context of anointing the Tabernacle's appurtenances for sacred use, is said to have "raised up his hands in the direction of the people and blessed them" (Leviticus 9:22). Is the text presented here, in Numbers, a transcript of the blessing pronounced there, in Leviticus? Or is this a different text entirely, one meant somehow to lessen the possibility of a recurrence of the kind of disaster recounted in the subsequent passage in Leviticus?[4] And what of the blessing Aaron and Moses are described in Leviticus as having together offered to the people after a brief visit to the Tent of Assignation—is the blessing referenced *there* the same as the one given here in Numbers?[5] To none of these questions does Scripture nod, even in passing—presumably preferring to allow countless generations of readers to puzzle over them and resolve them to the best of their ability. I will not here attempt to grapple with any of these questions, but will instead focus on a relatively straightforward issue: the simple meaning of one of the blessings Aaron and his sons are being instructed to convey to the Israelites.

The text at hand, Numbers 6:22–27, appears to imply that six specific blessings rest at the core of divine beneficence, and it is these six blessings that the priests of Israel are called upon to channel to their co-citizens. The blessings are a bit obscured in the standard English translations, but come to the fore when the text is translated specifically to identify them as the gifts God is prepared to offer to the faithful through the medium of a faithful priesthood:

May the Eternal grant you *b'rakhah and sh'mirah.*
May the Eternal grant you *ha·arat panim and hein.*
May the Eternal grant you *n'si·at panim and shalom.*

The text then goes on to characterize the bestowal of these six blessings as the functional equivalent of setting God's holy name "upon" the Israelites, presumably a poetic way of suggesting that the priestly effort to bestow these blessings on the people will effectively imbue them with a perceptible sense of ongoing divine presence.

With only one exception, saying what the six blessings mean is a relatively simple task. *B'rakhah* ("blessing") is divine beneficence itself and seems in the biblical context to imply primarily wealth (Proverbs 10:22), fecundity (Genesis 17:16), peace (Psalm 29:11), satiety (Exodus 23:25), and success, presumably of the commercial variety (Deuteronomy 23:21). *Sh'mirah* ("protection") is also relatively simple to define: the notion that God guards the blessed and makes them safe is at the core of any number of biblical passages, such as the psalmist's assurance that "the Eternal will guard you from all evil (Psalm 121:7).[6] *Ḥein* ("grace") is also simple to define: it is the quality of natural gracefulness that inspires the affection of others; indeed, the regular biblical idiom used to note that one party has successfully stimulated feelings of warmth and friendship in another is to say that the former has found *ḥein* in the eyes of the latter. *N'si·at panim* ("lifting the face") is a bit like *ḥein*, except that it appears to imply more precisely the experience of fostering after-the-fact affection rooted in forgiveness for past transgressions (Genesis 32:21) or of successfully garnering the respect of others (as, negatively, as Deuteronomy 28:50).[7] Nor is *shalom* ("peace") difficult to explain: it is the gift of peaceful existence to which all individuals, families, clans, tribes, and nations aspire, and which will be the hallmark of the messianic era when, as the prophet predicted, peace will come to the people as generously and unstoppably as flow the waters of a mighty river (Isaiah 66:12). The remaining blessing, *ha·arat panim*, is by far the most mysterious of the six, and it is specifically what I would like to attempt to elucidate in this essay by asking what Jews in Second Temple Jerusalem would have thought it to denote.

In Second Temple times, there was a widespread belief that God could symbolically be conceptualized as the light of the world.[8] When, for example, the psalmist noted that God was his "light and salvation" (Psalm 27:1), he most likely did not mean that God is light or even that God is in some profound way like light; more likely, he was merely acknowledging God as his source of spiritual illumination, that he felt himself to "see" in God's illuminating presence things that would otherwise have been invisible, thus hidden from him and unknown to him.[9] The famous line "In Your light shall we see light" (Psalm 34:10) should presumably be understood in like manner. And similar too are passages like Micah 7:8 and Isaiah 60:19–20, which imagine that the day will come when the light of God's presence will illuminate the entire world, heralding its ultimate redemption.

And it is precisely in line with such passages, as well as with the regular biblical predilection for anthropomorphic imagery, that we should seek to understand the reference in the Priestly Blessing to the illumination of the divine face. Indeed, by noting that God so favored Moses that their conversations took place face-to-face, the Torah seems merely to mean that their communion was personal, of the variety that would normally take place in human conversation when people speak to each other intimately and informally.[10] Moreover, references to God's face often denote little more than divine presence, as in the passage that commands every Israelite to appear three times annually "to see God's face" at the place that the Almighty shall choose (Exodus 23:17 and 34:23, and Deuteronomy 16:16). Indeed, the fact that the text is impossibly vocalized in two of those verses to avoid saying that the pilgrims actually "saw" God's face merely points to the fact that the text could easily be misconstrued by the theologically naïve and needed therefore to be masoretically "fixed" to avoid suggesting even obliquely that God actually has a face upon which the pious are being invited—or commanded—to gaze thrice annually.[11]

It would not be impossible, therefore, to explain the reference to *ha·arat panim* as meaning simply that among God's choicest blessings is the one that consists of feeling God's salvific presence—the so-called "face" of God—filling up one's personal space in the manner of light filling up a dark room so that one feels the redemptive potential of faith in God as a real, ongoing force for good in one's life, as a kind of heartening, quasi-luminescent presence capable of brightening up a life that might otherwise be characterized by the oppressive gloom occasioned by a sense of divine absence.

That, however, is only one way to interpret the text, because it is also possible to isolate any number of texts from the Psalter that seem to describe a Second Temple ritual designed not merely to inculcate faith but to go much further than that and actually to stimulate a sensory experience of perceptible divine light. In this context we must consider the argument set forth by such authors as Raymond J. Tourney to the effect that the Levites in Second Temple times pursued a kind of neo-prophetism that set them apart from their priestly overlords.[12] (Taking the Torah and the Psalter as complementary works, one suffused with neo-priestly and one with neo-prophetic spirituality, does not mean that they should *ipso facto* be taken as discrete works rooted in unrelated realms of distinct spiritual experience. Just the contrary is the case, in fact: both works derive from the same spiritual universe, merely from different ends of it, and can for that specific reason so profitably be read in each other's light.) For his part, the author of the Book of Chronicles, a resident of Second Temple Jerusalem with personal knowledge of the Temple and its workings, appears to have gone so far as to take an ancient text in the Book of Kings that mentions the priests and the prophets of old and update the passage by making it reference priests and Levites instead.[13]

Piecing together the evidence as collected by Tournay and others, including myself, a tentative picture emerges of a group yearning for sensory communion with God in the style of the prophets of old and whose efforts to achieve that level of intimacy with the divine realm were pursued within the precincts of the Jerusalem Temple.[14] Much remains unclear. Even what these people called themselves, for example, is hard to say. The most frequent Hebrew word for "prophet" (*navi*) barely appears at all in the Psalter, but many texts do seem to name the group, albeit inconsistently.[15] Sometimes they are "the Humble Ones," but other times they are "the Seekers of God" or "the Seekers of the Divine Face." Still other passages reference the group behind the mystic theology reflected in the Psalms as "the Upright," "the Pious," "the God-Fearers," "the Righteous," or "the Servants of God."[16] Regardless of how they referenced themselves, however, they seem clearly to have sought some sort of neo-prophetic communion with God. And, given the degree to which the Psalter is replete with divine oracles that appear to have been vouchsafed directly to the authors of the poems that preserve their gnomic texts, they appear also to have succeeded.

The prophetic experience sought by these individuals—perhaps like the model set for them in First Temple times by their spiritual forebears, the prophetic caste called the *b'nei ha-n'vi·im*—appears not only to have been aural in nature, but also visual. But what exactly these mystics sought to see is a more complicated question.[17] The sources are equivocal. When one psalmist, for example, writes that God appeared to him "from" Zion, the epicenter of earthly delight (Psalm 50:2), it is hard to know exactly what he means. Even more tantalizing in this regard is Psalm 17, in which the poet moves smoothly from the assertion that his supplication is guileless (verse 1) to the justification that his feet have followed the path toward God (verse 5), to the ultimate hope that he can reasonably expect—at least someday—to merit the experience of beholding the face of God, which experience the poet himself defines as seeing the divine *t'munah* in a waking state (verse 15). That the Torah specifies that it was precisely this experience visually of beholding the divine *t'munah*, apparently a visually perceptible image of God, in a waking state (as opposed to within the context of a dream that set aside Moses from all the other prophets) only makes the psalmist's point that much clearer in terms of the exalted level of communion he was hoping one day to experience.

Some biblical texts specify that this experience of the divine image is to be sought specifically within the confines of the Temple, presumably reflecting the fact that the levitical singers of the Second Temple period were not members of local prophetic castes like their pre-exilic (spiritual) forebears but rather Temple functionaries who pursued their religious quest within the context of service in the Jerusalem Temple.[18] When the author of Psalm 17 wrote about his fervent hope to behold God in the sanctuary, for example, he uses the specifically prophetic word *eḥezeh* to denote the experience of gazing on God, just as does the author of Psalm 63.[19] The rather obscure ending to Psalm 11 uses the same verb and must be interpreted, I think, along the lines of Psalms 17 and 63 as well, especially insofar as it too makes reference specifically to the divine face.[20] Psalm 27 preserves the same connection between the experience of gazing on God and physical presence in the Temple, but refines the idea somewhat: the poet longs to dwell in the Temple permanently not merely so that he might one day see the divine face, but specifically so that he might gaze (*la-ḥazot*) on the beauty (*no·am*) of God.[21] The key to all these passages, I believe, rests in the notion that God, like the Holy Ark, must be presumed to dwell (as King Solomon notes almost clearly at 1 Kings 8:12 [=2 Chronicles 6:1]) in darkness and can therefore only be seen by mortals when (and if) God deigns to illumine the divine face, thus making it seeable. It is this specific blessing of intimate communion with the perceptible Godhead that the priests are being commanded in *parashat Naso* to channel to the Israelites through the medium of the Priestly Benediction.

Psalms 11, 17, 27, and 63 are all "David" psalms, but it is not only within psalms ascribed or dedicated to David that the notion of gazing on God occurs. In Psalm 42, for example—a psalm whose superscription mentions the sons of Korach—the poet calls out, "My soul thirsts for God, for the living God; when shall I come and gaze on the face of God?"[22]

Other psalms offer more oblique references that are only explicable with reference to less guarded passages in the style of the verses mentioned above. Thus, when the author of Psalm 140 declares that the upright (*y'sharim*) shall surely dwell in the presence of the divine face (verse 14), the reference is probably to the same kind of mystical experience held out elsewhere in the Psalter as feasible and attainable. Indeed, Psalm 111:1 makes specific reference to a smaller conventicle of *y'sharim* within a larger congregation whose members worship God with all their hearts. Similarly, the reference in Psalm 24:6 to a specific circle of people[23] within the author's world who seek the divine face is probably intended to refer specifically to those who cultivated the kind of mystic epiphany referenced elsewhere in the Psalter.

The reader perusing these passages will naturally wonder what they are *really* about. Surely, it seems intuitive that citizens of Second Temple Jerusalem—and even the most mystically inclined among them—could not possibly have expected to "see" God or God's face in the Temple in the manner of pagans literally "seeing" their deities through the worshipful contemplation of their plastic images. To frame the issue differently, we might posit that the sought-after experience was called "seeing God's face" simply as a literary convention, but that only prompts us to ask ourselves what such a convention could have been imagined to denote. What, in other words, constituted the experience known literarily—and presumably popularly as well—as exposure to the light of God's face? What, if anything, did communicants actually see? Where did they see it? And how exactly did they know if the light was real or merely imaginary?

To pursue answers to these questions, we might turn to Psalm 80. The poem is dedicated to Asaph, of whom we know only what the

Chronicler tells us: that he was a "royal prophet" in David's court, that he was among the "trained singers of God" chosen to prophesy "with lyre, harp, and cymbal" by David and his generals,[24] that he was among the musicians who played when David first brought the Ark of the Covenant to Jerusalem (his instrument was the bronze cymbal), and that 128 of his personal descendants returned from exile in Babylon.[25] Furthermore, Asaph is the only one of his contemporaries to have his name linked specifically to David's by the Chronicler.[26] And Asaph was also the individual whose name appears in the superscriptions to twelve poems in the Psalter, psalms that (just like those attributed to David) were still being sung centuries after the lifetime of the original Asaph.[27] And among those twelve psalms is the poem we know as Psalm 80.

The poet's language is remarkably open: "Appear, You who are enthroned on the cherubs (*yosheiv ha-k'ruvim*)" he commands, perhaps using the language of imperiousness to mask his own nervousness (Psalm 80:2). And then, having said it once, he goes on to return again and again to the same notion in an amazingly unguarded refrain: "Illumine Your face so that we [may see it and] be saved," he declares, sounding just as if he means it simply and literally.[28]

The psalmist is unhappy and displays no reticence about explaining why a third of his daily drink is made up of his own tears. He is miserable. His neighbors hate him. His enemies treat him with open contempt. Nor is his unhappiness solely on the personal level. He writes of his nation, of Israel, as a vine *once* tended by God, but now left to fend for itself as marauders breach the wall once built to protect it, passers-by help themselves to its fruit, wild pigs gnaw at its runners, beasts feed on it, and malicious villains burn it at will—and indeed, when he does so, no one can fail to be moved by both the pathos *and* the bitter force of the poet's lament regarding his people's fate. And yet the poet's proposed solution to his and his nation's misery lies not in exacting revenge against those responsible, but rather in seeking communion with God. And the specific nature of the communion that he wishes to experience has to do, in some way, with the light of God's face.

The psalmist wants God to appear before his eyes. By that, he apparently means that he wishes specifically for God to make accessible the perceptible quality of concentrated divine presence so that the poet and his friends might experience it personally or, at the very least, for God to make possible the experience that the poet and his friends interpreted as seeing the light of God's face. Were they part of the group that gathered at night in the Temple courtyard to engage in this kind of esoteric endeavor?[29] For people gathering, perhaps surreptitiously, in the dark, light would constitute the obvious medium in which to perceive the reality of God's presence. But from where would the light issue forth? That, *in nuce*, is the question that churns and roils at the center of the matter...but it is one to which our poet offers no clear answer at all.

Can the answer be found elsewhere? Most of the psalmists held the theological presupposition that God dwells in heaven,[30] but also exists—concentrated in the way that a different psalmist referenced as being "very present"—in Jerusalem.[31] When the ancient poets referred to God dwelling "in" Jerusalem or "in" Zion, they undoubtedly meant to reference the notion that God's Presence is most fully perceptible in the inmost sanctum of the Temple, the Holiest of Holy Places in which the Ark was kept in First Temple times. According to the scriptural references to that holiest of chambers, the room was in a perpetual state of darkness. It had neither windows nor a skylight, nor any lighting fixtures. (The great golden lampstand, the *m'norat ha-zahav* as King Abiya called it,[32] was specifically *not* in the Holiest of Holy Places, but in the Holy Place immediately outside the curtain that separated the two rooms in the Temple.[33]) Indeed, when the High Priest entered the chamber on Yom Kippur carrying a golden censer of incense, the faint glow of the coals in the censer must apparently have served as the sole, scant source of illumination. The Ark itself may have disappeared into the maelstrom caused by the destruction of the First Temple, but the Second Temple featured a reconstructed inmost sanctum that, absent its sole appurtenance, nevertheless retained its least expected feature: its perpetual darkness.

The image of light coming forth from God to pierce bleak, impenetrable darkness provides the background to the Bible's opening tableau. And the notion that God's reality in the physical world is reasonably well symbolized by light—real, yet without physical bulk or dimension; existent, yet apparently unfettered by the natural laws that the ancients perceived to govern most other existent things; perceptible, yet not quite visible in the manner of illuminated things—is supported by all those scriptural passages that reference God as light.[34] Yet there is a somewhat different feel to the passages in the Psalms which seem not merely to reference God as a personal light source (in that God can illumine one's path, just as light itself can illuminate a dark road), but actually to seek to commune physically and fully really with God by being vouchsafed a glimpse of the light of God's presence, of God's face.

There are examples of both usages in the Psalms. When the author of Psalm 27 writes that God is "his" light, he presumably means that God guides him forward along a bright path that might otherwise be totally obscure.[35] There are many other such passages as well, but not all references to God's light seem simply to be metaphors for divine guidance through life's twists and turns. When, for example, the author of Psalm 4 specifically frames his prayer as an entreaty that God shine on the poet and his fellow travelers the light of the divine face, he sounds as though he is referencing some specific experience of perceptible divinity more than merely the need the pious all feel for divine guidance.[36] Nor need we assume that the communion sought with the perceptible God was limited to seeing. Psalm 81, for example, cited above with respect to the custom of gathering in the scant light of the New Moon, also references auditory experiences of various sorts: hearing a *shofar* blast, hearing speech in an unknown language, perceiving God's presence in the context of "secret thunder," and being invited personally to participate in prophetic speech.[37]

Nevertheless, the poets turn back again and again to the notion of knowing God through the experience of seeing divine light, sometimes referenced as the light of God's face and sometimes not. And we will best understand the third of the six blessings with which the priests of ancient Israel were commanded to bless their co-citizens in this sense: that the high road to sensory communion with the Divine consists—not poetically, but actually—in being vouchsafed a vision of the light of God's face. The psalmists, at any rate, return to the concept again and again: sometimes on the personal level, for example at Psalm 31:17 ("Let the light of Your face shine on me!") or Psalm 119:135 ("Shine the light of Your face upon Your servant…"); sometimes on the level of the group, for example at Psalm 67:2 ("…then illuminate the divine face for us, *selah*") or Psalm 80:4 ("Illumine Your face so that we may be saved"); and sometimes on the national level, for example when the psalmist at Psalm 44:4 uses that terminology ("With the light of Your face You showed them favor") to describe the Israelite warriors of Joshua's day.[38]

Moderns pondering the text of the Priestly Blessing as presented in Numbers 6 might do best to imagine themselves present in old Jerusalem when Ezra mounted the wooden platform set in place just before the Water Gate on the first day of the seventh month, the day we call Rosh Hashanah, to read aloud from the Torah of Moses, "which the Eternal had [previously] bequeathed to Israel" (Nehemiah 8:1).[39] He began reading, as the narrative in the Book of Nehemiah notes, at dawn's first light and he read until midday, addressing himself to "man, woman, and sage."[40] Clearly, this must have been a multi-day operation. (As any habitué of Sabbath services in any traditional synagogue can attest, it simply would not be physically possible to read the Torah aloud from beginning to end in the space of a few hours, no matter how quickly it were to be read.) And, indeed, reference is made later in the chapter to a second day (verse 13). Presumably, there were more. And then, on one of them, Ezra must finally have gotten to the passage in Numbers regarding the Priestly Benediction.

The assembled would surely have been listening with rapt attention when he got to that passage which formally identifies the choicest of God's blessings, the ones that collectively constitute the bestowal of God's sacred name upon the people (Numbers 6:27). This, the people gathered by the Water Gate must have felt, must be the essence of God's end of the bargain, the specific blessings God will grant the people if they uphold *their* end of the covenant. Would they have wondered why the text seems so intent on presenting as a priestly prerogative a set of blessings that includes at least one specific boon connected far more directly with the Levites' version of Israelite spirituality than the priestly version? Or was that the point—for the priests to indicate that however seductively any might proffer the ultimate experience of sensory communion with God or with the face of God or with its light, it is they and none other who can and may offer blessings in God's name to the faithful? Or perhaps is the explanation less overtly political and simply rooted in the fact that among the poetic blessings that tradition and later law instructed the priests offer the people was one that the authors of the Psalter would have understood as an oblique reference to the kind of communion with God that they themselves sought (and occasionally even achieved) but which the priests of Israel would have taken as a mere metaphor?

Nor are these the only unanswerable questions. What exactly the assembled crowd would have thought each specific blessing to imply is an excellent question, but not one that can be answered with certainty after so many intervening centuries. But Scripture makes a

point of noting that there were Levites listening to Ezra that day...
and, possessed as we are of their hymnal—it is our Book of Psalms—
and thus of their version of the spiritual heritage of Israel, we can
understand well what they, at least, would have taken the Torah
to mean when it numbers among the best of God's blessings the
opportunity to experience a glimpse of the light that emanates from
God's face. To them, it would have meant that among the greatest
of God's gifts is knowledge of the Divine rooted neither in theory
nor in learned dogma, but in sensory knowledge of the perceptible
Godhead, and principally in hearing—perhaps the secret thunder,
perhaps the heavenly *t'ruah*, perhaps an actual oracle (the Psalter
is filled with oracles in which God's words are openly quoted)—
and, even more convincingly and profoundly, in seeing the light of
God's perceptible Presence shining out in the cold night from deep
within the Holiest of Holy Places, a secret sanctum left in perpetual
darkness from which light could only emanate from one sacred
source: the living, perceptible Presence in that place of the God of
Israel, the God whom a psalmist labeled both Light and Salvation,
and for intimate communion with whom the psalmists and their
latter-day followers—which today surely includes the entire House
of Israel—have always yearned and still do yearn.[41]

NOTES

[1] "Renunciant" is my own neologism, one of several developed in the course of preparing my forthcoming Torah translation and commentary.

[2] For some midrashic attempts to justify the specific location of these laws in the narrative of Numbers, see some of the material gathered at Bemidbar Rabbah 10:1.

[3] Moses' permanent right to enter the Holiest of Holy Places is suggested by the final verse in *parashat Naso*, Numbers 7:89. See, e.g., the comment of Rabbi Ḥayyim ben Attar (1696–1743) in his Or *Ha-ḥayyim* commentary *ad loc.*: "[The way Numbers 7:89 is phrased] implies that Moses retained the right [to enter the Holiest of Holy Places] at will." The translation "Holiest of Holy Places" (for *kodesh ha-kodashim*, conventionally translated as "the Holy of Holies") also derives from my forthcoming Torah translation and commentary.

[4] The disaster referenced is the death of two of Aaron's sons recounted in Leviticus 10:1–2.

[5] Leviticus 9:23. Rashi understands the narrative in Leviticus to imply that Aaron offered the people the Priestly Blessing subsequently presented in Numbers, but Moses and Aaron together to have pronounced the blessing known to moderns as the final verse in Psalm 90. See his commentary to Leviticus 9:22, s.v. *va-y'var'kheim* and to verse 23, *s.v. va-yeitzu va-y'var'khu et ha-am.* The translation "Tent of Assignation" too is from my forthcoming Torah translation and commentary.

[6] Note that the Hebrew *yishmorkha* at Psalm 121:7 is nearly identical to the form found in the Priestly Blessing, *yishm'rekha.*

[7] See also, however, the passage at 2 Kings 5:1, where the phrase appears simply to reference respectful affection absent the notion of forgiveness, and cf. also Job 34:19.

[8] The Psalter, which contains at least some poetry that references the destruction of Jerusalem and the subsequent exile, clearly reached its final form during the Second Temple period. Undoubtedly earlier material was included, but in this essay I will reference the book itself as Second Temple work that was eventually canonized as sacred writ.

[9] Despite the Chronicler's bald assertion that there were women among the choristers in the Temple (and supposing that some version of the Psalter was used by such choristers in Second Temple times), I will refer to the psalmists here using masculine pronouns. The Second-Temple-period author of Chronicles was, at any rate, formally describing the First Temple at 1 Chronicles 25:4–7 rather than the one standing in his own day.

[10] This assertion appears both at Exodus 33:11, in the account of the setting up of the preliminary Tent of Assignation (set up by Moses outside the camp as the locus for prophetic communion with the God of Israel), and also at Deuteronomy 34:10 as part of the story of Moses' death.

[11] For readers without Hebrew, what this mean is that the vowels added to the

received consonantal text cannot be logically or reasonably deciphered as they appear and are clearly presented as they are to make the theological point that when the text speaks of "seeing" God, it means to imply that one is seen by God by virtue of being present in the Temple, the earthly locus of divine presence. In Exodus 23:17, the use of the preposition *el* in place of the pleonastic *et* makes the text read reasonably well as pointed. (This latter verse can profitably be read in light of Psalm 84:8.) Hebrew is written primarily with consonants; the effort to add vowels to the text to fix its pronunciation (and, in many cases, its meaning as well) was undertaken by a school of scholars in late antiquity primarily located in Tiberias and popularly referenced as the *ba·alei m'sorah*, in English "the Masoretes."

[12] Tourney's book, *Voir et entendre Dieu avec les Psaulmes ou La liturgie prophétique du Second Temple à Jérusalem*, was published in Paris by J. Gabalda & Co. in 1988 and was brought out in J. Edward Crowley's English translation as *Seeing and Hearing God with the Psalms: The Prophetic Liturgy of the Second Temple in Jerusalem* by the Journal of the Study of the Old Testament in 1991 as no. 118 in their Supplement Series.

[13] The passages are 2 Kings 23:2 and 2 Chronicles 34:30. The natural assonance of the Hebrew words *n'vi·im* ("prophets ") and *l'viyim* ("Levites ") is also worth noting.

[14] See my *Travels on the Road Not Taken: Towards a Bible-Based Theory of Jewish Spirituality* (London, Ontario: Moonstone Press, 1997), and cf. also Jon D. Levenson, "The Jerusalem Temple in Devotional and Visionary Experience," in *Jewish Spirituality from the Bible through the Middle Ages*, ed. Arthur Green (New York: Crossroad, 1986), pp. 32–61.

[15] The word *navi* appears three times in the Psalter: once in a superscription mentioning Nathan "the prophet" (Psalm 51:2), once to note that the despair the faithful felt when Jerusalem fell to the Babylonians had specifically to do with the sense that the absence of a Temple somehow implies the absence also of prophecy (Psalm 74:9), and once in a passage that treats the terms "prophet" and "anointed ones" (presumably, following Rashi and Radak, royal princes) in poetic parallelism and prays that God watch over them both (Psalm 105:15). An earlier term for prophet, *ro·eh* (cf. 1 Samuel 9:9), does not appear in any psalm.

[16] The humble ones/*anavim*: Psalm 69:33; seekers of God/*dor'shei Adonai*: Psalm 34:11; the upright/*y'sharim*: Psalm 140:14; the pious/*hasidim*: Psalm 132:9 (where the term is specifically used as the counterpart of *kohanim*, and cf. Deuteronomy 33:8, where the term *hasid* is specifically applied to the tribe of Levi); the God-fearers/*yirei Adonai*: Psalm 118:4 (where the group within the Temple population that aren't Israelites or priests, presumably Levites, are called God-fearers); the righteous/*tzadikim*: Psalm 118:20; the servants of God/*avdei Adonai*: Psalm 134:1. Regarding the name "God-fearers," it is worth noting that the sole time that the actual word "Levite" appears in the Psalter (at Psalm 135:20), it seems to be the functional equivalent of "God-fearers" at Psalm 115:11.

[17] For what it's worth, the Chronicler offers the fascinating detail that King Uzziah of Judah (mid-eighth century B.C.E.) actually sought out a certain Zechariah who

was adept at seeing God (if that is the right way to translate the Hebrew *ha-meivin bi-r'ot ha-elohim* at 2 Chronicles 26:5) so as to be able to do the same himself when seeking communion with the divine realm. But who this Zechariah was and whether he was formally connected to the prophetic caste in his day, none can say.

[18] The *b'nei ha-n'vi·im* mentioned above appear specifically *not* to have been tied to Jerusalem or to the Jerusalem Temple, but rather to other locales, such as Naiot (1 Samuel 20:19–20), Bethel (2 Kings 2:3), or Jericho (2 Kings 2:5).

[19] In Psalm 17:15 and Psalm 63:3, the specific form of the verb used is *ḥazitikha*, which usage seems to denote an experience actually had rather than merely yearned for. In this context, how interesting it is to note the Chronicler's comment at 2 Chronicles 35:15 that Jedutun, to whom Psalm 39 is attributed, bore the title of *ḥozeh ha-melekh* ("the royal visionary"), in which title *ḥozeh* is merely the nominal form of the verb used in Psalms 17 and 63 to denote the visual prophetic experience. (Cf. the superscriptions to Psalms 62 and 77, however, in which the word *y'dutun* appears to denote some kind of musical instrument.) The word *ḥozeh* itself does not appear in the Psalter.

[20] Psalm 11:7, following the comment of Rabbi David Kimḥi (1160–1235, called Radak) *ad locum*.

[21] Psalm 27:4; cf. Isaiah 33:17. References to the divine face and and divine beauty are brought together at the end Psalm 16 as well. (The word at Psalm 16:11 for divine beauty, *ne'imot*, is a version of the word *no·am* that appears in Psalm 27.)

[22] Psalm 42:3, reading *ereh* for *eira·eh* along with the traditional Targum to Psalms. The other "sons of Korach" psalms are Psalms 44–49, and 84, 85, 87, and 88.

[23] Using the NJPS translation of *dor* as "circle."

[24] That the singers had 288 descendants is no coincidence, that number being a neat multiple of seventy-two, the number of elders described by Scripture as constituting the original prophetic caste as ordained by Moses in the story presented in Numbers 11. (I am taking the reference to Eldad and Medad to be in addition to the seventy "upon whom the spirit rested" [Numbers 11:25] for a total of seventy-two.)

[25] David and his generals chose Asaph and his colleagues to become prophet/ singers: 1 Chronicles 25:1; Asaph designated "a royal prophet": 1 Chronicles 25:2; the number of descendants of Asaph, Heman, and Jedutun: 1 Chronicles 25:7; the first raft of public prophets ordained by Moses: Numbers 11:16–30; prophets singing in the Temple: 1 Chronicles 25:6; Asaph playing a bronze cymbal:1 Chronicles 15:19, cf. 1 Chronicles 6:16–33 and 16:37; 128 descendants of Asaph returned from exile in Babylon: Ezra 2:41 and Nehemiah 7:44.

[26] 2 Chronicles 29:30. It is unclear whether Nehemiah lived before or after the Chronicler, but he—Nehemiah—made the same point in his diary, noting specifically that the musical organization of Temple already existed "in the days of David and Asaph; see Nehemiah 12:46.

[27] The "Asaph psalms" are Psalms 50 and 73–83.

[28] The refrain appears three times in the poem, at verses 4, 8, and 20. The Hebrew is *ha·eir panekha v'nivashei·ah*.

[29] Such a group is mentioned in the following psalm in the Psalter (at Psalm 81:4), where the poet's circle is described as gathering by the meager light of the new moon on the eve of the festival celebrating, presumably, the new month.

[30] See Psalms 11:4, 73:25, 115:3 and 16, and 139:8.

[31] See Psalms 9:12, 76:3, 132:13–14, and 135:21, and cf. Joel 4:17 and 21, Zechariah 8:3, and 1 Chronicles 23:25. "Very present" is the Hebrew *nimtza me'od* at Psalm 46:2.

[32] 2 Chronicles 13:11.

[33] Regarding the curtain between the Holiest of Holy Places and the Holy Place, see Exodus 26:33.

[34] These passages are complemented by all those in which God's presence is symbolized by fire. Cf. Genesis 15:17, where God's legally binding presence in the establishment of the covenant with Abraham is signally by the appearance of "a smoking oven and a lighted torch," as well as those passages in which God's presence is symbolized by a giant pillar of fire (e.g., at Exodus 13:21 and 14:24 or Numbers 14:14, cf. Nehemiah 9:12) or, less grandly, by a single bush unnaturally aflame (at Exodus 3:4).

[35] Psalm 27:1. The poet, writing in the first person, references God as "my" (i.e., not "his") light. The prophet Micah was saying roughly the same thing when he declaimed hopefully, "Whenever I find myself dwelling in darkness, the Eternal serves as my light" (Micah 7:8).

[36] Psalm 4:7. The poet does not say who is group is exactly, but merely prays in the plural that God grant a glimpse of divine light to "us."

[37] The *shofar* blast: verse 4; speech in an unknown language: verse 6; perceiving God in "secret thunder": verse 8; an invitation to prophecy ("I am the Eternal your God, who bought you forth from the land of Egypt: open your mouth and I shall fill it up"): verse 11.

[38] In this regard, note too how the opening strophes of Psalm 67 resume three of the blessings assigned by Numbers to the priests of Israel. And cf. also Daniel 9:17, where Daniel prays for God to shine the light of the divine face on the ruined Temple in Jerusalem.

[39] For a very accessible survey of scholarly opinions relating to the date of Ezra's activity in Jerusalem, see John Bright, *A History of Israel* (4th edition published posthumously; Louisville, KY: Westminster John Knox Press, 2000), pp. 391–402.

[40] Nehemiah 8:2. That *meivin* here denotes the Levite is obvious from verses 7 and 9 later in the same chapter.

[41] Light and salvation: Psalm 27:1. Is the passing reference at Exodus 34:29–35 to Moses' face shining with light meant as the ultimate act of prophetic *imitatio Dei*? Maybe!

The "Other" Priestly Blessings Revisited[1]

Michael J. Broyde and Mark Goldfeder

Introduction

When most people hear the term "Priestly Blessing(s)," they imagine it to be referring to the blessings that God prescribed for Aaron and his descendants to bless Israel with. Those Priestly Blessings are described in Numbers 6:24–26, and read as follows: "The Eternal bless you and keep you; the Eternal make His face shine on you and be gracious to you; the Eternal turn His face toward you and give you peace." With their distinctive ritual chanting and melodies accompanying the symbolic raising of the hands, they are still performed to this day, only now in the synagogue and not in the Temple.

The Priestly Blessings as a genre, though, represent much more than just a ritual ceremony. They reflect one aspect of how the Divine Presence is meant to be manifest in this world. Unlike the job of the prophets, whose task it was to zero in on particular issues of the day and focus the hearts of the people, or the rabbis, whose legalistic function remains to faithfully apply God's timeless laws to shifting realities, the job of the priests was to remind the people that God is ever-present, and that all blessings really come from the Eternal One. This is true in times of peace, as reflected in the "regular" Priestly Blessings, but it is also true in times of conflict, and the people needed this reminded to them as well.[2]

Unlike the "regular" Priestly Blessings, which are only recited in times of joy,[3] there is another set of blessings that the priest is commanded to give to the Jewish people, specifically the Jewish army, right before they go to war. Deuteronomy 20 describes the process as follows:

> When you are about to go into battle, the priest shall come forward and address the army. He shall say: "Hear, Israel: Today you are going into battle against your enemies. Do not be faint-hearted or afraid; do not panic or be terrified by them. For the Eternal your God is the One who goes with you to fight for you against your enemies, to give you victory." (Deuteronomy 20:2–4)

The question this essay addresses is as follows: while the strict requirements for this priest, formally referenced as the Priest Anointed for War,[4] are certainly not followed today,[5] has the essence of the practice—and, for that matter, the Blessing itself—survived? And, if so, then under what circumstances and in what context has it done so?

Context

It is not far-fetched to assume that such an ancient law as the blessing of the Priest Anointed for War might have some modern-day resonance. The renewal of Jewish sovereignty in 1948 with the establishment of the State of Israel presented Jewish tradition with both grave historical challenges and unprecedented opportunities. Having wandered in exile since their crushing defeat at the hands of the Roman Empire, it had been literally millennia since the Jewish people had a state to call their own. Amidst the euphoria of a biblical homecoming, however, was the realization by the People of the Book that there was in fact a great lacuna in the text.

While some of the classic works of Jewish law—most notably the Talmud and the legal works of Maimonides (1135–1204)—do include some scattered references and a few brief guidelines about war, it became abundantly clear in the early days of the Zionist victory that Jewish law had never fully developed its own laws of *state*, with an accompanying code of military ethics.[6]

Rabbi Shlomo Goren (1917–1994), the first Chief Rabbi of the Israel Defense Forces (IDF) and later the Ashkenazic Chief Rabbi of Israel, believed that a vision of war through the ethical prism of the rabbinic sages was a realistic possibility, and that such a vision would effectively confer to the State and its armed forces a more valuable ethical code by which to conduct wars.[7] He also believed that such an ethical rejuvenation was religiously imperative; if Judaism really had laws of war (a fact which, as a believer in the all-encompassing nature of the system of *halakhah*, he was sure of), then they were just as binding as all other Jewish laws. And, similar in this respect to other aspects of Jewish law and ethics, they would serve to separate the "us" from the "other," even in the heat of the battlefield.

So began the legal resurrection. As Goren noted:

> It was necessary to gather, select, and organize, like the sheaves of wheat brought to the threshing floor, the shards of laws, customs, and practices that existed in the ancient armies of Israel—to resurrect them from the recesses of distant memory, from beneath the ruins of the kings of Israel, and to collect them from the holy books....We built practices brick by brick, establishing a firm foundation for a system of authoritative Jewish legal rulings based on the Torah of Israel.[8]

While much of the legal discussion involved answering the technical "theory of just war" questions of *jus ad bellum* and *jus in bellum* from a Jewish perspective, there were also some internal Jewish law points that needed to be hammered out. Primarily, this involved attempting to categorize the wars of the State of Israel as either "authorized" and "obligatory" wars, under the rubrics found in the Talmud and Maimonides. In addition though, there were ritual points, similar to the priestly war blessings, that also needed to be addressed.

The Talmud tells us that three primary ritual requirements must be met in order for an "authorized war" to be (rightly) permitted to commence. The first of these is the presence of an accepted king or ruler of Israel.[9] The second requirement is the consent of the Great Sanhedrin (the High Court in ancient Israel, composed of seventy-one elders),[10] and the third is consultation with the *urim* and *tummim*, a mystical and holy ornament that was worn as part of the High Priest's breastplate and was used to seek prophetic answers.[11] A legitimate theory of Jewish war must meet these requirements, even in the modern era.

The first requirement is perhaps the easiest to meet. Naḥmanides[12] is very clear that an official "king" is not actually needed. The decision to go to war can be made by "a king, judge, or whoever exercises jurisdiction over the people." After the destruction of the Temple, the Jews began their exilic existence in Babylonia, where there was no official position of Jewish royalty. Instead, the legal authorities established that "the exilarchs in Babylonia stand in place of the king."[13] To apply this nowadays and find a logical concurrence between the Babylonian exilarch and the modern government of Israel, we can turn to the talmudic authorities who already noted during the Middle Ages that the Jewish legal doctrine stating that "the law of the land is the law" (*dina d'malkhuta dina*) would not apply to a Jewish government.[14] Instead, a Jewish state would be "governed by the king's law, which applies to all forms of Jewish government as they continue to develop over the course of time."[15] As this pertains specifically to a modern State of Israel, Rabbi Abraham Isaac Kook (1865–1935), the first Chief Rabbi of the British Mandate for Palestine, points to the talmudic passage which states that "the king's law applies at all times and in every generation to the leaders of the time in their respective countries."[16] Rabbi Kook notes that the "royal prerogative governs the nation, and that 'king's law-making prerogatives revert to the nation as a whole…' The king's law applies to the government where they have flexibility to maintain order because the government is responsible for 'the totality of the needs of the people at any time for the general security.'"[17]

Using these standards, the government of Israel has the authority to rule the Jewish people under king's law. Thus, in an emergency situation, the Knesset is vested with the exact same powers and authority that King David himself would have been granted.

Regarding the requirement to seek the consent and approval of the Great Sanhedrin, the recently deceased Rabbi Yehudah Gershuni[18] advanced the thesis that the approval of the high court is only a requirement if the monarch finds it necessary to compel the populace to go to war against their will, and to conscript soldiers involuntarily. When the nation agrees to go to battle, the approval of the Sanhedrin is not necessary.

The comments of at least one influential early exegete seem to support this view. Rabbi Menaḥem Meiri (1249–c.1310), in his explanation of the relevant talmudic passage, notes that the approval of the Sanhedrin is required in order to compel the populace to go out to battle, but no approval is necessary for popularly supported wars.[19] In a similar vein, Rabbi Kook claimed that in a democratic era, the government—which expresses the will of the people—replaces the need for the approval of the high court.[20]

The last ritual requirement, consultation with the *urim* and *tummim*, is undoubtedly the most difficult to deal with. Whether or not the *urim* and *tummim* existed during the time of the Second Temple is a matter of scholarly debate,[21] but no one questions the fact that by the end of that era they had certainly gone missing. When approaching this problem though, it is important to note that in his legal discussions about the declaration of an "authorized war," Maimonides does not list the requirement of asking the *urim* and *tummim* at all.[22] Rabbi Yeḥiel Michel Epstein suggests that although biblically mandated, consultation with the *urim* and *tummim* is perhaps not a **necessary** condition of war;[23] although it constitutes a *mitzvah* and is required by virtue of the biblical command, failure to engage in prior consultation does not actually affect the legitimacy of the war itself.[24]

What, then, of the Priest Annointed for War? Is his a technical ritual that is biblically mandated but not required or necessary for war, along the lines of the *urim* and *tumim*? Or is it perhaps representative of some higher ideal and purpose, which can be legitimately reinterpreted to preserve the spirit if not the letter of the law?

The first thing we should note is that in general, while the idea of a military chaplain—someone to serve the army soldier's physical and spiritual needs—is a relatively new concept, the Priest Anointed for War is often seen as an early prototype. Indeed, according to the Office of the Chief of Chaplains,

> The Chaplaincy of the United States Army has its spiritual roots deep in the pages of the Old Testament, and prototypes for its institutional and organizational structure in the British military forces. The tradition of a specially appointed clergyman accompanying soldiers into battle dates from the Pentateuch, Deuteronomy 20:2: "And it shall be when ye are come nigh unto the battle, that the priest shall approach and speak unto the people." His message was to contain words of spiritual comfort for those soon to jeopardize their lives in combat, and patriotic sentiments suited to elevate morale.[26]

The religious chaplaincy of Israel Defense Force's Military Rabbinate would, then, in itself be a direct spiritual descendant of the Priest

Anointed for War. But it is not only a surface comparison. What made the Priest Anointed for War so special was not that he offered sacrifices or conducted rituals; his authority came from the fact that he actually went out to battle with his troops. The Israeli Army, unlike many other modern armies, trains its religious chaplains as soldiers, and many serve in combat units. This idea of priestly solidarity is rooted in the biblical text ("the priest shall approach the people," *v'nigash ha-kohein*) and it is not lost on the people of Israel. In 1967, after the Six Day War and the recapturing of Jerusalem, the lead article in *Amudim*, the newspaper of the Religious Kibbutz Movement, declared:

> Everyone who reads the newspapers today, everyone who listens today to the radio...is witness to the powerful eruption of faith in the Rock of Israel and its Redeemer... Rabbi Shlomo Goren [was] the "anointed priest of battle" who went before his armies in the conquest of the city of Gaza, who burst into the Ancient City of Jerusalem with a Torah scroll in his hand, and announced the good news of the redemption of the Land of Israel with a blast of the shofar...And none of the enemy could stand against them [i.e., the Israel Defense Forces]. All of their enemies, God put in their hand...[27]

Indeed, in their pep talks to the IDF forces right before they go into battle—designed, in the words of retired military Rabbi Lieutenant Shmuel Kaufman to "boost the spirit of the soldiers"[28]—the military chaplains sometimes even read the speech of Priest Anointed for War, and sound the *shofar*,[29] much as the priests were commanded to in the battle of Jericho[30] (as well as at other times).

But it is not only in the military chaplaincy that the "other" Priestly Blessing has survived; in synagogues around the word, both in Israel and in the Diaspora, many Jewish congregations of all denominations gather together for prayer, and add in a special blessing for the Israel Defense Forces. The prayer asks God to bless and protect the members of Israel's army. It reads, in full:

> He Who blessed our forefathers Abraham, Isaac and Jacob—may He bless the fighters of the Israel Defense Forces, who stand guard over our land and the cities of our God, from the border of the Lebanon to the desert of Egypt, and from the Great Sea unto the approach of the Aravah, on the land, in the air, and on the sea. May the Almighty cause the enemies who rise up against us to be struck down before them. May the Holy One, Blessed is He, preserve and rescue our fighters from every trouble and distress, and from every plague and illness, and may He send blessing and success in their every endeavor. May He lead our enemies under our soldiers' sway and may He grant them salvation and crown them with victory. And may there be fulfilled for them the verse: "For it is the Lord your God, Who goes with you to battle your enemies for you to save you" (Deuteronomy 20:4).[31]

And there it is, the second modern-day incarnation of the "other" Priestly Blessing, reminding Jews around the world that all blessings—both in times of peace and in times of conflict—come from heaven. May God watch over the IDF and bring them peace, and may the Priestly Blessings as we usually think of them be returned to their proper place, joyfully performed in the Temple, speedily in our days.

NOTES

[1] Parts of this essay have been adapted from Mark Goldfeder's "Defining and Defending Borders; Just and Legal Wars in Jewish Thought," a paper delivered at the 17th International Conference of the Jewish Law Association at Yale University on July 30, 2012, and subsequently published in Mark Goldfeder, "Defining and Defending Borders: Just and Legal Wars in Jewish Thought and Practice," in *Touro Law Review* 30:3, pp. 632–633, 636–637, 641–645.

[2] Although the text of Numbers 6:24–26 is universally referenced in Jewish literature as Birkat Kohanim, literally "the blessing of the priests" and commonly referred to as "the Priestly Blessing," in the singular, we prefer the plural ("Blessings") since the text actually does consist of discrete blessings and not just one. The text we reference as the Priestly Blessings is the same as the one widely referenced elsewhere in this volume in the singular.

[3] See commentary of Rabbi Moses Isserles (1520–1572), called the Rema, to the S.A., Oraḥ Ḥayyim 128:44.

[4] In Hebrew, *kohein mashu·aḥ milḥamah*.

[5] The Talmud at B. Sotah 42a, for instance, describes how the priest in question needs to be specifically appointed. According to Rabbi Naftali Tzvi Yehudah Berlin (called the Netziv), he must be appointed by the king; and cf. also Tosafot to B. Yoma 12b, s.v. *kohein gadol eivah*. The Netziv's comments can be found in his *Sefer M'romei Sadeh* (ed. Jerusalem, 1957), pp. 71a–b.

[6] See, e.g., M.T. Hilkhot Issurei Biah 17:1, Hilkhot K'lei Ha-mikdash V'ha-ovdim Bo 1:7 and 4:19, Hilkhot Rotzei·aḥ 7:9, and Hilkhot Melakhim U-milḥemoteihem 7:3.

[7] See Arye Edrei, "Spirit and Power: Rabbi Shlomo Goren and the Military Ethic of the Israel Defense Force," in *Theoretical Inquiries in Law* 7 (2005), pp. 255–297, and particularly the author's comments on p. 271.

[8] Rabbi Shlomo Goren, *Meishiv Milḥamah: She'eilot U-t'shuvot Be-iny'nei Tzava, Milḥamah U-vittaḥon* (Jerusalem: Ha-idra Rabba, 1983–1992), quoted in Edrei, "Spirit and Power," n. 38. Rabbi Goren's view is that *halakhah* has indigenous rules for waging war that, although covered by layers of dust from generations of disuse, are present and need to be fleshed out. See also his "Combat Morality and the *Halakhah*" in *Crossroads* 1 (1987), pp. 211–231. Of course, we recognize that the approach of Rabbi Goren to military and war law is not the only one in the Jewish tradition—indeed, it is just one of five views advanced by mainstream Jewish law authorities. In addition to Rabbi Goren's view, discussed in this essay, one may discern the following additional views on the matter:

(a) Rabbi Elazar Menaḥem Man Shach, leader of the Ponovezh yeshiva for decades, believed that there are no unique rules of how to fight a war and that war law simply consists of the general rules of self-defense writ large; see his

Kovetz B'zot Ani Botei·ah (1963; rpt. Bnei Brak, 1993), pp. 10–35. In his view, there is no priestly blessing in war time now, as there are no modern-day wars conducted consistent with Jewish law because—at the minimum—there are no *urim and tummim* but more generally because these rules are limited to messianic times. (The *urim* and *tummim* were the mystical and holy ornament worn as part of the High Priest's breastplate that were used to seek prophetic answers, including on questions of whether or not the nation should go to war; in this regard, see the talmudic material concentrated, e.g., at B. Yoma 73b, Sotah 48b, and Sanhedrin 16a–b.)

(b) Rabbi Shaul Yisraeli believed that *halakhah* has no **unique** rules of war, and that it accepts secular law norms as valid. He asserts that like many areas of *halakhah*, this realm too is governed only by the obligation to obey international law norms (much like the "law of the land" [*dina d'malkhuta dina*] writ large)—and international law certainly does not require a priestly blessing; See his "*Pe'ulot Tz'va·iyyot L'haganat Ha-m'dinah*," first published in *Ha-torah V'ha-m'dinah* 5/6 (1953–54), pp. 71–113, and now reprinted as chapter 16 in the author's *Ammud Ha-y'mini* (rev. ed., Tel Aviv: Moreshet, 1992), pp. 168–205.

(c) Rabbi Ovadia Yosef, who acknowledges that there are indigenous rules of war within *halakhah* but thinks that they are rules for the individual, not the state; as such, they are not related to the State of Israel *per se*, but govern Jewish soldiers in any army, whether Israel's or France's. See, e.g., his *Y'havveh Daat* 2:11 and 2:14 (Jerusalem: Makhon Y'havveh Daat, 1999), pp. 50–52 and 58–61. More generally, see Shlomo Fischer, "Excursus: Concerning the Rulings of R. Ovadia Yosef Pertaining to the Thanksgiving Prayer, The Settlement of the Land of Israel, and Middle East Peace," in *Cardozo Law Review* 28 (October 2006), pp. 229–244. In this model, a priestly blessing is, at the very least, not necessary.

(d) The Satmar rebbe, Rabbi Joel Teitelbaum, believes that fighting Jewish wars is prohibited by rabbinic decree after the "three talmudic oaths"; cf. B. Ketubbot 110b–111a, describing how Israel swore that they would not "storm the wall" or "rebel against the nations" until the coming of the Messiah. See his *Kuntres Al Ha-Ge'ulah V'al Ha-t'murah* (1970; rpt. Jerusalem and Brooklyn, 1985), particularly pp. 80–85. Certainly, in his understanding, a priestly blessing over a sin in not needed.

⁹ B. Sanhedrin 20a.

¹⁰ B. Sanhedrin 29b.

¹¹ B. Sanhedrin 16b and elsewhere; see above, note 8.

¹² Addendum to Maimonides' *Sefer Ha-mitzvot*, positive commandment #4.

¹³ Maimonides, M.T. Hilkhot Sanhedrin 4:13.

¹⁴ See, e.g., the commentary of R. Nissim of Gerona (1320-1376 and popularly called the Ran) to B. Nedarim 28a, s.v. *be-mokheis ha-omeid mei-eilav*.

¹⁵ Menachem Elon, *Jewish Law: History*, Sources, *Principles* (Philadelphia: Jewish Publication Society, 1994), vol. 1 (*The History and Elements of Jewish*

Law), p. 59, n. 28 (quoted in David Rosen, "Does Ariel Sharon Consult His Rabbi? How Israeli Responses to Terrorism Are Justified Under Jewish Law" [March 5, 2003], available online at jlaw.com/Articles/responseTerrorism.pdf). The book cites for their authority on this point the responsum of the Tosafot, published as #12 by Jacob Agus in his edition of the *T'shuvot Ba·alei Ha-tosafot* (New York: Yeshiva University, 1954), p. 58. The editors note that Rabbi Nissim ben Reuven, called the Ran (1320–1376), and Rabbi Shlomo ben Aderet, called the Rashba (1235–1310), follow this view that the king's law applies to the Jewish government.

[16] B. Sanhedrin 52b.

[17] Elon, p. 59 (cited in Rosen, "Does Ariel Sharon Consult His Rabbi"), citing Rabbi Abraham Isaac Kook, *Mishpat Kohen,* resp. no. 144 (1937; rpt. Jerusalem: Mossad Harav Kook, 1966), pp. 337–338.

[18] Yehudah Gershuni, "*Milḥemet R'shut U-milḥemet Mitzvah,*" in *Torah She-b'al Peh* 13 (1971), pp. 150ff. See also the *Einayim La-mishpat* commentary of Rabbi Yitzḥak Arieli to B. Sanhedrin 16a (Jerusalem: D'fus Ivri, 1971), p. 35, quoted in J. David Bleich, "Preventive War in Jewish Law," in *Tradition* 21:1 (Spring 1983), p. 34.

[19] *Beit Ha-b'ḥirah* to tractate Sanhedrin, ed. Yitzḥak Ralbag (ed. Jerusalem, 1974), p. 45. The talmudic reference itself is found at B. Sanhedrin 16a.

[20] Abraham Isaac Kook *Mishpat Kohein*, resp. no. 144, pp. 319–348 (quoted in Edrei, "Spirit and Power," p. 266). See also Rabbi Shaul Yisraeli, *Ammud Ha-y'mini*, no. 14, pp. 103–108, and no. 16, chap. 5, §§6–7, pp. 129–130; and cf. § 24, p. 137 (quoted in Bleich, "Preventive War," p. 34). See also generally Maimonides, who uses the expressions "according to the majority of Israel" and "according to the high court" throughout his code; e.g. at M.T. Hilkhot Terumot 1:2 or Hilkhot Melakhim U-milḥemoteihem 1:3.

[21] See, for instance, Josephus, *Jewish Antiquities* 3:8:9, in the Loeb Classical Library edition of Josephus, trans. H. St. J. Thackeray (1930; rpt. Cambridge, MA, and London: Harvard University Press and W. Heinemann, 1967), vol. 4 (*Jewish Antiquities, Books I–IV*), p. 421: "The [*urim and tummim*] ceased to shine two hundred years before I composed this work." Josephus completed his *Antiquities* in 93–94 C.E. after about fifteen years of work, cf. Thackaray's note, "b," pp. 420–421.

[22] M.T. Hilkhot Sanhedrin 5:1.

[23] Yeḥiel Michel Epstein, *Arukh Ha-shulḥan He-atid, Hilkhot Melakhim* 74:7 (Jerusalem: Mossad Harav Kook, 1973), p. 75.

[24] Bleich, "Preventive War," n. 7, citing Shlomo Yosef Zevin, *L'or Ha-halakhah* (Jerusalem: Mossad Harav Kook, 1957), p. 12; and cf. also the *Einayim La-mishpat* commentary of Rabbi Yitzḥak Arieli to B. Sanhedrin 16a, p. 35.

[25] See "Chaplains" in *The Oxford Dictionary of the Jewish Religion*, ed. Adele Berlin (New York: Oxford University Press, 2011), pp. 164–165.

[26] Parker C. Thompson, et al., *The United States Army Chaplaincy: From Its European Antecedents to 1791* (Washington, D.C.: Office of the Chief of Chaplains of the Department of the Army, 1977), vol. 1, p. xi, available online at the Internet Archive website at www.archive.org.

[27] Reuven Firestone, *Holy War in Judaism: The Fall and Rise of a Controversial Idea* (New York: Oxford University Press, 2012), p. 253.

[28] See video narrated by Katya Adler, "The Rise of Israel's Military Rabbis" (September 8, 2009), available online at the website of the British Broadcasting Company, www.bbc.com/news.

[29] Cf. Numbers 10:9, where we read: "When you go into battle in your own land against an enemy who is oppressing you, sound a blast on the trumpets. Then you will be remembered by the Eternal your God and rescued from your enemies."

[30] See Joshua 6:4–9: "And seven priests shall carry before the Ark seven *shofarot* of rams' horns; and the seventh day you shall go around the city seven times, and the priests shall blow with the *shofarot*. And it shall come to pass that when they make a long blast with the ram's horn, and when you hear the sound of the *shofar*, all the people shall shout with a great shout; and the wall of the city shall fall down flat, and the people shall ascend up every man straight before him. And Joshua the son of Nun called the priests, and said to them, 'Take the Ark of the covenant, and let seven priests carry seven *shofarot* of rams' horns before the Ark of the Eternal.' And he said to the people, 'Pass on and surround the city, and let those who are armed pass on before the Ark of the Eternal One.' And it came to pass, when Joshua had spoken to the people, that the seven priests carrying the seven *shofarot* of rams' horns passed before the Eternal, and blew with the *shofarot*; and the Ark of the covenant of the Eternal followed them. And the armed men went before the priests who blew with the *shofarot*, and the rear guard came after the Ark, the priests going on, and blowing with the *shofarot*."

[31] This text is reproduced here courtesy of the Orthodox Union. Aside from its prominent placement in many prayer books, the Orthodox Union had sold, as of the time of the writing, over 70,000 individual prayer cards with this blessing.

If Only Some May Bless, Can All Be Blessed?

Daniel Greyber

Many Jews possess a deep childhood memory of standing beneath their father's *tallit* or with their mother as the Priestly Blessing was recited in synagogue. I have no such memory. I grew up in an egalitarian synagogue in which rituals related to such "priests" were considered irrelevant, even counterproductive, to modern Judaism. In traditional Jewish communities, *kohanim* (Jewish men who, according to family tradition, are direct patrilineal descendants of the biblical Aaron) are given special honors and burdened with special restrictions. *Kohanim* are called up for the first honor when the Torah is read; they are invited to lead the Grace After Meals; they redeem all firstborn Jewish sons;[1] and it is the *kohanim* who stand before the congregation and pronounce Birkat Kohanim, the Priestly Blessing.[2] Furthermore, a *kohen* may not marry a divorcee, a convert, a non-virgin, or the descendant of a *kohen* who did not follow the priestly regulations.[3] They are also restricted from any contact with a corpse:[4] they may not be within four cubits (approximately seven feet) of a corpse, or in a chapel or near a grave in the cemetery, or be under the same roof with a corpse unless there is a permanent partition between the *kohen* and the corpse.[5] Levites—Jewish men who, according to family tradition, are direct patrilineal descendants of the biblical tribe of Levi, although not of the Aaronide line—are called up for the second honor when the Torah is read and, before the *kohanim* bless the congregation, the Levites perform a ritual hand-washing for the *kohanim* in preparation for the latter's recitation of the Priestly Blessing.

In the egalitarian synagogue of my youth, arbitrary distinctions among individuals—in this case, granting special privileges to people possessed of priestly ancestry in a post-priestly world—were considered counterproductive and off-putting. But I wonder about this basic assumption. Is Birkat Kohanim and all that it entails—the Levites washing the hands of the *kohanim*, who then pronounce the words of the Priestly Blessing for the community—*is* all that caste-based privilege inconsonant with egalitarianism? Over the past sixty or seventy years, Conservative rabbis have striven to build traditional communities that take seriously the fundamental and irreducible equality-of-personhood that is greater than either sex or gender—an agenda that emerges from the Torah itself, which describes each human being as created in the image of God who is beyond sex and gender.[6] In a recent paper for the Committee on Jewish Law and Standards for the Conservative movement, Rabbi Jeremy Kalmanofsky put it simply: "As a Conservative Jew, this is what I stand for: a traditional practice in which males and females are of equal status."[7] As efforts have been made to step away from inner-Jewish distinctions that diminish the personhood of one group or another, we can thoughtfully ask: Do the distinctions inherent in the ritual performance of Birkat Kohanim undermine the larger effort of many moderns to create unified, classless communities in which all are equal and equally welcome?

In one sense, yes. These are tasks not open to everyone; rather they are open only to those who are the sons—and, in more liberal communities, the daughters[8]—of *kohanim* or Levites.[9] The core concept then feels, at least *prima facie*, to be contrary to the egalitarian ideal. It also feels odd historically: the authority of the *kohanim* in Jewish life began to diminish as early as the Persian period (roughly, the two centuries from Cyrus' capture of Babylon in 539 to

Alexander's capture of Tyre in 332 B.C.E.), when people began to question if the same laws that pertained in Solomon's Temple had to be enforced, or even should be enforced, in a substitute structure. The diminution of priestly authority continued until the destruction of the Second Temple in 70 C.E. and the establishment of the rabbinic community in Yavneh, in which Jewish leadership was primarily earned by individuals through study and debate and not passed on through lineage. As Shaye Cohen explains,

> The destruction of the temple…facilitated the emergence of individuals as authority figures to replace the institutional authority previously exercised by the temple and sects, and the emergence of the ideology of pluralism to replace the monism which previously characterized the temple and the sects. The net effect of these developments was the end of sectarianism and the creation of a society marked by legal disputes between individual teachers who nevertheless respected each other's right to disagree.[10]

Rabbinic culture, from which modern Judaism has inherited so many of its mores and values, is a meritocracy in which people are evaluated in terms of their own deeds and accomplishments. In a famous story from the Mishnah,[11] Akaviah ben Mehallalel's son begs his father, "Recommend me to your colleagues." When Akaviah refuses, his son asks, "Have you found any wrong in me?" To which the sage responds, "No. Your own deeds will bring you close [to the sages] and your own deeds will distance you [from the sages]." There were no favors for family: no one was born a rabbi, and neither was it possible to acquire the title of rabbi by virtue of one's wealth or power. One became a rabbi only by virtue of one's own dedication to, and achievement in, the study of Torah. The Mishnah teaches emphatically that Torah can be earned—and in forty-eight different ways!—by any who desire to give of themselves with sufficient ardor and assiduity (Pirkei Avot 6:6).

The concept of awarding special privileges to *kohanim* and Levites thus appears to stand in sharp contrast to at least some core values of the rabbinic system. It is thus a strange—but also, at least in my opinion, a very beautiful—twist of fate that the victorious rabbis left in place a remnant of the very system they replaced. The rabbis of classical antiquity may have rejected the model of priestly authority for leadership of the Jewish community, but they could not ignore it completely, as it was embedded in the very Torah laws the rabbis valued and to which they dedicated their lives.

Nobody can become a *kohen*; thus, there is something inherently un-egalitarian about according a special status to *kohanim* and Levites. Yet, it is also possible to argue that allowing those who believe themselves to be *kohanim* to offer the Priestly Blessing (and similarly self-identified Levites to wash their hands beforehand) is in fact the most egalitarian thing we can do. Indeed, bringing the *mitzvah* of Birkat Kohanim into our community is "anti-egalitarian" only if egalitarian means that everyone must be the same and do the same things. But what if egalitarianism does not mean that at all? What if, for example, egalitarianism were to be taken to mean that we should strive to create communities in which all individuals are given the best opportunity to fully express their Jewish selves and their humanity in the world? Each person would then be presumed to have a special, holy role to play in the world—his or her own *avodat hashem*, service of God—but each person's holy task would not necessarily need to be construed as the same. The infinite number of God's tasks unique to each person would thus reflect the infinite nature of God's greatness. It is arrogance of the highest degree to presume that being a rabbi or a *kohen* or a prayer leader makes one *better* or *more important* than a person who is a Levite or a simple Israelite.

I remember going to see my rabbi once, when I was trying to figure out what I should do with my life. I had listed for him many different professions I was considering when he stopped the conversation and told me I was making a fundamental mistake: "You are equating what you do for a career with what your life is about," he said to me. "Daniel, you can be a grocery store clerk and be a good Jew and live a good life." The same point is made in the famous, perhaps too-often-told story of Reb Zusya, who on his deathbed fears not that he will be asked why he wasn't Moses but rather why he wasn't Reb Zusya: why he wasn't the man he could have been, had he made more of an effort to meet his own destiny.[12]

Too often, our society ascribes importance to particular *things*. In the secular world, what appears to matter the most is going to the best school or driving the biggest car, having the slimmest body or winning the most awards in school. In the Jewish world, we try to step past that kind of hierarchy and instead to valorize those who study lots of Torah, and those who keep Shabbat and *kashrut* punctiliously. Maybe some would even include in this category those who stand up in front of the community beneath a large *tallit* and intone the ancient words of Birkat Kohanim. But Pirkei Avot teaches that we should not make false distinctions between major commandments and minor ones, for we cannot know their importance in God's eyes, or the possible reward their performance might entail. The blessing of the *kohanim* is only one out of 613 *mitzvot*—each of which is an equal and holy path to God.[13]

In a truly egalitarian community, we should focus on making space for more people in the community to find a path to God and fully live out their role in the world—by providing a space *both* for *kohanim* to pronounce their blessing *and* for the community to hear it, and thus to be blessed not by the *kohanim* at all but by God.

Interestingly, the *halakhah* ascribes no more importance to the *kohen* who recites the words of the Priestly Blessing than to the community that hears and receives the blessing. For example, *Sefer Ḥareidim* states: "It is not only the *kohanim* who fulfill the *mitzvah* when it is done, but rather all of the community standing in silence and [listening] with focused intent and who then answer 'amen' after the blessing [of the *kohanim*]—they are all partners in fulfilling this *mitzvah* of the Torah."[14] Acknowledging the task of the *kohanim* need not—and does not, in my own mind—imply a higher or lower status with respect to "lay" Jewish people not of priestly descent. Theirs is a particular task offered them by some combination of ancestry, destiny, and happenstance. But just as saying that the Jewish people are a kingdom of priests does not imply that Jews are better than everyone else, but rather that we have a special task or role to play in the world—so too do the *kohanim*, the priests of priests, have a special task: to utter the words of this blessing.[15] Accepting the burden of destiny does not imply untoward favoritism; it merely acknowledges that each Israelite has a different role to play in the great mission of Israel, to bring the world to the brink of redemption.

Rabbi David Wolpe tells a story of a time, early in his rabbinate, when he was called to the bedside of a dying person.[16] When he got to the hospital the person was unconscious. The family was gathered around and they asked him to say the Viddui, the deathbed confessional. Rabbi Wolpe returned home and told his wife how uncomfortable, how unworthy, he had felt reciting the deathbed confession for someone he'd never met before. "I don't feel worthy to do that for someone else," he said, to which his wise wife Elie responded, "You're right—you're not worthy. Anyone would be unworthy. But it is ok, because you are not doing it. The Viddui is being done through you." This story reminds us that it is not the *kohanim* who provide God's blessing. God's blessing is not magic. When the *kohanim* say the blessing, they shape their hands in a special way beneath their *tallitot*. But Birkat Kohanim is not a secret procedure to make something physical flow from the hands of the *kohanim* into the air over the listeners' heads because those hands are shaped in a certain way, or because they pronounce the words at a particular time or in a particular way. The blessing is being given *through* them, not offered *by* them. The more that ego is a part of the blessing, the less room there is for God. The more we aim, both in this ritual and in life, to make of ourselves a vessel for God's blessing, the more room there is for blessing to come into the world.

I will conclude with one more law about this ritual as found in the Shulḥan Arukh—a law that at first glance may seem unfair, but that I have nontheless come to consider both profoundly beautiful and important. Rabbi Joseph Karo teaches: "One who has a defect in his face or hands…should not raise his hands [to bless] because the people will [be distracted from the blessing and will] look at it [the defect]." [17] That surely *sounds* like discrimination against a *kohen* who is physically deformed, whose hands or face are not perfect in color or shape. But what may appear at first glance to be discriminatory or even harsh is softened somewhat as Rabbi Karo continues to explain: "If the custom of the place is for all *kohanim* to cover their faces and hands with a *tallit* [as is now the universal custom], however, even if there are several defects on his face and hands, he should go up to bless [because the defects will be covered]." [18] But one may ask: what if the *kohen* has another kind of blemish or deformity—for example, in his voice, or in a part of his body that is not covered? Rabbi Karo says that *if the community* will not be distracted, then that person may bless. [19] What does this mean? In a community with just one *kohen*, it would mean that if the community is tolerant and able to see beyond the physical and attune itself to the true source of the blessing—God—instead of being distracted by physical deformities, then that community will be able to receive God's blessing. But if the community is unable able to get past the physical difference of that *kohen*, then they will not be blessed. This law thus teaches us that people who are different can indeed be sources of blessing for us, but only if we are worthy to be blessed—and only if we teach ourselves to see the potential for God's blessing within each and every member of our community. That is egalitarianism at its best.

Such a law is also an important reminder about what does, or does not, happen each time Birkat Kohanim takes place. In the Zohar, the canonical book of the Jewish mystical tradition, it is taught: *b'it·aruta di-l'tata itar l'eila* ("by means of an awakening below comes an awakening above").[20] Birkat Kohanim is not magic, not some magical set of motions and words that cause this magical thing called "blessing" to descend into the world from heaven. The blessing does not happen if we just wave our hands and speak a spell; rather, *the blessing depends upon us*. Can we see past what is physical in a physical world? Can set aside our egos and make room for God to be found in a sacred moment? Can we prepare ourselves to receive God's love? God has commanded the *kohanim* to bless Israel with love. The more we desire to receive God's blessing, the more God's desire to bless us will be awakened above.

NOTES

[1] In accordance with Exodus 13:13, which reads: "Every firstborn of a donkey you shall redeem with a lamb, or if you will not redeem it you shall break its neck. Every firstborn of man among your sons you shall redeem."

[2] In accordance with Numbers 6:22–27, which reads: "The Eternal spoke to Moses, saying: Speak to Aaron and his sons and say to them: Thus shall you bless the people of Israel. Say to them: *The Eternal bless you and protect you! The Eternal deal kindly and graciously with you! The Eternal bestow His favor upon you and grant you peace!* Thus they all link My name with the people of Israel, and I will bless them."

[3] Based on Leviticus 21:13–15, which reads: "[The priest] shall take a wife in her virginity. A widow, or a divorced woman, or defiled, or a harlot, these shall he not take; but he shall take a virgin of his own people to wife. Neither shall he defile his seed among his people; for I the Eternal do sanctify him."

[4] Following Leviticus 21:1, which reads: "And the Eternal said unto Moses, Speak unto the priests the sons of Aaron, and say to them, 'There shall none be defiled for the dead among his people.'"

[5] See S.A. Yoreh Dei·ah 371 for a full analysis of these rules.

[6] Genesis 1:27.

[7] Jeremy Kalmanofsky, "An Egalitarian Abstention." This paper was submitted in May 2014 as a dissent to "Women and Mitzvot" by Rabbi Pamela Barmash. Dissenting and Concurring papers are not official positions of the CJLS. The paper may be consulted on the website of the Rabbinical Assembly at www. rabbinicalassembly.org, where it is catalogued as Y.D. 246:6.2014b.

[8] For analysis of the daughters of a *kohen* or Levite being called up for these special *aliyot*, see the following two responsa submitted to and approved by the Rabbinical Assembly's Committee on Jewish Law and Standards: (1) Joel Roth, "The Status of Daughters of *Kohanim* and *Leviyim* for *Aliyot*" (1989), which permits daughters of *kohanim* and Levites to be called up first and second to the Torah respectively; and (2) Mayer Rabinowitz, "Rishon or Kohen" (1990), which concludes that the categories of *kohanim* and Levites are based in Jewish law on the sociological category of *mi-p'nei darkhei shalom* (literally, "for the sake of the ways of peace"), which changes with time and circumstances and can therefore be upheld or cancelled at the discretion of the community rabbi. Both papers are available online at www.rabbinicalassembly.org; Roth's *t'shuvah* is catalogued as O.H 135:3.1989a and Rabinowitz's as O.H. 135:3.1990.

[9] Regarding the permission of daughters of *kohanim* offering the priestly blessing, see the responsum by Mayer Rabinowitz, "Women Raise Your Hands" (1994). See also the opposing position by Stanley Bramnick and Judah Kogen in "Should N'siat Kapayim Include B'not Kohanim?" (also approved by the CJLS), in which the authors argue that the modern priestly blessing is a continuation

of the Temple ritual in which women did not participate and therefore there is no precedent to allow women to do so in modern times. Rabinowitz's *t'shuvah* is catalogued as O.H 128:2.1994a, and that of Bramnick and Kogen as O.H. 128:2.1994b.

[10] Shaye J. D. Cohen, "The Significance of Yavneh: Pharisees, Yavneh, and the End of Jewish Sectarianism," originally published in *Hebrew Union College Annual LV* (1984), pp. 27–53, but now conveniently available in the author's volume of collected essays, *The Significance of Yavneh* and *Other Essays in Jewish Hellenism* (Tübingen: Mohr Siebeck, 2010), pp. 44–70. The quote cited here is on page 45 in its original setting and on page 62 in the volume of collected essays.

[11] M. Eduyyot 5:6 7.

[12] The story may be found in Martin Buber, *Tales of the Hasidim*, trans. Olga Marx (New York: Schocken, 1947), p. 251.

[13] Pirkei Avot 2:1 and 4:2, and cf. M. Ḥullin 12:5.

[14] Rabbi Eleazar ben Mose Azikri, *Sefer Ḥareidim* 12:8 (ed. Venice, 1601), p. 22b. *Sefer Ḥareidim* (literally, "The Book of the Pious") was written by Rabbi Eleazar ben Moshe Azikri, one of the great kabbalists in Safed during the late 1500s, and first Ḥareidim published in Venice just one year after his death in 1600. The book's introduction lists seventeen different conditions for a commandment to be fulfilled in the proper manner, and the book itself categorizes the commandments according to the various organs and limbs of the body with which they are to be fulfilled.

[15] The reference to Israel as a Kingdom of priests is at Exodus 19:6

[16] David J. Wolpe, *Why Faith Matters* (New York: HarperOne, 2008), pp. 110–111.

[17] S.A. Oraḥ Ḥayyim 128:30.

[18] S.A. Oraḥ Ḥayyim 128:31.

[19] S.A. Oraḥ Ḥayyim 128:30.

[20] For example, Zohar I 77b, 86b, 88a, or 164a

Birkat Kohanim: How Humans Reframe Traditions

Michael Graetz

The text known as Birkat Kohanim is usually called "the Priestly Blessing" in English, but that translation obscures—at least slightly—the simple meaning of the Hebrew, which literally means "the blessing of the priests." It is not, after all, a blessing that has a "priestly" feel to it or "priestly" provenance. It is a blessing formula presented as a divine oracle vouchsafed directly to the prophet Moses—thus a specific text framed as a blessing—which Scripture ordains be recited only by members of priestly families. In the Bible, the tribe of Levi is accorded special status by being assigned oversight and stewardship of all matters pertaining to sacrificial worship, matters of holiness status, and issues relating to purity and impurity. The tribe of Levi is itself subdivided into the *kohanim* (priests), the sons of Aaron and their descendants, and the other male descendants of Levi son of Jacob, who are depicted in Scripture as the priests' adjuncts and assistants.

The text of this blessing is found in Numbers 6:22–27:

The Eternal spoke to Moses, saying: Speak to Aaron and his sons as follows.
Thus shall you bless the people of Israel; say to them:
The Eternal bless you and keep you!
The Eternal deal kindly [literally, "make His face shine upon you"] and graciously with you!

*The Eternal bestow divine favor upon you [literally, "lift
up His face toward you"] and grant you peace!*
And they shall link My name with [literally, "put My name
upon"] the people Israel, and I will bless them.

One fascinating aspect of this passage is its literary setting. The
passage that immediately precedes it is a description of a complicated
ritual involving holiness, purity, and impurity, all in the case of the
accidental violation of nazirite vows. Furthermore, the passage
following the text of the blessing is the long and repetitive passage
describing the dedication of the Tabernacle in the wilderness,
a twelve-day operation in which the head of each tribe brought a
tribute for the benefit of the Tabernacle and (presumably) its priests.

It is easy to fit the blessing of the *kohanim* into the following
narrative, the one regarding the dedication of the Tabernacle, by
supposing that the blessing given by the priests is intended to be part
of that narrative. But it is also possible to read the text as a kind of
coda to the preceding story of the hapless nazirite, who has suffered
the unexpected misfortune of standing next to someone who suddenly
dies. In that case, the text could be read as a reassuring promise of God's
grace to someone who has suffered an accidental setback to the serious
desire to dedicate oneself to God. In both cases, we are given a hint as
to the power of a blessing. Indeed, the passage itself stresses that this
blessing text will be "put upon the people Israel," using the language
of physical placement[1]—in the wake of which a state of blessing will
devolve upon the people who have had this "garment" put upon them.
So perhaps the most basic question to ask in considering this text has
to do with the concept of "blessing" itself. What does it actually mean
to "put" a blessing on someone or something?

What Is a Blessing?

Words derived from the Hebrew root *bet-resh-kaf* are commonly translated into English as some form of the word "blessing." It is not an easy concept to define. In many passages, the word *b'rakhah* itself, usually translated as "blessing," is juxtaposed with its apparent antonym, *k'lalah*, usually translated as "curse" and derived from a different verbal root, *kaf-lamed-lamed*. In one famous passage from the Book of Deuteronomy, the two are presented by God as distinct choices available to human beings:

> Behold, I set before you this day a blessing and a curse: a blessing, if you obey the commandments of the Eternal your God, which I command you this day; but a curse, if you will not obey the commandments of the Eternal your God, and turn aside from the way, which I command you this day, to go after other gods, which you have not known. (Deuteronomy 11:26 28)

Most probably, the idea is that the choices made result in either a "blessing" or a "curse." The paths are also identified: the former consists of following the commandments of God, while the latter consists of turning aside from them.

Some individuals are referenced in Scripture as being "blessed," but these are not invariably people who have chosen the path of blessing by being faithful to the commandments—because it turns out that the act of blessing may be performed by a person acting unilaterally, the object of whose efforts is then called "blessed."[2] But, strikingly, human beings are also depicted as blessing God.[3] Nor may humans bless God only indirectly, but also, as my teacher Rabbi Max Kadushin pointed out in his writings on prayer, they may do so in direct address, in the second person: "When the individual addresses God with the words of the *b'rakhah*, he feels that God is before him, and hence he can use the pronoun, 'Thou.'"[4]

All of these verses, and there are many more, form a response to our question: blessing is a positive state, the opposite of a cursed state, which one may attain either through one's own deeds or through the pronouncement of another (or an Other). One can therefore bless oneself, although that language is not actually used, by doing certain deeds, usually described as somehow connected to God's commands, or even by saying certain words. The only hitch seems to be that one does not know if one is in fact "blessed" until after the fact. What is common to all blessings is that they express, in words, a state of improvement, satisfaction, or achievement different from and better than the state that the person being blessed is in at the moment. Blessing is the bestowing of positive benefits to a person by stating them out loud. It seems obvious that the power that might turn these words into reality is God, but the words are uttered by humans.

Some people point out that the usage of the root *bet-resh-kaf* implies "praise"; indeed, if people "bless" God then that is a clear interpretation of the meaning of "blessing." I submit, however, that Jewish theology also allows the idea of effecting improvement in God's own self via a blessing offered by human beings—for example, when we bless God as merciful, helping God to leave a state of anger.

What Is the Function of the Priestly Blessing?

The blessing is structured as an incantation whose recitation opens up the forces of blessing for those being addressed. There are three verses, consisting of three, five, and seven words each. In each verse there are two verbs whose subject is God, whose name is invariably the second word of each verse. If we present the verses vertically, we get the outline of a pyramid:

Y'varekh·kha YHVH v'yishm'rekha.
Ya·eir YHVH panav eilekha vi-ḥunneka.
Yissa YHVH panav eilekha v'yaseim l'kha shalom.[5]

Both the wording and the structure imply an incantation of the apotropaic kind—that is, a formula whose purpose is to guard against evil. Indeed, the use of formula of God's face and the benefits that one derives from it is a clear indication of an apotropaic formula.[6]

Another feature of the blessing that suggests it be read as incantation is the ceremony of *n'si·at kappayim*, literally "the raising of hands," engaged in by the priests while reciting the blessing: tradition dictates that they are to raise their arms, straight forward to the height of their shoulders, and spread their fingers in a unique way. This practice is spelled out in rabbinic literature, but may well inhere unspoken within the biblical text.[8] Such motions by "holy men" of various sorts are well documented by anthropologists as being part of incantation rituals.

The Mishnah sets Birkat Kohanim into the ritual of the Temple, where it is described as being part of the prayer service that accompanied the daily sacrifice.[9] As such, it has strict laws governing who says it, as well as when and how it may be recited. Just as with any other Temple ritual, the recitation of Birkat Kohanim is esoteric; its rules are kept private as a way of guarding it from degradation. Most crucial of all are the strictures regarding its recitation solely by *kohanim*: a non-priest who raises his hands and recites the words of the blessing is deemed to have committed a grievous sin. At Ketubot 2:7, for example, the Mishnah sets out rules to define how to determine if a person who claims that he is a *kohen* is to be accepted as such. In the talmudic discussion of this *mishnah*, there is a long and involved investigation of what actions may imply that a person is genuinely a *kohen*, and how we may use those actions to determine priestly status.[10] The discussion there about the ritual recitation of Birkat Kohanim raises the question of whether or not participation in the *n'si·at kappayim* ritual can be taken as proof of priestly status. Clearly, a non-*kohen* who raises his hands has transgressed. And yet, today, the words of the Priestly Blessing may be spoken quite freely by any Jew, even non-priests, on many occasions, most notably in the ritual blessing of children on Shabbat eve.

Is There Any Evidence for Use of the Formula in the Past?

One of the most exciting archeological find of the past few decades is the discovery, in a burial cave in Ketef Hinnom (an area of Jerusalem close to the Temple Mount), of two strips of silver upon which are etched, in ancient Hebrew script, the text of Birkat Kohanim. At the time of its discovery, the strips were considered to constitute the oldest physical example of a biblical text ever found.[11] Because of the site and epigraphical evidence of the lettering, Gabriel Barkay, the archaeologist who found the strips, pronounced them to be from the last years of the First Temple, which was destroyed in 586 B.C.E.

Subsequently, as is always the case with archaeological finds, different parts of Barkay's conclusions were challenged. Furthermore, with the development of advanced imaging technology, the strips were re-examined and much clearer images of the lettering were produced. Barkay himself published an update of his original findings, in which he admitted that some of his original conclusions might have been overstated.[12] Yet subsequent scholarship has once again shown that these strips might well be pre-exilic and date from the end of the First Temple era.

In any case, these silver strips are certainly one of the most ancient physical finds of a biblical text in existence. But the enhanced imaging of the strips revealed that other biblical verses also appeared on the strips, which discovery suggested that much more investigation was necessary in order to establish their original purpose. Most researchers, however, continue to accept Barkay's initial thesis that the strips were some form of amulets worn to ward off evil. Barkay even proposed that they were forerunners of *t'fillin*.

Following the revised publication of the texts, it became possible to discuss the literary and religious meaning of these strips in a new light—and thus also to discuss the concept of Birkat Kohanim being used in First Temple times as an apotropaic formula. Most intriguing to me, though, is that the discovery suggests a possible use of the Priestly Blessings in a context that is not connected directly to Temple ritual. That is: the words of the Priestly Blessing appear to have been used in a context that is not specifically priestly at all, and not connected to Temple ritual. In turn, this suggests that their importance lies, or at least eventually came to lie, in what the words themselves say and in the sentiments and ideas that they convey, and not in the formal framework of sacred ritual. This is the most ancient evidence we have for the usage of the formula of the Priestly Blessing outside of a formal priestly setting, and it dates from a period when a Temple stood and priestly classes were operating!

What Light Do the Ketef Hinnom Strips Shed on Birkat Kohanim?

Barkay's article from 2004 expands our understanding of the texts, based upon the clearer reading of the writing on the amulets. Most importantly, it makes it clear what other texts sharing language found elsewhere in the Bible are used in conjunction with Birkat Kohanim. For example, the line that precedes Birkat Kohanim on the strips, *ha-eil ha-gadol shomeir ha-b'rit v'ha-ḥesed*, resonates with the language found in Daniel 9:4 and Nehemiah 1:5, both of which hark back to Deuteronomy 7:9. In Daniel and Nehemiah, however, this phrase appears in the context of a prayer for God's mercy at a time of disaster for Israel, rooted in God's obligations to observe the covenant with Israel. The common theme in all of these texts is the motif of God's merciful redemption of Israel from bondage in Egypt. This is our first clear evidence of Birkat Kohanim being used as a reminder of God's protection, particularly in times of trouble or disaster. Birkat Kohanim was thus taken, at least in some sense, as an antidote to evil suffered by Israel.[13] However, there is no attestation of the blessing being used against anything, or to remove something.[14] It thus seems—at least with respect to the first strip—as if God's protection is in the positive aspects of the blessing, and does not actively remove any of the evil that might befall the wearer of the amulet. The translation of the second strip reads as follows:

1[For PN, (the son/daughter of) [xxxx]lh/hu. May h[e]/
2sh[e] be blessed by YHVH,
3the warrior [or: helper] and
4and the rebuker of
5[E]vil: May YHVH bless you,
6keep you.
7May YHVH make his face shine upon you and
8grant you p[ea]ce.[15]

The interpretation of the whole text, and the citation of Birkat Kohanim at the end, is summed up by Barkay as follows: "Hence, while neither inscription makes specific reference to Satan, demons, or other agents of wickedness, they do offer God's protection from Evil through the invocation of his holy name and the text of his most solemn of protective blessings. Given that context, it is safe to conclude that these artifacts both served as amulets and that their function falls in line with similar amulets whose inscriptions invoke divine protection for the wearer through the use of one of the tradition's most famous prayers."[16]

Do These Artifacts Shed Light
on Birkat Kohanim in Other Literature?

The analysis of this question in relation to Psalms relies on an article by Jeremy Smoak.[17] (I will present his ideas in quotation marks, even when the language is my own.) Any comments about Jewish usage of Birkat Kohanim and rabbinic literature are totally my own, however.

"One of the main characteristics of ancient Jewish magical incantations which seems to be found in Birkat Kohanim is protection against evil."[18] As noted above, there is no claim that Birkat Kohanim removes evil, but it does offer some protection *against* evil. This protection is connected to God's love (which will emotionally help sustain a person beset by evil), to divine abundance (which may help one cope with evil), and to God's compassion (which might bring about some spiritual support for being beset by evil—or, at the very least, provide enough comfort and strength that one would not succumb to evil or disaster).

The biblical story of the conflict between Jacob and Esau over their father's blessing suggests the high value placed upon the blessing of a patriarch, and invites us to suppose that even more value would have been placed on the blessing of a priest deemed able to channel God's own blessing. Indeed, the opening lines of the rabbinic midrash on Birkat Kohanim recall the struggle between Jacob and Esau in precisely this context:

> "In this wise you shall bless the people Israel, etc." (Numbers 6:23). This bears on what is written in Scripture, "Envy not the man of violence, and choose none of his ways" (Proverbs 3:31). "The man of violence" refers to the wicked Esau....And the reason it says "envy not" is because it is manifest to the blessed Holy One that Israel is destined to be enslaved under the power of Edom [the rabbinic appellation of Esau] and will be oppressed and crushed in its midst, and that Israel will at some time raise angry protest against this....Accordingly the Holy Spirit, speaking through Solomon, said, "Envy not the

man of violence"—envy not the peace enjoyed by the wicked Esau! "And choose none of his ways"—that is, you must not do according to their deeds![19]

In this midrash, the very act of "placing" Birkat Kohanim "on" Israel is to aid them in eschewing the evil ways of Esau in favor of the sacred ways of Jacob. Thus, Birkat Kohanim is here depicted as a kind of a "power drink" that gives one the strength necessary to stand up to evil or to the temptations that evil presents. The blessing is not so much a magical formula as it is a kind of spiritual supplement for a weary and vulnerable person, or perhaps an additive that helps such a person to stand up to temptation and the lure of quick fixes to difficult problems.

This perspective is most notable in the following fascinating talmudic passage: "Our rabbis taught: Twelve questions did the Alexandrians address to Rabbi Joshua son of Ḥinanah [or perhaps: Ḥananiah]. Three were about wisdom [*halakhah*], three were matters of *aggadah*, three were mere nonsense, and three were about matters of conduct."[20] In the questions about *aggadah*, Rabbi Joshua is asked about biblical verses that seem to contradict each other—since, after all, one of the roles of *aggadah* is to supply a philosophical or a theological explanation of such seeming contradictions. And one of the three questions about *aggadah* references Birkat Kohanim: "One verse says, 'God, who shows no favor [*lo yissa panim*] and takes no bribe'(Deuteronomy 10:19), but another verse says, 'The Eternal bestows His favor [*yissa adonai panav*] upon you' (Numbers 6:26). [How can the discrepancy be resolved? By positing that] the former refers to the time before sentence is passed, while the latter refers to the time after the sentence has been passed."[21]

The Hebrew expression *yissa panim*, literally "to lift up (or: show) a face," means to bestow favor, and there seems to be an inconsistency in how this notion is understood in the Torah. Although the first verse cited, from Deuteronomy, claims that God does *not* bestow favor, in Numbers—at least in the framework of Birkat Kohanim—God does just that! What is striking is the juxtaposition of the act of showing favoritism and of accepting bribes: God is praised for eschewing both in Deuteronomy, but God is depicted in Numbers as bestowing favors, thus being open to bribery! This surely must be questioned, and the Alexandrians jump at the chance.

Rabbi Joshua's aggadic explanation is that there is no contradiction between the two verses, for God's relationship to an individual changes according to the individual's personal circumstances. God *does* do both, both withholding and bestowing favor—but there are times when one mode is appropriate, and other times when the opposite mode is appropriate. God shows no favoritism "before sentence is passed," but will be merciful "after sentence is passed."

The debate here has to do with the efficacy of blessing, and even more so with the perceived inefficacy of blessing. The notion that a sentence is passed on an individual, or on a larger group, is a well-known theme in rabbinic literature. In our day, this notion may be more abstract, something along the line of randomness or chance, the workings of the universe but not necessarily as the result of a heavenly court (*beit din*) passing a sentence. In either case the outcome is the same; what happens is inevitable. The main difference is that in the case of the sentence by a *beit din*, supposedly we should be able to understand the actions that led to the sentence. At the very least the *beit din* could, at least theoretically, supply the reasoning and the considerations that went into passing the specific sentence. The Book of Job calls this idea into question; yet we still tend automatically to suppose that there is rhyme and reason to the decision of the *beit din*. However, in the case of randomness (that is, our modern version of sentencing), the best we can do to express any understanding of what "caused" it is through a statistical mathematical formula. In other words, perhaps people may accept the sentence as an inevitable outcome of the workings of the universe.

A similar talmudic passage concerns praying for the sick to be healed, even though each person's fate is written down on Rosh Hashanah and sealed on Yom Kippur. It reads as follows: "Rabbi Joseph said: Whose authority do we follow nowadays in praying [daily] for the sick and for the ailing? That of Rabbi Yosi, [who holds that people are judged daily].[22] Or, if you like, I can say that it is, after all that, actually the opinion of the rabbis, but that at the same time we follow the counsel of Rabbi Isaac, who said: 'Supplication is good for an individual, whether before the sentence is pronounced or after it is pronounced [so that daily prayer for the sick is of some effect, though judgment has already been pronounced on Rosh Hashanah.]'"[23]

Clearly this passage relates to prayer or blessing, totally apart from what actually happens to a person in reality. There is no guarantee of health, but even after the "sentence" has been passed, or the random occurrence occurs, one should not eschew prayer or blessing. They are good in and of themselves! Keeping the possibility of healing, compassion, support, nearness, and love out in the open, despite any evil going on, is a worthy enterprise in itself.

We can thus begin to understand the development of Birkat Kohanim from its beginning, in priestly ritual, to the present, as a vehicle for blessing one's children every Shabbat. Reciting it highlights and focuses our attention on any thought or action that exhibits compassion, and that is meant to grant and/or enhance life. "Putting" a blessing into the world helps to make life safe and secure.

Blessing Children on Shabbat Evening

The custom of blessing the children of a family on Shabbat, including a symbolic laying of one's hands on the child's head while reciting Birkat Kohanim, seems to be of a relatively late provenance. The earliest reference that I know of is in the kabbalistic book *Sefer Ma·avar*

Yabbok, by Rabbi Aaron Berekhiah bar Moshe of Modena (d. 1639), who justifies the use of the fifteen words of Birkat Kohanim by parents on Friday night with reference to the fifteen joints of the hand.

Some rabbis question the propriety of this custom, as it was clearly deemed a halakhic transgression for a non-priest to recite Birkat Kohanim. However, in the Talmud we find the following statement: "Rabbi Yosi also said, 'I have never disregarded the words of my neighbors. I know of myself that I am not a priest, [yet] if my neighbors were to tell me to ascend the dais [to recite Birkat Kohanim with the priests in the synagogue], I would ascend [it]."[24]

Different interpretations of this puzzling text have been proposed. According to one, Rabbi Yosi went up to the dais in order not to embarrass his neighbor, but he did not in fact participate in the recitation of Birkat Kohanim. According to another, it is indeed permitted to say the words of the Birkat Kohanim, as long as it is done without the attendant lifting up of the hands.[25] And according to yet another, the text of the Talmud is corrupt, and instead of the word *kohen*, "priest," we should read *k'dai*, meaning "worthy." On this reading, Rabbi Yosi would be noting that although he was a priest, he nevertheless did not consider himself worthy.[26]

In any case, the custom to bless the children is based on the concept of the rest of Shabbat being a whole and complete rest, and thus there must be peace and feelings of support and love between parents and children. A parent may well have scolded a child during the week or become angry with a child over some matter, yet the warm embrace and the words of blessing change that residue to one of peace and harmony, which is the goal of Shabbat.[27] Others have noted that the custom is for parents to continue to bless even adult children, and specifically daughters as well as sons.[28]

The custom is clearly another example of how humans have reframed traditions. Birkat Kohanim, even in the earliest period of the First Temple, was reframed by whoever created the spectacular silver strips found in Ketef Hinnom. In my opinion, this is also further testimony to the demystifying of Temple ritual and priestly status over the course of Jewish history. The Jewish people assume a more direct relationship to God, and to the rituals formerly reserved for a priestly caste. Thus the power of this biblical text continues to inspire a ritual that enhances and tightens the relationship between parents and children.

NOTES

[1] The same verb is used to denote the putting a bandage on a wound at Ezekiel 30:21.

[2] Cf., e.g., Genesis 14:19 or 27:23. God can also bless individuals, presumably at will; see, e.g., Genesis 26:12 or Judges 13:24.

[3] E.g., at Psalm 119:12, 134:1-3, 135:19-21 or 1 Chronicles 29:10, which latter verse is the origin of the blessing formula that became the norm for Jewish religious practice.

[4] Max Kadushin, *Worship and Ethics* (1964; rpt: Binghamton, NY: Global Publications, 2001), pp.166-167. Kadushin makes this same point in almost all of his other writing on the fixed formula of blessing.

[5] "YHVH" here represents the Hebrew letters *yod-hei-vav-hei*, known at the Tetragrammaton, which constitute the proper name of God. In Jewish tradition, the Tetragrammaton is spoken aloud (during the recitation of Birkat Kohanim, as well as in other liturgical contexts) as "*Adonai*" (meaning "my Lord").

[6] To understand the text of Birkat Kohanim as an apotropaic formula or a form of incantation, see Gabriel Barkay, "The Priestly Benediction on Silver Plaques from Ketef Hinnom in Jerusalem," in *Tel Aviv* 19 (1992), pp. 139-192, and Jeremy D. Smoak, "May YHWH Bless You and Keep You from Evil: The Rhetorical Argument of Ketef Hinnom Amulet I and the Form of the Prayers for Deliverance in the Psalms," in *Journal of Ancient Near Eastern Religions* 12 (2012), pp. 202–236.

[7] Readers will recognize something of the traditional stance in Mr. Spock's greeting pose from the popular Star Trek movies and television show.

[8] Cf. Leviticus 9:22, where we read that "Aaron lifted up his hands toward the people and blessed them."

[9] M. Tamid 5:1.

[10] B. Ketubot 24b–26b.

[11] Gabriel Barkay, "The Priestly Benediction on Silver Plaques" (note 6 above).

[12] Gabriel Barkay, Marilyn J. Lundberg, Andrew G. Vaughn, and Bruce Zuckerman, "The Amulets from Ketef Hinnom: A New Edition and Evaluation," in *Bulletin of the American Schools of Oriental Research* 334 (May 2004), pp. 41–71.

[13] Cf. Barkay, "The Amulets from Ketef Hinnom," p. 55, column 2 (top).

[14] Ibid., pp. 59, col. 2–60, col. 1.

[15] Ibid., p. 68, column 1. Brackets around letter indicate that those letters are not totally clear in the original document and are presented by the scholars as the most likely letters at this place. The "xxxx" siglum represents four illegible letters.

[16] Ibid., p. 68, column 2.

[17] Jeremy D. Smoak, "May YHWH Bless You and Keep You from Evil," see above, note 6.

[18] Ibid., p. 209, n. 15.

[19] Bemidbar Rabbah 11:1.

20 B. Niddah 69b.

21 B. Niddah 70b.

22 Cf. B. Nedarim 49a.

23 B. Rosh Hashanah 16a.

24 B. Shabbat 118b.

25 Cf. in this regard the comments of Rabbi Jacob Joshua Falk (1680–1756) in his monumental *P'nei Yehoshua* volume to B. Ketubot 24b (ed. Warsaw, 5621 [1860/1861]), p. 20b, s.v. *ba-g'mara*.

26 In this regard, cf. the comment of the Baruch Halevi Epstein (1860-1941) in his *Torah T'mimah* to Numbers 6, note 131.

27 Cf. the commentary on the traditional prayerbook entitled *B'samim Rosh* by Rabbi Ḥanokh Zundel ben Yosef, as published in the siddur *Otzar Ha-t'fillot, Nusaḥ Ashk'naz* (Vilna: Romm, 5688 [1927/1928], p. 614.

28 Cf. the *Imrei Shefer* commentary included in the *Siddur Ha-g'ra*, (New York: Kol Torah, 5714 [1953/1954], p. 87b.

Receptivity, Dependence, Love, and the Healing Power of Blessing: In Defense of Birkat Kohanim

James Jacobson-Maisels

Passivity, Dependence, and Healing

In the midst of the morning service, near the end of the prayer leader's repetition of the Amidah, the *kohanim*, the hereditary priests, ascend to bless the congregation. Having removed their shoes and having had their hands washed by the *leviyim* (that is, the Levites), they cover themselves in their *tallitot*, raise their hands in a special incantory gesture, and, echoing the prayer leader word by word, bless the congregation. The congregation—quiet, eyes averted, many covered in their own *tallitot*—receive the blessing. It is an extraordinary and unusual moment of staging and ritual power in the service and one of the few moments (unfortunately) in my experience that the congregation takes unusually seriously: stopping talking, arranging their bodies in particular reverent postures, and focusing on the moment of prayer and blessing.[1] It is a ceremony filled with mystery, awe, and even superstition, and one that feels particularly archaic and atavistic in its ritual components. As I live in Israel, it is a ceremony that I experience in its fullness more regularly than my diaspora brothers and sisters, for its frequency increases as one comes closer to the precincts of holiness, though an attenuated version recited by the prayer leader is regularly experienced by us all.[2] It is a ceremony that has unfortunately, in my view, fallen into disuse and even disrepute in liberal Jewish circles, but one I that want to champion in this essay as a crucial spiritual practice of blessing and transformation, and the bearer of an important message about the nature of who we are and the power of love.

I wish to highlight the receptivity, passivity, and even dependence that are part of the ritual of Birkat Kohanim. This moment is one of the few times that many of us are blessed, passively receiving a blessing sent forth by another. For those of us for whom neither amulets, rebbes, nor faith-healing is a normative part of our religious lives, Birkat Kohanim is a unique moment when we are formally, ritualistically, and lovingly blessed—as dependents—with well-being. The very structure of Birkat Kohanim, what seems to me its various atavistic elements, strengthens this aspect of its performance. The strong separation and preparation of those who offer blessing (as their hands are washed and they remove their shoes), the formal distinction between blesser and blessed (priests vs. lay Israelites), the mysterious and esoteric nature of the rite (the priests covering themselves with *tallitot* so their hands are not seen), and the deferential and reverential posture and distinction of those being blessed (standing in front of the *kohanim*, averting the eyes, being covered by a *tallit*)—all of these elements create a tableau, a formal ritual structure, that emphasizes the passivity, dependence, receptivity, and humility of those receiving the blessing. For those of us who receive the blessing, the ritual structure encourages us to let the blessing wash over us and penetrate us, to be passive receivers of the blessing...putting us in the unusual position, as modern adults, to be graced with blessing.

Perhaps this receptivity can be best felt by comparing the receiving of this blessing of love from the Divine, channeled through the *kohanim*, to a Tibetan Buddhist practice from the Dzogchen tradition, in which a blessing is received from spiritual benefactors (beings of great love, whether personally known to you or figures like the Buddha). This practice is described by John Makransky, a professor of Buddhism and Comparative Theology at Boston College and a Tibetan Buddhist meditation teacher, in his book *Awakening Through Love*. Makransky describes the practice of calling up such figures and opening oneself to the love and blessings they will send. He then writes:

> Receive the gentle, healing energy of that radiance. As other thoughts or feelings arise, let them be enveloped in this loving luminosity. No matter who you think you are, what you think you deserve, all such thoughts are irrelevant now—just accept the benefactors' wish of love for your deepest happiness. Trusting this wish more than any limiting thoughts of yourself, receive it into your whole being.
> Let yourself rely upon this love, the goodness it comes from, and the goodness it meets in your heart. To rely upon this love more than on your own defensive reactions is to find profound refuge.
> Be at ease, open, and accepting, like a puppy lying in the morning sun, passively soaking up its rays. Absorb the soft, healing energy of love into every cell of your body, every corner of your mind. Bathe in this, heal in this, rest in this. [3]

Here one can feel, quite clearly, the profound dependence, passivity, and softening that such a practice calls for, as well as the healing it can potentially bring. The practitioner is instructed to "rely upon this love," to trust the love and the practice in a posture of dependence. Similarly, one should, in a delightful image, "Be at ease, open, and accepting, like a puppy lying in the morning sun, passively soaking up its rays." The spiritual posture is one of receptivity and, I suggest, one can feel how that posture of receptivity allows one to genuinely "absorb the soft, healing energy of love into every cell of your body," to genuinely take in the blessing.

Nor is this posture of dependence limited only to those who formally receive the Priestly Blessing. The priests themselves—as

channels for divine blessing, rather than actual sources of blessing—
are also properly seen as passive, as they open themselves so that the
Divine might pass through them. This is clear from the very language
of the blessing: "May the Eternal bless you and guard you. May the
Eternal shine God's face upon you and be gracious to you. May the
Eternal lift God's face to you and grant you peace" (Numbers 6:24–26).
It is God who is properly the blesser, the source of blessing. The priests
only invoke the wish for God's blessing to be manifest. In this sense,
the priests are most properly seen as channels for divine blessing.

This is not a unique posture in the Jewish tradition. Indeed, Rabbi
Moshe Cordovero (1522–1570) understands the central goal of the
kabbalistic practitioner as becoming a channel for the divine flow,
the divine energy that kabbalists believed to flow down from heaven
into the earthly realm. This flow (*shefa*) is connected to the s'*firot*,
divine personalities and qualities which together constitute the very
nature of God. Unfortunately, the s'*firot*, as reflected in our broken
world, are estranged from one another and in discord. The goal of
the kabbalistic practitioner is to bring them back into unity. As
Cordovero describes in *Pardes Rimmonim*, the perfected practitioner
"will unify the s'*firot* and bind them with a strong tie, and thus, in
his soul, will be a channel through which the s'*firot* will flow…"[4] The
perfected practitioner thus brings the divine flow into the world and
unifies the s'*firot*. Yet it is not an active pulling down that Cordovero
describes, but rather a passive opening to allow the Divine to flow
through the practitioner. To enable this divine flow, the channel of
course must be empty; that is, the perfected practitioner must be
"clear" or "pure."[5] Any "self" that is filling the channel, any attempt by
individuals to insert themselves in this process, blocks the flow. We
can see this in another of Cordovero's works, the *Tomer D'vorah*, in his
discussion of the s'*firah* Tiferet. Speaking of Torah, the paradigmatic
divine gift which the teacher must transfer or allow to flow to the
student, Cordovero stresses that humility is essential in this process.

If the scholar becomes prideful through the learning of Torah, such a one causes Tiferet, the central *s'firah*, to separate from the *s'firot* Nezaḥ and Hod; if humble and loving, then Tiferet will send its effluence (*shefa*) to Nezaḥ and Hod and there will be no interruption in the divine flow.[6] That is, humility brings about the unification of the *s'firot* by allowing the divine flow to continue uninterrupted, while arrogance causes a separation in the *s'firot* as it blocks the flow from the higher to the lower *s'firot* and so separates the lower *s'firot* from their source. Only through the "open channel" of humility can the divine flow create unity and connection. Yet in Birkat Kohanim, this role is accentuated and brought into relief through the structure of the rite: the *kohanim* channeling the blessing physically, orally, emotionally, and spiritually to the congregation. The preparations the *kohanim* undergo can be seen as ways to purify them and prepare them for the divine encounter, allowing the blessing to be channeled to the congregation rather than being trapped in the priests' egos.[7] For both parties, then, Birkat Kohanim is in many ways about surrender, passivity, and receptivity.

It is perhaps this very quality that has led contemporary Judaism, particularly in its American variety, to put aside this practice. There are, of course, many aspects of this ritual that may not sit well with a "modern" audience, including its seemingly atavistic or shamanic elements and its hierarchical nature. Yet one additional difficulty I would like to highlight is the passivity and dependence that are built into the ritual's structure—traits that are deeply at odds with the image of the autonomous individual championed by modern Western civilization, and particularly by American mythology that so valorizes the self-made individual pulled up by that person's own bootstraps. Indeed, this championing of autonomy and (pathological)[8] resistance to dependence can be seen, quite worryingly, in American attitudes about gratitude, particularly among American men. Indeed, a study investigating "which emotions they [the participants] most like to experience, which they most dread having, which they prefer to 'keep in,' and which they view as constructive and destructive" found that "Americans in general ranked gratitude comparatively low in desirability and constructiveness, and...American men, in particular, tended to view the experience of gratitude as unpleasant. Some, in fact, found gratitude to be a humiliating emotion....Over one-third of American men reported a preference for concealing feelings of gratefulness."[9]

According to this study, many Americans (and particularly American men) found gratitude—an emotion that expresses dependence and challenges our illusion of autonomy by recognizing that which we have received from someone else—to be undesirable, unpleasant, unconstructive, worthy of concealment, and even humiliating. The posture of dependence, as a valorized and worthwhile disposition, is foreign to contemporary Western, particularly masculinist, ideology. Yet, the power of Birkat Kohanim, at least in part, is precisely its cultivation of this posture.

Indeed, the suspicion toward Birkat Kohanim that is so prevalent in liberal Judaism is part of a larger project of the demythologization and de-atavization of Judaism (which may express itself liturgically, for example, by replacing references to "a redeemer" with "redemption," or by removing references to sacrifices). While this is a complex and intricate topic, it can also be linked, in part, to this fear of dependence. Myth, religious myth, places us in a larger trans-temporal and trans-spatial context in which we hold a paradoxical dual position. On the one hand, placing our lives in a cosmic context means that we are merely bit players, insignificant aspects of an extraordinarily grandiose universe. On the other hand, myth tells us that we are also the very integrated substance of the divine universe, avatars of the Divine of a sort—playing out, enacting, and actualizing the myth in our lives.[10] In both cases, whether small (bit players) or colossal (divine avatars), we are never independent but always pieces of a larger story. In both cases our autonomy and individuality, our centrality as individuals, are brought into question.

This stance of dependence and passivity is perhaps highlighted in one traditional use of the Birkat Kohanim: as the blessing that parents give to their children on the Sabbath eve. In receiving the blessing, whether from our parents at home or from the priests in the synagogue, we are all, in a sense, made to be children. Yet, that childlike dependent posture is not one with which we are culturally comfortable, as adults. We can all imagine, for instance, how parents (especially men, given modern gender roles), while blessing their children, could become uncomfortable, awkward, or even humorous as their children grow older and eventually become adults. Indeed, we live in a culture where even children are expected and encouraged to be independent: going to bed by themselves at extremely young ages, turning in their tweens to peer (rather than parental) culture, receiving praise when they are able to do things themselves and being criticized and even shamed when they "act like a baby" by being "needy" or requesting help that is not deemed age-appropriate.[11] To be blessed is to recognize not only that one is needy, but also that one cannot meet all of one's needs by oneself. It is, in many ways, the fundamental posture of prayer. Yet unlike the mostly personal prayers of our tradition, it is a posture starkly highlighted communally by the ritual structure of Birkat Kohanim.

The centrality of dependence, passivity, and receptivity can be seen in the various usages of Birkat Kohanim. In ancient times, for instance, Birkat Kohanim was inscribed on apotropaic amulets to confer health, prosperity, and well-being on their wearers.[12] Indeed, one midrash describes this as the very nature of the Priestly Blessing:

> "On the day that Moses finished (*kallot*) [setting up the Tabernacle]" (Numbers 7:1). What is written before this matter? "May the Eternal bless you..." (Numbers 6:24). Rabbi Joshua of Sikhnin said: It is a parable of a king who betrothed (*kiddeish*) his daughter and performed the ceremony, and she then fell

under the control of the evil eye. When the king went to marry off his daughter, what did he do? He made an amulet for her and said to her, "Wear this amulet, so that you do not fall under the control of the evil eye." So too, when the blessed Holy One gave the Torah to Israel, God made for them a public display: "The whole nation saw the thunder" (Exodus 20:15), which was none other than betrothal (*kiddushin*), as it says: "God said to Moses: Go to the people and sanctify them (*v'kiddashtam*)…" (Exodus 19:10). But they fell under the influence of the evil eye and broke the tablets, as it says, "It was when he approached the camp and saw the calf and the dancing, that Moses grew angry and threw the tablets from his hands and shattered them at the foot of the mountain" (Exodus 32:19). When they came and made for them a Tabernacle, God first gave them blessings so that they would not fall under the control of the evil eye. Therefore it is written: "May the Eternal bless you and guard you" first, and [only] after the priestly blessing does it say, "On the day that Moses finished (*kallot*) [the Tabernacle]."[13]

Playing on the similarity between the Hebrew words for "finished" (*kallot*) and "bride(s)" (*kallah* or *kallot*), the midrash sees the completion of the Tabernacle as a wedding ceremony/sanctification (*kiddushin*), with the Tabernacle serving as the *huppah* (wedding canopy) underneath which God and Israel are wed. Why does the Priestly Blessing precede the text describing the completion of the Tabernacle? Because the words of the blessing are an amulet, which protects the already-betrothed bride (Israel) from forces of evil and therefore allows her to complete the marriage. The blessing prevents Israel from once more falling into the sin of idolatry. The blessing is thus literally a form of protection that allows the consummation (*kallot*) of the marriage.

Similarly, the Talmud recommends recitation of the Priestly Blessing as a way to transform an uncertain dream into a blessing, explaining:

If one has seen a dream and does not remember what one has

seen, let that person stand before the priests at the time when they spread out their hands, and say as follows: "Sovereign of the Universe, I am Yours and my dreams are Yours. I have dreamt a dream and I do not know what it is. Whether I have dreamt about myself or my companions have dreamt about me, or I have dreamt about others—if they are good dreams, confirm them and reinforce them like the dreams of Joseph; and if they require a remedy, heal them, as the waters of Marah were healed by Moses, our teacher, and as Miriam was healed of her leprosy and Hezekiah of his sickness, and the waters of Jericho by Elisha. As You did turn the curse of the wicked Balaam into a blessing, so may You turn all my dreams into something good for me." One should conclude the prayer along with the priests, so that the congregation may answer, "Amen!"[14]

Here, in a lovely display of dependence and surrender, one who has had an uncertain dream simply asks that it be made beneficial in whatever way is appropriate, whether through its fulfillment or through its transformation and healing. Birkat Kohanim is considered the perfect time for this request, for such transformation, fulfillment and protection is the very nature of the priestly blessings.[15]

Similarly, Rabbi Isaiah Horowitz (1565–1630) describes a beautiful healing ceremony that utilizes the Priestly Blessing, which he details as "a beautiful ritual to do with a sick person who is *in extremis* (*li-g'sos*)." In this ceremony, the sick person is to recite a number of biblical verses (if possible), which are then completed by the person at the bedside.[16] The sick person then says, "Thus shall you bless the children of Israel; say to them..." (Numbers 6:23), which is the introduction to the biblical Priestly Blessing. The person at the bedside then continues by reciting the text of Birkat Kohanim (Numbers 6:24–26), and they both conclude by then reciting another series of verses.[17] It is noteworthy that the Priestly Blessing occupies a central place in the ritual; moreover, it is the only place where, utilizing the words of the verse, a sick person invites another to bestow a blessing, and the person responds with explicit words of blessing.[18] Echoing the Talmud's dictum, conveyed precisely in a discussion of healing, that "a prisoner cannot free himself from the prison,"[19] here an individual in a vulnerable and dependent position invites another person to recite the Priestly Blessing, so that the former can fully receive the blessing—which is meant either to aid in the person's recovery, or to provide succor in finding acceptance and peace in the midst of the illness. The roles here are significant. Though in both wording and choice of verses it is abundantly clear that the blessing and healing comes from God, still the sick person explicitly instructs the companion to offer the blessing—thus placing him or herself in a position of receptivity and dependence, in being blessed by his or her fellow.

This passivity and dependence, the receptivity of receiving a blessing, is crucial to the very content of the blessing itself, love and peace. Here form serves function, receptivity enabling the only true peace attainable: not the peacefulness of knowing that things will turn out all right (for we never know if things will turn out all right), but rather the peacefulness of knowing that we can be all right, that we can be present however things turn out. The true blessing is the ability to relax in the midst of the struggle, to find peace in the uncertainty, to receive what is. Passivity and receptivity, and the protection of equanimity that they help engender, similarly make possible genuine love—the ability to truly be loved, receive love, be helped, feel gratitude, and enable true vulnerability and intimacy. It helps us relinquish our illusion of autonomy and our illusion of control, two barriers that prevent us from awakening to sincere equanimity and love. This passivity is neither disempowering nor about being weak or helpless. Rather, it is about recognizing that no matter how efficacious we can be, we are never in control—and that the striving, fear, and tension of control has no place for peace or love. This posture of receptivity empowers us to respond, from a place of balance and compassion, with wisdom and clarity. I will return to support this argument below; for now, we must turn to the place of love and peace in Birkat Kohanim, from which we can then see the profound connection between its posture of receptivity and the love and peace with which it blesses us.

Love, Protection, Peace, and Blessing

The Priestly Blessing is essentially a blessing of love, incanted in love, and expressing divine love and care for the recipients. The hasidic master Rabbi Kalonymus Kalman Halevi Epstein of Krakow (b. c. 1753) beautifully presents this idea of the centrality of love in his work *Maor Va-shemesh*, in a homily on the priestly blessings. He explains:

> Torah commentators have already remarked as to why it is written "Say to them" (Numbers 6:22) and not "Speak to them." Concerning this, it seems to me that the verse hints that one who comes to bless Israel must have this quality, that he loves them with a love as powerful as he loves his soul and heart. Even the lowest of the low among Israel he loves like his soul. And through this he glorifies them before their Father in heaven with a plethora of virtues. And through this he arouses compassion and great forces of lovingkindness, and draws down upon them all manner of blessings. And this is hinted at in the words "Say to them"—that is to say, the word "say" (*emor*) comes from the language of "you have affirmed (*he·emarta*) the Eternal this day [as your God]" (Deuteronomy 26:17). And its explanation is that God commanded the priests, "Thus shall you bless the children of Israel; say to them…" (Numbers 6:22)—meaning that with this quality you will bless the children of Israel; that is to say, that you will love them. Then you will be fit to bless Israel.[20]

The meaning of "thus" in the verse, the Maor Va-shemesh explains, is that the blessing must be done with a particular quality, the quality of love. Only *thus*, in this way—with love—must you (the priests) bless Israel. Indeed, the priests are only fit to bless Israel when that love is present. This love is not merely a mild generic caring but rather a passionate concern, like one's love for one's own soul and heart. Such love, he explains, is a powerful force, pulling down compassion, love, and blessings through the channel of the priest and into the world. Such love glorifies its recipients, allowing their inherent virtue and goodness to be seen and extolled. Indeed, that is the nature of love: to allow ourselves and others to see and be seen through the eyes of love, to acknowledge our fundamental virtue and worthiness. Similarly, the Zohar teaches: "Any priest who does not love the people or whom the people do not love should not spread out his hands to bless the people."[21]

Indeed, the necessity of love is expressed in the very ritual formulation of Birkat Kohanim, which requires that the priests begin the ceremony by reciting the blessing, "Blessed are You, Adonai our God, Sovereign of the world, who sanctified us through the sanctity of Aaron and commanded us to bless the people Israel with *love*," in which context the word love (*ahavah*) rings out and permeates the space then filled by the Priestly Blessing. This command to bless with love can of course be read two ways. On the one hand it is a command, as the Zohar and the Maor Va-shemesh suggest, that the priest must himself feel love for those he is blessing, that the blessing itself must be performed with love. On the other hand, as the hasidic master Rabbi Yeraḥmiel Yisrael Yitzḥak Danzinger (1853–1910) teaches, it can also be read as blessing its recipients with the experience of love, "that there will be between them love and unity and each one will love the other."[22] Perhaps it is this requirement of love that disqualifies a priest who has committed manslaughter from performing the priestly blessing.[23]

As the Maor Va-shemesh makes clear concerning the priest who pronounces the blessing, it is the love of the *kohen* that arouses and brings down the heavenly love and blessing, because

he loves them [i.e., the people whom he is blessing] with a

love as powerful as he loves his own soul and heart. Even the lowest of the low among Israel he loves like his soul. And through this he glorifies them before their Father in heaven with a plethora of virtues. And through this he arouses compassion and great forces of lovingkindness and draws down upon them all manner of blessings.[24]

This is to say: whatever our metaphysical commitments, the love and blessings bestowed here are, at least initially, the love of one human being for another. How can such love, a loving vision that truly sees, appreciates, glorifies, and extols everyone it encounters—no matter how seemingly low or unworthy—not bring forth boundless compassion, lovingkindness, and blessing? How can such a love not extend beyond itself to cause, in kabbalistic language, an arousal above?[25] Whether understood metaphysically or empirically, we can see how intentions and acts of love extend beyond themselves to affect more than what seems to be their limited borders. We can see how the Priestly Blessing itself is an act of love, communicating and bringing love to both blessed and blesser.

Indeed, the blessing itself not only communicates love but is itself an act of love. As Gerald Janzen explains, "The Priestly Blessing... exemplifies what Austin characterizes as 'performative speech': words do not simply refer to something, but actually do what they say. 'I love you' not only reports the speaker's affections, but enacts them verbally; their efficacy is to be felt by one to whom they are addressed. Likewise, 'God bless you' is a verbal act whose efficacy is conveyed in those words."[26]

The performative speech act of blessing itself not only conveys the love of the speaker for the one blessed but is itself an act of love. It is a moment of genuine intimacy and care. This is why the Talmud insists that the blessing be said face to face: "'Thus shall you bless' (Numbers 6:22)—face to face. You say 'face to face,' but perhaps it should be face to back? The verse teaches us, 'Say to them'—like someone speaking to a friend."[27] In other words, the blessing must be said in a posture of intimacy, the way one would talk to a friend. Despite the formal and hierarchical nature of the ceremony, there is no intent to distance or estrange, but rather to enable a genuine intimate encounter. Indeed, the language of "face to face" is particularly striking and powerful. This is so for two reasons. First, speaking face to face is precisely how the relationship between Moses and God is described, and is the ultimate sign of divine intimacy;[28] and second, because of the prominent place of the face in the priestly blessings. In three short lines, the divine face is mentioned twice: "May the Eternal bless you and guard you. May the Eternal shine God's *face* upon you and be gracious to you. May the Eternal lift God's *face* to you and grant you peace." The shining of the diving face and its lifting toward those blessed indicate divine love, care, and attention flowing toward the blessed.

What, then, is the connection between the two ideas discussed so far—the centrality of receptivity, dependence, and passivity in the Priestly Blessing; and the centrality of love—and how do they both relate to the wish for peace that is the ultimate end of the Priestly Blessing? In brief, I want to maintain that the protection and blessing that Birkat Kohanim provides is precisely love. Love is the blessing and healing, and it is the peace that is the promise of the blessing. The surrender, dependence, receptivity, and passivity structured into the Priestly Blessing are what enables that love, and the peace that is its fruit, to be actualized. That is: love is actualized through receptivity and surrender. The protection of love, the peace it provides, is the deep knowing that we are held in love, held from outside, in a posture of dependence and passivity.

We can see this aspect of the Priestly Blessing by turning again to the Tibetan blessing practice discussed above. Makransky describes how the posture of receptivity enables the transformation of love, which the practice provides. He explains:

Tibetan Buddhists generally begin their meditations by

recalling spiritual benefactors who embody for them the enlightened qualities of the infinite, non-conceptual nature of mind. Their reverence and receptivity to the qualities of these benefactors becomes so strong that they learn to trust the mysterious, infinite ground of those qualities: the vast expanse of openness and cognizance beyond self-clinging. Through the power of such receptivity and trust, they are enabled to release their egos into the infinite nature of mind itself. Tibetans do this by envisioning their spiritual benefactors—their lamas[30] and buddhas[31] and · bodhisattvas[32]—as a radiant field of refuge before them. Then they receive the luminous blessings and energies of their benefactors' enduring love, compassion, liberating wisdom, and spiritual power into their whole being. The warm, radiant energy of those qualities helps them to relax their ego-centeredness, to melt away their self-protectiveness, and to sense the radiant ground of those qualities as absolute goodness. Pulled beyond themselves in this gentle way, they merge joyfully into oneness with their benefactors within that ground, which is the infinite, non-conceptual nature of mind beyond separation (buddha mind, *dharmakaya*).[33] In this way, a conceptual practice of devotion to the goodness of spiritual benefactors, and to the infinite ground of that goodness, provides the most effective entry into non-conceptual meditation.[34]

It is the receiving of love, a conceptual practice of reverence, receptivity, and devotion, which evokes enough trust in the basic goodness of reality that we can take refuge in that reality and relax into its mystery.[35] The more deeply we learn to receive the unconditional love that accepts us just as we are, the more we can trust and let be into just what is, to relax into an intuitive knowing beyond anxieties of self-concern.[36]

Here, Makransky makes clear the connection between receptivity, blessing, love, and peace. It is when we are able to genuinely receive the love bestowed on us, to really take in the blessing of love, that peace arises as a fundamental trust in the nature of what is. This is not some Pollyannaish certainty that everything will turn out all right, but rather a strong, centered knowledge—founded on love—that we can be all right, however things turn out. This Tibetan practice also helps us to understand the importance of the dependence, hierarchy, formalism, and surrender that we have noted in Birkat Kohanim. That is to say (as Makransky points out): reverence and receptivity are key. It is reverence which enables the kind of open-hearted, non-striving receptivity that is fundamental to this practice and which allows, in the Jewish context, the practitioner to receive the "enduring love, compassion, liberating wisdom, and spiritual power" not of their benefactor directly, but rather of the Divine as channeled through the priests. It is the posture of reverence, dependence, trust, and surrender that can allow the practitioner to "melt away their self-protectiveness, and to sense the radiant ground of those qualities as absolute goodness." Indeed, it is this absolute goodness that, the Maor Va-shemesh tells us, is reflected in the loving gaze of the priest bestowing the blessing.

When performed properly, or perhaps ideally, the relative formal postures and positioning of the blessing priest and the blessed congregant, and the love that the priest must bring to the blessing, allow for a special and childlike softening of the heart in the blessed. This allows the individual to genuinely take in and embody the love and blessing being sent forth, to trust the blessing and the love, and so to experience the peace and equanimity that come with such a deep opening, softening, and trust. Here, to use Makransky's phrase, Birkat Kohanim helps enable the practitioner, the one blessed, "to trust…the vast expanse of openness and cognizance beyond self-clinging."[37] That is, Birkat Kohanim invites the blessed to simply let go: to no longer be in control, to give up self-protection, to relinquish the illusion of ultimate autonomy…and so to be opened to love, blessing, and peace; to be opened to the vastness of divinity. As Makransky explains, "It is the receiving of love, a conceptual practice of reverence, receptivity, and devotion, which evokes enough trust in the basic goodness of reality that we can take refuge in that reality and relax into its mystery."[38] This, I believe, is the promise of Birkat Kohanim: that we might, through our "reverence, receptivity, and devotion," truly receive the love which is its nature, evoking for us sufficient trust so that we relax into the Reality and its basic goodness, so that we can experience the peace which is the promise of the Priestly Blessing. Birkat Kohanim is a precious and relatively rare opportunity to open and receive the love that is being sent to us. It is an opportunity to stop doing, controlling, and making and instead to take a few moments, a recurring Shabbat, to soften, open, surrender, relax, and receive.

Blessing and Being Blessed:
Birkat Kohanim and Blessing as a Spiritual Practice

Having discussed the central importance of the posture of receptivity I want now, in a sense, to turn our discussion on its head and consider how what we have discovered might be applicable more generally to a practice of blessing and to the very stance of the blesser. That is: having considered ourselves as the blessed, can we take what we have learned and become in turn blessers ourselves—making Birkat Kohanim, in an extended way, a more everyday and widespread practice for ourselves and others? Doing so is not an innovation, but rather an extension of two pre-existing liturgical facts surrounding Birkat Kohanim.

The first is the fact that the priests themselves are blessed in their very blessing. As we learn in the Talmud:

Rabbi Joshua ben Levi also said, "Every *kohen* who pronounces the benediction is himself blessed, but if he does not pronounce it he is not blessed, as it is said, 'I will bless them that bless you.'" Rabbi Joshua ben Levi also said, "Any *kohen* who refuses to ascend the platform transgresses three positive commandments, namely: 'Thus shall you bless,' 'Say to them,' and 'So shall they put My name on the Israelites [and I will bless them].'"[39]

The priests themselves are blessed in their blessing, but only if they themselves bless. Here the priest is the receiver of the blessing but also its channel—and his receptivity, the passive aspect, is dependent on his blessing, his active aspect. Indeed, the blessing itself is a described as a "performative commandment" (that is, as a positive commandment, one of the *mitzvot aseih*) in three ways,[40] one that must be actively done in order to be fulfilled. The priest can then be both active and passive at the same time, both calling down and also receiving the blessing.

This stance of the priest is reflected in the stance of praying Jew who, in reciting the Sim Shalom prayer (the final blessing of the Amidah, which immediately follows the Priestly Blessing), mirrors Birkat Kohanim itself.[41] Let us compare the two blessings.

The Priestly Blessing	Sim Shalom
May the Eternal *bless* you and guard you. May the Eternal *shine (ya-eir) God's face* upon you and be *gracious* to you. May the Eternal lift God's *face* to you and grant you *peace*.	Place *peace*, goodness and *blessing;* life, *grace*, lovingkindness and compassion, upon us and on all the people Israel. Bless all of us as one, our Father, with *the light (or) of Your Face*. For by *the light of Your face* you have given us, Eternal our God, a Torah of life, love of kindness, charity, *blessing*, compassion, life, and *peace*. May it be good in Your eyes to bless all of Israel at every time and every hour with Your *peace*. Blessed are You, Eternal, who *blesses* the people Israel with *peace*.

The Sim Shalom prayer, in its repetition of almost every element of the Priestly Blessing—its particular echoing of the illumined face of God, and its parallel conclusion with the blessing of peace—can be seen as a kind of extended adaption of the Priestly Blessing for the lay practitioner. Whether in a liturgical context that includes the Priestly Blessing or not, lay practitioners similarly request blessing for themselves and their people. The Sim Shalom prayer, in this sense, is thus a kind of extension of the Priestly Blessing, the receiving of blessing from outside into lay practice, where lay practitioners continue the practice of blessing for themselves and their people.

This process is paralleled in the Tibetan practice we have been exploring. Makransky instructs, following the receiving of the blessing from the benefactors, as follows:

> After a little while, join your benefactors in their wish for you. While receiving the radiance of their love, mentally repeat the wish for yourself, using words like these: "May this one have deepest well-being, happiness, and joy." Affirm the words repeatedly in your mind. Try to mean them as you say them, just as your benefactors mean them for you. Like everyone else in this world, you most deeply need and deserve happiness and well-being. Repeat the wish for yourself while accepting your benefactors' love even more deeply into body and mind, communing with them through its radiance.[42]

Similarly, in the Sim Shalom prayer we are invited to join in the well-wishing of the priests' channeling of the divine blessing. We ourselves becomes as we are, one of a "kingdom of priests" (Exodus 19:6).

This points to the way in which the practice of blessing—in our prayer life (where the Amidah, the "prayer" *par excellence*, is structured as a series of blessings) and in our spiritual life more broadly—can be a powerful spiritual practice. It encourages us to take seriously the blessing of ourselves and others with love and well-wishing, whatever our metaphysical positions, as a transformative practice of love, protection, and peace. That is, we are to understand our own practice of blessing, though structurally different and lacking many of the elements of the Priestly Blessing, as parallel to those blessings themselves. By this I mean that even in our own enactment of blessings, passivity, dependence, and receptivity are crucial and are the very mechanisms by which the healing of the blessing is manifested, the way that the love, protection, and peace come into the world.

We can see this clearly in the instructions that Rabbi Kalonymus Kalmish Shapira, the Piaseczner Rebbe (1889–1943), gives concerning a blessing practice he taught, a practice of cultivating certain qualities by saying phrases that invite in those qualities. He teaches concerning the repetition of a particular phrase: "One repeats this several times, but not forcefully. The whole point here is to quiet one's thoughts. Speaking with great forcefulness is liable to arouse the self;[43] rather, on the contrary, one utters the phrase with great gentleness."[44] Here, in the saying of the blessing itself, in the calling down of the change or the inviting in of the quality, one still takes on a stance of receptivity. The words must be said gently. It is not a practice of strength and force, but rather a kind of receptive activity. There is a kind of non-self action here, which acts and blesses in a way that is consonant with the receptive and dependent stance of the receiver of blessings. Even in our own action, in our own blessing and cultivation, in our own premeditated "autonomous" acts, the blessings only work, the Piaseczner Rebbe tells us, when we approach this act with a passive, inviting, and soft texture, *sans* any illusion of control.

In this way, the Priestly Blessing is a model more broadly for a kind of spiritual practice that can be present in our lives, however often we are actually able to experience the ritual of the blessings themselves. We can actualize this model in our traditional prayer lives, as well as in concrete meditative practices of blessing and cultivation—both blessing and being blessed—as ways to manifest the love, protection, and peace of the Priestly Blessing, as well as innumerable other qualities. At the same time, we can bring a new intention and presence to the ritual of Birkat Kohanim itself, opening ourselves more fully to receiving the blessings that are offered and channeled to us. In both cases, we are presented with the possibility of being held in something wider and deeper than our normal small sense of self, something beyond the "me" that is desperately striving to control and dominate the world. In both cases, we are given the possibility of truly receiving blessing and, in that receiving, being healed.

NOTES

[1] The focused intentionality, including cessation of all talking and other distractions, during Birkat Kohanim is comparable, in my experience, only to the congregation's comportment, in traditional settings, during the Kedushah.

[2] In the Ashkenazic tradition, Birkat Kohanim is recited in the Diaspora only on festivals, but in the north of Israel every week on Shabbat, and in Jerusalem (and other parts of Israel) every day. Though there are significant halakhic objections to this minhag, see Rabbi Yeḥiel Mikhel Epstein (1829–1908), *Arukh Ha-shulḥan,* Oraḥ Ḥayyim 128:63–64.

[3] John Makransky, *Awakening Through Love: Unveiling Your Deepest Goodness* (Boston: Wisdom Publications, 2007), pp. 26–27.

[4] *Pardes Rimmonim,* Sha·ar Ha-kavvanah §32 (Jerusalem: Yerid Ha-s'farim, 2000), p. 482.

[5] Ibid., p. 482. The Hebrew for "pure" in this passage is *zakh.*

[6] *Sefer Tomer D'vorah* (Brooklyn: Mesivta Publication Society, 5703 (1942/1943), chap. 7, p. 26. By "central s'firah," I mean to refer to the literal place of Tiferet within the schema of the s'firot flow, and not to its importance. The particularities of the significance of Tiferet, Nezaḥ, and Hod and their interactions are not important to our discussion here; the point is simply that one need recognize that separation or connection depends on the level of humility and "emptiness" of the practitioner.

[7] Note the spiritual cleansing effected through hand-washing and the removal of shoes. (The latter resonates with the command for Moses to remove his shoes when approaching the sanctified space of the burning bush; cf. Exodus 3:5.)

[8] Pathological in the sense that independence is seen as a supreme value, which displaces other crucial values (such as compassion) and is, moreover, illusory—as there never has been and never will be a completely independent human being, if only for the simple reason that no human being has ever brought him or herself into the world.

[9] Robert Emmons, *Thanks!: How Practicing Gratitude Can Make You Happier* (Boston and New York: Houghton Mifflin, 2008), p. 130, citing Corinne Kosmitzki and Shula Sommers's essay, "Emotion and Social Context: An American-German Comparison," in *British Journal of Social Psychology* 27 (1988), pp. 35–49.

[10] This is most strongly true in Kabbalah, where the practitioner is, at times, quite literally an avatar of one of the s'firot.

[11] See the analysis of this phenomenon in Gordon Neufeld and Gabor Mate, *Hold On to Your Kids: Why Parents Need to Matter More Than Peers* (New York: Ballantine Books), 2008.

[12] See Barry Ross, "Notes on Some Jewish Amulets: *Ayin Ha-ra* and the Priestly Blessing," in *Journal of Associated Graduates in Near Eastern Studies* 2:2 (1991),

pp. 34–40, and see the essay by Michael Graetz elsewhere in this volume.

[13] *Midrash Tanḥuma, Naso* §17.

[14] B. Berakhot 55b.

[15] For more on the role of the Priestly Blessing in the realm of dreams, see the essay by Howard Addison elsewhere in this volume.

[16] *Sh'nei Luḥot Ha-b'rit*, vol. 2, *P'saḥim, Shoresh Y'sod Amud Ha-ḥesed, Perek Neir Mitzvah*, chap. 1 (ed. Warsaw 5690 [1929/1930]), p. 3b.

[17] Ibid.

[18] Interestingly, this ceremony is not particular to a *kohen*; rather, it seems that any Jew is encouraged to utilize the Priestly Blessing in this way.

[19] B. Berakhot 5b.

[20] *Ma·or Va-shemesh, Parshat Naso*, s.v. *va-y'dabbeir...dabbeir el aharon.*

[21] Zohar III 147b.

[22] *Yismaḥ Yisrael, Parshat Naso*, s.v. *v'zeh she-omeir.*

[23] B. Berakhot 32b.

[24] *Ma·or Va-shemesh, Parashat Naso*, s.v. *va-y'dabbeir...el mosheh leimor.*

[25] See just such a comment on Birkat Kohanim in Rabbi Yaakov Yosef of Polonne (1710–1784), *Sefer Tol'dot Yaakov Yosef, Parashat Naso* §8.

[26] J. Gerald Janzen, "What Does the Priestly Blessing Do?" in, *From Babel to Babylon: Essays on Biblical History and Literature in Honour of Brian Peckham*, eds. Joyce Rilett Wood, John E. Harvey, and Mark Leuchter (New York: T & T Clark, 2006), p. 26, citing J. L. Austin, *How to Do Things With Words*, 2d ed. (Oxford: Clarendon, 1976).

[27] B. Sotah 38a.

[28] Note, though, that the Hebrew is slightly different in the two formuations. In speaking of Moses' encounter with God, it is *panim el panim* (Exodus 33:11); in the Talmudic passage, it is *panim k'neged panim.*

[29] The centrality of peace, *shalom*, in the blessing can be seen both in the fact that the blessing concludes with the idea of peace and also in how the other elements of the blessing all lead toward and contribute to peace. Moreover, Birkat Kohanim is followed liturgically by the Sim Shalom prayer, which (as we will discuss below) is a kind of echo and reformulation of the Priestly Bessing.

[30] Teachers of dharma.

[31] The various enlightened beings who inspire Tibetan Buddhists.

[32] Those who strive for enlightenment of themselves and others.

[33] Buddha mind or *dharmakaya* is the infinite, non-conceptual nature of mind beyond separation.

[34] Makransky, *Awakening Through Love*, p .48.

[35] Ibid., pp. 49–50.

[36] Ibid., p. 63.

[37] Ibid., p. 48.

[38] Ibid., p. 49.

[39] B. Sotah 38b (quoting Genesis 12:3 and Numbers 6:23, 27), based on the Soncino Press translation, trans. A. Cohen (London: Soncino Press, 1936).

[40] "Thus shall you bless," "Say to them," and "So shall they put My name [and I will bless them]" are all distinct positive commandments according to the Talmud.

[41] See Michael Fishbane's comments in this regard in "Form and Reformulation of the Biblical Priestly Blessing [Num 6:23]," in *Journal of the American Oriental Society* 103:1 (1983), p. 120.

[42] Makransky, Awakening Through Love, pp. 26–27.

[43] The Hebrew for "self" here is *anokhi·ut*, literally "I-ness."

[44] "The Subject of Quieting," in *Derekh Ha-melekh* (Jerusalem: Va·ad ḥasidei Piaseczno, 1995), p. 451.

The Natural Limits of Freedom:
On the Tight Structure and Comprehensive Contents of Birkat Kohanim[1]

David Mescheloff

Preface

At first blush, the three verses of Birkat Kohanim might seem to be an almost random collection of good wishes (Numbers 6:24–26):

> May the Eternal bless you and protect you.
> May the Eternal make His face shine light toward you and be gracious to you.
> May the Eternal lift His face toward you and give you peace.

We will show, however—in two distinct but overlapping ways—that Birkat Kohanim is, in fact, so tightly structured and comprehensive as to direct all of God's blessings into every corner of a meaningful human life—that is, a life characterized by free choices made under five types of constraint.

The Plain Meaning

First, let us reflect on the plain meaning of the text, as explained by Rashi[2] in his classic Torah commentary. We will see that Birkat Kohanim can be thought of as structured in concentric rings—beginning with the outermost ring of human activity, and spiraling in step by step toward a human being's most personal and intimate internal life. Each verse contains two verbs, calling God's blessings upon the individual who stands before the *kohen*.[3] We will examine the plain meaning of each verse, considering each verbal phrase separately.

The First Verse (Numbers 6:24)

VERSE 24A: "MAY THE ETERNAL BLESS YOU." The fundamental meaning of the Hebrew root *bet-resh-kaf*, translated as "bless," denotes increase. Also derived from the same root is the word *b'reikhah*,[4] a natural or artificial pool into which the waters of a spring flow gently, filling the pool via an ever-increasing accumulation.[5] Since a natural spring may ebb and flow, the pool in which the water accumulates serves as a reservoir, making it possible to regulate the water supply so that one can provide a steady supply of life-giving water to one's fields, vineyards, and orchards. Such pools, constructed at the mouth of springs centuries and millennia ago, are a common sight in the hill and mountain regions of Judea and Samaria. Thus, Rashi explains, "May the Eternal bless you" means "may God increase your possessions."

VERSE 24B: "AND [MAY THE ETERNAL] PROTECT YOU." God's blessing of possessions is followed by "and [may the Eternal] protect you." That is, Rashi writes, "may no robbers come to take away your property." He continues: "If a human being gives a gift to a servant, the human giver cannot guard it from everyone. If a band of robbers attacks and takes away the gift, then of what benefit is it to the recipient? But God both gives and guards that no one will take the gifts away from you." Of course, robbers are only one of a great many potential dangers that may threaten one's accumulated possessions and wealth. This part of Birkat Kohanim, then, is a prayer that the Eternal protect from all possible harm all of those material blessings that God showers upon us.

One's possessions are in the outermost ring of one's life. They are surely not the essence of one's life. Possessions come and go. They may make one's life more comfortable, but only for a while. When a person has possessions, they mediate between one's body and one's self on the one hand, and the rest of the world around oneself on the other. Possessions serve as tools that one can use to engage the world—creating, molding the material world to the benefit of oneself and others, improving the quality of life on earth, and bringing blessing to the world.

The Second Verse (Numbers 6:25)

VERSE 25A: "MAY THE ETERNAL MAKE HIS FACE SHINE LIGHT TOWARD YOU." Rashi explains this metaphor as follows: "May God show you a smiling face, a yellow face." Rashi's use of this modern image is astounding; his description is precisely that of the graphic image, the "smiley" that hundreds of millions of human beings recognize from the internet and countless other arenas of public culture.

It is generally thought that Harvey Ball created the smiley in 1963, but, apparently, the idea has been around for millennia.[6] The smiley brings a smile to the viewer's face. It conveys a feeling that the world is smiling at you. It expresses a sense of general well-being, of joy, that all is well with the world. The priestly prayer that God should "make His face shine" toward you means that you should feel pleased in your encounter with the material world around you, that your efforts should be crowned with success. "Smile, because the world is smiling at you; things are working out well for you!" Those actions and deeds that one does with one's own body are closer to one's person than one's possessions—which, as we have noted, are attached only externally, and which may come and go. By way of contrast, one is bound to one's body throughout one's life. Through one's body, one interacts with the surrounding world and engages it in direct physical contact. The ring of one's deeds in the world is closer to one's self than the ring of one's possessions.

VERSE 25B: "AND [MAY THE ETERNAL] BE GRACIOUS TO YOU." This common translation implies that this is an additional blessing, calling upon God to show favor to the recipient of the blessing. But Rashi, basing himself on the Sifrei on our verse,[7] suggests that a more accurate translation would be: "May God grant you good favor." This is an intentional ambiguity, for it means both "may the Eternal grant that you find favor in the eyes of others" and also "may the Eternal grant that others find favor in your eyes." Thus, this blessing calls for mutual pleasure in our relationships with other people: may we all like each other, may God grant that we all get along well.

Other human beings—who live, breathe, feel, and think, like us; who share our humanity; who, like us, choose freely how to live— are closer to us than are the inanimate objects and the non-human animals that serve us for utilitarian purposes in the world. Only with other human beings can we create the personal "I–Thou" human relationship of which Buber wrote, a relationship of trust and love. The quality of our lives as social creatures is determined by the nature of our interactions with our family members, our friends and neighbors, our work colleagues, and our communities in general. And the nature of these interactions is a responsibility shared by us and those others.

Thus this single Hebrew word *vi-ḥunneka* ("and may [the Eternal] grant you good favor") encompasses the entire area of our interpersonal, social, work, and communal relationships. It is a prayer that both we and others succeed in creating a social world that is pleasant for us all. And thus, Birkat Kohanim has moved one step closer to our inner selves.

We should note, too, that the Hebrew word *ḥein* (derived from the same root as *vi-ḥunneka*), usually translated as "grace" or "favor," has a connotation of being an unpredictable type of relationship. It is something that one "finds," almost as one finds a lost object by chance. Thus of Noah it is written, "And Noah found favor (*ḥein*) in God's eyes" (Genesis 6:8). Similarly, the unpredictability of finding favor in one's eyes is emphasized in God's self-description, "I will show favor [or: grace, *ḥein*] to whomever I will show favor [or: grace]" (Exodus

33:19). This part of Birkat Kohanim, then, is, like the blessings for prosperity and success that precede it: a wish that we be blessed by God with something that we cannot achieve on our own, although our own input is necessary. And the third verse of Birkat Kohanim continues in this same vein.

The Third Verse (Numbers 6:26)

VERSE 26A: "MAY THE ETERNAL LIFT HIS FACE TOWARD YOU." This metaphor describes the behavior of someone who was so furious that he or she could not look directly at the object of his or her anger. After bringing the rage under control, the angry person becomes able to lift his or her face again, and look at the other person directly—or, as we say, "in the face." Thus Rashi explains this part of Birkat Kohanim with two Hebrew words: *yikhbosh ka·aso*, "may [the Eternal] suppress His anger [toward you]." This is a highly startling "blessing"! Would it not be more of a blessing if the *kohanim* were to say "May the Eternal not be angry with you"?

To understand this idiom, let us examine a different, yet similarly startling, biblical expression. Whereas Birkat Kohanim addresses its blessings to each individual, Leviticus 26:3–13 is a passage of blessings addressed to the people of Israel as a whole. It opens with the conditional "If you will walk in My statutes, and observe My commandments, and do them," and then follows a long list of blessings addressed to the entire nation. The list begins with rain and an abundance of produce, and continues to enumerate security, success in war, regional peace, and more abundant prosperity. As the list of blessings nears its climax, we read: "And I will place My sanctuary in your midst, and My soul will not detest [or: abhor/loathe] you" (verse 11). Again, one is startled by God's promise—near the climax of the blessing—not to abhor us. That would have been more understandable at the very beginning, before the blessings of rain and produce, peace and security. What can this mean?

The key to understanding this lies in the context. Note that the promise not to abhor us comes between "I will place My sanctuary in your midst" and "I shall walk in your midst, and I will be your God, and you will become My people" (verse 12). Thus, the risk of abhorrence, loathing, and disgust is actually another measure of God's closeness! One cannot be disgusted by one with whom one has no contact. Indeed, one can love billions of human beings easily—in the abstract, from afar. But spouses, parents and children, friends and neighbors, who live together in close quarters—or, at least, experience close, personal, intimate emotional contact—find it more challenging to ignore the sometimes offensive behaviors, or even natural physical phenomena, to which they are exposed. Familiarity breeds contempt.

If that is true of relations among human beings, all of whom share common physical behaviors and similar emotional and behavioral patterns, how much more so can this be expected in the relationship between human beings and the utterly transcendental God, who experiences only the purest of abstract spiritual existence! God's disgust, loathing, and abhorrence are to be expected if human beings come close to God; indeed, the expectation of such responses is a measure of closeness. Thus, when the blessings in Leviticus reach their climax, with God's sanctuary in our midst and God walking among us, then it is most appropriate to be told "My soul will not detest you." It is as if God is telling us, "We will be so close to each other that My soul *should* be disgusted—because you are so human and ungodly—but it will not be so! I know that you are human, I made you that way, I will accept you for what you are—and if you will walk in My statutes, then I will not be disgusted by you, even as I and My sanctuary are in your midst!"

Birkat Kohanim is to be understood in the same way. In the first part of this third verse, the priests are blessing each individual with closeness to God. It is not possible for a human being to be truly close to God while yet remaining human, without in some way angering God. If Birkat Kohanim were to include a wish to the effect that God not be angry with human beings, then that could only mean that a deep chasm would separate those being blessed from God. So instead, acknowledging the risks that come with closeness, Birkat Kohanim wishes that although we, as humans, will inevitably anger God in some way—that is a measure of how close we will be to God—nevertheless, may God understand, accept, forgive, and suppress any anger we may arouse. And may we do our share in repairing our relationships with God through t'shuvah (repentance). Thus, Birkat Kohanim has moved one step closer to our deepest internal lives by blessing each of us in our relationship with God.

VERSE 26B: "AND [MAY THE ETERNAL] GIVE YOU PEACE." Concluding with the blessing of personal peace of mind, Birkat Kohanim encompasses all of human life. Rashi makes no comment on this phrase, for the necessity of internal peace—in order for all of the other blessings to be meaningful—is clear. A life of material prosperity, success in all one's endeavors, friendly relations all around, and even acceptance by God are not blessings for a person who suffers internal torment. On the other hand, the equanimity, calm, self-assurance, and confidence that come with a state of internal peace of mind will allow all the other blessings to be appreciated, to be truly blessings.

Thus we have seen that in its plain meaning Birkat Kohanim has a simple, clear structure, and constitutes a comprehensive formula for a blessed life in every possible way. We will now take a deeper look into the meaning of the blessing.

A Meaningful Human Life: Freedom and Its Limiting Factors[9]

<u>Freedom: The Sine Qua Non for Meaningful Human Existence</u>
Maimonides (1135–1204) was generally quite sparing with his words, trying to squeeze as much meaning as he could into as few words as possible. Yet in his discussion of the foundation of the Jewish notion of repentance, he repeated the following idea at least four times, in very similar terms (three of these appear below, typeset in capital letters):

EVERY PERSON IS ABLE, IF HE OR SHE SO DESIRES, TO INCLINE ONESELF TOWARD A GOOD PATH AND TO BE RIGHTEOUS; OR, IF HE OR SHE SO DESIRES, TO INCLINE ONESELF TOWARD AN EVIL PATH AND TO BE WICKED... the human species is unique in that A HUMAN BEING KNOWS INDEPENDENTLY, OF HIS OR HER OWN MIND AND THINKING, WHAT IS GOOD AND WHAT IS EVIL, AND DOES WHATEVER HE OR SHE DESIRES, AND THERE IS NONE WHO HOLDS HIM OR HER BACK FROM DOING GOOD OR EVIL...AND THERE IS NONE WHO COERCES, OR PREORDAINS, OR WHO DRAWS HIM OR HER ONTO ONE OF THE TWO PATHS; ONLY THE PERSON, OF HIS OR HER OWN SELF AND MIND, WILL DIRECT HIM OR HERSELF TO WHICHEVER PATH HE OR SHE WANTS.... And this is a great fundamental principle, the pillar upon which the Torah and the commandments rest...If God were to decree that a person would be righteous or wicked, or if there were something that drew a person by virtue of his or her birth to a certain path, or to a given knowledge, or to a certain attitude, or to given deeds...then how could prophets command us to do certain things and to refrain from others, if we were not able to do so? What point would there be to the entire Torah? What justice would there be in punishing the wicked and rewarding the righteous?...Just as God desired the other laws of nature to be as they are, so did God desire that HUMAN BEINGS HAVE THE ABILITY TO CHOOSE THEIR OWN PATHS, THAT WHAT THEY DO SHOULD BE UNDER THEIR CONTROL, AND THAT THERE IS NONE TO COERCE THEM OR TO DRAW THEM; HUMAN BEINGS OF THEIR OWN [FREE] WILL AND THEIR OWN GOD-GIVEN MIND DO WHATEVER HUMAN BEINGS ARE ABLE TO DO...[10]

It is human free will that gives meaning to human life. Indeed, from Maimonides' statement about Torah, the commandments, and divine justice, it follows that at least nine of the thirteen principles of faith that he enumerated rest on the realization that humans have free will. The very idea of free will has been challenged, debated, and examined in different ways by many scholars and thinkers over the millennia, and we shall not discuss it here. But why did Maimonides repeat so extreme a position—that nothing coerces a person, and that nothing draws him or her to a given behavior, or deed, or attitude, or knowledge, or path in life? Perhaps it was for didactic reasons. Perhaps it was an attempt to counterbalance a human tendency—common to this very day—to deny responsibility for one's choices by attributing one's choices to some other factor. Perhaps Maimonides meant only to negate extreme claims, such as "So-and-so forced me to do it," or "Such-and-such drew me with irresistible attraction into a certain path or deed."[11]

The Limits of Freedom

Whatever may have motivated Maimonides, it is clear that there are things that do push a person onto a wrong path and there are things that prevent one from doing what is right.[12] Indeed, freedom is not a binary matter, as if there are only two possibilities: one is either completely free, or one has no freedom at all. Rather, there is a range of levels of freedom, from completely free to reduced freedom to no freedom at all.

I suggest that the natural, necessary limitations to human freedom can be classified into four principal observable groups, with a fifth almost inaccessible element that I will describe later. The limitations will be presented here descriptively, not prescriptively—that is, I will speak of necessary limits of freedom, which apply universally to all human beings. I will not speak of limits that ought to be placed on individual freedom for ethical, moral, social, or religious considerations of one type or another.

One may thus speak of four "spheres" or "spaces" within which people live their entire free lives (plus a fifth sphere, to be described subsequently). Human freedom is exercised in the form of choices made well within the spheres, and choices made at the edges or surface boundaries of the spheres; however, leaving the spheres is not a possible choice. Any given situation may call for a person to make decisions related simultaneously to more than one of the spheres, and in this sense the spheres may overlap. However, all of the spheres are conceptually quite distinct. What follows is a description of these spheres.[13]

(A) THE LIMITS OF FREEDOM— THE PHYSICAL LAWS OF NATURE

One cannot choose to convert iron into gold by chemical means—even if it were for a higher spiritual purpose, such as to support a yeshiva or to bring an end to human poverty. One cannot choose to avoid death forever—even for the ethical aim of studying and teaching more Torah. One cannot choose to walk through a solid wall—even for the *mitzvah* of saving a life. One cannot choose to call out with one's own unamplified voice halfway around the world—even for the purpose of honoring one's parents. One cannot fly with one's unassisted arms—even for the purpose of burning *hameitz* that is up in a tree in one's backyard as Passover approaches. One cannot change one's given genetic makeup—even for the purpose of marrying and having children, or of improving a character flaw that may have a genetic component. And many more such examples could be adduced.

Our choices must be made within the confines of the laws of nature, which we cannot change merely because they limit our free choices, even in matters of human happiness. Being free does not mean that we can violate physical laws, even for purposes of doing good or evil, or for choosing a good path...or an evil one.[14] Thus we live our lives and make our ethical choices among various options, all of which are within the laws of nature, and all of which have natural consequences.

On the other hand, we can choose to push at the boundaries. Since we do not know all the laws of nature, and since we don't like the limitations that the ones we do know place on us, we seem to be constantly striving to learn more about them, so as to extend what we thought were the limits. In other words, we seek to expand the boundaries of the space of physical laws within which we live freely. This drive for greater freedom lies behind all progress in medicine: we want to avoid disease, to enable and to hasten healing, and to delay death, by understanding how those laws really work. We don't like the limitations that other physical laws place on us, either; since we want to move about freely and we want to communicate with other human beings, we keep pushing the limits as we explore and innovate impressive technological advances in transportation and in communications.

When we come up against a boundary that resists being extended, we can choose freely how to respond. For example, if one were to be diagnosed with a fatal disease, one could choose to accept reality with some degree or other of equanimity, or one could choose to challenge it and struggle against it, trying—more successfully or less so—to find ways around it. Alternatively, one might choose to rebel against the fact of mortality—doing the equivalent of banging one's head against a stone wall, getting nowhere but increasing frustration, and perhaps even harming oneself. How we respond to our encounters with the boundaries of this sphere is our choice.

Finally, it should be noted that the laws of nature establish that choices have consequences; the more "rigid" the law, the more certain that the consequences will follow. If one chooses to throw a heavy object out of a high floor in a building, then it will fall, and it may hit someone on the way down—even if one sees the tragic accident coming and would like the heavy object to stop in mid-air or move to the side.

(B)   THE LIMITS OF FREEDOM—THE FREE WILLS OF OTHERS: INDIVIDUALS AND SOCIETIES

Each individual is free to choose his or her own goals, and to work to achieve them. But so is every other human being. By definition, this means that one cannot choose another's goals, attitudes, paths, moral values, or deeds, and cannot implement another's goals in his or her stead. One person's free will ends where (or before) the next one's begins. Generally, we live with other people cooperatively, within the boundaries that their choices create for us.

The same is true of groups of people. One cannot decide, for example, that it is all right to drive through a red light—for example, because one is in a hurry and there is no other car and no police officer in sight—after a society has determined that driving through a red light is against the law. Here, too, in general people make their life choices within the space whose boundaries are set by law.

This is not to say that one is unable to violate the free choice of another human being or of a society. As in the case of the limitations placed by the laws of nature, one can choose how to face the limitation of being unable to make choices for another person. One could choose to accept and submit to this limitation. Alternatively, one could attempt to influence the choice of the other—using the "laws" that govern how humans influence one another (ranging from persuasion to assertion, perhaps even of the aggressive variety). There is also the unhappy option of force, of violating another's choice, giving preference to one's own choice over that of another. But none of those options is the same as making the other person's choice.

On the one hand, the result of such violations is often untold pain. One might choose, for example, to hire ruffians to take hold of a person and physically force him or her to sign a deed of sale, conveying the rights to a given piece of property—but one cannot make the choice in the heart and mind of the victim in his or her place. Another example: untold harm may result when parents make choices for their young adult children, preventing them from learning to take responsibility for their own choices; but on the other hand, parents can often spare their young adult children untold harm by making decisions for them and implementing them. This does not mean that the parent has made the child's choice, though, or *vice versa*. Again, it only means that one has chosen to override the other's preference: one person thus carries out his or her own choice against the will of the other. People often miscalculate the consequences of choosing to behave in this way.

In other words: although the free will of one person limits that of another, nevertheless, one can choose to "test" this limitation on one's own free will and see whether it can be pushed, and one can choose how one will respond to that boundary—whether by acceptance or by rebellious refusal to accept that boundary, even if such rejection of the fact of the other's choice is to no avail. Choices have consequences, in both the realms of human relationships and the laws of nature, and there are interpersonal, social, and political processes that, once set in motion, may not be stoppable. On an individual level, for example, parents who choose to deprive their children of Jewish education may set them on a trajectory that leads them to assimilation. On an international level, think of the consequences for tens of millions of people of choices made by Hitler, Stalin, and others like them.

(C)   THE LIMITS OF FREEDOM—GOD'S FREEDOM

Two fundamental principles of Jewish faith are the freedom of human beings and the freedom of God.[15] As with other free human beings, this does not mean that one is unable to choose to implement one's own choice rather than that of the other; that is a matter of how one chooses to deal with the limitations at the boundary of this sphere of human freedom. The fact that there is a boundary means that one cannot make God's choices in God's place. God has chosen to make humans free, and so one is free to say, "No, God, I don't want to do what You want me to do"; but one is not free to say, "No, God, You don't want me to do what You said that You want me to do, but, rather, something else—what *I* say You want me to do."[16] That would be overstepping the bounds of God's freedom. God states what God wants, and we can state what we want. But we cannot dictate to the other—to God—what it is that the Divine wants.

Yet, here too people often test the boundaries, perhaps wondering, "Is that what God really wants, or does God want something else?" And we humans, in our freedom, can choose how to respond to the experience of coming up against the limitations placed on us by God's free expression of what God wants: we can accept the limitations, or we can grumble about them, or we can deny their existence, or we can rebel against them—or we can choose another possibility, somewhere in between these.

As with the laws of nature, the freedom of others, and the laws of societies, we spend our lives as free agents making choices within the boundaries expressed by God's choices, and in our encounters with those boundaries.

(D) THE LIMITS OF FREEDOM—THE INHERENT LIMITATIONS OF FREEDOM ITSELF

Free will is often thought to mean that one can do whatever one chooses, with the emphasis on "whatever." However, having a variety of options is only a necessary—but not a sufficient—requirement for there to be free choice. For free choice to be real, not only potential and theoretical, one must actually choose from among the various options available. That means that the essence of free choice is an act of self-limitation, choosing one option from among more than one possibility, or choosing one combination of possibilities over more than one possible combination.

Exercising one's freedom can be difficult, since people often feel freer when they are unfettered by limitations—even self-imposed limitations. Making decisions can be difficult, too, when choosing one option from among others occurs against a background of uncertainty—that is, a lack of knowledge of all of the consequences of making the choice.[17] Indeed, very often, after making one choice one will need to make other choices, in order for the first choice to work out for the best. For example, a young person may say, "I am free to marry anyone I want!" But until the actual choice of spouse is made, that "freedom" is only theoretical; it has not been exercised. And one might say, "How do I know whether the person I am about to choose is the best possible one for me? Perhaps a better one is waiting around the corner!" To this one must respond, "You are right! You won't have to choose in the dark, in complete ignorance. But even though your choice may be made with as much knowledge as is reasonable, fair, ethical, and moral for you to gather, you will still be without full knowledge of all the consequences of your choice. To the contrary: after you make your choice of mate, you will have many choices to make about your relationship with your spouse that will go into making the choice you made of a spouse successful—or not."

Thus we live our free lives within a space whose boundaries are set by freedom itself, making numerous decisions daily with no special difficulty, far from the boundaries, but occasionally bumping up against the limitations that require us to choose, although we might prefer not to limit our options. And we may choose to respond to the challenges of having to choose in numerous ways. One may accept the fact, and choose. One may procrastinate constantly, and avoid commitments. One may just refuse to choose—which is itself a choice. In other words, paradoxically, to be truly free one must choose, must limit one's self, must leave fewer options open. This is no small challenge.

Birkat Kohanim and Freedom

Birkat Kohanim addresses all of the challenges that a free person must face, both in living life within the four frameworks enumerated above and also in dealing with those situations in which one confronts the borders of those spaces.

The first verse, "May the Eternal bless you and protect you," addresses the challenges that people face in dealing with the physical laws that govern material things. One cannot increase one's possessions magically, but must work within the laws of nature (including the laws of economics) in order to succeed. Birkat Kohanim blesses us, that we make the wisest possible decisions. It also recognizes a basic truth: we are never able to fully guarantee that all our efforts will bear fruit. God's blessing is necessary for our material success.

The first part of the second verse, "May the Eternal make His face shine light toward you," continues the theme of our acting as free agents within the limitations of the laws of nature. As we saw above, it speaks of the success of our personal efforts, those in which we use our bodies to effect changes in the world around us. Here too God's blessing is needed, so that we make wise, meaningful, and effective choices.

The end of the second verse, "[May the Eternal] be gracious to you," addresses the meaning of human lives as free agents living in a sphere whose limits are the boundaries between the free wills of separate individuals and between individuals and societies. May you find favor in others' eyes, and may they find favor in your eyes. May your choices in this sphere create a world of pleasant relationships between you and others. May your lives blend smoothly with those of other human beings, so that you live together meaningfully, with mutual respect for each other's freedom, in cooperation and pleasantness.

The first part of the last verse of Birkat Kohanim, "May the Eternal lift His face toward you," addresses the life one lives within the space whose boundaries are defined by God's free choices. If your humanity creates clashes between you and God, whether by choices you make that are within the boundaries or whether by choices you make at the edges, then may you find the way to make amends with God, and may God— after the fact and after being angry—accept you, with your flaws, mistakes, and weaknesses, suppress anger, and "lift His face toward you" again.

Finally, Birkat Kohanim concludes with the words "and give you peace," expressing the wish that God bless us in that area where we have to face the challenges of limiting ourselves. May we be at peace with ourselves in having to limit ourselves. May we not be filled with regrets over decisions we have made in the past and their consequences. (We made past choices based on all the knowledge available to us at the time, and so there is no point regretting what we could not have realistically chosen differently; and if we can correct mistaken choices—through *t'shuvah*, repentance, for example—then let us do so.) May the incomplete and imperfect knowledge that we have when we make our decisions not prevent us from making the best decisions possible, one after another.

Thus, Birkat Kohanim addresses us in the full range of our meaningful lives as humans, praying that our freedom be exercised well and with God's blessing in every "space" within which we operate, allowing us to freely decide how to live within the limitations that are imposed on us by the material world, by people, by society, by God, and by the very nature of freedom itself.

The Fifth Element

It might appear, at first blush, that this analysis of the universal, inherent limitations of freedom is exhaustive. Yet our ancient sages pointed out, in their inimitable fashion, that there is one more space in which we human beings spend our lives, free to act and make changes within the space, even though it is sharply limited by its boundaries. The Talmud, after noting that it is often good people who have bad dreams that they cannot recall or understand, relates the following story:[19]

> Amemar, Mar Zutra, and Rav Ashi were sitting together. They said, "Let each one of us say something that his friends [i.e., the rest of us] have not heard."[20] One began, "[If] a person had a dream and doesn't know what he or she saw,[21] let that person stand before the *kohanim* as they spread their hands [to recite Birkat Kohanim], and say as follows: "Master of the universe! I am Yours, and my dreams are Yours! I dreamt a dream, and I don't know what it is![22] Whether I dreamed about myself or whether my comrades dreamed about me, or whether I dreamed about others—if the dreams were good, reinforce them and make them be strong and come true, like the dreams of Joseph; and if they need healing, then heal them as [You healed] the bitter waters of Marah, through Moses our teacher, and as [You healed] Miriam from her *tzara·at*, and as [You healed King] Hezekiah from his illness, and as [You healed] the waters of Jericho through Elisha, and as You reversed Balaam's curse to a blessing—so may You turn all my dreams into good [ones]!" And he or she should conclude [this prayer] together with the *kohanim*, so that the congregation will respond, 'Amen!' [to the dream prayer at

the same time as they say 'Amen!' to Birkat Kohanim]."[23]
Why did our sages link the unremembered—or not understood—bad
dreams of a good person to Birkat Kohanim?[24] I believe they were
aware of the interpretation I suggested above: that through Birkat
Kohanim God is being called upon to bless us in all the activities in
which we act with free will, within and at the limiting boundaries of
four spheres: the physical, deterministic laws of nature; the freedom
of all human beings;[25] God's freedom; and the inherent nature of
freedom itself.

I believe our sages may have been calling our attention to one
more space in which we are free, but restricted: our selves. On the
one hand, "we"—as free agents—are what we are. As free agents, it
is we who choose freely whatever may be within reach of our ability
to choose. That chooser—each individual "I"—is a given, the sum
total of all our givens (by birth, nature, rearing, culture, personal
inclinations, and faith) and all of our choices and their consequences,
up to the given moment of our next choice.

"Who we are," or "what we are," or "how we are"—in that sense—
can be a highly restrictive reality. Is there a way that one can choose,
freely, to act not only in the world, not only in relation to others and
to God, and not only in relation to one's self as a free chooser—but
also in relation to one's very self, the very chooser? Can one choose
to mold, to make changes, in the one who chooses—directly, rather
than only indirectly by acting in the four other spheres?

I believe that our sages may have been hinting that the answer to
these questions is "Yes!" But how does one do that? Am I, the free
chooser, not a permanently fixed, given identity? And so the sages
instruct us: "Bring your dreams to Birkat Kohanim! Your dreams are
a window into your very self, your unconscious, your personality, your
soul. You can reach inside that narrow sphere, and mold your own
image. You can choose to act within the sphere of your self, just as
you can in the other spheres."

When God approached the task of creating men and women "in the image of God"—that is, as free agents, free to choose independently of the deterministic laws of nature, within the limitations set by each of the other four spheres of human existence, especially free to choose to limit themselves—God said, "Let us make humankind in our image!" (Genesis 1:26). Commentators have interpreted the plural in that declaration in different ways. Some suggest that it should be understood as "the royal we," while others suggest that it be taken as a call to the angels in God's heavenly court. One can also suggest that God was turning to the human creation, to men and to women, and calling upon them to join the Divine in the act of creating human beings. This notion can be found in midrashic understandings of more than one of our traditional sources.[26]

In recent generations, humanity has been blessed with numerous attempts to develop theories concerning the human "self": how it begins, develops, and changes. Many of these theories are associated with methods intended to help relieve psychological distress. The hope is that by restoring people to a state of wholeness and emotional health, they will be able to act with full freedom, responsible both to themselves and to their material, social, and spiritual worlds. Many of these techniques make use of a person's dreams as a means of seeing into the internal life of the person, so as to help him or her regain emotional health.[27] These processes are, on the whole, compatible in principle with the thinking reflected in the directive of our sages that one bring one's dreams to the liturgical recitation of Birkat Kohanim. One may freely choose to change one's own choosing self!

Conclusion

We have shown that Birkat Kohanim is a structured set of blessings that encompasses all aspects of human life. One understanding sees the blessings converging from a person's outermost extension to one's most inner self: blessing one with possessions, success in one's endeavors, pleasant human relations, closeness and acceptance by God, and peace of mind. A second way is to see the blessings applying to every meaningfully human aspect of life, as defined by free choice and its inherent limitations: the bounds of the laws of nature, the limits each person's freedom places on every other's, social limits, the bounds set by God's free expression of the divine will; and the self-limitation required for a person to be genuinely free. Concerning the second way, we showed that our ancient sages suggested that one is also free to make changes in one's self, thus sharing in God's creation of each and every human being. May God bless the people of Israel in every way—and may there be peace on Israel—so that Israel may be a source of blessing to all the peoples of the world.

NOTES

[1] In memory of my father, Rabbi Dr. Moses Mescheloff, of blessed memory, and my mother, Rebbetzin Magda Mescheloff, of blessed memory, whose blessings sustain me daily.

[2] Rabbi Shlomo Yitzḥaki (France, 1040–1105).

[3] Many parents, too, recite Birkat Kohanim to bless each of their children on Friday evenings, calling down God's blessing on each child.

[4] It has been suggested that many three-letter Hebrew roots may have been constructed from two-letter pairs, where the second letter of the first pair is the same as the first letter of the second pair. Thus bet-resh-khaf, the root that denotes increase, may derive formed from the two letter pairs bet-resh, "external, flowing outward," and resh-kaf, "soft."

[5] See 2 Kings 20 20; and B. Mo·eid Katan 4b and Gittin 68a.

[6] See http://en.wikipedia.org/wiki/Smiley and http://en.wikipedia.org/wiki/Harvey_Ball for possible modern precursors to Ball's "smiley." Although Ball (1921–2001) was not Jewish, he reported being deeply influenced by the Worcester, Massachusetts sign painter to whom he was apprenticed while in high school. See www.worcesterhistory.org/sidebar-exhibitions/smiley-face, where it is reported that "In his junior year he apprenticed himself to a local sign painter who taught him how to create visual images with strong impact. He won a scholarship to attend the Worcester Art Museum School in 1940, where he received training in fine arts. In his view, working at the sign shop may have been better preparation for his commercial art career than the formal training he received at the Worcester Art Museum School." I cannot help but wonder whether that sign painter was Jewish, or whether Ball was influenced by members of the Jewish immigrant community that flourished in Worcester during his youth.

[7] Rashi to Numbers 6:25, s.v. vi-ḥunneka, paraphrasing Sifrei Bemidbar §41. The Sifrei is an early rabbinic halakhic midrash based on the biblical books of Numbers and Deuteronomy.

[8] Not uncharacteristically, many words are required to render into English what is conveyed in a single Hebrew word. This is common in translating from Hebrew to English, for Hebrew is a tightly compact language, rich in associations, and making liberal use of prefixes and suffixes to represent whole English words.

[9] I hope to write about this in more detail in a later volume in this series.

[10] Maimonides, M.T. Hilkhot Teshuvah 5:1–3.

[11] To this theme, too, I hope to return in a later volume in this series.

[12] Indeed, Maimonides hinted at this in this very chapter of the Mishneh Torah. One hint is at the very end of the sections quoted above, "human beings of their own [free] will and their own God-given mind do *whatever human beings are able to do*." Thus, Maimonides acknowledged that things do exist that human

beings are not able to do—that is, that are not within the range of human free will.

[13] I will write briefly of this here, since my primary purpose here is to illuminate Birkat Kohanim. In a subsequent essay, I hope to return to this topic in greater detail.

[14] This truth is often distorted, in more than one direction, in ways that I will not elaborate on here. Some misuse it in order to excuse immoral choices. Others deny this truth, claiming that exceptionally admired moral leaders—even Torah leaders—perform wonders.

[15] See Samson Raphael Hirsch (1808–1888, Germany), *Commentary to the Torah* (New York: Judaica Press [second revised edition], 1989), vol. 1, commenting on Genesis 6:6. In a subsequent essay, I hope to discuss the observations of Rabbi Hirsch and of Rabbi Avraham Yitzhak Hakohen Kook, and others, about this. I also hope to examine how the giving of the Torah established limitations on our freedom of will by establishing the ways in which God wants us to live a life of service before God.

[16] Thus, for example, God has commanded us not to eat the flesh of swine; one cannot say, "No, God, it is all right with You if we do that"; or, given that God has commanded us in the Torah not to slander, one cannot say, "No, God, it is all right with You if we do that." One may choose to eat the flesh of swine, or to slander—but one is not free to say that God wants that which God has expressly forbidden.

[17] This is not to say that no choosing takes place where one knows with certainty what the consequences may be. One might choose to harm one's self, even though one knows what pain will follow. One might choose not to marry, even though one knows what loneliness will follow. One might choose willfully to harm others, as well.

[18] Free will places other inherent limitations on free agents, to which topic I hope to return in a later essay in this series.

[19] B. Berakhot 55b. The story continues beyond the section we bring here, but I quote only the part relevant to Birkat Kohanim, the subject of this essay.

[20] A different possible translation: "that the others don't consider reasonable."

[21] A possible different translation: "doesn't understand what he or she saw."

[22] Or: "I don't understand it."

[23] This prayer appears in many *siddurim*, especially in *maḥzorim* for the festivals and for the High Holy Days, to be said during Birkat Kohanim during the cantor's public repetition of the Musaf Amidah. For more on the connection between Birkat Kohanim and dreams, see the essay elsewhere in this volume by Howard Avruhm Addison.

[24] Indeed, this passage raises many interesting questions, including: What is the significance that the statement needs to be new to the friends (or disputed by them)? What is the significance of each of the analogies in the prayer to

biblical dreams or to biblical stories of repair? Why is it important that the entire congregation reply "Amen" to the dreamer's prayer? Our answer to the one question that we do address here should hint at possible directions for some answers to some of these and other questions about this passage.

[25] This is distinct from the probabilistic laws of subatomic nature, which some have suggested might be a link—at least conceptually—between the other laws of nature and human free will. Recognizing probability as a measure of our lack of knowledge, which has been shown to be inherent in the realm of the atom and below—where energies and masses appear interchangeable, and where the energy waves that serve as a means of measuring and knowing affect unpredictably the velocity and location of the particles we are trying to observe—seems an appropriate analogy, at least, to the sometimes unpredictable nature of human free will.

[26] Esau, Jacob's older twin, was born "red, all over like a hairy robe" (Genesis 25:25). His name, Esau, indicated both that he was *asu·i* ("made" or "done")— that is, at least in terms of his hair, fully developed and complete. It has been suggested that Esau's name indicated metaphorically that he was born "a finished product," to be accepted as is, rather than as a human being whose free choices would and could mold his personality. It has been suggested that precisely this attitude is why Esau became identified in the course of Jewish history as the archetype of a wicked person.

[27] How dreams do this is also a fascinating question, with which I hope to deal more fully elsewhere.

A Priestly Blessing of Love and the Question of Pure Consciousness in Judaism

Aubrey L. Glazer

There are those moments we experience in life that remain etched in our hearts forever and the time of that etching stands still. Oftentimes those experiences can be transformative to the point where we actually shift in our own awareness of the world and the role our consciousness plays in processing the "big picture." This essay will explore precisely that subtle shift in our awareness from the "thinking I"—that bold declaration of modernity within Rene Descartes' *cogito ergo sum*, "I think therefore I am"—which creates our perception of reality as moderns, to a pure consciousness of love which permeates the entire constitution of self and universe. I will argue in this essay that Judaism provides avenues for glimpsing such transformation of consciousness through liturgical moments, like the Priestly Blessing. I will offer anecdotal encounters with remarkable poets reflecting upon their verse and with teachings of spiritual masters, as well as my own constructive approach to all these elements, in order to address the question of the (im)possibility of pure consciousness in Judaism. To accomplish this, I will argue that it is possible to read the Montreal bard, Leonard Cohen, against Rabbi Mordecai Yosef Leiner (known as the Ishbitzer Rebbe) to sense the beginning of an answer. In turn, my discussion of Leonard Cohen will be explored against the backdrop of the Israeli poet Yehuda Amichai, and I will then turn to an exploration of the work and thought of Integral Yogi Sri Aurobindo in order to enrich my understanding of the Ishbitzer Rebbe. By taking this constructivist approach, I am searching for the experiences that inspired the poetic verse and homiletic teachings under consideration. My juxtaposition of these "texts" will strike many readers as somewhat unconventional, but it is all part of an attempt to get behind the words of the Priestly Blessing into the experience to which that powerful blessing points—an experience largely inaccessible to most moderns. If I have been successful, by the close of this exploration, you will never read the Ishbitzer's homilies the same way again, and you will never listen to Leonard Cohen the same way again; something in your relationship to Judaism and the pure consciousness of love transmitted through the Priestly Blessing will (hopefully) have shifted.

Let me begin by recalling two remarkable encounters with poets who explored the pure consciousness of love. One is Montreal singer–songwriter Leonard Norman Cohen (b. 1934), and the other is the late Israeli poet Yehuda Amichai (1924-2000). Despite the fact that I am now distanced from each of these encounters by significant space and time, I can actually put my finger on what it was that touched me so in both of them: an outpouring of pure love. It may sound strange, especially given that both Amichai and Cohen were both in their seventies at the time that these meetings took place, but these meetings with remarkable men touched me like no other.

The Montreal bard Leonard Cohen had just returned to stage performances as a singer–songwriter after more than a decade of living as a reclusive Jewish monk meditating on Mount Baldy on the outskirts of Los Angeles. The reasons for Cohen coming down the mountain were not that complex, and were, in fact, even antithetical to his contemplative life: his longtime manager had been embezzling the equivalent of millions from this cult folk-singer. When he was ready to retire and turned to his savings, Cohen realized that he had been swindled by his own manager. True, this incident was only one bump on the road, as Cohen's life had been marked by bouts of depression, which he had attempted to alleviate through various means, including spiritual practices. Sitting in a café with Cohen, surrounded by a few fellow academics at a conference of the Association of Jewish Studies a few years ago, and watching him interact with his daughter Sasha, everyone present could feel him emitting an energy that palpably changed the room. Years later, I invited a close friend of mine (who happens to be a cantor) to join me at Barclays Center in Brooklyn to hear Leonard Cohen on what may turn out to have been his last tour. This friend told me excitedly that he had seen Cohen perform at Madison Square Garden in Manhattan a few nights earlier, and it had been one of the most spiritual experiences he'd had in quite a while. This sounded a bit hyperbolic to me, but I did not want to miss this apparent finale (and of course, the notion of a "finale" to Cohen's career keeps shifting, as his creativity proves boundless and more songs emerging daily). After three straight hours of performing music drawn from his entire oeuvre, at times prostrating himself on his knees in prayerful positions, I had to agree with my friend: this was a truly transformational experience. Something palpable happened in that arena; Cohen was transmitting an energy of love that could only come from one place—pure consciousness.

Perhaps Cohen's ability to channel such pure consciousness emerged after he was introduced by a close Jewish friend to a Zen Buddhist master called Roshi.[1] Cohen was immediately drawn to follow this master because, he relates, there was something about this teacher that had captivated him for decades. Although Cohen does not use this language, he clearly experienced a common Tantric phenomena known as *shakti-pat* or an "energy-descent"—namely, a mind-to-mind release of pure consciousness transmitted by master to disciple.[2] Interestingly enough, the more Cohen advanced in his Zen studies and rigorous meditation, the more deeply anchored he became to his Jewish identity. In part, this was a function of Roshi wanting his student to be authentic to what the Zen *koan* describes as his "original face," and partly because Cohen remained aware of his own priestly lineage (as indicated by his last name).

Cohen claims to have had "a very messianic childhood"[4] growing up on Belmont Street in Westmount, a suburb of Montreal. A classmate recalls how much "Leonard was embedded in religion, deeply connected with the *shul* through his grandfather, who was president of the synagogue, and because of his respect for the elders; I remember how Leonard used to recount how his grandfather could put a pin through the Torah and be able to recite every word on each page it touched…"[5] In addition to providing his grandson with regular exposure to traditional synagogue life, Leonard's grandfather, Rabbi Solomon Klonitzki-Kline—himself a writer—was supportive of his grandson's literary endeavors, and the two of them would often sit together in the evening "going through the Book of Isaiah, which the rabbi knew by heart and which Leonard came to love for its poetry, imagery, and prophecy."[6] This inspiration, which flowed both from his priestly lineage and the prophetic calling to be a poet, can be felt in the following prelude to a song proffered by Cohen during his concert in Jerusalem in the early 1970s, replete with Jewish mystical imagery:

> It says in the Kabbalah that if you can't get off the ground you should stay on the ground. It says in the Kabbalah that unless Adam and Eve face each other, God does not sit in his throne, and somehow the male and female part of me refuse to encounter one another tonight and God does not sit on his throne and this is a terrible thing to happen in Jerusalem. So listen, we're going to leave the stage now and try to profoundly meditate in the dressing room to try to get ourselves back into shape…if we can manage we'll be back.

Cohen's decades-long dedication to Zen practice can be seen as a commitment to redeeming the Jewish tradition through the rigor of a Buddhist lens, rather than succumbing to its betrayal through a Judaism that he considered at times to be xenophobic or triumphalist.

His master, Joshu Sasaki Roshi, instructed Cohen that there is ultimately no contradiction between the prayerful worship of Judaism and atheistic practice of Zen. Notwithstanding his deep involvement with Buddhist thought, Cohen always insisted to anyone who asked that he remained a Jew, fully satisfied in having a perfectly good religion; this can be seen, for example, in the following lines of his poetry:

> Anyone who says
> I'm not a Jew
> is not a Jew
> I'm very sorry
> but this decision is final.[8]

Cohen also pointed out that Roshi never made any attempt to give "this Jewish monk a new religion."[9]

With the outbreak of the Yom Kippur War on October 6, 1973, Leonard Cohen immediately left his family on the tranquil Greek island of Hydra in the house he has retreated to since the 1960s and flew from Athens to Tel Aviv to volunteer for service in the Israel Defense Forces, explaining: "I've never disguised the fact that I'm Jewish and in any crisis in Israel I would be there…I am committed to the survival of the Jewish people."[10] For the next few weeks, Leonard joined up with Israeli musicians Oshik Levi, Matti Caspi, Mordechai "Pupik" Arnon, and Ilana Rovina to sing for the IDF soldiers in "outposts, encampments, aircraft hangars, field hospitals, anywhere they saw soldiers, and performed for them up to eight times a day."[11]

What is most intriguing about the Montreal bard is his process of song writing. While Cohen appears to be a prolific songwriter, his drafts most often go through grueling stretches of agonizing rewrites until the song emerged complete. By contrast, this Yom Kippur War trip to Israel remains one of the few times when Cohen was able to compose a song quickly. Indeed, he improvised the song "Lover Lover Lover" in front of the soldiers during his second performance with the band of Israeli musicians, and the through the lyrics, he was able to express the effects of war in Zion:

> May the spirit of this song
> May it rise up pure and free
> May it be a shield for you
> A shield against the enemy.[12]

Clearly, this ability to feel love and transmit such pure consciousness in a time of war was Cohen's own Priestly Blessing, even evoking its liturgical format. And this ability became even more evident once the Montreal bard actually returned again to Zion, despite his earlier (post-Yom Kippur War) poetic reflections on the impossibility of reaching Jerusalem: "I won't be going to Jerusalem after all. You will have to go to Jerusalem alone. It is yours. It was given to you by the angels of culture and time. But I can't go."[13] This feeling of love, and the ability to transmit such pure consciousness in a time of war through his own Priestly Blessing, emerged anew when Cohen travelled to Israel three decades later, at the end of his 2009 European tour. Playing the finale of his concert in Tel Aviv, Cohen—wearing his signature black suit and fedora—gave this preamble to his invocation of the Priestly Benediction:

> I want to draw our attention to the Israeli and Palestinian member[s] of the Bereaved Parents For Peace...and those other men and women, some of whom have been called foolish, irrelevant, defeatist, but no, no, not at all friends! They have achieved the victory, perhaps the only victory available—the victory of the heart over its own inclinations for despair, revenge, and hatred. So dear friends...[positioning his fingers into the

priestly formation and bowing with his musicians onstage he begins reciting the benediction:] *Y'varekh·kha Adonai…*

This return to Zion, with its invocation of the Priestly Blessing in Tel Aviv rather than at the Western Wall in Jerusalem, is telling of Cohen's own journey from exile to redemption. The universalist tone of his poetics, which was incubated in the early 1960s in Montreal, resounded decades later—while remaining imbedded in his particular religious path. After the finale to end all finales—assuming the role of a priest, invoking his Priestly Blessing in Tel Aviv—the particular has become universalized with *"Leonard Cohens* everywhere."[14]

That expansiveness, intrinsic to the Priestly Blessing of the pure consciousness of love, is something I also felt when I first met Amichai, then in his seventies, a few years before he passed away. Being in this poet's presence, I felt constantly embraced by unending love. He was visiting my university for a poetry reading, and we were involved in a deep conversation about translating his radio play, "The Day Martin Buber Was Buried,"[15] into a film script that I was then planning to direct. What was it that allowed this gentle septuagenarian soul to be so full of love? Born in Würzburg, Germany to an Orthodox Jewish family, Amichai was raised speaking both Hebrew and German. Perhaps it was a childhood trauma in Germany that caused him to dedicate his life to writing poetry of pure love. Apparently, Amichai had an argument with a childhood friend of his, Ruth Hanover, that caused her to bike home angrily; she fell and as a result of injuries sustained in the accident had her leg amputated. Several years later, because of her missing leg she was unable to join the rest of her family when they fled the Nazi takeover; she was killed in the Holocaust. Amichai would later write of that experience, of love lost with his childhood friend, in poems such as "Little Ruth."[16] Premonitions of becoming a writer began for Amichai while he was stationed with the British army in Egypt, as he confronted death in the trenches as the other side of love about which he would continually be writing poetry. As a soldier he happened to find an anthology of modern British poetry, and the works of Dylan Thomas, T. S. Eliot, and W. H. Auden all inspired and confirmed his first serious thoughts about becoming a writer of love poetry. In 1956 Amichai served in the Sinai War, and in 1973 he served in the Yom Kippur War. He later became an advocate of peace and reconciliation in the Middle East, working with Arab writers. How could a Hebrew poet steeped in the machinations of war and death be so open to pure love, as permeates all of his poetry?

Such openness to pure love for Amichai finds its framework within a devotion to examining the intricacy of the human condition. Consider, for example, the powerful poetic expressions of this pure consciousness of love as found in the seventh stanza in his cycle, *Open, Closed, Open*:

> I believe with perfect faith that at this very moment
> millions of human beings are standing at crossroads
> and intersections, in jungles and deserts,
> showing each other where to turn, what the right way is,
> which direction. They explain exactly where to go,
> what is the quickest way to get there, when to stop
> and ask again. There, over there. The second
> turnoff, not the first, and from there left or right,
> near the white house, by the oak tree.
> They explain with excited voices, with a wave of the hand
> and a nod of the head: There, over there, not *that* there, the *other* there,
> as in some ancient rite. This too is a new religion.
> I believe with perfect faith that at this very moment.[17]

The poet's unstinting faith in the moment within which he stands and contemplates existence allows for an opening of his consciousness to a different experience of time. That experience is one that transcends his own subjective sense of self, allowing him to connect with millions of others facing crossroads and "showing each other where to turn, what the right way is." The consciousness of each individual involved in the search for "what the right way is" in life is guided by a process of continual turning to follow the direction of the moment. That pulsation of turning and returning throughout the universe is a pulse that precedes its creation and continues guiding existence. This pulse of continual turning, *t'shuvah*, within pure consciousness is something that fascinates the poet, but he also channels it as a universal force that abides within his view of existence.

It is precisely this pulse of continual turning, this *t'shuvah*, within pure consciousness that frees the poet from being trapped at intersections of binary thinking and getting entangled in the web of dualism. Amichai's non-dual view of the world is seen clearly in another poem, "A Man in His Life," where he proclaims:

> A man needs to love and to hate at the same moment,
> to laugh and cry with the same eyes,
> with the same hands to throw stones and to gather them,
> to make love in war and war in love.
> And to hate and forgive and remember and forget,
> to arrange and confuse, to eat and to digest
> what history
> takes years and years to do.[18]

The poet here identifies with pure consciousness, where there is no longer any sense of dualism between loving and hating, remembering and forgetting. The poet conjures concluding verses here that open once again to a pure consciousness of eternal time within his experience of mundane temporality:

> …He will die as figs die in autumn,
> shriveled and full of himself and sweet,

the leaves growing dry on the ground,
the bare branches pointing to the place
where there's time for everything.[19]

These encounters with remarkable Jewish poets, Leonard Cohen and Yehuda Amichai, may strike the reader as idiosyncratic, but I think they serve as helpful signposts along the path of the present investigation into the Priestly Blessing of love and the question of pure consciousness in Judaism. Truth be told, for most moderns, it is no small challenge to scour through those mystical texts on the Jewish bookshelf, like Daniel Matt's pathbreaking translation of the body of the Zohar or Aryeh Kaplan's translation of *Sefer Yetzirah* and the *Bahir*, that convey such experiences of pure consciousness.[20] That is not to say that states of pure consciousness have not been experienced by adepts and mystics in the Jewish tradition; rather, the issue is whether these experiences have been considered worthy or even safe enough to transmit through a textual record. If these experiences do exist in Judaism, then certainly the most we will find in our search is a delicious hinting, always more concealed than revealed.[21]

Even with a cursory search of Jewish liturgy, we find that the only word that repeats as frequently as *b'ahavah* ("with love") is probably *b'shalom* ("with peace"). Why is that? And, more to the point: Why is it that priests to this day during prayer services recite at appointed times the benediction "Blessed are You, Eternal One, Master of the Cosmos, who has sanctified us through the holiness of Aaron, and commanded us to bless His people Israel with love (*b'ahavah*)"?

The answer to this question is complex. Let us first outline the contextual meaning (*p'shat*) through translation of the Priestly Blessing itself (Numbers 6:24–27), as follows:

24: May YHVH bless you and protect you!

25: May YHVH deal kindly and graciously with you!

26: May YHVH bestow favor upon you and grant you peace!

27: Thus they shall link My name with the people of Israel, and I will bless them.[22]

We are aided in understanding the power of this blessing by seeing these words in their historical context, as uncovered in recent archaeological discoveries at Ketef Hinnom, a hill overlooking the Hinnom Valley to the southwest of the Old City of Jerusalem. Silver plaques were found at the site that contain benediction formulas in paleo-Hebrew script (that is, the ancient Hebrew characters used in the Second Temple period). The major discovery of the Ketef Hinnom excavations were several rock-hewn burial caves, dating from the end of the First Temple period (seventh century B.C.E.). One of the larger tombs, which probably belonged to a wealthy family, was found almost intact, with over a thousand objects in it— the most important of which are two small silver scrolls that were placed in the tomb. Considering these finds, Jacob Milgrom offers the following insightful reading of Numbers 6:27:

> Literally, "And they (the priests) shall place My Name on." In light of the Ketef Hinnom silver plaques, which demonstrate that in the seventh- (or sixth-) century Jerusalem the Priestly Benediction was worn on the body in the form of amulets, the possibility exists that the literal meaning of this phrase is the correct one, that is, that the Priestly Benediction delivered by the priests in the sanctuary was also to be placed on the Israelites as prophylactics. The usual interpretation, adopted in translation, is that God's Name is figuratively "placed" by the priests on the Israelites through the medium of benediction. Alternatively, God's name is *nikra*, "called" upon

Israel (Deuteronomy 28:10). Both verbs imply ownership
(Deuteronomy 12:5; Jeremiah 7:10).[23]

This description of the historical reality surrounding how this
Priestly Blessing was actually used is instructive, insofar as the words
were worn and embodied by each person constituting the tribe of
Israel. The assumption, of course, is not only that "clothes make the
man" but in fact that these kinds of amulets do more than simply
protect the wearer: they bring the Divine Presence into one's life.
So, what happens when we do not live up to the call to live in the
pure consciousness of love? The prophet Malachi hurls this blessing
as invective against the hypocritical priests by decrying:

> ...will [God] lift your countenance (*ha-yissa panekh*a)...
> that He may be gracious to us (*vi-honneinu*)...will He lift
> His countenance (*ha-yissa panim*)? Would that you not light
> (*ta·iru*) My altar in vain (*hinnam*)!

Undoubtedly, this stands as a scathing prophetic critique of
priestly corruption of their powerful blessing. One could argue,
however, that both the priest and the prophet—in their own
way and time—attempted to link the divine name to their
own being, and in so doing, to embody pure consciousness.

Pure Priestly Consciousness As "Soft Antinomianism" in Ishbitz/Radzin Hasidism

The language of the benediction preceding the Priestly Blessing
invokes the formula "blessing His people with love," giving rise to the
following questions: Is the priest the only channel of transmission for
such a blessing? What (or who) is the source of that blessing? If the

transmission leads to a state of pure consciousness imbued with love, then what does this suggest about the constitution of the Divine? Do emotions like anger and jealousy exist within a God that stands as the very source of this flow of love? We now turn to one of the most creative and radical schools of hasidic thought in Judaism Izbice/Radzin hasidism, and particularly to the Ishbitzer Rebbe, to explore possible answers to these questions.[25]

The original thinker in this lineage was Rabbi Mordecai Yosef Leiner (1800–1854), known as the Ishbitzer Rebbe, so named for the town of Izbica (Ishbitz in Yiddish), where he taught and wrote his homiletical commentaries to Scripture and Talmud known as *Mei Ha-shilo·ah* (which translates roughly as "The Waters of Release"). The Ishbitzer dynasty is an offshoot of the Pryzsucha school (lead by Rabbi Jacob Isaac ben Asher Rabinowitz, and transmitted through the dynasty of Kotzk (lead by Rabbi Mendel).[26] The Ishbitzer dynasty flourished during a tumultuous time in Polish history, which is a testament to how Jewish ingenuity survived—and was inspired by—the face of tragedy. This time period was characterized by rapid modernization; moreover, tolerance and emancipation were facilitated by Pope Pius IX's election to the papacy in 1846, as well as by the coronation of Alexander II as Czar of Russia in 1855.[27] Hasidic communities in Congress Poland, like that of the Ishbitzer Rebbe, did not necessarily participate fully in Polish culture and politics, and they remained disenchanted with access to Enlightenment thinking, which was now virtually inescapable elsewhere in Europe.[28] While modernization brought with it the advantages of technological advances, travel, and increased availability of printed books and manuscripts, it also posed challenges to these staunchly conservative Hasidic communities, in the guise of military service and secularism. It is important to note here the degree to which messianic overtones imbue the teachings of the Ishbitzer Rebbe, beginning already with a contentious split between Rabbi Menaḥem and Rabbi Mordecai Yosef in 1839 and 1840.

What is the nature of this messianism, and how does it relate to pure consciousness? One first needs to recall that messianism in Judaism is often a yearning to redeem the world in the final eschaton through a cycle of redeemers, beginning with the Messiah son of David and followed by the Messiah son of Joseph.[29] One traditional way of understanding the roles of these redeemers is to see them as part of a narrative that culminates with the apocalyptic vision of Armageddon's final battle, led by the Messiah son of David. Following his death in battle, a new eschaton of peace will follow, ruled by the ensuing Messiah son of Joseph. Some Jewish thinkers, like the Ishbitzer Rebbe, have sought to bring that yearning to redeem the world in the final eschaton closer to the here and now, in what we might term the proto-messianic era.

Secondly, one must keep in mind that the messianic era in general is considered to be a time when the commandments are no longer in effect and are thus nullified;[30] it then becomes intertwined with an antinomianism, whereby the law itself is suspended and no longer practiced—as it has been fulfilled. The system of *mitzvot* assumes free will, whereby one has the freedom to choose between good and evil, thus reinforcing values and consequences that make its observance worthwhile. Once the human and divine will are unified through messianism, the *mitzvot* as a system no longer obtain, given that free human will itself has dissolved into a unified will.[31] Both Rabbi Mordecai Yosef and his grandson, Rabbi Gershon Henokh, articulate a "tension between illumined experience and the authority of *halakhah*."[32] That tension arises once human and divine wills have been unified, because *halakhah* is a system meant to legislate submission to the divine will through human will and agency. Once the tension between competing wills has been resolved through unification, what then remains is a life that is completely and utterly free of any yoke of *mitzvot*, "as it will become clear that God is directing" the individual.[33] Rather than resulting in an outright transgression of Jewish law, what emerges is a "soft antinomianism"—that is, by redefining "piety as acting in accordance with divine will," it thus "can extend beyond the law." [34] Such a soft antinomianism is "capable of living with *halakhah* while challenging its basic tenet—that is, its exclusive right to divine will." [35]

There is a blurring of the boundaries between the messianic era and the person of the Messiah in Ishbitz/Radzin Hasidism, whereby the one who has refined the self through humility and piety becomes the messianic archetype acting outside the confines of *halakhah* in a pre-messianic world. [36] This kind of soft antinomianism is a sanctified transgression of the law, whereby the communal experience of revelation at Sinai gives way to individual illumination as guiding force. What, then, is the purpose of following the commandments, if one is guided by the unified will of illumination rather than by human free will yoked to the divine law? The devotional way of life serves as a touchstone for piety: "the submission to the over-arching principle of *mitzvot*—[which is] to occupy oneself with God, even as the specific *mitzvah* may no longer serve any constructive function." [37] Shaul Magid concludes, from his study of Ishbitz/Radzin Hasidism, that

> ...personal illumination generally shares the same basic values with the halakhic system and, in most cases, enhances rather than opposes halakhic norms....Therefore, acting outside (and against) the system "for the sake of heaven" (i.e., to oblige the divine will) is built into the system and is always possible. Therefore, it seems that *mitzvot* function best when performed by someone who no longer needs them. [38]

With this approach to soft antinomianism now in mind, the question remains: how does living a life guided by such personal illumination then manifest the love of pure consciousness?

To answer this question, we now return to our opening concern with the Priestly Blessing of Love as a manifestation of living with pure consciousness. Commenting on the eight components of the priestly vestments[39] and their mystical symbolism, the Mei Ha-shilo·aḥ notes a parallel between these dressings and the eight spiritual modalities in the blessing preceding the recitation of the Shema.[40] As we shall see, the unspoken link between the two is that of love. In this symbolic matrix, the Breastplate of Judgment (*hoshen mishpat*) aligns with "discernment," for as the Mei Ha-shilo·aḥ teaches:

> Every human needs to contemplate in order to realize that within divine consciousness anger against the Israelites is non-existent, "for He is angry but a moment, and when He is pleased there is life" (Psalm 30:6).[41]

Love is the natural spiritual state of reality and anything other than love—especially anger—is non-existent. What is remarkable in this comment is the degree to which the Ishbitzer Rebbe is willing to recast the cosmos as a manifestation of pure consciousness: love. The Priestly Blessing then serves as a perpetual witness beyond its liturgical invocation, speaking to this spiritual reality of love that courses through the cosmos. The necessary re-alignment of dual consciousness into non-dual unity is catalyzed by this Priestly Blessing and in a sense unveils the larger purpose of the contemplative prayer process in Judaism.

A further look into the language of the Priestly Blessing in its component parts invites the Ishbitzer Rebbe to reflect on the divine names as a matrix of the cosmos. From his granular look at the letters within the words of the Priestly Blessing, the Ishbitzer Rebbe makes the following nuanced comment on the invocation in Numbers 6:26:

> "*May YHVH bestow favor upon you*"—where the language of "bestowal" (*yissa*) implies that the Divine should supply you with

a "spiritual elevation" (*hitnassut*). "*And grant you peace*"—namely, you will have an even greater "spiritual elevation" (*hitnassut*), even in the midst of dialectical opposition have no fear from the opposition because God is with you. So this is the meaning of "[grant] you"—namely, within yourself.[42]

In this hyper-literal reading of the Priestly Blessing, the Ishbitzer Rebbe is spiritualizing the blessing. By this process, the one invoking the blessing is engaged in an act of turning the *outward* blessing of the priest exoterically directed to the Israelites toward an *inward* esoteric blessing of the one invoking the blessing within oneself. Through this inner transformation of the body as a "temple in miniature" (*mikdash me'at*), the contemplative gesture allows for the pure love channeled through Priestly Blessing to expand throughout the macrocosmic structure of the individual, rather than through the collective. As one becomes imbued with pure consciousness by this self-reflexive energy transmission, the very constitution of subjectivity shifts from its previous dichotomy of human will and divine will to a unified will of love. Through the dissolution of human free will into nothing but divine will, the Ishbitzer Rebbe is making a compelling case for the possible reconciliation between the pre-messianic consciousness of exile and a proto-messianic consciousness of redeemed living in the here and now.[43] To gain a better understanding of the very texture of this pure consciousness, we will have to turn outside of Judaism, before returning to the Priestly Blessing more deeply.

Embodying Pure Consciousness in Sri Aurobindo

What the Jewish mystic experiences in the state of *d'veikut*, or merging of the human mind state with that of the divine, does not seem that dissimilar to what the Integral Yogi Sri Aurobindo might have experienced in the Nirvana state. What both states of *unio mystica* (mystical union) do certainly share is the cessation of ego-consciousness in the all-pervading peace of what for the former is the *Ein Sof* (or Without End) and for the latter is the silent Brahman. Upon the disappearance of the ego in this state of unitive consciousness, the mystic must then grapple with the sense of unreality of the external world. Notwithstanding the nuances in stages and states of consciousness within each spiritual path, these mystics share the reality that this experience of unitive consciousness generally lasts only a short while—*and then what?* Jewish mystics tend to be highly attuned to the ebb and flow of unitive consciousness inherent in this state of cleaving (called *d'veikut*), while in contrast an Integral Yogi, like Aurobindo, notices how the transient experience of unitive consciousness is replaced by more integral experiences of an "immense Divine Reality" behind, above, and within everything that had initially appeared illusory.[44] This is a realization that consciousness is the ultimate reality in the universe, of which all existence itself is but a manifestation, while beyond any final qualification. Pure consciousness, while unqualifiable, is nevertheless real; Aurobindo describes it as follows:

> In the state of pure consciousness and pure being we are aware of that only simple, immutable, self-existent, without form or object, and we feel that to be alone true and real. In the other or dynamic state we feel its dynamism, to be perfectly true and natural and are even capable of thinking that no such experience as that of pure consciousness is possible. Yet it is now that to the Infinite Consciousness both the static and the dynamic are possible; these are two of its statuses and both can be present simultaneously in the universal awareness...[45]

It is precisely here, in this state which is the ultimate ontological category and the material cause of all that exists, that Judaism appears to rub up against the (im)possibility of pure consciousness. The challenge that such a state of integral consciousness poses for Judaism is how to then relate to the distinct categories of Creator–creation–creature. It is precisely this challenge that emerges within the *d'veikut* state that I would like to explore within a hasidic re-reading of the Priestly Blessing. While the Jewish mystic yearns to reach and remain in a state of *d'veikut*, the Jewish conception of consciousness would seem to dictate that a return to dual consciousness is intrinsic to its distinct categories of Creator–creation–creature.

With this understanding in mind, consider now the re-reading of the Priestly Blessing by the Ishbitzer Rebbe—who is himself one of the rare mystical voices in Judaism that advocates for cultivating and remaining in a state of pure consciousness. Remaining in such a perpetual *d'veikut* state, for the Ishbitzer Rebbe, is cultivated by entering into a single commanded act of a *mitzvah* with deeper consciousness; this very immersion leads to a cessation of all further commandments. There is no longer a need for commanded acts in such a state of pure consciousness, as the distinct categories of Creator–creation–creature no longer exist. While the Ishbitzer Rebbe may be the most radical exponent of this antinomian tendency in Judaism, one could argue that this direction is at the heart of all forms of Hasidism. This spiritual renaissance movement that swept through Eastern Europe in the mid-1700s had already posited that one could serve the Divine either through the 613 commandments (*taryag mitzvot*) or through "integral immersion" (*m'sirat nefesh*). Notwithstanding the ban on Hasidism and its wild mystical spirituality promulgated by the Gaon of Vilna in 1772, one can only speculate as to whether Jewish mystics after Hasidism would have eventually followed the path of integral immersion in consciousness.

Conclusion

In considering the question as to whether Judaism makes space for the cultivation of a state of the pure consciousness of love, we have encountered some remarkable, if not disorienting, teachings. Our investigation began with anecdotal encounters with two remarkable Jewish poets, Leonard Cohen and Yehuda Amichai, and explored how such seekers, so embroiled in the darkness of depression and death, can possibly come to continue writing and singing love poems. From these encounters, which already confirm experiences of pure consciousness in Judaism, we then turned our attention to the word *b'ahavah* ("with love"), seeking to understand why it is repeated so frequently within Jewish liturgy. The deepest layer of meaning appears to abide in the most unexpected of places: within the Priestly Blessing. By examining the contextual meaning of this biblical blessing, we then turned to a hyper-literal reading found in the homiletical commentaries of the Ishbitzer Rebbe. In the process of unpacking his commentary, *Mei Ha-shilo·ah*, to the Priestly Blessing, we discovered that an overarching "soft antinomianism" emerges, whereby the illuminated personality allows for a unification of the human will with the divine and, in the process, changes the praxis of *halakhah*. The change takes place in a twofold manner, as Magid explains:

> First, it keeps the messianic personality rooted in the proto-messianic world, preventing him from moving beyond the boundaries of legitimate Judaism until the world catches up to him. Second, by living in tension inside the *halakhah*, the messianic personality destabilizes the law, thereby extending the elasticity of the *halakhic* tradition.[46]

From this vantage point, straddling the pure consciousness of the illuminated personality within Judaism, we then turned to a comparison of the Ishbitzer Rebbe's teachings with the tradition of Integral Yoga formulated by Sri Aurobindo. This point of contrast was instructive insofar as it sets into relief the difference between the two traditions: straddling with pure consciousness as a proto-messianic posture in Judaism is a struggle to maintain, whereas Integral Yoga provides a state of pure consciousness that, once cultivated, is never lost. Whereas pure consciousness allows the mystic to remain tuned in with clear reception to a channel constantly broadcasting love, the halakhic system of *mitzvot* in Judaism serves as both an anchor and a prophylactic from remaining tuned into that channel of pure consciousness.[47] In the cases of Leonard Cohen and Yehuda Amichai, who have by and large left behind Judaism's halakhic system of *mitzvot* while still remaining creative Jews, each poet is able to manifest and create poetry of pure love. More than the hasidic mystic, it is the Jewish poet—as seen in Amichai's transformation of Hebrew liturgical language and Cohen's invocation of the Priestly Blessing—who truly embodies the messianic personality rooted in the proto-messianic world, yet is continually catching the world up to live in that state of love emanating from pure consciousness.

NOTES

[1] Kyozan Joshu Sasaki (1907–2014), also called Joshu Sasaki Roshi. "Roshi" in an honorific title used for Zen masters.

[2] For more about the notion of *shakti-pat* or an *"energy-descent,"* which I am interpolating into the context of this analysis, see Jeffrey J. Kripal, *Esalen: America and the Religion of No Religion* (Chicago: University of Chicago Press, 2007), pp. 262 and 485.

[3] Thomas F. Cleary, *Classics of Buddhism and Zen: The Collected Translations of Thomas Cleary* (Boston: Shambhala, 2001).

[4] Sylvie Simmons, *I'm Your Man: The Life of Leonard Cohen* (New York: Ecco Press, 2012), p. 72.

[5] Ibid, p. 37.

[6] Ibid.

[7] Ibid, pp. 262–263.

[8] Leonard Cohen, "Not a Jew," in *Book of Longing* (Toronto: McClelland & Stuart, 2006), p. 158.

[9] Simmons, *I'm Your Man*, p. 316.

[10] Ibid., p. 272.

[11] Ibid., pp. 272–273.

[12] Leonard Cohen, "Lover Lover Lover," on *New Skin for the Old Ceremony* (released August 11, 1974).

[13] Leonard Cohen, "The Politics of this Book," in *Stranger Music: Selected Poems and Songs* (New York: Pantheon, 1993), p. 291.

[14] Nathan Jeffay writes: "Even that wasn't the last that concert-goers saw of Leonard Cohen. On the way out of the stadium, there were Leonard Cohens everywhere. Next to the shopping carts purloined from supermarkets by street sellers using them to sell hot bagels was a stall offering black fedora hats, Cohen's trademark. It sold hundreds, and so Leonard Cohen has left a behind a different Israel to the one that greeted him. Today, you don't have to be Haredi to wear a black hat." See also his *"Hallelujah* in Tel Aviv: Leonard Cohen Energizes Diverse Crowd," in *The Jewish Daily Forward* of September 25, 2009, available online at www.forward.com.

[15] Yehuda Amichai, *Pa·amonim V'rakavot: Maḥazot V'taskitim* (Jerusalem: Shocken, 1992).

[16] Nili Scharf Gold, *Yehuda Amichai: The Making of Israel's National Poet* (Waltham, MA: Brandeis University Press, 2008), pp. 78–98.

[17] Yehuda Amichai, "I Wasn't One of the Six Million: And What is My Life Span? Open Closed Open," in *Open Closed Open*, trans. Chana Bloch and Chana Kronfeld (New York: Harcourt, 2000), pp. 7–8.

[18] Yehuda Amichai, "A Man in His Life," in *The Selected Poetry of Yehuda Amichai*, trans. Chana Bloch and Stephen Mitchell (New York: Harcourt, 1986), pp. 158–159.

[19] Ibid.

[20] Daniel Matt, *The Zohar* (Stanford: Stanford University Press, 2004–present); Aryeh Kaplan, *Sefer Yeẓirah: The Book of Creation in Theory and Practice* (York Beach, ME: S. Weiser, 1997); idem, *The Bahir* (Northvale, NJ: Jason Aronson, 1995).

[21] Kripal suggests that mystical texts do two things very skillfully: "(1) rhetorically both reveal and conceal the religious experiences of their authors, and (2) such texts have the power to semantically re-enact analogous 'experiences' in the hermeneutical events of their readings." See Jeffrey J. Kripal, *Roads of Excess, Palaces of Wisdom: Eroticism and Reflexivity in the Study of Mysticism* (Chicago: University of Chicago Press, 2001), p. 9.

[22] YHVH is my rendition of the Tetragrammaton, the four-letter name of God (*yod-hei-vav-hei*) that appears in the Hebrew text but is traditionally left unpronounced.

[23] Jacob Milgrom, *JPS Bible Commentary: Numbers* (Philadelphia: Jewish Publication Society, 1990), p. 52. In this context, the word "prophylactics" denotes an amulet capable of protecting its bearer from spiritual damage by evil spirits.

[24] Malachi 1:9–10, and cf. 1:6–7 and 11–14; and 2:2–9.

[25] In this essay I refer to the spiritual lineage known as Izbica/Radzin Hasidism in general, while the main focus of the particular homilies I address are from the specific link in that Izbica/Radzin hasidic dynasty known and expounded by the Ishbitzer Rebbe. As Shaul Magid explains, the villages of Izbica and Radzin were both integral settings for the version of Hasidism I am referencing: "After R. Mordecai Yosef's death, his circle of close disciples scattered....R. Jacob Leiner [R. Mordecai Yosef's son] led the community in Izbica for the next twenty-four years, during which time he moved to Radzin, a small city almost due north of Kotzk and Lublin in the northern corner of the province. This brought him closer to the growing Izbica community already established in Lublin. R. Jacob Leiner remained in Radzin until his passing in the summer of 1878." (See the introduction to Magid's *Hasidism on the Margin: Reconciliation, Antinomianism, and Messianism in Ishbitzer Rebbe/Radzin Hasidism* [Madison, WI: and London: University of Wisconsin Press, 2003], p. xx.)

[26] Shaul Magid, *Hasidism on the Margin*, pp. xviii–xix.

[27] Ibid., p. xvii.

[28] There is a distinctly "Polish" Jewry that remained identifiable throughout what is known by historians as Congress Poland. After 1815, this Congress consisted of ten Russian-ruled provinces, as well as the areas incorporated into the Austrian province of Galicia. For more information, see Gershon Bacon, "Poland from 1795 to 1939," in the *YIVO Encyclopedia*, ed. Gershon D. Hundert, available online at www.yivoencyclopedia.org.

[29] Steven S. Schwarzschild and Menachem Kellner, "On Jewish Eschatology,"

in *The Pursuit of the Ideal: Jewish Writings of Steven Schwarzschild* (Albany: State University of New York Press, 1990), pp. 209–228.

[30] B. Niddah 61b, *mitzvot b'teilot le-atid lavo.*

[31] This recurring motif of the unified will appears over fifty times in the Ishbitzer Rebbe's *Mei Ha-Shilo·aḥ* commentary to the Torah, to be discussed below; see Magid, *Hasidism on the Margin*, pp. 205–207.

[32] Magid, *Hasidism on the Margin*, p. 216.

[33] *Mei Ha-Shilo·aḥ*, vol. 1, 51d–52a as quoted in Magid, *Hasidism on the Margin*, p. 223.

[34] Ibid., p. 217.

[35] Ibid, p. 227.

[36] Ibid, p. 224.

[37] Ibid, p. 233.

[38] Ibid, pp. 237–238.

[39] This eightfold division of the priestly garbing, described in Exodus 28:1–43, consists of the following: (1) the *ephod*, verses 6–12; (2) the breastplate of judgment and the *urim* and *tummim*, verses 13–30; (3) the robe, verses 31–35; (4) the frontlet, verses 36–38; (5) the tunic, verse 39; (6) the headdress, verse 39; (7) the sash, verse 39; and (8) the turban, verse 40.

[40] This eightfold division of spiritual qualities is divided in the liturgy as follows: "Endow us with (1) understanding (2) and discernment, (3) that we may study (4) and teach your Torah with devotion, (5) heed its words, (6) transmit its precepts, (7) follow its instruction, and (8) fulfill its teachings in love."

[41] *Mei Ha-shilo·aḥ, Parshat Tetzaveh* (B'nei Brak: Meishor Publications, 5755 [1994/1995]), p. 89a.

[42] *Mei Ha-Shilo·aḥ, Parshat Naso*, p. 146a.

[43] The Ishbitzer Rebbe tends to refer to a reconciliation between the exilic messianic consciousness of Joseph and the redeeming messianic consciousness symbolized by Judah; see Magid, *Hasidism on the Margin*, p. 205.

[44] Sri Aurobindo Ghose, *On Himself* (Pondicherry, India: Sri Aurobindo Ashram, 1972), p. 102.

[45] Sri Aurobindo Ghose, *The Divine Life* (Pondicherry, India: Sri Aurobiondo Ashram, 1973), p. 345. See also Ernest L. Simmons, Jr., "Mystical Consciousness in a Process Perspective," *Process Studies* 14:1 (Spring 1984), pp. 1–14, now available online at www.religion-online.org/showarticle.asp?title=2585.

[46] Magid, *Hasidism on the Margin*, p. 240.

[47] This nuanced point of straddling the struggle for pure consciousness in contemplative and mystical Judaism is something that still needs to be redressed in light of recent popular works. For example, see Jay Michaelson, *Everything Is God: The Radical Path of Nondual Judaism* (Boston: Trumpeter, 2009); and idem, *Evolving Dharma: Meditation, Buddhism, and the Next Generation of Enlightenment* (Berkeley, CA: Evolver Editions, 2013).

What's In a Blessing?
Rashi and the Priestly Benediction of Numbers 6:22–27

Robert A. Harris

Birkat Kohanim, the three-fold "priestly benediction," is often thought of as the aggregate of the greatest of God's blessings:

> The Eternal spoke to Moses: Speak to Aaron and his sons:
> Thus shall you bless the people of Israel. Say to them:
> > *The Eternal bless you and protect you!*
> > *The Eternal deal kindly and graciously with you!*
> > *The Eternal bestow His favor upon you and grant you peace!*
> Thus they shall link My name with the people of Israel, and
> I will bless them.[1]

But what do these verses really mean? And what is the implication of this particular text for our larger understanding of biblical and post-biblical theology? One of the foundational Jewish treatments of this prominent biblical passage that offers anything like comprehensive answers to those questions is found in Rashi's Torah commentary. In order to assess Rashi's evaluation, let us first consider a different biblical text that features a divine blessing.

Toward the end of Abraham's life, the Torah reports that the patriarch was "old, advanced in days, and the Eternal had blessed Abraham in everything" (Genesis 24:1). In this particular passage, as in so many others, the language of Scripture is delightfully ambiguous, enabling traditional Jewish exegesis to have a field day. The famous twelfth-century commentator Rabbi Abraham ibn Ezra (1089–c. 1167) interprets the unspecified blessing according to what he senses to be the contextual (*p'shat*) meaning: "God blessed Abraham in all things: with length of days, wealth and honor, and children—and this is all a person can wish for!" While this explanation certainly makes sense, and considers the divine blessing in terms that incorporate bounties for which many people might wish, a later commentator, Rabbi David Kimḥi (1160–1235, called Radak), interprets the passage in a way that perhaps even more closely follows the ambiguous meaning of the verse: "God did not deprive Abraham of anything, nor was he in want of anything, save for [the business of] marrying off his son Isaac to a woman worthy of him." Since Genesis 24 relates the efforts that Abraham (and his servant) took to ensure that Isaac be married off "properly," Radak's explanation may fit the verse's context even better than that of Ibn Ezra. In Radak's estimation, a "complete divine blessing" in this case was one that did not deprive Abraham of any (positive) human aspiration or experience, save for finding a wife for his precious son, and he was about to experience also that. Not to be outdone, an even later commentator, Rabbi Moshe ben Naḥman (1194–1270, called Ramban) stated that it was not specifically concern for the proper marriage of his son that motivated Abraham to arrange with his servant to find Isaac a wife, but rather his desire to experience the joy of grandchildren: "Scripture records this matter to recount that Abraham's life was complete in every way, nothing was missing— other than seeing children [born] to his son...." Unsurprisingly, other rabbinic exegetes examine this identical ambiguity in the biblical narrative, and each posits his own unique interpretation of precisely how God blessed Abraham at this temporal juncture.

In thinking about this interpretive arc (Ibn Ezra to Radak to Ramban), and the seemingly never-ending wish to refine the sense of what constitutes the completeness of a divine blessing, I am reminded of an old Borsht Belt joke. Walking along the shore, a mother is aghast when her young son is swept out to sea by a sudden large wave. Falling to her knees, she cries out to God to spare her child. On this particular occasion (as on few others, it seems!), God answers her pleas, reverses the course of the wave, and deposits the boy back on the shore, directly into the arms of the mother. After a moment of grateful tears, the mother steps back to examine her son, turns back to God and says, "He had a hat!"

Beyond the humor, the story conveys an awareness of both the tangible and intangible dimensions of God's blessings. On other occasions, the biblical narrator seems to make a distinction between formulating blessings that are material in character and others that are more generally covenantal in nature. For example, when the blind Isaac mistakenly blesses Jacob with the blessing intended for his favored son, Esau, Isaac stipulates items mostly of a material nature: "May God give you of the dew of heaven and the fat of the earth, abundance of new grain and wine. Let peoples serve you, and nations bow to you; be master over your brothers and let your mother's sons bow to you. Cursed be they who curse you, and blessed they who bless you" (Genesis 27:28–29). However, when patently aware of Jacob's identity only a few verses later, Isaac offers Jacob an intentional, covenantal blessing: "May El Shaddai bless you, make you fertile and numerous, so that you become an assembly of peoples. May He grant the blessing of Abraham to you and your offspring, that you may possess the land where you are sojourning, which God assigned to Abraham" (Genesis 28:3).[3]

There are, of course, numerous instances of all kinds of blessings being issued in biblical literature—both of the covenantal and spiritual type, as well as blessings oriented toward material beneficence. When turning toward the three-part "Priestly Blessing" (Numbers 6:22–27), a central question that we ought to consider is: what type of blessing does the biblical author intend through these particular words, material or spiritual? Another way of considering this question would be to ask it from the vantage point of the blessing's recipients: out of all the possible blessings for which ancient Israel could have hoped, why would they have wanted these in particular?

There are, of course, many ways in which one could attempt to answer such questions. This essay will consider these and related questions primarily from the perspective of one of the great medieval rabbinic exegetes of the Bible from northern France, Rabbi Solomon ben Isaac, universally called Rashi (1040–1105). Our questions, thus refined, will therefore be as follows: how does Rashi construe these blessings, and why does he think ancient Israelites—or his contemporary Jewish audience—would wish to be blessed with *these* specific blessings? Since Numbers 6:22–27 represent the only instance of biblical commands that mandate the issuance of cultic-sourced blessings (whether or not they were considered to be a constituent part of the actual service), one might well ask, as a follow-up: does Rashi think these blessings represent a kind of *summa*, as it were, "blessings *par excellence*"? Or does he consider them to be, if not actually "random," essentially isolated wishes for specific beneficent acts with which priests are to express the hope that Israel will be blessed?

Before proceeding directly to Rashi's interpretation, we ought to consider the nature of Rashi's commentary as it has come down to us through the ages. Whatever Rashi's intent when he began the process of Torah exegesis, and whatever the specific social circumstances in which he did so, in many ways it is appropriate to think of Rashi's commentary as a twelfth-century "Renaissance project" more than as a singularly authored text—and it is a "century" that in a sense lasted hundreds of years, into the age of printed editions (i.e., the fifteenth century and beyond). Although there is in popular imagination (and in the world of the yeshiva, in particular) widespread agreement on the text of most of Rashi's Torah commentary, this was by no means always the case. With hundreds of medieval manuscripts and printed editions in existence, some with remarkable variants, it is virtually impossible to imagine a truly "critical" edition of the commentary. For the most part, I have relied in this essay on what is generally considered the most accurate medieval manuscript, ms. Leipzig 1.[4]

As we shall see, Rashi does not approach these verses as initially conveying any sense of a summa of divine beneficence, but rather understands them to speak of specific, concrete measures of goodness. He begins, however, with what amounts to an exhortation of God, as it were, by Israel:[5]

> **So shall you bless.** A *midrash aggadah*:[6] Said Israel [to God]: "To the priests You say that they shall bless! We have no need to be blessed by anyone except Your mouth! *Look down from the abode of Your holiness and bless [Your people Israel]* (Deuteronomy 26:15). So, too, does David state: *And now undertake to bless the house of Your servant...* (2 Samuel 7:29)." The Holy One said: "With them do I stand and bless, as it is said: *...but I will bless them* (Numbers 6:27)." Therefore the priests spread their hands, as though to say that the Holy One stands behind them, as it is said, *There He stands behind our wall, gazing through the window* (Song of Songs 2:9)— from between the fingers of the priests.

By citing this midrash, Rashi addresses an obvious question that might undermine the very ritual the Torah mandates: if God is the source of all blessing, what need is there for the priest to take any role in the ritual? To be sure, Rashi's citation anticipates his interpretation of the end of the biblical passage (Numbers 6:27), to which we will return. But it also serves to explicate his understanding of the word "bless" right at the outset: what does it mean for any human being, priest or otherwise, to "bless"? In reality, Rashi would aver, all blessing emanates from God, and when people employ the verb "to bless" with themselves as the subject, it is either to invoke the blessing of God or to serve as a conduit through which God's blessing may pass. That is certainly the clear message of the midrash that Rashi invokes.

Following this introductory comment, Rashi then addresses the manner in which the Torah prescribes how the priests should deliver the blessings and how the people ought to receive them[7]: "**Say to them**: so that they can all hear." Rashi roots this brief initial gloss on our actual text in the soil of ancient rabbinic midrash. In and of itself, this is not surprising: in approximately 70% of his Torah commentary, as he does with regards to Numbers 6:22–27, Rashi refracts his understanding of Scripture through rabbinic midrash. While he drew on Midrash Tanḥuma in his introductory comment, in the body of his actual explication of the words of the blessing he mainly (although not exclusively) adduces the early midrash called Sifrei Bemidbar.[8] What might be surprising to the casual reader of Rashi's commentary, however, is the degree to which Rashi adduces only particular *midrashim* in his reading of Scripture. In addition to various other sundry observations, Sifrei Bemidbar derives no fewer than five important lessons from the specific wording of Numbers 6:23: that the priests stand when reciting the blessing; that they must raise their hands; that they must express the fully spelled out name of God; and that they must directly face the people at the moment of blessing.[9] However, Rashi ignores all of these other interpretations and selects only one, namely: "that all of the congregation will hear." He does this probably because most of Sifrei's interpretations reflect no specific scriptural language and thus do not fit the selection process he outlines most famously in his methodological comment on Genesis 3:8: "…whereas I have only come for the plain sense of Scripture and the *aggadah* that settles a word of Scripture and its sense…"[10] As is his way, Rashi modifies the language of the midrash, and glosses "so that all of them hear"; the midrash employs the term "congregation" (*kahal*), whereas Scripture merely uses a pronoun ("to them," *lahem*). Rashi's comment thus hews even more precisely to the language of the Torah than does that of the midrash.

The continuation of Rashi's comment in many manuscript versions and printed editions contains an additional gloss on the word "say," this time rooting his midrashic interpretation in a Tanḥuma tradition:

> **Say**: The word *amor* is written in its full form [i.e., including the Hebrew letter *vav*, which functions here as a vowel], indicating that they should not bless them hastily or in a hurried manner, but with concentration and with wholeheartedness—in order that the blessing should have dominion over them; therefore it is written *to them*.[11]

One may wonder why Rashi offers more than one interpretation of the same word. Generally, this is due to Rashi's desire to offer the fullest possible accounting of scriptural language, and if he knows of multiple midrashic insights that root themselves in the actual language of Scripture, he may choose to offer more than one; similarly, if he intuits a plain-sense meaning (*p'shuto*) of a word or phrase, he may choose to present this alongside of his midrashically channeled insight.[12] On the other hand, sometimes an additional interpretation may originate through the hands of a glossator later than Rashi, whose comment was subsequently incorporated into the manuscript traditions. In this case, since ms. Leipzig includes both glosses, I will choose to think of them both as originating within Rashi's own purview. In any case, Rashi interprets the plene[13] form of the verb via the *midrash* to mean that the priests should pronounce the divine blessing with a high degree of deliberation and intentionality.

Rashi next turns his attention to the initial word in the Priestly Blessing itself (*y'varekh·kha*, "may [the Eternal] bless you") and again bases himself on Sifrei, commenting "may your possessions be blessed." One could not imagine a more prosaic interpretation, in a sense, and he seconds it with a similar interpretation of the following verb (*v'yishm'rekha*, "may [the Eternal] protect you"), though this time rooted in the Tanḥuma, a different midrash:[15]

> **May [the Eternal] protect you**: that robbers should not come upon you and take your money, for one who gives a gift to a servant is not able to protect that servant from any person, and since bandits may come upon the servant and take the gift away, what benefit does such a servant have through the gift? Rather, the blessed Holy One gives and protects.

Thus, Rashi sees divine blessing as resulting in divine protection.[16] Although Rashi may not address what might be the ethereal or "spiritual" blessings that our culture might aspire to find in this initial expression of the Priestly Blessing, he does interpret as a man of his own dangerous world, where the roads were not safe and material possessions were often difficult to secure. Moreover, Rashi accurately represents what is likely the concrete nature of this blessing in its own ancient Israelite context. As Jacob Milgrom writes, "Generally in the Bible, God's blessing comprises mainly material bounty," and he specifically enumerates examples of these: posterity, possessions and wealth, land, fertility, health, victory, strength and peace.[17] Coincidence or not, in this circumstance, Rashi's interpretation of the opening of the Priestly Blessing is remarkably similar to the conclusions of Milgrom's presentation of modern historical-critical scholarship.[18]

In the version of Rashi's commentary contained in ms. Leipzig 1, Rashi concludes his exegesis of the first blessing with an interpretation that some in our day would not consider to be politically correct. Nevertheless, in the service of accurately representing the tradition, let us examine it here: "May [the Eternal] bless you—with [regard to] sons, and may He protect you—with [regard to] daughters, for daughters require protection."[19] There are a number of rabbinic statements that underlie Rashi's sentiment here. For example, with reference to the verse with which we began our investigation of blessing, Genesis 24:1 ("the Eternal had blessed Abraham in everything"), recall that one of the commentators, Ramban (Naḥmanides), offered an interpretation that God had not deprived Abraham even of grandchildren! As it happens, Ramban offered an additional interpretation that is similar to the one Rashi expresses here, and it is based in what the Babylonian Talmud relates in Bava Batra 16b: "Rabbi Meir said that [Abraham was blessed in all things in that] he didn't have a daughter. Rabbi Judah said that [he was blessed in all things in that] he did have a daughter." Now, it's quite possible to interpret that Rabbi Meir saw male children as a greater blessing than females, whereas Rabbi Judah couldn't imagine that God could have blessed Abraham without having "arranged" for Abraham to know the joys of fathering a daughter! In his commentary on Genesis 24:1, Ramban teases out what really may have motivated the ancient rabbinic debate:

> Rabbi Meir explained that not having a daughter was a blessing, in that [Abraham] didn't have to marry a daughter to one of the cursed Canaanites, and if he had sent her back to Mesopotamia she would also there end up worshipping idols, since [in those days] a woman was in the domain of her husband [and would have to do what he did]. Rabbi Judah explained that he had a daughter, and that God did not deprive Abraham even of the blessing of having a daughter…

In other words, since at most times in human history up to our present day women were generally considered to be under the authority of the most important man in their life (typically either a father, brother, or a husband), that person held the responsibility of "protecting" them. For the various rabbinic arbiters of earlier biblical traditions, this meant (*inter alia*) ensuring that Jewish women married Jewish men, and were also "protected" against the possibility of social interaction with gentile men and any dangers associated with that contact. We should, therefore, understand Rashi's additional comment about women needing protection in the light of those circumstances. Whether we approve of those standards in our society is a different matter altogether!

Rashi next turns to the second verse of the three-part blessing, that God should "shine His face" upon the Israelites. Unlike the very material way in which he understood the first blessing, Rashi interprets this phrase to express the hope that God will "show you[21] a face of laughing, a face of radiance." But he does not elaborate beyond this somewhat surprising locution.[22] One might have imagined that Rashi would have chosen to illuminate his explanation, as he does so often, with reference to a biblical verse—for example: "May God be gracious to us and bless us; may He show us favor" (Psalm 67:2).[23] Indeed, such a verse might help us find in the Priestly Blessing the kind of connection between "blessing" and "deliverance" for which we may have originally hoped. (The fuller syntactic unit of Psalm 67:2–3 also includes the following verse: "May God be gracious to us and bless us; may He show us favor…that Your way be known on earth, Your deliverance among all nations.") But that is not "Rashi's job," so to speak; rather, he wants to help us see the immediate meaning of the biblical passage in question, insofar as his intuition and his knowledge of midrash enable him to do so.

Turning to the final word of verse 25 (*vi-ḥunneka,* a single-word verbal phrase that consists of a prefix, a verb, and a suffix that serves as its object), and again drawing on Sifrei Bemidbar, Rashi explains that this means "may He give you grace." Thus, for Rashi, the wish is not, as is generally interpreted, that God should "favor" or "show graciousness" to the recipient of the blessing.[24] Rather, Rashi states that the blessing will be that God will bestow (the quality of or the capacity for) "grace" on the Israelites, interpreting the word as a nominal, not a verbal, phrase. Thus, before we move on to the third blessing, we should pause to consider that, whereas Rashi explained the first blessing as conferring material benefits, he understands the second blessing to express the hope for more ethereal blessings, a kind of "altered state," as it were, though Rashi himself does not define precisely what that might mean.[25]

Rashi approaches the third blessing in legal terms. Whereas he explained the expression *l'ha·ir panim,* "to shine the face" in rabbinic Hebrew as God will "show" a favorable countenance to the Israelites, he understands the biblical Hebrew idiom *la-seit panim,* "to lift the face," as an action that would take place "before the decree of judgment. But after the decree of judgment, He [=God] will not 'lift the face.'" What was Rashi thinking of with this interpretation? The underlying midrash (Sifrei Bemidbar 42) helps us understand Rashi more fully:

> One verse states that *He will lift up His face* (Numbers 6:26) while another verse states that *He will not lift up His face* (Deuteronomy 10:17).[26] How may these two verses be reconciled? When Israel does the will of the Omnipresent, *He will lift up His face*; when Israel does not do the will of the Omnipresent, *He will not lift up His face.* Another interpretation: until the decree is sealed, *He will lift up His face*; after the decree is sealed, *He will not lift up His face.*

As we see, the midrash understands the biblical expression to constitute a legal idiom: "to lift the face" means to pardon or show mercy, whereas "to refuse to lift the face" essentially means to convict. Given the midrashic predilection for homogenizing any and all conflicts and contradictions between biblical verses, the midrash needs to determine in what circumstances God would agree to "lift His face" and show mercy in a courtroom, while refusing to do so in other circumstances. Therefore the midrash suggests two possibilities to resolve the conflict, and Rashi chooses to include one of these in his commentary:[27] while "court is still in session," as it were, God will take every opportunity to "lift His face" and forgive/show mercy to the defendant. Once God issues His decree, and it is "sealed," however, then there is no deviation from the judgment.[28]

It may be over-reading, but I cannot help but think that Rashi is deliberately contrasting the role that the Torah mandates for human judges, and the way in which he imagines the priests hope that God acts when he functions as Divine Judge. When it comes to considering how a human judge ought to decide a case in an Israelite courtroom, the Torah is quite clear: "You are not to commit corruption in justice; you are not to lift-up-in-favor the face of the poor, you are not to overly-honor the face of the great; with equity you are to judge your fellow!" (Leviticus 19:15).[29] Another iteration of the expectation that human judges must decide cases before them with an utter dedication to the facts is found in Deuteronomy 16:18–20:

> Judges and officials you are to provide for yourselves, within all your gates that YHWH your God is giving you, for your tribal-districts; they are to judge the people (with) equitable justice.
> You are not to cast aside a case-for-judgment, you are not to (specially) recognize (anyone's) face, and you are not to take a bribe—for a bribe blinds the eyes of the wise, and twists the words of the equitable.

Equity, equity you are to pursue, in order that you may live
and possess the land that the Eternal your God is giving you!

Thus, the biblical Hebrew idiom "lifting up the face" means "to show
favor." Moreover, both from the perspective of priestly Torah and
Deuteronomy, the Torah commands as complete a dedication to
impartiality as can be aspired to when it comes to functioning in
an Israelite court of law. However, paradoxically, when it comes to
entering the divine court, as it were, the rabbis expressed the hope
(both in midrash and in liturgy) that God would **not** function with
impartiality! As is completely natural, when facing God and when
considering one's misdeeds, one hopes for a merciful judge, one who
does "lift up the face," and **not** one who assesses only the facts of
the case! Thus, in presenting the third blessing (in which the priests
express the wish that God "lift up his face") in a juridical context,
Rashi wishes readers to think that—following both a material and
a spiritual blessing—the recipients of the Priestly Blessing will also
receive the best gift of all: *shalom* (peace), here construed as a pardon
for past sins.

Rashi follows this legal interpretation, as is his custom, with a
second interpretation (somewhat related to the preceding) that
understands this last part of the Priestly Blessing as a wish that
God will "conquer His anger."[31] It is not immediately clear what
Rashi means precisely, or why he chooses this specific explanation
(in addition to the previous selection) in lieu of all the others he
might have adduced. However, the significance may become clear by
considering the midrashic context from which Rashi has culled this
brief comment. The midrash states that "God will lift up His face
to you," meaning that God "will cause His anger to pass away from
you"—a formulation close in sentiment to Rashi's gloss, although
not identical in exact wording. However, what is striking is that it
comes at the very end of a long passage that tries to harmonize a

series of contradictory verses (as we have already seen) that depict Israelite sin as the cause of the rupture between God and Israel, that urge Israel to repent for its crimes, and that mention more than in passing the possibility of the death penalty for Israelite trespasses. Rashi's comment that in "lifting up His face" God will in fact be "conquering His anger" now makes perfect sense: in the eyes of the midrash, the people had committed sins that had caused a distancing between them and God's presence—and God has every right to be angry with them! Therefore, Israel is in great need of a blessing that will result in God "lifting up His face" and "conquering His anger" so as not to punish them, but instead bring them peace—the final result of the divine blessing.

Ironically, Rashi has nothing to say about that final blessing of peace! The primary midrash upon which Rashi relies in commenting on the Priestly Blessing has a great many things to say about the importance of peace—in fact, it repeats the pronouncement "Great is peace..." no fewer than twenty times in the remaining thematic half of its discourse; nonetheless, Rashi seems to be true to the game plan he outlined in his comment on Genesis 3:8 (above), and will only resort to midrash to "settle" the meaning of biblical language, to offer "the fullest possible accounting of it," but will not present *midrashim*, however great the values they teach, only for the sake of teaching those values. That is, simply put, not his purpose in composing his commentary. We are left, therefore, to intuit how he imagines this *shalom*/peace, based on his own formulation, as "the feeling of well-being when one exits from a court room, vindicated or pardoned."[32]

So it is that Rashi turns to the final verse in the biblical passage: "So shall they place My name upon the people of Israel, and I will bless them" (Numbers 6:27). With regard to this verse, Rashi is interested in clarifying two of its aspects. The first of these is: what does it mean for the priests to place the name of God upon the people of Israel? Once again, Rashi relies on Sifrei Bemidbar and explains that the priests must "bless the Israelites using the divine name," YHWH.[33] There is power in the name, and the priests must not invoke God using any euphemism or substitute. The second item on Rashi's agenda for this verse is to clarify the referent to the pronoun (in Hebrew, a pronominal suffix only) at the end of the verse: when the Torah states, "and I will bless **them**": to whom does it refer? The immediate antecedent is, of course, Israel—and to our ears this is, perhaps, obvious.[34] Rashi states, "**And I will bless them,** i.e., Israel, and I shall agree with the priests." However, as Rashi's ancient rabbinic predecessors acknowledge, it is also possible to read the pronoun as a reference to the priests themselves—that is, God states "I will bless the priests" and, by implication, they shall transfer that blessing to the Israelites.

We can summarize Rashi's exegesis of the Priestly Blessing as follows. Rashi primarily interprets the passage according to ancient rabbinic midrash, which frames the pericope (Numbers 6:22–27) as a dialogue between Israel and God, with Israel initially objecting to priests blessing them at all, and preferring to be blessed only, and directly, by God personally, who then reassures Israel that the divine intention is for God to continue to be the source of all blessings, including the ones spoken by the priests. Rashi references this dialogue both at the beginning and end of his exegesis, analogous to the way in which the biblical text itself (Numbers 6:22–23 and 27) frames the blessing formula (Numbers 6:24–26). In his interpretation of the individual components of the blessing, Rashi proceeds along the lines suggested by the midrash, and treats the first blessing (Numbers 6:24) as one in which the priests invoke God to bestow material well-being, and the second blessing (less grounded in concrete imagery) as one that speaks more to an emotional or ethereal state of being. In the third and final blessing, Rashi depicts Israel in a juridical setting, the priests expressing the hope, actually, that God will **not** function as a good human judge is expected to function, with an eye only to justice and not to the particular circumstances of the defendant, but will pardon the Israelites for any and all sins, granting them the "peace" of a favorable verdict.

We have traversed the length and breadth, as it were, of Rashi's commentary on the Priestly Blessing. We now return to the questions we posed at the beginning of this essay: how does Rashi construe these blessings, and why does he think ancient Israelites (or his contemporary Jewish audience) would wish to be blessed with *these* specific blessings? In a sense, perhaps, we were asking the wrong questions of Rashi, though they seemed logical enough to us at the outset. Let us recall what Rashi himself states quite clearly about the goals of his Torah commentary (at Genesis 3:8), "I have only come for the plain sense of Scripture and the *aggadah* that settles a word of Scripture and its sense." When Rashi states his interest in "plain sense" interpretation, he could not have had in mind what ancient Israel thought—because the very notion of a fixed, historical/contextual interpretation had not yet been invented in European Jewish circles. As the late, great Israeli scholar Sarah Kamin demonstrated, for Rashi, the terms *p'shuto* and *midrasho* ("plain sense interpretation" and "midrash") had not yet achieved the degree of interpretive categories that they did later in the twelfth century, and it is highly misleading and anachronistic to apply to Rashi as sophisticated a distinction among levels of interpretation and methodologies as developed two and three generations after him.[36]

In order to more fully appreciate Rashi's achievement in his own time, let us briefly contrast his commentary with that of another northern French rabbinic exegete of the Bible who, at a remove of three generations from Rashi, presented what we might think of as an accurate contextual understanding of the Priestly Blessing. This commentator, Rabbi Joseph Bekhor Shor, was a disciple of another of Rashi's grandsons, Rabbeinu Tam (the younger brother of Rashbam, discussed above). When writing about the blessing's opening verse, Bekhor Shor interprets as follows:

May the Eternal bless you and keep you: May God bless you with children,[37] with a [healthy] body, with wisdom, with length of days, and with wealth;[38] and [may God bless you] in your going forth and in your returning, and in the city and in the field, in your basket and your kneading-bowl (see Deuteronomy 28:3–6)—that your heart may be joyful in your portion/lot-in-life. For in all of these belongs the language of blessing.[39]

One can distinguish at a glance between the type of contextual commentary Bekhor Shor provided (in the late twelfth century) and the very distinctive style of Rashi (in the eleventh). Rashi does not think of "blessing" in the abstract, and then apply that notion to his interpretation of the Bible; nor does Rashi first scan all of the various biblical contexts in which a notion of blessing occurs (although of course he knows all of those verses!)—but Bekhor Shor does both of these things before his pen hits the page. Instead, Rashi does just what we would expect him to do, given what he says about the goals and methodology of his enterprise: rooting his understanding primarily in ancient rabbinic midrash, Rashi conveys that meaning in a clear-flowing and lucid prose. To be sure, that is no mean achievement, and one that has lasted some 900 years as the fundamental, first reading of the Bible for Jews all over the world.

One might ask: Why should we care about what Rashi had to say, if commentaries that show greater fidelity to literary and historical context have been written since? My response to this question comes from several different directions. First, because of the exceedingly prominent role that study of Rashi's Torah commentary has played in the lives of Jewish communities all around the world and from the Middle Ages until our very day, Rashi has become what may be considered a self-validating source. We no more ask this question about Rashi than we do about the Torah itself, or about any other Jewish classic composed since the day the Israelites are first said to have gathered at the foot of Mount Sinai. These works, Rashi among them, are the life-blood of the Jewish people. In a sense, we live to study these works. True, we transform their finest thoughts into our ongoing and reinvented Jewish civilization and we discard elements that we no longer consider worthy of retaining in our contemporary understanding and practice of Judaism. But we preserve the sources and make them all available for study—and perhaps we live precisely because we try so hard to maintain the fullest possible library and accounting of Jewish civilization.

Rashi was himself one of the great exemplars of this process, and this observation leads me to my second response to the question of why we should study Rashi. Rashi refracted all of ancient rabbinic wisdom in his Torah commentary—Talmud and midrash, law and lore, Targum and *piyyut*, and more—but cast his learning in what was in his time a completely new genre of literature for the Jews of his day: the *ad locum* gloss.[40]

I will illustrate what I mean by this via a personal story. I was once lecturing at a university in Israel, attempting to explain what I found to be utterly new in Rashi's Torah commentary. Frustrated that I could not convince one of the members of my audience, I exclaimed, "Don't forget—Rashi didn't study 'Ḥumash (Pentateuch) with Rashi!" While the vast majority of the *content* of Rashi's Torah commentary was ancient midrash, the *form* in which Rashi presented his exegesis—the commentary or gloss—was all but utterly new. I have always been bothered when rabbis and professors alike refer to "ancient biblical commentaries" in the Talmud and other rabbinic works. These works are replete with interpretations, to be sure; however, the genre through which the rabbis cast these interpretations are not "commentaries" *per se*, and are completely midrashic in nature and form. Indeed, midrash is "the original" rabbinic form of "reading" or, rather, "interpreting the biblical text."[41] What Rashi did in creating a running interpretation right there on the page was nothing short of extraordinary (at least in a Jewish cultural and intellectual milieu).[42] Rashi was in many ways the originator of what I call the "two-finger method of reading," requiring one finger following along the reading of the biblical text, while another finger followed along in the interpretive gloss. Jews did not read that way before Rashi—and they have hardly read any other way (at least when reading traditional and "authoritative" texts) ever since.

My second response to the question "Why study Rashi?" leads to a third observation. What is even more startling and revolutionary was that, in employing the commentary form (both in his biblical and in his talmudic exegesis), Rashi essentially adopted what was for all intents and purposes a Christian hermeneutic. Christians had employed the commentary form, in one iteration or another, for hundreds of years, essentially adopting and adapting Greco-Roman literary conventions that preceded them. Yet even Christians in Rashi's time and geographical locale, sharing the same cultural and intellectual world, were changing the ways in which they used the form to interpret the Bible.[43] Let me mention only one remarkable analogy to Rashi's interpretive works, the *Glossa Ordinaria* ("Ordinary Gloss"). The Gloss is a remarkable and vast work of Christian biblical scholarship and, roughly speaking, was a project that took hundreds of years to complete. Moreover, the Christian scholars who composed the Gloss essentially "lived down the street" from Rashi and his family (in medieval Paris, Champagne county and the Loire River valley).[44] But perhaps the most telling point of comparison with Rashi's commentary is its composition; approximately 70–80% of its contents were culled from ancient patristic works of Christian homily and allegory, while a smaller percentage were ad *litteram* ("according to the letter") comments that by the eleventh and twelfth centuries had developed into a "plain sense" commentary (especially as this developed outside the bounds of the Gloss, but existed even within its pages). This is not the place to elaborate further, but the analogies to Rashi's exegetical program (or Rashi's to the Gloss) are abundant enough to see.[45]

My point in addressing the points of contact between Rashi and contemporary Christian exegesis is not to try to determine precedence or even influence—it is clear beyond debate that Christians and Jews were in close cultural and intellectual contact and learned from one another; indeed, it almost defies belief to imagine it could be otherwise—but only to help us understand the ingenuity of Rashi in adapting ancient Jewish content to the new forms of literacy and cultural presentations that were current in his time and locale. And I think that matters. To truly appreciate Rashi's genius, we need to consider not only the words in the commentary itself, but we also need to imagine the world in which he lived and the challenges that he faced. And the fact remains: studying "Ḥumash with Rashi" is today universally recognized as a quintessential Jewish act of both erudition and piety. And yet our very ability to engage in this study is due to Rashi's own creative and brilliant adaptation of Christian intellectual and religious mores—and that is as timeless and important a message as one can imagine, as Judaism faces its own contemporary challenges.

I wish to conclude with one final thought about Rashi, as man and as exegete. Anyone who has ever studied Rashi's commentary knows that there are many verses for which there is no comment. Apparently, Rashi felt that those verses were self-explanatory and did not require any elaboration on his part. However, on other occasions, Rashi will confess about some matter or another, *lo yadati peirusho*, "I do not know its explanation." Rashi was well-known as an extremely humble man, and he did not hide behind the veneer of learning's prestige (and he surely could have)! Instead of allowing his students and readers to think that that reason he did not provide commentary for a given verse because its meaning was "self-explanatory," he went out of his way to call attention to his lack of knowledge—and this was one of the ways in which he opened the door for critical thinking among his disciples and followers. But Rashi's dedication to truthful investigation went even further than this. It is relatively well known that Rashi rewrote and changed his commentaries during his lifetime (which is one of the many reasons that it is virtually impossible to arrive at "an original text" of the commentary). What is not as well known is the pride of place he gave to new interpretations that were proffered in his community. His grandson, Rashbam, famously wrote in his own commentary (on Genesis 37:2): "...Our Master, Rabbi Solomon, my mother's father (i.e., Rashi), who illumined the eyes of all those in exile, and who wrote commentaries on the Torah, Prophets and the Writings, also set himself the task of elucidating the contextual meaning of Scripture [*p'shat*]. And I, Samuel, son of his son-in-law Meir, may the memory of the righteous be for a blessing, argued it out with him (Rashi, i.e., privately) and in his presence (i.e., publicly, in the *beit midrash*). He admitted to me that if he had the time he would have written new commentaries in accordance with the fresh interpretations of the contextual meaning that are innovated day by day...." But this is not merely Rashbam "telling tales" that vindicated his own approach over that of his illustrious grandfather, for we also have contemporary evidence that suggests that what Rashbam claims was true. In reviewing such poetic passages as Genesis 49 and Exodus 15 that he had glossed as a younger man, Rashi saw fit to incorporate some of the insights that his grandson, Rashbam, had proposed about parallelistic syntax that are an essential marker of biblical poetry. (Recall that although we consider those chapters to be poetic compositions, this distinction was only being rediscovered in northern European Jewish circles in the eleventh and twelfth centuries.) In drawing upon Rashbam's methodologically sophisticated understanding, Rashi did not do so stealthily, but proudly proclaimed his indebtedness to his grandson by calling those new interpretations "Samuel's verses."[46]

Thus, the image of Rashi is one of a brilliant scholar; dedicated to transmission of Torah; and open to the virtue of new ideas and incorporating them into his world view; humble in self-consideration; and selfless in seeing the broader purpose of the pursuit of truth and the survival of an ancient covenant.

Insofar as the Priestly Blessing itself is concerned, Rashi matters here as well. Think of Rashi's commentary on Birkat Kohanim as a microcosm of the macro-importance of Rashi for which I have just argued. The blessing of Numbers 6:22–27 continues to function as a kind of liturgical fulcrum—daily, in the prayer services; familially, in the parental blessing of children each Shabbat eve; and in a host of other prayer-filled and cultural contexts. These liturgies balance divine beneficence and human gratitude for God's blessings. Rashi provides us with a way of understanding how exactly that works, and taking his thoughts into account can help a modern person interpret the concept of being blessed with those ancient words in a way that might otherwise elude even the most savvy modern reader. Through Rashi's commentary, we learn that we needn't feel guilty for hoping for material blessings alongside those of a more spiritual nature; that we may imagine God as smiling or even "laughing" with delight at us human creations, an image that few of us may have received through institutional religious representations; and that whatever our relationship with those who claim to represent God through traditional religious structures, we may imagine God's own blessing showering down upon us directly, as the power to bless ultimately resides in God alone. This—and much more! As was originally stated about the Bible itself, generations of students have discovered about Rashi's biblical commentaries: *hafokh bah va-hafokh bah, d'khulla bah*, "Turn it over and over, for all is in it."[47]

NOTES

[1] The translation is taken from the NJPS, although rendering the four-letter name of God as "the Eternal" (rather than "Lord"), in keeping with the conventions of this volume.

[2] Unless otherwise noted, all translations of ancient sources (including biblical passages) are those of the author.

[3] I do not address here the approach to this distinction taken by advocates of the Documentary Hypothesis, who assign different authors or sources to these two passages. I first became aware of the distinction between the material blessing of Genesis 27 and the covenantal blessing of Genesis 28 in 1976, in a course I took with Nehama Leibowitz; see Nehama Leibowitz and Aryeh Newman, *Studies in Bereshit (Genesis): In the Context of Ancient and Modern Jewish Bible Commentary* (Jerusalem: World Zionist Organisation Department for Torah Education and Culture, 1981), pp. 275–279.

[4] I am grateful to my student Dr. Yedida Eisenstat for providing me with a digital edition of the manuscript she obtained in the course of writing her dissertation, *Rashi's Midrashic Anthology: The Torah Commentary Re-Examined* (Jewish Theological Seminary, 2014). There is a prominent recent scholarly debate about the importance of this commentary, in particular by two Israeli professors, Avraham Grossman and Elazar Touitou; unfortunately for the English reader, all of this research is published in Hebrew only. For now, about Rashi's life and works, see Avraham Grossman, *Rashi*, trans. Joel A. Linsider (Oxford and Portland, OR: Littman Library of Jewish Civilization, 2012); for particular reference to ms. Leipzig 1, see pp. 77–78. By far the best edition of all medieval rabbinic commentaries on the Bible are the ones published in *Mikra·ot G'dolot "Ha-keter": A Revised and Augmented Scientific Edition of Mikra·ot G'dolot Based on the Aleppo Codex and Early Medieval Mss: Numbers*, ed. Menachem Cohen (Ramat Gan: Bar Ilan University Press, 2011). This series now covers much of the Hebrew Bible. The classic study of the historical period in which Rashi produced his masterpiece is Charles H. Haskins, *The Renaissance of the Twelfth Century* (Cambridge, MA and London: Harvard University Press, 1927). A crucial and much more recent study is Brian Stock, *The Implications of Literacy: Written Language and Models of Interpretation in the Eleventh and Twelfth Centuries* (Princeton: Princeton University Press, 1983).

[5] Please note that none of the printed editions incorporate Rashi's introduction to the Priestly Blessing, which I present here in English for the first time, based on ms. Leipzig 1.

[6] A version of the midrash that Rashi brings is found in Tanḥuma Naso 8.

[7] Actually, Rashi initially addresses the grammatical form of the verb "say" (*amor*), and notes that it is not an imperative but rather an infinitive, analogous to the form of the verbs *zakhor*, "remember" (Exodus 20:8) and *shamor*, "observe"

(Deuteronomy 5:12), in the so-called "Fourth Commandment" to remember and observe the Sabbath. As is his oft-practiced custom, Rashi also proposes an Old French equivalent (*disant*), for the benefit of his contemporary, French-speaking Jewish audience. I am grateful to my colleague, Dr. Kirsten Fudeman, for confirming that this is the OF present participle for "saying" (related to the Modern French verb "dire"). However, Rashi does not appear to tease any broader observation, either theological or otherwise, from any perceived grammatical connection between Numbers 6:23 and the Sabbath commandment.

[8] For an English translation of this midrash, see Jacob Neusner, *Sifré to Numbers* (Atlanta: Scholars Press, 1986).

[9] See Neusner, *Sifré to Numbers*, pp. 187–190.

[10] This translation incorporates a slight conjectural emendation I have advocated (see Robert A. Harris, "Rashi's Introductions to His Biblical Commentaries," in *Shai L'Sarah Japhet: Studies in the Bible, Its Exegesis and Its Language*, eds. Moshe Bar-Asher, Dalit Rom-Shiloni, Emanuel Tov, and Nili Wayzana, 219*–241* (Jerusalem: The Bialik Institute, 2007, p. 294, n. 17). Rashi's commentary on Genesis 3:8 does not survive in ms. Leipzig 1, and I have transcribed it according to my corrected reading of the version found in *Mikra·ot G'dolot Ha-keter*. To this version, I have added one letter (*a mem*) in order to make greater sense of the comment. Thus, in place of Haketer's reading of *v'la-aggadah ha-m'yashevet d'var ha-mikra u-sh'mu·o*, I read: *v'la-aggadah ha-m'yshevet d'var ha-mikra u-mashma·o*, ושמע[מ]י, noting that elsewhere (e.g. in his introduction to the Song of Songs) Rashi employs the term *mashma* as a synonym for *p'shat*. Moreover, the midrashic tradition that Rashi goes on to cite, in close proximity to this methodological question, asks the rhetorical question *mah sham'u*, "What did they [Adam and Eve] hear?" with reference to the Hebrew verb *va-yishm'u*, "and they [Adam and Eve] heard" in Genesis 3:8. On Rashi's methodology, and the manner in which he navigates between reliance on ancient midrash and the presentation of his own intuitive sense of the "plain meaning," see Edward L. Greenstein, "Sensitivity to Language in Rashi's Commentary on the Torah," in *The Solomon Goldman Lectures* (vol. 6), ed. Mayer I. Gruber (Chicago: The Spertus College of Judaica Press, 1993), pp. 51–71.

[11] This last phrase ("in order that the blessing…") is found in ms. Leipzig 1, but not in the standard printed editions.

[12] For the observation about Rashi wishing to offer the fullest possible accounting, see Greenstein, "Sensitivity to Language," p. 54 and passim.

[13] In this context, the Latin word *plene* refers to a word being written out "fully," with helping letters that stand for vowels. Here, for example, *emor* is written out as *alef-mem-vav-resh*; since the *vav* is not, strictly speaking, necessary, the midrash (and Rashi, in its wake) fleshes out its apparent superfluity with extra meaning.

[14] Alternatively, one might see the influence of Targum Pseudo-Jonathan, which translates as "May the Eternal bless you in all your [business?] matters…."

[15] For English translations of the Tanḥuma *midrashim*, see Avrohom Davis

and Yaakov Y. H. Pupko, *The Metsudah Midrash Tanchuma* (Lakewood, NJ: Metsudah Publications, 2004); and Salomon Buber, *Midrash Tanhuma*, trans. John T. Townsend (Hoboken, NJ: Ktav Publishing House, 1989).

[16] See Jacob Milgrom, *The JPS Torah Commentary: Numbers* (Philadelphia: Jewish Publication Society, 1990), p. 51: "The first part of each line invokes the movement of God toward His people, the second, His activity on their behalf... God initiates six actions: bless *and* protect; shine *and* be gracious; bestow *and* grant peace. However, the transitional *and* may indicate consequence: blessing results in protection; God's shining face results in grace; the bestowal of God's favor results in peace. Thus the Priestly Blessing may actually express three actions."

[17] Milgrom, p. 51, cites a series of biblical verses that substantiate his assertion, and points to Deuteronomy 28:3–14 as a text that encompasses what "blessing" might generally mean in ancient Israel.

[18] For a definition of what is meant by the term "modern historical-critical scholarship," see Marc Zvi Brettler's *How to Read the Bible* (Philadelphia: Jewish Publication Society, 2005), p. 3.

[19] The source for Rashi's comment is likely *Tanḥuma Naso* 10.

[20] NJPS renders idiomatically, "The LORD deal kindly and graciously with you!"

[21] Rashi has confused two biblical Hebrew roots, employing here a word whose root is *resh-alef-hei* (actually *resh-alef-yod*), whereas the biblical root is *alef-vav-resh*. Whether these roots are related bi-literally is beyond the scope of our discussion.

[22] Rashi's formulation, "a face of radiance," is an idiom in rabbinic, not biblical, Hebrew; see, e.g., B. Ḥullin 7b, Pesaḥim 113b, etc. Ironically, the root for radiance can also indicate anger in rabbinic Hebrew (e.g., B. Sanhedrin 105a). However, Rashi indicates his contextual use of the phrase to mean "happy" by including the explanatory expression "a face of laughing."

[23] See also Psalms 31:17 and 80:4, 8, 20; Daniel 9:17.

[24] See, e.g., Targum Onkelos and Targum Pseudo-Jonathan, which both choose different verbs to render "be compassionate." Among the various *midrashim* found in ancient through early medieval literature, one source, nearly contemporary with Rashi, comes closest to him. That is one of the interpretations found in Bemidbar Rabbah (11:6), which states: "May God grant you the capacity/understanding to show grace to each other, and show compassion to one another..."

[25] In both ms. Leipzig 1 and in many of the printed editions, Rashi concludes his gloss of the second blessing with the notice that the rabbis have "expounded many facets (Hebrew: *panim*)/*midrashim* about this in Sifrei."

[26] In fact, many editions of Rashi cite this very verse here in this comment, as well as the conclusion of the midrash.

[27] It is likely the legal language of Deuteronomy 10:17 that leads Rashi to incorporate into his commentary the more overtly juridical interpretation of the two possibilities the midrash offered.

[28] A different tack was taken by Rashi's grandson, the great *p'shat* commentator Rabbi Samuel ben Meir (Rashbam). Here, as throughout his plain-sense commentary on the Torah, Rashbam covertly critiques his grandfather's reliance on midrash to make sense of biblical composition, and instead interprets solely on the basis of his intuition of the Bible's contextual meaning. Rashbam holds that the so-called contradiction that Rashi attempted to resolve via the midrash is, in reality, no contradiction at all. Thus, Rashbam comments: "*May the LORD lift His face to you*: [This is similar to what] is written, *I will turn [My face] toward you* (Leviticus 26:9), i.e., that [God] will not hide His face from you. And regarding that which is written *[God] will not lift up a face* (Deuteronomy 10:17), this means that the blessed Holy One will not lift up the face of a person to wipe him or clean him from all sins. But God does lift up His own face toward one whom He loves, in that He will turn to face such a one to pardon him, as it is written, *I will turn-my-face toward you and multiply you; and I will maintain My covenant with you* (Leviticus 26:9)." For further reading about Rashbam's Torah commentary, see the fine translation by Martin Lockshin, which contains many explanatory notes and essays: Martin I. Lockshin, *Rabbi Samuel Ben Meir's Commentary on Genesis: An Annotated Translation* (Lewiston, NY: Edwin Mellen Press, 1989); followed by companion volumes on Exodus (Atlanta: Scholars Press, 1997); Leviticus and Numbers (Providence: Brown Judaic Studies, 2001); and Deuteronomy (Providence: Brown Judaic Studies, 2004).

[29] Translation according to Everett Fox, *The Schocken Bible: Volume I: The Five Books of Moses* (New York: Schocken Books, 1995).

[30] Ibid.

[31] Again, Rashi bases himself on Sifrei Bemidbar §42. In many editions, the order of Rashi's two interpretations is reversed; in general, there is no significance to the order of interpretations in the commentaries, whether between plain-sense (*p'shuto*) interpretations and *midrashim*, or between multiple midrashic explanations.

[32] Jacob Milgrom defines "peace" in its biblical context as follows: "Hebrew *shalom* means in its negative sense the freedom from all disasters (Leviticus 26:6; Job 21:9). But in its broadest scope it encompasses the positive blessings of prosperity (Deuteronomy 23:7; Proverb 3:2); good health (Psalm 38:4); friendship (Jeremiah 20:10; 38:22); and general well-being...." (*JPS Torah Commentary: Numbers*, p. 52). For an English translation of the midrashic formulations that Rashi here ignores, see Neusner, *Sifré to Numbers*, pp.197–199.

[33] By this Rashi means the divine name pronounced according to its four Hebrew letters, not with any of the traditional ellipses or circumlocutions (e.g., Adonai, "Lord," and the like).

[34] It was also obvious to Rashbam. He disagrees with Rashi's contention that the pronoun is ambiguous, and instead claims that what God has stated in verses 23 and 27, God has stated clearly: "I will hear your (priestly) voices when

you say those words, and then I will bless the Israelites....When the priests bless the Israelites in My name, not in their own name, then **I will bless them**, i.e. Israel, as the priests prayed for when they said *"May the Eternal bless you* (Numbers 6:24)." Rashbam's insightful and pithy comment also has the virtue of connecting the Priestly Blessing's framing verses (Numbers 6:22–23 and 6:27) and framing the literary sense of the entire pericope.

[35] The sentiment for Rashi's gloss is found in Sifrei Bemidbar 43, although a more direct source may be B. Ḥullin 49b.

[36] Kamin mostly wrote in Hebrew. The English abstract of her great monograph on Rashi's Torah commentary may be found in Sarah Kamin, "Rashi's Exegetical Categorization With Respect to the Distinction Between Peshat and Derash" in *Immanuel* 11 (1980), pp. 16–32. A posthumous collection of her essays, some in English, may be found in Sarah Kamin, *Bein Y'hudim L'notz'rim B'farshanut Ha-mikra* (Jerusalem: Magnes Press, 2008).

[37] Literally, Bekhor Shor writes *banim*, that is, "sons," though I think he has in mind both male and female children.

[38] Literally *g'dullah*, "greatness."

[39] I have translated only a brief portion of Bekhor Shor's very long comment, according to the text provided in Cohen, *Mikra·ot G'dolot Ha-keter.*

[40] As I have already noted, a full English presentation of this idea in book form will have to await the publication of the dissertation of my doctoral student, Yedida Eisenstat.

[41] For several years I have been reconsidering the distinction between what it meant "to read" in rabbinic antiquity, as opposed to what it meant as a result of developments that took place in the twelfth-century Renaissance. These changes essentially mark the transition "from *d'rash* to *p'shat.*" See, e.g., Robert A. Harris, "Twelfth-Century Biblical Exegetes and the Invention of Literature," in *The Multiple Meaning of Scripture: The Role of Exegesis in Early Christian and Medieval Culture*, ed. Ienje van't Spijker (Leiden and Boston: Brill, 2009), pp. 311–329 ; and idem, "The Reception of Ezekiel Among Twelfth-Century Northern French Rabbinic Exegetes," in *After Ezekiel: Essays on the Reception of a Difficult Prophet*, eds. Andrew Mein and Paul M. Joyce (New York, London: T&T Clark International, 2011), pp. 71–88.

[42] Of course, the fact that there was "a page" to begin with (as opposed to an aural interaction between master and disciple) is itself a crucial development in the history of "reading." See, for example, what David Stern has observed: "The one element which has not yet been included in this discussion, however, is the adoption of the codex. Just as aurality was a basic condition for *midrash*, so too—I venture to propose—the reading of the text on a page is the basic condition for all types of medieval exegesis, especially for those traditionally characterized under the rubric of *p'shat*. This is the case whether *p'shat* refers to the colloquial or popular sense (as in Saadiah), the grammatical sense (as

in Abraham Ibn Ezra), or the contextual sense (as in Rashbam). In all these interpretive approaches, the text is read as it appears visually and spatially on the page." David Stern, "The First Jewish Books and the Early History of Jewish Reading," in *Jewish Quarterly Review* 98:2 (2008), pp. 163–202 (quoted material appears on p. 199). For a recent provocative thesis about how twelfth-century study of the Talmud factored into the changes I am describing with respect to Bible study, see Talya Fishman, *Becoming the People of the Talmud : Oral Torah as Written Tradition in Medieval Jewish Cultures* (Philadelphia: University of Pennsylvania Press, 2011), especially pp. 91–155.

[43] The classic study of this phenomenon remains Beryl Smalley, *The Study of the Bible in the Middle Ages* (Oxford: Basil Blackwell, 1952), although much has been written since, as would be expected.

[44] A recent and brilliant book on the composition of the Gloss is Lesley Smith, *The Glossa Ordinaria: The Making of a Medieval Bible Commentary* (Leiden, Boston: Brill, 2009). For a different, yet still insightful, approach to the Gloss in the context of medieval literary theory, see David A. Salomon, *An Introduction to the Glossa Ordinaria as Medieval Hypertext* (Cardiff: University of Wales Press, 2012).

[45] A recent attempt to systematically compare Rashi and the Gloss is Devorah Schoenfeld, *Isaac on Jewish and Christian Altars: Polemic and Exegesis in Rashi and the Glossa Ordinaria* (New York: Fordham University Press, 2013).

[46] For a more detailed accounting of this, see Robert A. Harris, *Discerning Parallelism: A Study in Northern French Medieval Jewish Biblical Exegesis* (Providence, RI: Brown Judaic Studies, 2004), pp. 35–40.

[47] The famous teaching of Pirkei Avot 5:21: "Ben Bag Bag would say: turn it over and turn it over (perpetually), for all is in it; see with it; grow old and worn in it; do not budge from it, for there is nothing better."

Birkat Kohanim in the *S'fat Emet*

Nehemia Polen

The root *bet-resh-kaf* in its various forms appears about 450 times in the Hebrew Bible, and the Priestly Blessing may be seen as the highest expression of this core concept. Powerful in its simplicity and elegance, the increasing sequence of three-five-seven words bespeaks assurance of divine protection, grace, and peace. While the family narratives in Genesis are propelled largely by siblings' struggles to receive their parents' blessing, the Priestly Blessing is striking in its universal scope and equal applicability to every individual. Composed in the second-person singular, each listener is addressed individually and hears the "you" of the blessing as meant for himself or herself. The patriarchal blessings in Genesis seem to be a zero-sum game, provoking envy because the special favor bestowed on one brother appears to detract from what remains for the others. By contrast, in its sweeping generality and embracing language, the Priestly Blessing prompts benevolence rather than competition, dissolving much of the dynamic tension of the Genesis story.

Yet there are aspects of the Priestly Blessing that seem alien to moderns. There is the fact that in the Bible, the mandate to bless the people is awarded to Aaron and his children: the right to invoke these potent words appears to be limited to them. This of course is part of the wider puzzle of the election of Aaron in the Book of Exodus (28:1). As Jeffrey Tigay has observed, "The Bible never explains why Aaron was granted the priesthood."[1] The priesthood is hereditary, promised to

Aaron's sons and later descendants: "And the priesthood shall be theirs for a perpetual statute" (Exodus 29:9). The Aaronides are the ones who, the first-person voice of God says in Numbers, should "place My name upon the Children of Israel" (Numbers 6:27).

The notion of a hereditary priesthood is perplexing in our day and age. We are suspicious of inherited privilege of all kinds, and many people find the idea of innate distinction between individuals to be troubling and problematic. Yet while the special election of Aaron and his progeny is a central feature of all the priestly texts, hardly anything remains in today's Judaism of the priestly sacrificial system; since the destruction of the Jerusalem Temple almost two thousand years ago, Rabbinic Judaism has placed prayer and Torah study at the center of religious life. But the rite of the Priestly Blessing is still practiced in traditional synagogues, chanted by those claiming descent from Aaron. It is almost the only surviving element of ancient Temple-based, priestly-centered ritual in contemporary Jewish practice. What are we to make of this sacred endowed prerogative in our egalitarian society? To be sure, the tendency in Jewish tradition has been to democratize the Blessing, widening the circle of those authorized to pronounce it. It is a long-standing custom for parents to bless their children using these words, and in many congregations it is the rabbi who invokes the Priestly Blessing at life-cycle events and during services. Yet the question remains: are these uses of the Blessing disruptive adaptations, appropriations of an ancient biblical practice but largely discontinuous from it, or is there a way to understand them as natural and organic extensions of the ancient biblical (and Second Temple) rite?

Another problem relates to the very idea of blessing, whose efficacy is based on pronouncing certain words. From the days of classical antiquity's philosophical schools, we have been taught to be suspicious of claims that words in themselves have power; it is considered a mark of archaic, unenlightened thinking to confuse words and things. Jacob Milgrom, the late and renowned Bible scholar, acknowledges that some narratives in Genesis assume that the patriarchal blessings have "inherent powers of fulfillment"; once uttered, they take effect ineluctably.[2] Yet in an essay on our topic, he asserts that in general blessings are nothing more than prayers, and that the Priestly Blessing specifically should be understood as the priests' prayer on behalf of Israel.[3] This position appears to be motivated by apologetic considerations and is difficult to maintain: when biblical narrative wishes to have an eminent figure pray on behalf of another, it says so explicitly.[4] While they may be closely related and sometimes overlap, prayer and blessing are really different concepts; each is too important in the biblical world for the two to be confused or for one to be collapsed into the other. How then do we understand the Priestly Blessing? Does the implied biblical theology of this practice take the words to have magical efficacy, and if so, how do we relate to this claim?

These issues are addressed in a series of teachings by a late nineteenth- and early twentieth-century hasidic master, Rabbi Yehudah Aryeh Leib Alter, known as the Gerer Rebbe (1847–1905).[5] Perhaps the most prominent rebbe of his day, he was a noble exemplar of the Przysucha school of Polish Hasidism, which emphasized intellectual attainment in talmudic study, cultivated a certain independence of thinking, demoted the centrality of belief in paranormal powers, and stressed (as Abraham Joshua Heschel put it) a "passion for truth."[6] As Arthur Green has pointed out, Rabbi Aryeh Leib developed a language at once devout and sophisticated, which spoke to not only the pious faithful but also to the newly urbanized and somewhat acculturated Jewish residents of large population centers such as Warsaw. The collection of his Torah discourses, the *S'fat Emet*, published shortly after his death, is widely considered one of the greatest hasidic Torah commentaries, distinguished by mastery of classic sources, profundity and freshness of insight, literary flair, and economy of expression. Eschewing technical kabbalistic terminology, it is elusive without being arcane or esoteric—a breathtaking combination of concise exposition and sublime spiritual vision.

Like nearly all hasidic masters, the S'fat Emet follows in the footsteps of the founders of Hasidism, especially the Baal Shem Tov, in emphasizing the presence of God everywhere. God is the essential reality of the cosmos, and the human religious task is to become ever more fully aware of this reality. The omnipresence of God might be taken as a theological doctrine, an article of faith whose truth requires assent. But it is closer to the spirit of Hasidism to think of omnipresence as a way of seeing the world, an inner disposition and perspective on life to be constantly cultivated rather than a theological proposition commanding agreement once and for all. The S'fat Emet stands firmly within this early hasidic tradition, but he develops his own characteristic language to express and enhance it.

Rabbi Aryeh Leib was situated at the very center of a large and devoted hasidic community of the most traditional stripe, the kind that today would be called *ḥaredi*. Indeed, he was its leader. Yet in his *S'fat Emet*, he avoided the rhetorical tropes typical of pietistic books of the time: exhortations to more meticulous fulfillment of the commandments, calls to belief in the classic articles of faith, threats of punishment and promises of reward in the afterlife, and even traditional God-language. His piety and holy devotion were exemplary, but his discourse cast a much wider net. By highlighting the centrality of mindful awareness in daily life, by stressing the importance of inner preparation for every religious act even more than the act itself, by softening if not collapsing the distinctions between the holy and the profane, by emphasizing the interdependence and interpenetration of Sabbath and weekday, he sounds remarkably contemporary, having anticipated and articulated a modern and even postmodern religious sensibility.

In the *S'fat Emet*, polar opposites are not collapsed or absorbed one into the other, but rather come into full mutuality as each faces the other dialogically, respectfully acknowledges the other, and beckons the other to more sublime possibility. This theological posture is often referred to as monism, the assertion of ultimate unity beyond the multitudinous, contentious surface that the world seems to present. But it is important to note that for the S'fat Emet, polar positions do not disappear; rather, they are acknowledged as they are brought into ever-closer proximity and dialogue with each other. Boundaries are bridged, rigid categories are tunneled through, without erasing the boundaries or destroying the categories. Spirit crowns but does not replace the physical; the sacred caps the mundane without trumping it.

This stance is inherently difficult to maintain, insofar as it cannot struggle too vigorously with opposing views. Were it to fight against other perspectives, it would thereby confirm their dualism and undermine its own claim of unity. Hence the monistic viewpoint must be satisfied with speaking its own truth with clarity and vitality. When opposition emerges, it is viewed as a cutting edge of growth, the horizon of further opportunity. This is the way the *S'fat Emet* understands election and the special roles in space, time, and person of Temple, Sabbath, and priest. They are not defined in opposition to a presumed estranged Other but rather as vectors pointing asymptotically to unity, never fully attained and therefore always present, always dynamically attractive.

A key term conveying this approach is *n'kudah p'nimit*, the "innermost point." The *n'kudah p'nimit* is a beckoning to interiority, a reminder to avoid superficiality of all kinds. As Arthur Green has noted, the term has a range of meanings and can be variously translated "core of being," "inward reality," or, when combined with another key term, *ḥayyim*, "inner life-point."[8] The *n'kudah* is a fundamental element of consciousness that, when recognized and nurtured, opens the individual to more profound awareness of self, the world, and divinity. Rabbi Aryeh Leib's interest is more phenomenological than metaphysical, more call to awareness than theological assertion. He invites his readers (originally his audience)[9] to develop sublime perception and inhabit a gracious, inclusive mode of seeing ever more securely, opening eyes to truth, the ultimate unity of all things. An important aspect of that truth is that the inner point was always within the individual who discovers it, waiting to be awakened; and the process of discovery and awakening never end. We already possess the *n'kudah p'nimit* but at the same time we need to work to make it manifest. Reaching for the *n'kudah p'nimit* is what today is often called a spiritual practice: the *n'kudah* is not a goal, a prize to be seized and captured, but a wisdom path of constant effort on which every milestone of success leads immediately to others, and in which no lapse is ever ruinous beyond recovery.

This brief introduction to the *S'fat Emet* will assist us in entering his thought on the Priestly Blessing, which departs radically from the traditional approach, and will be seen to speak to the questions that opened this essay[10]. He does this by a daring reframing of three key words: "face," "hands," and the final, all-important word of the Blessing, *shalom*.

Face

The Priestly Blessing refers twice to the "face [of God]," with the possessive pronoun, "His face" (*panav*): once in Numbers 6:25, and again in 6:26. In his comment to verse 25, "may the Eternal make His face shine upon you and be gracious to you," the S'fat Emet associates the word for "face," *panim*, with *p'nimiyut*, "inwardness." At first glance this move may seem unjustified philologically, a homiletical flight of fancy not grounded in the plain meaning of the words. But like many such exegetical associations, beginning with the classical midrash, what initially strikes the reader as an unconvincing act of lexical legerdemain may upon further consideration turn out to uncover deeper resonances of the text. The S'fat Emet directs us to

Deuteronomy 5:4, the verse introducing Deuteronomy's account of the revelation at Sinai, which states: "Face to face (*panim b'fanim*) the Eternal spoke to you on the mountain out of the fire." The language of "face to face" surely means to convey an unmediated encounter with God,[11] and that in turn suggests that the people confronted God in the totality of their being, without barriers, poses, or veils. One could hardly imagine a direct rendezvous with divinity with one's attention distracted. Indeed, that seems to be the point of the verse, even on the level of *p'shat*, the so-called plain or simple meaning of the text.[12] So while the notion of interiority surely underwent significant development over the millennia up to our own day, the S'fat Emet is persuasive in pointing to the Torah itself for the kernel of the notion that experiencing the divine Face directed toward oneself, shining and smiling, is meant to be a catalyst for total presence and touching the depths of one's own being.

By referencing Deuteronomy 5:4, Rabbi Aryeh Leib suggests that genuine revelation, aside from any specific communicative content (such as the words of the Decalogue), brings us face to face with the life-force of the cosmos—with, as he puts it, the source of vitality (*shoresh ha-ḥiyyut*). In the face-to-face encounter at Sinai, the people achieved a state of interiority, the fullness of their own being turned lovingly, joyously to the reality of supernal Presence. Since this is the Face that the Priestly Blessing pronounces as directed our way, it follows that, indeed, what is being elicited is our own inwardness.

The S'fat Emet then addresses the second occurrence of the word panav in Birkat Kohanim, "May the Eternal lift up His face toward you" (*yissa Adonai panav eilekha*, Numbers 6:25). The midrash[13] understands this as a promise to treat Israel favorably—that is, preferentially. This leads to a midrashic exploration of the question of how preferential treatment is consistent with divine justice. The midrash has God say: "How can I not treat Israel preferentially when they do more than expected, going above and beyond the requirements of the Torah's rules? I asked them to recite Grace after a bountiful, filling meal, but they bless Me even after the smallest morsel, even when they don't have enough to satisfy themselves and their families. In light of their graciousness to Me, how can I—God—not treat them with favor?"

Based on a tradition from his grandfather, the S'fat Emet frames this midrashic motif as associated with *p'nimiyut*, interiority. Awareness that food is a gift from God gives satisfaction and a sense of bounty, of blessedness. This promotes a feeling of satiety: the alertness to God's nourishing presence is a better channel of plenitude than the amount of food ingested. When we are connected to *p'nimiyut*, inwardness, and to *shoresh ha-ḥiyyut*, the source of vitality, then we know that food is divinity materialized, and that's what gives it its sustaining power. Eating can be an act that is primarily a quest for interiority, rather than a craving for taste and satisfaction of appetite. We are nourished by mindful awareness more than by ingestion. Eating is a paradigm of all our interactions with the physical world; what *p'nimiyut* calls for is a stance that does not seek to incorporate the objects of this world into the self. Rather than merely fulfilling desire, one can cultivate appreciative awareness of divinity in whatever it is that graciously provides nourishment. God indeed looks with favor at a person who constantly subordinates one's personal appetites in order to be attached to *p'nimiyut ha-ḥiyyut*, the vital force of interiority. Since the core being of such a person is Godly, occasional flaws and missteps are forgiven as not reflective of one's essence. So, responding to the midrash's question, God is quite justified in looking at us favorably when we refrain from chasing superficial desires, rather focusing on that "vital force of interiority." This is just what Numbers 6:26 promises: divine recognition of our own deep and sweet savoring of the Presence. That is not playing favorites—it is mutual attunement and sympathetic resonance, Divinity recognizing Itself.

Scripture often associates blessing with bounty and abundance, with images of overflowing granaries and flocks covering the hillsides.

There is a long and impressive interpretive tradition that understands the Priestly Blessing in precisely this way. Rashi's very first comment on Numbers 6:24 is: "May your possessions increase." This emphasis is not surprising in light of the fragile economic circumstances of biblical agrarian society, always on the edge. The situation in pre-war Poland was hardly much better: many Jews were never far from destitution, and starvation was a constant threat. Yet here, Rabbi Aryeh Leib completely reframes the meaning of blessing: there is no mention of material abundance, only of mindfulness, including the practice of mindful eating—which assures that every small morsel of food is savored not for gustatory delight but as divine gift, a delight of the spirit rather than the palate.

Hand

Another lexical focus of the *S'fat Emet* is the word "hands." His point of departure is Leviticus 9:22, "Aaron lifted his hands (*yadav*) toward the people and blessed them," which verse is understood by the midrash (as well as many modern commentators) to be identical with or closely associated with the Priestly Blessing.[15] Indeed, in rabbinic literature this priestly rite is often called *n'si·at kappayim*, "raising the hands (literally: palms)." Midrashic texts see this posture as one of channeling the Shekhinah toward the people; the Presence stands behind the priests and the effusion of blessing comes through the cracks formed by the characteristic finger-formation that the priests adopt. That is why the congregation is warned against gazing at the fingers of the priests: one should not look at the dazzling light of the Divine Presence.[16]

This approach, with its air of shamanistic transmission, is avoided by the *S'fat Emet*. Rather, he sees the raised hands as a posture of yielding, of receiving, of humility. He notes that Aaron's hands were lifted "toward the people"—which he takes as a gesture of gratitude, acknowledging that the greatness and the distinction he had just attained (the passage refers to the inauguration day of the priests and Tabernacle service) are due to the people as a whole. That is: in Leviticus 9:22 Aaron was saluting the people, acknowledging the centrality of their role in his own elevation. Although in Leviticus 9 Aaron had himself offered an entire series of sacrifices, he realized, at the end of the day, that God had granted him authority only because of the people—which fact he acknowledged by lifting his hands, saluting them. Greatness comes from, and requires constant nurturance from, surrender.

Everyone can and should take on the role of the priest, affirming and confirming blessing for those who are not aware that they are already blessed. To the extent of one's certainty—in the place of clarity about blessedness—one is invited to bless those who are not yet clear that they are also already blessed. The role of the priest is to empower others to face forward and bless still others, ultimately inviting all into the great chain of united being, the cascading flow of blessing.

Shalom

Our attention now moves to the last word of Birkat Kohanim: *shalom*, "peace." It is axiomatic that peace is not just the absence of conflict but in fact a positive state of wholeness or well-being. The *S'fat Emet* takes this insight further, noting that *shalom* is called "the vessel that embraces blessing,"[17] and that Shabbat—the blessed capstone of creation (Genesis 2:3), is also associated with *shalom*. (To this day, the practice in many communities is to greet one another with the words Shabbat Shalom.) This enables the S'fat Emet to call *shalom* "inner vitality" (*ḥiyyut p'nimit*[18]), the "point that gives life to every living being" (*n'kudah ha-notenet ḥayyim l'khol ḥai*), "the fulfillment of everything" (*sh'leimut ha-kol*). The Gerer employs his characteristic language of inwardness with generosity, linking it to *shalom* in a way that makes the Priestly Blessing a call to all-inclusiveness, an invitation to appreciate the soaring range and interconnectedness of all being. As Michael Fishbane has written in an important essay on the *S'fat Emet*, "to penetrate the mystery of *shabbes* is to bring to mindfulness the transcendental unity and totality of divine Reality that lies at the core of all things—despite the apparent multiplicity of the phenomenal world and the scattered perceptions of the unfocused mind."[19] Furthermore, he states: "The proper perception of divine unity behind the phenomenal obscurities of the world is the task incumbent upon the spiritual seeker in the here and now."[20] It is necessary "for the seeker to detach himself from the outer world of flux and form, and devote himself to the divine principle of vitality (*ha-bittul el ko·aḥ ha-ḥiyyut*), at the still center of all being. Only in this way may a person escape the frenetic externality of earthly existence—and return to God, who is the deep presence of the All in all [things]."[21] Fishbane notes that on Shabbat, "which has the stillness and wholeness of *shalom*, one perceives how 'all things complete' or perfect one another."[22]

It is striking that all this is accomplished in the *S'fat Emet* without recourse to the technical language of Kabbalah; some readers may be familiar with the connection between Shabbat and the last divine manifestation or *s'firah*, known as Malkhut ("Kingdom"). But the Gerer's exposition does not depend on this knowledge, and in some ways the teachings do their work of consciousness-transformation better without it.

It would not have been at all difficult for Rabbi Aryeh Leib to have provided precise kabbalistic terminology for his ideas, but he chose not to do so. Rather than definition, all is allusion and gesture. The fertile ground is encircled but is not surveyed with instruments. This may be to some degree a matter of disposition and sentiment—his style is essentially poetic and midrashic, not technical—but it also is utterly determined by the essence of his views. For the inner point is to be nurtured, not manufactured. It is not a formula to be replicated, but an elusive quality that is slowly teased out of the soul and grasped as the fabric of reality. It cannot be measured by quantity or produced by algorithm; it emerges gradually, if at all.

Summary and Conclusions

The thread that unites the teachings of the S'fat Emet on Birkat Kohanim is that of interiority. The quest for the inner point, the *n'kudah p'nimit*, invites us to achieve suspended moments out of quotidian time when we inhabit the self more deeply and see above more acutely. The *n'kudah p'nimit* enables us to obtain a purchase on reality beyond the accidents of our geographical location, and to envision a self more richly aware of its sacred origins and vital possibilities. The focus is on God's "face" (*panav*), but rather than engaging the literal, anthropomorphic sense of the word, the S'fat Emet consistently links it with *p'nimiyut*, inwardness. There is also a focus on the "hands" of the priests (as in Leviticus 9:22), but here too the S'fat Emet confounds our expectations. One might have anticipated an exploration of "laying on of hands" and the power of hands to channel desired beneficence. Instead, hands elevated are a posture of receptivity and surrender, emblematic recognition that all our attainments derive from the One. The raised hands beckon the people to mindfulness and attachment to the cosmic unity. The hands of the priest tilt upward, above the head, opening the vessels of receptivity more capaciously, more generously, more robustly. We are bidden to loosen the hold that the surface appearance of things has on one's consciousness, to go both deeper and higher than the plane of the obvious, escaping the tyranny of the facade and its dazzle, linking heaven and earth.

It is striking that this approach leaves little room for a more conventional understanding of blessing as relational transaction, where the one giving the blessing bestows something (material or spiritual) onto the recipient. The S'fat Emet's focus is resolutely on the monistic aspects of the Birkat Kohanim: the task of the priests is to draw the people into the state of unity. This unity is the *n'kudah p'nimit*—the focal point, the point where everything comes into true perspective, where all things can be seen in bare integrity without distracting casings.

Nowhere does the S'fat Emet construe the blessing as promising a good in the sense of an advantage or commodity, whether material or spiritual. The Priestly Blessing is more solicitation than transmission. Since all that is offered is a mode of perception, the blesser cannot convey what he or she does not already have. Even more arrestingly, the blesser cannot bestow what the *receiver* does not already have, within, waiting to be awakened and cultivated.

The inner point is nestled in each of the three foundational axes of being: space, time, and person. Within each axis, the inner point is elect, chosen, distinct, special. At the very same time, the specialness is precisely the ability to transform everything else, to see the supposedly unchosen as brimming with the glow of emergent possibility. Time and again the S'fat Emet invokes the rabbinic exegetical maxim: *kol ha-yotzei min ha-k'lal…l'ammeid al ha-k'lal yatza*, "Whatever has been taken out of a general category, has been taken to teach about the category as a whole." Originally this appears as a technical hermeneutical rule,[23] but the S'fat Emet deploys it as an overarching theological principle: election is always for the non-elect. Moreover, it is not just for the benefit of the non-elect, but is in fact to enable a new view of what is perceived to be the non-sacred, the common, what remained in the cosmic urn and was apparently left over by the divine choosing Hand. Shabbat is for the week; the priesthood is for Israel; Israel's election is for the world; and the Holy Temple is to transform our view of place. The expansiveness we seek comes not so much by widening boundaries as by rising to a place beyond worldly metrics, finding a purchase on reality that in its infinitesimal smallness holds limitless capaciousness.

In this light, it is not surprising that the S'fat Emet does not emphasize the unique qualities of the lineage of the Aaronide priesthood. Aaron and his sons are chosen to give blessing; that is true. But that chosenness is little more than the confidence to welcome others into the ever-expanding blessed circle. Only when the priests realize that their election is grounded in the supposedly non-elect, only when the priests surrender their sense of specialness—only then do they justify and secure their election. At the end of the day, we are all priests. By engaging in humble surrender to God and the putative "other"; by realizing that we must work to cultivate the sublime spirit, the inner point; and at the same time mindful that our attainments must immediately be offered back as gift—by this constant shuttling between struggle and assurance, between achievement and surrender, do we find ourselves worthy to be the resting-place for the name of God.

The view of the S'fat Emet is clearly mystical, but this is an unusual variety of mysticism. The doors of perception are flung open and what is revealed is not a cosmos of angels and demons, not a dewy paradise, nor even an intricate array of ten-spoked kabbalistic wheels-within-wheels. What comes into view is the world as it is and the person as he or she is: beheld in clarity, in sober truth, the better to do what we already know needs to be done, and to struggle to be what we hope to discover we already really are. That is truly a blessing.

NOTES

[1] Jeffrey H. Tigay, annotations on Exodus in *The Jewish Study Bible*, ed. Adele Berlin and Marc Zvi Bretler (Oxford and New York: Oxford University Press, 2004), p. 171.

[2] Jacob Milgrom, *The JPS Torah Commentary: Numbers* (Philadelphia: Jewish Publication Society, 1990), p. 360.

[3] Ibid., "Excursus 13: The Priestly Blessing," p. 360.

[4] See, for example, Genesis 20:7 and 17, where Abraham prays on behalf of Abimelekh; and Numbers 12:13, where Moses prays on behalf of his sister Miriam. The former instance uses the verbal root *pei-lamed-lamed*; the latter, *tzadi-ayin-kof*.

[5] In this essay, I will refer to him by his full name, as "Rabbi Yehudah Aryeh Leib," or simply as "the Gerer," or as the S'fat Emet.

[6] *A Passion for Truth* is the title of Heschel's 1973 work on the Kotzker rebbe.

[7] Arthur Green, *The Language of Truth: The Torah Commentary of the S'fat Emet, Rabbi Yehudah Leib Alter of Ger* (Philadelphia: Jewish Publication Society, 1998), pp. xlvi–xlviii.

[8] Green, *The Language of Truth*, "Introduction," pp. xv–lviii. The discussion of the term *n'kudah* can be found on pp. xxxi–xxxix. My thanks to Rabbi Jonathan Slater for a fruitful discussion on *n'kudah p'nimit*.

[9] For an analysis of how the original orally delivered Yiddish discourses were shaped into the published Hebrew texts, see Daniel Reiser and Ariel Evan Mayse, "The Last Sermon of R. Judah Leib Alter of Ger and the Role of Yiddish for the Study of Hasidic Sermons" (Hebrew), in *Kabbalah: Journal for the Study of Jewish Mystical Texts* 30 (2013), pp. 127-160.

[10] In keeping with the traditional Jewish practice of referring to authors bn y the names of their most famous works, "the S'fat Emet" in this essay refers not just to the book but also to its author, Rabbi Yehudah Aryeh Leib Alter. The title of the book is italicized; the phrase "S'far Emet" used to denote the book's author is printed in Roman type.

[11] Cf. Exodus 33:11, speaking of Moses' direct encounter with God.

[12] The point is so striking that the very next verse appears to qualify and perhaps even contradict it. As Bernard M. Levinson writes, the following verse ("I [Moses] stood between the Eternal and you at that time to convey God's word to you") "neither continues nor supplements v. 4 but presents an alternative perspective inconsistent with" it. Levinson's comment appears in his work on Deuteronomy in the *Jewish Study Bible* (supra, n. 1), p. 374. It is as if the notion of each individual Israelite having an unmediated encounter with God was so radical that the text could not let it stand. This of course does nothing to undercut the *S'fat Emet's* point—and, in fact, supports it.

[13] At Bemidbar Rabbah 11:7; cf. B. Berakhot 20b.

[14] See Deuteronomy 8:10, "When you have eaten your fill, give thanks to the Eternal your God."

[15] For one example among many, see Sifrei Bemidbar §39.

[16] See, e.g., the midrashic comments based on Song of Songs 2:9, where the words *meitzitz bein ha-ḥarakhim* ("he peeps through the latticework") are immediately glossed with the phrase *mi-bein etzbe'oteihem shel ha-kohanim*, e.g. at Bemidbar Rabbah 11:2 or Shir Ha-shirim Rabbah 2:24.

[17] M. Uktzin 3:12.

[18] The original text reads *ḥiyyut p'nimiyut*, which I take for a typographical error for the text as presented here.

[19] Michael Fishbane, "Transcendental Consciousness and Stillness in the Mystical Theology of R. Yehudah Aryeh Leib of Gur," in *Sabbath: Idea, History, Reality*, ed. Gerald J. Blidstein (Beer Sheva: Ben-Gurion University of the Negev Press, 2004), pp. 119–129; quotation appears on pp. 120–121. *Shabbes* is a variant on the more usual *shabbos*, the Yiddish for Sabbath.

[20] Ibid., p. 123.

[21] Ibid., p. 124.

[22] Ibid.

[23] It is one of the Thirteen Hermeneutic Principles of Rabbi Ishmael, which introduces the tannaitic midrash on Leviticus known as the Sifra.

The Intense and Splendiferous Light of the Shekhinah
as Reflected in the Ancient Priestly Blessing

Admiel Kosman

Translated from the Hebrew by Martin S. Cohen

In the footsteps of Martin Buber, who generally understood myths as fragments of spiritual events that took place in the inner lives of the ancients, I would like to direct my focus in this essay on something that the tradition forbids us to gaze on at all—that is, the priests as they bless the people with the words preserved at Numbers 6:24–26 and known liturgically as Birkat Kohanim ("The Priestly Blessing")—in an attempt to reconstruct some sense of the original core conception of a ritual that has morphed forward through many different versions and iterations over the course of the many years that separate the biblical period from our own day.[1]

Nevertheless, in contradistinction to Buber (who was at constant loggerheads with the intellectual world of his day, a world that strongly favored a positivist approach that discouraged accepting at face value information culled from ancient documents), I tend these days—after spending about three decades studying the aggadic testimony of Jewish antiquity—to accept this kind of material at face value, and thus to presume that this kind of ancient testimony was possessed in the distant past of a fully real, even tangible, dimension that can under certain circumstances still be recovered today. (Buber, like so many rationalist thinkers that preceded him, felt obliged to consider such information as merely metaphoric—that is to say, as the record of internal feelings or events; but that is precisely the approach I do *not* wish to take.)

This study, which shall concern the belief that the divine indwelling (the Shekhinah) becomes physically present when the *kohanim* bless the people, will serve as an excellent example of the approach to ancient texts I wish to set forward for my readers to consider.

Rabbi Judah, the son of Rabbi Naḥmani, lived in third-century C.E. Galilee and a tradition is preserved in the Talmud in his name, to the effect that "there are three groups of individuals whose eyesight becomes dim because of what they have gazed upon…[and one of these is made up of those who,] when the Temple still stood, would gaze upon the *kohanim* when they stood on their platform and blessed Israel using the explicit [four-letter] name [of God].[2]

This source is undoubtedly dependent on ancillary traditions according to which the Shekhinah hovered over the *kohanim* when they blessed the people in God's name.[3] This tradition is also cited by Rashi who, using the following language, explains the Mishnah's remark that one of the differences in practice between the synagogues of antiquity and the Jerusalem Temple was that, although in the Temple the priests would lift their hands up over their heads, in the synagogue ritual the priests would only lift their arms to shoulder-height:

> *Above their heads.* [Why was it that the *kohanim* in the Temple lifted their hands up over their heads?] Because [it was only there, in the Temple that] the priests would bless the people using the explicit [four-letter] name, in which context *the Shekhinah hovered directly over their knuckles.*[4]

This tradition was hardy an invention of the sages of medieval Ashkenaz, nor does Rashi suggest that it was. In my opinion, it should properly be understood as a reflex of an old midrash deriving from the Land of Israel and preserved in the ancient collection of texts relating to the Song of Songs, Shir Ha-shirim Rabbah. There, we find the following:

*My lover is like a gazelle or a young buck. And suddenly there he
was, standing behind our walls, watching through the windows,
peering through the latticework. And then my beloved called out
and said to me, "Come, my beloved, my beauty, and hurry off."*
Rabbi Yosi son of Rabbi Ḥanina [said]…"Standing behind
our walls" refers to the walls of synagogues and study halls;
"watching through the windows" means that [God is present]
between the shoulders of the *kohanim*; "peering through the
latticework" means that [God is present] amidst the fingers
of the *kohanim*. And [then we read:] "And then my beloved
called out and said to me." What [exactly] did he say to me?
"May the Eternal bless you and guard you" (Numbers 6:24).[5]

This text, however, brings another question in its wake: if the
ancients understood this concept of the presence of the Shekhinah
as something fully spiritual and abstract, thus as something lacking
all physicality and sensual reality, then why should it be forbidden to
gaze at the *kohanim* when they pronounce the blessing—let alone to
the point of threatening any who dare do so with dimmed eyesight?[6]

From this jumping-off point, I would like to proceed now to put
forward an argument that I know will, at least at first, sound far-
fetched. Nevertheless, I find myself unable to think about traditions
that have come down to us from antiquity in any other way; and so
I wish to propose that the concept of the presence of the Shekhinah
mentioned above be taken neither metaphorically nor poetically, but
simply as a statement of sensually perceptible reality. And it seems
reasonable to me also to assume that this ancient experience of divine
presence was accompanied by a parallel experience of effulgent light—a
phenomenon that, as I shall attempt to demonstrate presently, is widely
taken in many different cultures as indicative of divine presence.

If I am correct in this assumption, it seems logical to suppose
that the obligation to avert one's eyes from the priests pronouncing

the blessing, prohibiting one from gazing upon the *kohanim* as they pronounced the Priestly Blessing, was not understood by the ancients as an expression of polite deference prompted by respect and awe, but rather as a prohibition that derived directly from the simple fact that it is not possible for human eyes to gaze directly at the source of such powerful, blinding light without coming to harm. It was for this specific reason that tradition tells us, almost in the style of simple reportage, that the eyesight of those who dared to gaze upon the *kohanim* as they pronounced the blessing became noticeably weakened—the Hebrew literally means "his eyes dimmed"—as a result of staring into the blinding effulgence.[7]

I also believe that it is possible to see, in another of the traditions of our classical sages, a kind of oblique reference to a similar feature of life in the Temple precincts witnessed in its day by many. This tradition, preserved in Vayikra Rabbah, tells us that the face of the High Priest "burned like torches ablaze when the holy spirit descended upon him" on Yom Kippur.[8]

The Bible itself reports several similar events. When, for example, Moses encountered the divine Presence "in a fiery flame from within the bush" (Exodus 3:2)—which is to say that the bush, which "was not consumed," was the source of the fire—the narrative also reports immediately that "Moses covered his face, for he was afraid to gaze directly at God" (3:6). It is obviously possible to understand Moses' instant response of covering his face as an expression of respect toward God and nothing else, but my point is that it is no less reasonable to read the text as reporting an instance in which Moses was confronted with light of such awesome intensity that he naturally feared that its blinding effulgence might well damage his eyesight—perhaps even permanently.[9]

Later, we hear that Moses *himself* was granted this kind of photic effulgence—which image I believe readers are intended to take literally—when the Bible's most holy of men began to exude light, which actually shone off him in rays. Well known, of course, is the text that relates how Moses, after descending from Mount Sinai, "knew not that the skin of his face was giving off rays [of light]" (Exodus 34:29). The point there is that this new development was an immediate effect of Moses having spoken directly with God, as the text specifically says that the light began to emanate from his skin "when He [i.e., God] spoke to him" (Exodus 34:30).[10] And the same verse also says that Aaron and the Israelites "feared approaching him."[11]

In another incident, we find that the angelic visitors who come to see Lot in Sodom are able to inflict blindness—the ultimate "dimming" of one's eyesight—on the unruly mob that surrounds Lot's home.[12] The implication here is that Lot's would-be attackers were struck with blindness caused by a sudden effulgence of light that flowed directly to them from the visitors. And we may compare to this the story of the prophet Elisha smiting the armies of Aram with blindness.[13]

It also bears recalling that God was conceived of in ancient times as being visible as pure photic effulgence. This assertion can be demonstrated with reference to many different passages in the Bible, but for the sake of brevity I will only point out two: "For with You is the source of life; in Your light shall we see light" (Psalm 36:10) and "The sun shall not provide you light by day nor shall the shining moon illumine you, but instead shall the Eternal be your everlasting light, your God [whose existence is] your splendor" (Isaiah 60:19).[14]

Indeed, it is in light of such passages that biblical scholars have interpreted the expression found uniquely in the Priestly Blessing, "May the Eternal illumine for you the divine face" (Numbers 6:25); and similarly the text of Psalm 67:2, "God shall act beneficently toward us and shall bless us; God shall illumine the divine face for us, *selah*."[15] In fact, biblical scholars have pointed out that this concept actually pre-dates the biblical text, insofar as an enveloping aura of shining light was already attributed to the gods in Mesopotamian texts at the end of the Assyrian period (i.e., the seventh century B.C.E).[16]

In the writings of our ancient sages we also find many similar expressions of the same idea, but here I will only mention a few of them. Rabbi Samuel bar Naḥman, for example, is cited as having remarked that "the blessed Holy One self-swathed in light as though it were a robe, and the brightness of [the consequent] divine splendor shone forth from one end of the universe to the other."[17] And in the Yerushalmi we find the interesting statement to the effect that once, when Rabbi Eliezer and Rabbi Joshua were studying Torah, there suddenly "came down from heaven fire that surrounded them."[18] In my opinion, this story is about a kind of spiritual light that enveloped the sages with a kind of body-halo that, instead of encircling their heads, actually covered their entire bodies.[19] And a final example of this kind of story is preserved in the Bavli, where it is reported that once, when Rabbi Yoḥanan found himself in a gloomy room, he simply "exposed his arm and light streamed out [into the dark space]."[20] Concerning the talmudic stories that feature light flowing out of the body of a holy individual: I do not think that it is reasonable to understand these texts other than literally and simply, nor do I believe there are reasonable grounds for considering these stories as mere allegories intended poetically to illustrate their subjects' fine inner virtues.

I will turn to several brief anecdotes that demonstrate that such discussions continued well into the Middle Ages. But first I would like to highlight the common theme shared by the first two sources I am going to cite—which they also share with other texts by medieval kabbalists. It is the case, as Moshe Idel concluded after analyzing them himself, that "light appears [in kabbalistic Jewish texts of this specific sort] in connection with the activity of writing or of combining the letters of the Ineffable Name in writing."[21] This point is crucial for my analysis as well because, as I have tried to demonstrate, these kabbalistic lessons have their roots in the talmudic tradition relating to the use of the ineffable four-letter name of God in the Priestly Blessing.[22] Indeed, just as Rashi understood from the midrash, they are tightly tied to the traditions

regarding the physical presence of the Shekhinah made perceptible by
the appearance of intensely splendiferous brilliance of light or fire.

Now, to the sources themselves. Rabbi Natan ben Saadiah Harar,
the author of *Shaarei Tzedek* and a student of Abraham Abulafia,[23]
describes the moment that this wondrous light appeared in his home
once after midnight:

> The third night, after midnight, I nodded off a little, quill in
> hand and paper on my knees. Then I noticed that the candle
> was about to go out. I rose to put it right, as oftentimes
> happens to a person awake. Then I saw that the light
> continued. I was greatly astonished, as though, after close
> examination, I saw that it issued *from myself*. I said, "I do not
> believe it." I walked to and fro all through the house and,
> behold, the light was with me. I lay on a couch and covered
> myself up, and behold, the light was with me all the while.[24]

Similar to this text is a parallel account by Rabbi Isaac of Acre, who
writes as follows in his *Otzar Ḥayyim*:

> Moreover, in the third watch, when I was half asleep, I saw the
> house in which I was sleeping full of a light which was very
> sweet and pleasant, for this light was not like the light which
> emanates from the sun, but was [bright] as the light of day,
> which is the light of dawn before the sun rises. And this light
> was before me for about three hours, and I hastened to open
> my eyes to see whether the dawn had broken or not, so that
> I might rise and pray, and I saw that it was yet night, and I
> returned to my sleep with joy, and after I rose from my bed in
> order to pray, I suddenly saw a secret of the letter *alef*.[25]

From the traditions of medieval Ashkenaz, I shall reference only the
short anecdote from *Sefer Ḥasidim* that describes how one of the local
ḥasidim was washing himself in a bathtub when suddenly "a shaft of light
smacked the head of this righteous man while he was still in the water."[26]

***

Testimonies from ancient and medieval times like the ones cited above must be paired with the large number of extant non-Jewish sources— both literary and artistic—to which they are parallel. Indeed, we can find such parallels in cultures that derive from every corner of the world, including different sorts of shamanistic religions, in Central American culture,[27] in Hinduism,[28] in Buddhism,[29] in Christianity,[30] and in Islam.[31] Common to all of these passages is the depiction of the holy individual who experiences the physically real indwelling of divine presence (what Jewish sources call the Shekhinah) as a flaming lamp, as a pillar surrounded by fire, or as someone from whose head radiates a halo of light.[32]

As stated at the beginning of this essay, I have come to believe that Jewish tradition (in this respect similar to many other world cultures) has preserved accurately the original ideational framework that underlay the ancient ritual of the Priestly Blessing, by maintaining the recollection of that ritual as an entirely sensory experience of the intense light upon which no mortal, or at least no "regular" mortal, may gaze.[33] And I have also come to believe that there is no rational way to interpret these traditions, at least in their ancient settings, as merely abstraction and metaphor.

***

I wish to embellish my argument with a telling anecdote. A close friend tells me that once, back in the 1990s, she regularly attended the classes of Yemima Avital, a spiritual teacher whose method contained many kabbalistic elements.[34] In the course of one of those classes, my friend tells me that she lifted up her head from her notebook and saw a very strong blue light adhering to the wall facing her, just in front of which Yemima was standing. My friend further says that she

was so shocked by the experience that she automatically lowered her
head and looked directly into her notebook, whereupon she heard
Yemima's voice addressing her personally and by name, asking "Did
you see something on the wall?"

* * *

Before I conclude, I would like to address a question that flows
naturally from the argument put forward in this essay but which I
have not yet discussed: So what? Even if we were to accept as proven
all the suggestions made above, we are still left with the challenge of
explaining the meaning of these supernatural occurrences and their
significance for Jews today who have no personal experience of any
of this and who, even if they *were* to have such experiences, might
well respond by shrugging their shoulders. Would that gesture imply
a lack of faith or a lack of certainty? Since such a discussion could
easily become very long and complex, however, I will limit myself
here to a line of thought that strikes me as the most potentially useful
for members of our own generation facing the challenge inherent in
these supernatural phenomena (insofar as they can be demonstrated
to constitute actual spiritual events and not mere illusory tricks).

    Given the intense emotion that history has embedded in the harsh
story of Jewish efforts to find a place for Judaism among the religions
of the world (and this is particularly so if we take into account the
painful history of Jewish-Christian and Jewish-Muslim relations in
the medieval period), I wish to begin by saying clearly that I am not
proposing anything here that is especially incompatible with what
one might hear in traditional Jewish circles. Indeed, many medieval
Jewish sages adopted a similar stance toward the supernatural
phenomena that they perceived as functions of the presence and
power of the holy individual.

Of all those medievals I could cite, I will quote here the words of Rabbi Joseph Albo (1380–1444),[35] who wrote as follows in his masterwork, *Sefer Ha-ikkarim*:

> A prophet who offers a [supernatural] sign to demonstrate the legitimacy of his prophetic calling—for example, one who "proves" his status by walking through fire without being burnt or by means of some similar stunt—has, in so doing, only really offered a sign that he is the kind of individual capable of provoking miraculous signs and wonders. Such, however, should not be taken to constitute verification of his status as a true prophet. Nor, needless to say, should it be taken to constitute a sign of legitimate ability to offer a [new] Torah to the world, because, indeed, there are many instances of wonders and signs of that ilk being provoked by sorcery or magic, or being performed by truly righteous individuals who nonetheless were not prophets. Examples of this are given, for example, in the Talmud, where we read about the effort of Rabbi Eliezer to demonstrate the correctness of his position by successfully ordering a carob tree to uproot itself or commanding a stream of water to reverse the direction of its flow. But even in that instance they specifically did not fix the *halakhah* in accordance with his opinion, [because such wondrous signs were not deemed to constitute evidence of prophetic status].[36]

Albo's argument is as follows: the fact that a holy individual can perform (or at least provoke) a miracle—or, as we today would say, the fact that supernatural phenomena appear to attend a specific holy individual—merely demonstrates that that person is someone "capable of provoking miraculous signs and wonders." In other words, such signs merely demonstrate that the individual capable of provoking them is not a "regular" individual like the rest of us, but rather someone close enough to God for divine behavior in his ambit specifically *not* to be bound by the regular laws of nature. To make this specific point, Albo brings the example of Rabbi Eliezer ben Hyrcanus who, in the context of his famous debate regarding the halakhic status of the specific kind of clay oven called an "Akhnai" oven, was able to provoke remarkable examples of "miraculous" behavior—and yet his views were still not accepted as authoritative based on those supernatural "proofs," and precisely because it does not go without saying that even an individual capable of such feats was necessarily a legitimate spokesperson for God. Therefore, there is no specific reason to believe the claims even of such a wonder-worker to have received direct instructions from God regarding a new revelation merely because he or she was able to perform a supernatural feat.

It seems obvious that Albo, a medieval well ensconced in his own world, was aiming his remarks directly at Christians and Muslims. Seen in this light, his argument—if I may restate it in unambiguous modern terms—is simply this: even if we accept that Jesus or Muhammed were holy men who were able to provoke impressive supernatural events in their followers' presence, this ability alone does not grant them the right to promulgate a *torah* different from the Torah revealed to Israel at Sinai. Therefore we, the Jewish people, are justified in rejecting these "new" revelations as legitimate *torah* from God.[37]

Basing myself on Albo's formulation, I can formulate a response in the classical Jewish style to the issue at hand as follows. Traditional Judaism recognizes that there are, in every corner of the world, holy individuals in whose ambit supernatural occurrences of various sorts may occasionally occur. We there have no specific obligation, both as moderns living in an age of ever-advancing technology and also as faithful Jews, to respond to reports of such incidents in knee-jerk fashion or by denying their possibility. Indeed, may we reasonably accept as possible the reality of holy individuals possessed of supernatural abilities, without abandoning our integrity.

On the other hand, we also recognize that the intellectually and spiritually naïve in our midst may be so overwhelmed with such supernatural events that they find themselves almost involuntarily swept along in the wake of such holy individuals to the point at which they conclude that their spiritual teachings "must" constitute absolute truths. (In such category, for example, would be those naïfs who feel drawn to Sufi mystics, even to the point of abandoning their own faith for the sake of embracing Islamic truth instead.) The "correct" Jewish response to such individuals need not involve an absolute denial of the holiness of the Sufi sage in question. Rather, since there is no compelling reason *not* to embrace both the fact that some specific Sufi sage is a truly holy person *and* that he or she has come to that stage of holiness in the Sufi context because that is the religious framework in which that individual lives and labors, it stands to reason that an individual can grow into holiness in the context of any spiritual society, faith group, ideological school, or religious civilization. However, the fact that an individual attains holiness—even to the point of being rationally considered to be a true intimate of God—does not necessarily imply that the ideology, religion, or religious sect to which he or she belongs *itself* was vouchsafed the authentic word of God more powerfully or really than any other such group.

On the other hand, accepting that there are holy individuals in the world—and that such virtuous people wholly given over to the service of God are plausibly to be found among every people or faith group across the globe—is a profoundly meaningful step for modern (or, more precisely, post-modern) believers to take. Such a step can open wide the gate to new approaches to the worship of God, regardless of the ethnicity or religious context from which they derive. Indeed, the sole requirement for such a role in our lives should be the holiness, virtue, and integrity of the teacher—none of which should be supposed to be the exclusive province of only one group or sect.

Perhaps one could say the same thing using the language of Hasidism. Indeed, in light of the well-known hasidic belief that the sparks of divine holiness are scattered all across the world, we could conclude that one may well seek to come close to the service of God in any place in which individuals of personal merit and virtue gather, regardless of which faith group they belong to…as long as they prove themselves able to raise up at least some of the holy sparks that are to scattered in every corner of the sublunary world.[38]

NOTES

[1] With regard to Buber's belief regarding the myth as a remnant of some sort of spiritual event, see in far more detail the sources cited in my essay "*Shamati Mimori: Al Musag Ha-masoret V'al Ha-mashma·ut Ha-p'nimit Shel Mitzvat Talmud Torah*," in *Dimmui* 27 (2005–2006), pp. 4–40.

[2] B. Ḥagigah 16a.

[3] The clear implication is that the priests used the ineffable name (i.e., the Tetragrammaton) when pronouncing the blessing; cf. M. Sotah 7:6, which explicitly notes that "in the Temple, the name [i.e., the four-letter name of God] was pronounced out loud." In other words, none of the traditional circumlocutions was employed. And cf. also the interesting ideas regarding Birkat Kohanim set forward by Michael Schneider in his *Mareh Kohen: Tei-ofaniah, Apotei-ozah V'tei¬ologia Binarit Bein He-Hagut Ha-kohanit Bi-t'kufat Ha-bayit Ha-sheini L'vein Ha-mistikah Ha-y'hudit Ha-k'dumah* (Los Angeles: Cherub Press, 2012), p. 114. Regarding the pronunciation of the Tetragrammaton in late Second Temple times, see Gedalyahu Alon's *Meḥkarim B'toldot Yisrael Bimei Bayit Sheini U-vi-t'kufat Ha-mishnah V'ha-talmud* (Tel Aviv: Ha-kibbutz Ha-me¬uḥad, 1957), vol. 1, pp. 194-205.

[4] Rashi to B. Sotah 38a, s.v. *u-va-mikdash*, referencing M. Sotah 7:6. As far as the custom today goes, the Tosafot (commenting on B. Ḥagigah 16a, s.v. *ba-kohanim*) follow Rashi and instruct us that the fear that "the eyes of the onlooker may be dimmed" only pertained in ancient times and in the Temple, but that even in antiquity there was no need for anyone outside the Temple to worry that someone who gazed upon the priests as they pronounce the blessing risked poor vision, let alone blindness. Nevertheless, even though the *halakhah* forbidding gazing on the priests was limited to the Temple, it remains customary not to gaze upon the priests as they pronounce the blessing, lest one be distracted by some unusual feature of the *kohanim's* appearance and as a result be unable fully to concentrate mindfully on the blessing as it is spoken aloud. (Cf. also in this regard M. Megillah 4:7.) In addition, see Rabbi Israel Ha-kohen of Radin's comment in his *Mishnah B'rurah* to S.A. Oraḥ Ḥayyim 128:23, §89: "From a strictly legal standpoint, all that is forbidden is overly focusing on the *kohanim* in a way that might distract one's attention [from the blessing at hand], but a quick glance is permitted. This is so because, when the Temple stood, they [the *kohanim*] would pronounce the blessing using the explicit [four-letter] name [of God], whereupon the Shekhinah would hover over their hands, and it was in that specific context that even a casual glance [at them] was forbidden; but this has no pertinence today. Nevertheless, it remains customary [to avert one's eyes from the *kohanim* as they pronounce the blessing and] not to look at them at all, as a kind of homage to Temple practice." It seems likely to me that a comment in the Zohar (II 147a) was probably influential in the retention of the custom to not

look at all. There, Rabbi Yitzḥak asks: "If one cannot actually see the Shekhinah,
why should it matter [if one looks at the priests as they pronounce the blessing
or not]?" The Zohar's answer is that the Tetragrammaton is allusively present
amidst the priests' fingers even today—and that one should therefore not gaze
on them out of a sense of awe, and also because one who would dare gaze upon
them would be guilty of displaying unwarranted insolence toward heaven. (On
the specific custom of the *kohanim* spreading out their fingers in the traditional
way, see Alon, *Meḥkarim*, pp. 181-182.) It is also well worth noting that there
were kabbalists who attempted to re-create the version of the Priestly Blessing
that was in use in the Temple. Indeed, we know that the kabbalists of Beit-El
(a group with origins in the eighteenth century and still in existence), following
the lesson of Rabbi Isaac Luria (1534–1572) as preserved in the *Sha·ar Ha-
kavvanot* of Rabbi Ḥayyim Vital (1543–1620), required that the *kohanim* lift
their hands over their heads when pronouncing the blessing, just as was the
practice in the Temple. (Regarding this practice and its theoretical justification,
see Naftali Hoffner, *N'si·at Kappayim V'taḥanun* [Tel Aviv: Mossad Eliezer
Hoffner, 5761 [2000–2001], p. 80.) Later, the custom of averting one's eyes from
the priests as they pronounced the blessing was considered by some halakhic
decisor requisite as *halakhah l'ma·aseh*, as is obvious from the comment of Rabbi
Shalom Mordechai Schwadron in his *Da·at Torah* to S.A. Oraḥ Ḥayyim 128:23
(ed. Jerusalem, 5718 [1957–1958], pp. 177–178). He bases himself there on the
fact that Rabbi Abraham of Narbonne in his *Sefer Ha-eshkol* (ed. Halberstadt,
5628 [1867–1868], part 1, *Hilkhot Birkat Kohanim*, p. 30) does not formulate
the prohibition of gazing on the hands of the priests in the past tense, but uses
instead present-tense verbs—suggesting that he understood the prohibition of
gazing on the Shekhinah to remain in full force in his own day (and cf. the
comment in the *Naḥal Eshkol* commentary by Rabbi Tzvi Auerbach [*ad locum*
§3] in this regard).

⁵ Shir Ha-shirim Rabbah 2:2 (commenting on Song of Songs 2:9–10), s.v. *davar
aḥeir: domeh*. And cf. the text as it appears in Shir Ha-shirim Rabbah (=*Midrash
Ḥazit*) 2:21, ed. Shimshon Dunsky (Jerusalem: Dvir, 1980), p. 67.

⁶ See my discussion above of B. Ḥagigah 16a.

⁷ The phrase *einav keihot* appears in the Talmud at B. Ḥagigah 16a, and cf. the comments
of the Tosafot *ad locum*, s.v. *ba-kohanim bi-z'man she-beit ha-mikdash kayyam*.

⁸ See Vayikra Rabbah 21:12, ed. Mordechai Margoliot (1953–1960; rpt. New
York: Jewish Theological Seminary, 1993), p. 493.

⁹ Regarding a similar progression of ideas, beginning with the sensory
apprehension of the otherwise ethereal notions of *kavod* (taken here as
something no less tangible than any ordinary material object) and *hod* (the
term in this context denoting a deity's halo of light) and leading directly to the
abstract use of both terms to denote the God of Israel in the biblical context, see
Menachem Haran's *Mikra V'olamo: Mivḥar Meḥkarim Sifrutiyim V'historiyim*
(Jerusalem: Magnes Press, 2009), p. 408, n. 13.

[10] The text could also be read as "when he [Moses] spoke to Him [i.e., God]," but the point is the same. Perhaps the midrash is suggesting that Moses, who earlier on (i.e., at the burning bush) was unable to gaze upon the effulgence of the Shekhinah, later ascended to a higher plane when he was permitted to encounter God directly when receiving the Torah atop Mount Sinai. It is important to note that, according to this line of exegetical thinking, the language used to describe the shining-forth of Moses' skin implies that henceforth he himself *would* be able to gaze upon the effulgent light of the Shekhinah; cf. the midrash preserved in Devarim Rabbah 11:3 that reads: "Isaac said to Moses, 'I am greater than you, for I [willingly] stretched out my neck atop the altar and [at that moment] saw the face of the Shekhinah.' Moses responded, 'I have ascended to greater heights than you, for your eyes dimmed when you gazed upon the face of the Shekhinah but I encountered the Shekhinah face to face and my eyes did not grow dim.' [And how do we know that Isaac's eyes grew dim?] From the verse in which it is explicitly written, 'And it came to pass that Isaac grew old and his eyes grew too dim to see' (Genesis 27:1). [Instead of reading the Hebrew *mei-re'ot* as translated here 'to see,' take it to read that his eyes grew dim '*from* seeing.'] And from seeing what did Isaac's eyes grow dim, if not from seeing the Shekhinah? [And whence do we know this about Moses?] From the verse that reads 'And Moses knew not that the skin of his face [was giving off] rays [of light]' (Exodus 34:29)."

[11] It is worth noting, however, that several Christian exegetes, including Jerome (who was simply following the lead of the *targum* of Aquila), understood from the passage here that Moses actually grew horns, which interpretation found its most classical and widely known expression in Michelangelo's Moses. Nevertheless, most other interpreters took the verse to mean that Moses was endowed with some sort of glowing halo. In this regard, see Menachem Haran, *Mikra V'olamo*, pp. 402–403. For a detailed survey of other biblical interpreters who comment on this passage, see Yaakov Gertner, "*U-moshe Lo Yada Ki Karan Or Panav*," in *Mipeirot Ha-ilan Al Parashat Ha-shavua*, eds. Yehoshua Schwarz and David Algavish (Ramat Gan [Israel]: Bar Ilan University Press, 1998), pp. 278–279.

[12] See Genesis 19:11: "And they smote the men who stood at the gateway of the house with blindness, young and old alike, so that they eventually tired of ever finding the gateway."

[13] See 2 Kings 6, especially verse 18.

[14] For a more detailed account of these points and for biblical sources in their regard, see Menachem Haran, *Mikra V'olamo*, pp. 407–409. And cf. also Nahum M. Waldman, "Hebrew עד and the Divine Aura," in *Graetz College Annual of Jewish Studies* 1 (1972), pp. 7–13.

[15] Cf. George Buchanan Gray, *A Critical and Exegetical Commentary on Numbers* (Edinburgh: T. & T. Clark, 1912), p. 73; and, similarly, Menachem Haran, *Mikra V'olamo*, p. 408.

[16] See, e.g., Umberto (Moshe David) Cassuto, *Peirush Al Sefer Sh'mot* (Jerusalem: Magnes Press, 1962), p. 313, available in Israel Abrahams' English-language translation (Jerusalem: Magnes Press, 1967), p. 448. And cf. also Menachem Haran, *Mikra V'olamo*, p. 408; Avigdor Victor Horowitz, "*L'diyukano Shel Ha-eil Ha-mesopotami*," in *Eilei Kedem: Ha-politeiyizm B'eretz Yisrael U-sh'kheinoteha Min Ha-elef Ha-sheini Lifnei Ha-s'firah V'ad Ha-t'kufah Ha-muslamit,* eds. Menachem Kister, et al. (Jerusalem: Yad Yitzḥak Ben Tzvi, 2008), pp. 22–25; and Thomas Podella, *Das Lichtkleid JHWHs: Untersuchungen zur Gestalthaftigkeit Gottes im Alten Testament und seiner altorientalischen Umwelt* (Tübingen: J.C.B. Mohr [Paul Siebeck], 1996).

[17] Bereishit Rabbah 3:4, ed. Theodor–Albeck, pp. 19–20. And cf. the analysis of Ḥananel Mack, *Mi-reishit Le-Bereishit Rabbah* (Jerusalem: Carmel, 2010), pp. 57–61. Regarding the concept of divine light too powerful to be seen by human eyes, see the material collected by Louis Ginzberg in his *Legends of the Jews*, trans. Henrietta Szold (Philadelphia: Jewish Publication Society, 1909–1938), vol. 5, p. 338, n. 102.

[18] Y. Ḥagigah 2:1, 77a. Regarding the correct text for this passage, see Nurit Beeri, *Yatza L'tarbut Ra·ah: Elisha Ben Abuya, Aḥeir* (Tel Aviv: Yediot Aḥaronot, 2007), p. 36. And cf. also the comments of William D. Davies in his *Paul and Rabbinic Judaism* (London: S.P.C.K., 1962), p. 185 n. 1, regarding the revelation of the Holy Spirit to Paul as fire, and see too the discussion of Davies there on p. 184 where he claims that the same perception was held by the Rabbis.

[19] There is even a source (B. Niddah 30a) about the "light of wisdom" that shines forth from the human head, found in the description of the unborn fetus that, in the rabbinic conception—and this idea appears in non-Jewish sources as well—knows everything while still in its mother's womb, insofar as it is able "to see from one end of the universe to the other"—hence the description of the fetus as having a lighted lamp on its head.

[20] B. Berakhot 5a. For other talmudic sources that feature this motif, see my book *Massekhet Nashim* (Jerusalem: Keter, 2007), pp. 101–106.

[21] Moshe Idel, *The Mystical Experience in Abraham Abulafia*, trans. Jonathan Chipman (Albany, NY: State University of New York Press, 1988), pp. 81–82.

[22] In the book cited in the previous note, Idel specifically does not make this point—even though it could have served him as one of the more important sources for the later kabbalistic traditions he discusses. Regarding the link between visible fire and the audible names of God, see also the midrashic text *Otiyyot D'rabbi Akiva*, text A, published by Abraham Wertheimer in his *Battei Midrashot* (1950–1953; rpt. Jerusalem: Ketav Va-sefer, 1968), vol. 2, p. 365: "… and the blessed Holy One is seated upon a throne of fire and all around in every direction are the explicit divine names in the form of pillars of fire…such that, when an individual uses [i.e., speaks aloud] these names, every [intermediary layer of] firmament is [immediately] filled with fire that descends to burn the

world…when an individual uses these name, the world is instantly filled with fire." And cf. Moshe Idel's comments in *Mystical Experience*, p. 106, n. 236.

[23] See Moshe Idel, "*Rabbi Natan Ben Saadia Harar V'hashpa·ato B'eretz Yisrael*," in *Shalem* 7 (2001), pp. 47–58. (I thank Rabbi Martin S. Cohen for this reference.)

[24] This passage is cited in Idel, *Mystical Experience*, p. 79, from the original manuscript that had previously been published by Gershom Scholem in *Kiryat Sefer* 1 (1924–1925), p. 134; emphasis added.

[25] This citation comes from Idel, *Mystical Experience*, p. 81, where he cites the text from Moscow-Ginzburg ms. 775, p. 197a. The phrase "third watch" references the final third of the night, cf. B. Berakhot 3b.

[26] *Sefer Ḥasidim* §370, ed. Reuven Margoliot (Jerusalem: Mossad Harav Kook, 1957), p. 272. Moshe Idel, who collected some of the more pertinent medieval kabbalistic sources relating to the link between having a mystical experience and seeing the intense light, notes that in his estimation this is a very wide-spread phenomenon in world culture, and merely bringing together a few sources that can at best serve to limn the larger topic for their readers will hardly be sufficient to understand it fully. In his summary of the matter in *Mystical Experience*, Idel states that, in his estimation, "the subject of the specific kind of 'illumination' vouchsafed the mystic as part of the mystic experience itself would make a worth subject for a [full-length] study" (p. 148, n. 38).

[27] For the fascinating personal account by contemporary anthropologist Nachum Meged of the Hebrew University of Jerusalem of his own experience of supernatural light in the context of shamanistic ritual, see Nachum Meged, *Sha·arei Tikvah V'sha·arei Eimah: Shamanizm, Magia, V'khishuf Bi-d'rom U-merkaz Amerika* (Tel Aviv: Modan, 1998), p. 165.

[28] Cf. Stella Kramrisch, "The Triple Structure of Creation in the Ṛg Veda," in *History of Religions* 2:1–2 (1962–1963), pp. 140–175, and particularly her comment on p. 172: "The light of Vaisvanara is seen here in this world and it is the inner light of the seers. It passes through their filters…in the heart, on the road of meditation, on the road of illumination." And cf. also Weston La Barre, *Muelos: A Stone Age Superstition about Sexuality* (New York: Columbia University Press, 1984), pp. 80–82, where the author presents various traditions (including from shamanistic religions) regarding fire coming forth from the head of the holy individual.

[29] Cf., e.g., Sogyal Rinpoche, *The Tibetan Book of Living and Dying*, ed. Partick Gaffney and Andrew Harvey (New York: HarperCollins, 1993), pp. 278–290, "Intrinsic Radiance," and especially the section entitled "The Duration of the Ground Luminosity," on pp. 269–270. And cf. also the interesting account on p. 275: "Then something extraordinary happened. An incandescent, milky light, looking like a thin and luminous fog, began to appear and gradually spread everywhere. The palace temple had four large electric lamps outside; normally at that time of the evening they shone brightly, as it was already dark by seven o'clock. Yet they were dimmed by this mysterious light. Apa Pant, who was then Political

Officer to Sikkim, was the first to ring and inquire what on earth it could be. Then many others started to call; this strange, unearthly light was seen by hundreds of people. One of the other masters then told us that such manifestations of light are said in the Tantras to be a sign of someone attaining Buddhahood."

[30] Cf. Mircea Eliade, *The Two and the One*, trans. J. M. Cohen (Chicago: University of Chicago Press), 1962, pp. 61–65.

[31] For a source in the Koran in which God is described as light, see *sura* 24 (called "The Light"), and particularly line 35: "God is the light of the heavens and the earth; his light may be compared to a niche that enshrines a lamp, the lamp within a crystal of star-like brilliance" (*The Koran*, trans. N. J. Dawood [London: Penguin, 1990], p. 353).

[32] For a general analysis of sources featuring the halo, see Avidov Lipsker's essay, "*Or Zarua La-tzaddik*," in *Entziklopedia Shel Ha-sippur Ha-y'hudi—Sippur Okev Sippur*, eds. Yoav Elstein, Avidov Lipsker, and Rella Kushelevsky (Ramat Gan: Bar Ilan University Press, 2004–2013), vol. 1, pp. 105–134. In Lipsker's own rich and illuminating essay, from which I myself first learned of some of the sources I have cited here, the reader will find many references to cross-cultural material regarding the concept of the halo that crowns the head of the righteous individual with light. See in particular the material regarding the specific connection between the righteous individual and light (p. 107, n. 3), and the material regarding the ancient belief according to which the sun or the moon themselves originally emanated from the head of ancient kings or priests (pp. 106–107); and see there also Lipsker's reference to the Egyptian hieroglyphs in this regard, as well as his comments about archaeological finds in Mykonos and India, as well as his reference to the image of the halo on the drawings found at Dura-Europos (p. 111, n. 7). In this regard, see also Marthe Collinet-Guérin's *Histoire du nimbe: des origins aux temps modernes* (Paris: Nouvelles Editions Latines, 1961), in which that author discusses the image of the halo in many different world cultures. In addition, cf. also Stith Thompson's *Motif-Index of Folk-Literature, Vol. 5 (L-Z)* (Bloomington, IN: Indiana University Press, 1955), p. 455.

[33] I am obviously not arguing that this phenomenon recurred over and over throughout the long period of the Temple's existence. Nevertheless, it hardly matters for my argument even if we are speaking of the recollection of something that happened one single time that was subsequently presented in the annals of Jewish legend as though it were an ongoing, oft-repeating feature of the Priestly Blessing in the Temple. Regarding the tantalizing historical question of whether the Priestly Blessing was performed in the First Temple, see the remarks of Menachem Haran, *Mikra V'olamo*, pp. 421–432.

[34] Yemima Avital was born in 1929 in Casablanca and died in 1999 in Herzliya. She was a spiritual teacher, as well as a kabbalistically-oriented religious mystic, who developed the school of mystic thought known as "consciousness

awareness" or simply "the Yemima method." I heard of a similar experience from a different friend who attended the classes of Jean Klein; cf. what I wrote in my column *"Merḥavim"* in the Israeli newspaper *Maariv* on Friday, November 29, 2013, p. 15. For yet another report, see the book by Friedrich Weinreb (himself also a Jewish mystic), *Begegnungen mit Engeln und Menschen—Mysterium des Tuns: Autobiographische Aufzeichnungen* 1910–1936 (Bern: Origo, 1988), p 198. Weinreb's comments were summarized by Israel Koren in his essay *"Y'sodot Mistiyim U-n'vi·iyim Eitzel Friedrich Weinreb,"* published in *Kabbalah* 4 (1999), p. 371: "Weinreb writes about an experience he had in the prayer house in Scheveningen, Holland, in 1932 when he was twenty-two years old, an experience that, like the majority of his mystical experiences, came to him unheralded and unexpected. Weinreb tells that, in the course of the prayer service in the study hall, the room filled with bright light unlike anything one would normally see with one's own eyes. He tells how, at that very minute, he understood for the first time what light really is. And the presence of this light exerted an influence as well on the words of the liturgy themselves which appeared themselves to be radiating the light. Weinreb instantly understood that this experience was tied to the presence of a different man, a guest who had arrived in that place whom Weinreb only noticed when the prayer service ended. When he shook that man's hand, Weinreb felt himself to be intimately connected to this stranger. Then, the next day, they met again and began to speak to each other. It turned out that the man's name was Rabinov and that he had been a student of the Ḥafetz Ḥayyim [Rabbi Israel Meir HaKohen Kagan, 1838–1933] but was now working as a congregational rabbi in Hamburg. The conversation between the two men took on a distinct mystic overtone" (emphasis added).

[35] Regarding Albo and his philosophy, see most recently Dror Ehrlich's *Haguto Shel Rav Yosef Albo: K'tivah Ezoteirit B'shilhei Y'mei Ha-beinayim* (Ramat Gan: Bar Ilan University Press, 2009), and especially his discussion of the philosopher's exact dates on p. 15, n. 2.

[36] Rabbi Joseph Albo, *Sefer Ha-ikkarim* 1:18 (ed. Warsaw 1847), p. 76. The talmudic passage cited may be found at B. Bava Metzia 59b.

[37] It should be noted that Rabbi Joseph Albo served as one of the Jewish representatives in the disputation at Tortosa, the great public debate held between Jews and Christians in the years 1413 and 1414 in Tortosa, a town in Catalonia. See R. Ben Shalom, *"Vikku·aḥ Tortosa: Vincente Ferrer U-v'ayat Ha-anusim Al-pi Eiduto Shel Yitzḥak Natan,"* in Zion 56:1 (1991), pp. 21–46. Regarding the specific role of Rabbi Albo at Tortosa, see Ehrlich, *Haguto*, p. 16.

[38] Regarding the scattered sparks, see Louis Jacobs's essay, "The Uplifting of the Sparks in Later Jewish Mysticism," in *Jewish Spirituality*, ed. Arthur Green (New York: Crossroad, 1987), vol. 2, pp. 99–126.

Universalism and Particularism in Birkat Kohanim

Yeshaya Dalsace
Translated from the French by Martin S. Cohen

From Text to Spoken Word

When we look at a Torah scroll that has been unrolled before us, we find ourselves facing an endless sea of letters. Here and there, some brief bits of empty space provide a bit of a respite. And in the scroll we also find many longer spaces as well—most (but not all) of them places at which the scribe has stopped to begin a new section on a new line. These white spaces, as much a part of the ensemble as the black letters, are something like the foam that aerates the surface of the sea without destroying the endless monotony of the seascape. But what does catch the eye as we peruse the scroll are some few passages that are written out on the parchment in a distinctive way which sets them apart from the immense sea of text that surrounds them. There are very few of these anomalous passages, and they generally feature a particularly poetic text. For example, the Song of the Sea in Exodus 15 is presented to the reader as interlocking bricks of text, to suggest the water-walls that the Eternal created to fashion a path to safety for the Israelites "on their right and on their left" (Exodus 14:22 and 29); and at the end of the Torah, Moses' closing hymn to future salvation (Deuteronomy 32) is also written in a very distinctive style, a two-column layout.[1] There are other examples as well. And the very short text presenting the blessing of the *kohanim* (Numbers 6:24–26), the priests of ancient Israel, is one of them: each of the three short verses that constitute this text is set off by a gap in the text, the equivalent of nine letters' length.

This should not be passed lightly by: it is both anomalous and unique, this feature of the written scroll in which the monotony of the textual surface is suddenly broken by a series of small text-waves that appear one after the next, waves that—if one really were at sea—would indicate to the eye of the practiced sailor the presence of a hidden reef just beneath the otherwise placid surface. This benedictory passage has clearly been set out by the Masoretic tradition that governs the writing of sacred scrolls in a way that wordlessly (but also unmistakably) invites us to dive beneath the calm surface to see what lies below.

This sense that there is something worth exploring beneath the textual surface is reinforced by two unexpected features of the text: the three verses appear to be formulated in a kind of arithmetic progression so that they consist—we can suppose not accidentally—of lines consisting of exactly three, five, and seven words respectively, in which the most sacred of God's names appears as the second word of each line.

It is also worth noting that the text of the Priestly Blessing is the oldest biblical text that has been found; an amazing archeological discovery of two silver amulets has reliably been dated back to First Temple times and they are currently on display in the Israel Museum in Jerusalem. This text effectively proves the antiquity of the benedictory formulary and points almost as conclusively at its ancient ceremonial usage.[2]

The descendants of Aaron, the *kohanim*, were to recite this specific benedictory formulary in the Temple as a way of conveying God's blessing to the people assembled there. No doubt constituting one of the peak experiences of Temple worship, the liturgical formula itself is presented cursorily in the biblical Book of Numbers, and the ceremony in which it is pronounced is developed in much greater detail in a long talmudic passage.[3] This was, therefore, originally a Temple rite, but early on it was introduced into the synagogue, where it has remained a feature of Jewish liturgical practice ever since. Indeed, even today hundreds of *kohanim* gather at the Western Wall in Jerusalem three times annually—during Passover, Shavuot, and Sukkot—to pronounce the blessing before thousands of pilgrims.

Although textually rooted, the blessing lives on in the context of spoken language: it appears in the written Torah but escapes from its scriptural frame the moment it is pronounced aloud. In its ritual enactment, the words of the blessing must be pronounced aloud (and specifically *not* read from a printed text): they are repeated by the *kohanim*, word for word, as prompted by the prayer leader, and are then heard by a congregation of individuals, who may not gaze upon the *kohanim*—who, in any event, are hidden beneath the folds of their own prayer shawls. The effect, especially for the uninitiated, is startling—somewhat suggestive of a snowy field, or perhaps even the sea covered in white foam. In other words, the written version of Birkat Kohanim is there in the scroll, obviously, where it has been copied and recopied with the greatest precision by generations of scribes; but in the context of worship, it exists solely as spoken language. And the transition of the text from the realm of the written word to the one of spoken language is not a mere detail; in fact, it has the effect of liberating the blessing from its narrative frame, and thus also from the context in which the biblical text embeds its words. Indeed, in the mouths of the *kohanim* offering the blessing to the public, the text is simply devoid of any context or referential frame, which ephemeral feature lends to the larger enterprise a suggestion of eternity, of existence outside of literary history, perhaps even outside of time itself. At the same time, however, the creative power of the spoken blessing reinforces a sense of communal solidarity among all those present who hear the blessing pronounced. And that too suggests that this specific text exists in its own liturgical category: it is independent of the scriptural passage in which it is embedded and its oral recitation makes it unlike the rest of the Torah—which specifically may *not* be recited from memory, but which must instead be read verbatim from the scroll. The Torah read aloud exists in its own sphere of orality, of course. But it is an orality that is anchored in the written word that is read aloud *from* a written text.

What is the origin of this unusual blessing? And what meaning can it have for moderns contemplating it in our own day? It is to these questions that I wish now to turn.

The Blessing of Abraham

The first promise made by God to Abraham was that he, Abraham, would become "a blessing for all the families of the earth" (Genesis 12:2–3). This essential promise underscores the positive and universal character of Judaism in just a few words by defining the faith of Abraham's descendants not as the particularistic religion of a small group of individual members of the human family but rather as a message for "*all* the families of the earth" that, by its nature, can transcend the cultural differences and spiritual particularities of those families. This notion of Israel as the bearer of divine benediction to the world recurs in several different scriptural contexts and eventually became the foundational idea upon which rests the ritual blessing of the people by the *kohanim* in the Jerusalem Temple.

But the *kohanim* were not Abraham-like at all: Abraham by his very nature embodied a kind of divine blessing, but the *kohanim* in ancient times were nothing more than ritual functionaries obliged by custom and law to recite the benedictory formula precisely and with ritual exactitude. And, indeed, their specific task was to bless the house of Israel—and specifically *not* all the families of the earth. Abraham, on the other hand, "is" a blessing, as Scripture states at Genesis 12:2 ("…and you shall be a blessing"). Thus, even though he is depicted as the father of several nations within the human family, he is also described as a figure that transcends all ages and peoples. The *kohanim*, in this way unlike Abraham, neither embody blessing personally nor are deemed capable of transmitting it as part of their genetic heritage to their descendants; instead, they must pronounce the blessing aloud. They must speak the blessing plainly, and they transmit to their descendants not the blessing itself (which is offered freely to all), but the right to offer the blessing to future generations. Unlike Abraham, Scripture depicts the *kohanim* as faceless, mostly unnamed, functionaries—but not necessarily as role models.[5] The public attends the ritual and hears the blessing that only the *kohanim* may execute, and the community identifies not with the priests personally but rather with the words solemnly pronounced by the priests as God's blessing for the house of Israel.

It also bears saying that there is something paradoxical in the way Abraham is presented in Scripture. It is true that he embodies a universal blessing, but he only transmits—at least as far as the biblical narrative relates—membership in the *b'rit*, the covenant with God, to one single descendant among his eventually innumerable progeny: Isaac, who then transmits it to Jacob/Israel.[6] Abraham thus personifies a kind of paradox relating to the realization of the divine promise: the blessing of all the families of the earth boils down to the blessing of one single family, the family of Abraham. This contradiction would eventually come to be considered scandalous, at least in some quarters, as both Christians and Mulslims would come to reject the notion of the election of Israel and use it as the basis of anti-Jewish theologizing. From the vantage point of history, the consequences of this tension—which feels so innocuous in the context of the scriptural narrative—become enormous, and it remains problematic in terms of interfaith relations to this very day.

For their part, the *kohanim* bless solely Israel: "...and thus shall you bless the Israelites" (Numbers 6:23) is meant to be taken simply. Yet the wording of the blessing is specifically non-particularistic and entirely universal, suggesting that it could in fact be offered to anyone at all. The text itself (Numbers 6:24–26) reads as follows:

May the Eternal bless you and guard you.

May the Eternal illumine the divine face in your direction

and be gracious unto you.

May the Eternal lift up the divine face in your regard and grant you peace. There is nothing here at all that concerns Israel specifically. And precisely the opposite seems to be the case: it would be more than reasonable to construe the blessing as truly Abrahamic—that is, as a benedictory formula redolent of the universalism attributed by Scripture to Abraham. One could even posit that the real point of the ritual is for the *kohanim* to use the benediction to integrate Israel into the universal Abrahamic blessing, thus repeatedly and insistently calling Israel to its universalist mission to bring blessing to the world. What, after all, could be more universal than the specific blessings included in the scriptural formulary: light, graciousness, protection, and peace? These ideas will eventually echoed by the prophets of Israel, who will call their people to become a "light unto the nations" and to promote universal peace among the nations of the world.[7]

The Love of Israel

It is also worth noting that the current practice is for the *kohanim* to pronounce a blessing before they recite the Priestly Blessing itself. At first blush, this "blessing of a blessing" looks like the standard benediction often recited before the performance of a commandment. That resemblance is, however, only superficial; indeed, there are anomalous features that suggest that this is a special blessing with its own ideational foundation.

The blessing itself, cited already in the Talmud, reads as follows: "Blessed are You, O Eternal God and Sovereign of the universe, who, having sanctified us with the holiness of Aaron, has commanded us to bless God's people Israel in love."[8] Once this blessing is pronounced, the *kohanim* then, as the prayer-leader prompts them word by word, solemnly declaim the actual formula of the biblical blessing. As a result, there is a kind of double blessing to consider: the actual biblical blessing for the people, and the "pre-benedictory" blessing fixed by rabbinic tradition, which introduces the ritual pronunciation of the ancient biblical text. This latter blessing is constructed, for the most part, like the blessings pronounced before fulfilling a commandment: "Blessed are You, Eternal God and sovereign of the universe, who, having sanctified us with divine commandments, has commanded us to...." However, this latter blessing differs from the blessing that precedes Birkat Kohanim in two important ways: firstly, in the latter the source of sanctification is not said to be the commandments themselves but rather the holiness of Aaron personally; and secondly, the latter blessing concludes with the bald statement that the commandment is not merely to bless the people, but to bless them *b'ahavah*, "in love."

The traditional formula for the blessing that precedes the performance of "regular" commandments (as given above) reflects the fundamental Jewish notion that sanctity in this world derives from action—and specifically from acting according to the path of observance ordained by Scripture and developed over centuries by rabbinic tradition. This path is open to all, provided that an individual is prepared to submit to the rigorous discipline of the commandments. Thus, the holiness of Israel does not derive from its heritable nature and neither does it have any specific ontological basis; instead, it derives solely from the fact that Israel has self-constituted itself as a nation that generates holiness through fidelity to the Torah's sacred commandments. This is why Judaism remains open to all who are prepared to live under the yoke of the commandments. Indeed, it is the acceptance of that complex set of ritual, ethical, and spiritual obligations that serves even today as the litmus test of the willing convert to Judaism. The holiness of Israel is thus available to all who are prepared to join in the performance of the *mitzvot*. In that sense, this holiness can reasonably be qualified as universal—and thus as the natural extension of the covenant established millennia ago between God and Abraham.

The introductory blessing pronounced by the *kohanim* specifies that it is not the *mitzvah*, not the commandment *per se*, that creates holiness in the world (which idea is suggested by the classical formula mentioned above that references God as sanctifying Israel "with divine commandments"), but rather the "holiness of Aaron" that does so. Nor does the *kohen* maintain his status by virtue either of his actions or his exemplary behavior, but rather by virtue of his ancestry, by the circumstances of his birth. This is unexpected, but appears to be how things are: the holiness of the *kohen* is intrinsic sanctity that can only be obtained by being born to it; the holiness of the *kohen* is completely unrelated to his deeds or to his personal worthiness. One cannot acquire the status of *kohen* through any conversion ritual. But this heritable sanctity, which may be traceable back to Aaron, has no intrinsic value; rather, it exists solely for the sake of Israel, the transcendent people— or, as the introductory blessing references them, "God's people Israel" (which is to say: the people of the universal God, rather than the people of the *kohen*—which is, at best, a nationalist concept). The sanctity of Aaron and his descendants is only meaningful in terms of the function of the *kohen* with respect to the collective—that is to say, with respect to its ability to offer God's blessing to Israel, which itself will only acquire its eventual sanctity through such acts. Finally, the last word of this introductory blessing bears a precise meaning: the blessing can only be offered with love, in love, in the context of love. This final word, signaling one final requirement, is totally unique among the many blessings that are to be recited before performing commandments.

We can thus see that the ceremonial surrounding the Priestly Blessing is anomalous, both with respect to the specific language of the blessing that introduces it and also with respect to the notion of *ahavat yisrael* ("the love of Israel") that is the requisite context for the blessing's pronouncement. It is, in fact, precisely because they are called upon to summon up feelings of love with respect to the Jewish people that the *kohanim* are entitled to declaim the blessing, which only truly makes sense in the context of that love.

After centuries of development, the notion of *ahavat yisrael* has become an important Jewish value. A Jew must love other Jews. Our halakhic decisors saw in the commandment to love one's neighbor one of the fundamental principles of the Torah (just as Rabbi Akiva taught in his day), but others sought to limit the application of the scriptural injunction to people with whom one has values and a Torah in common.[9] When viewed in this context, the love of Israel *is* the love of one's neighbor, of one's other.[10] Nonetheless, it is important to me to distinguish between these two concepts. It seems to me that the love of one's neighbor cannot reasonably be restricted—with all due respect to the medieval sources that teach to the contrary—to apply solely to the observant Jew; the concept must be broadened to include all of humankind, each and every individual being created in the divine image.[11] To be meaningful as a religious concept, the love in question cannot be restricted to only some part of God's creation. Nevertheless, Israel—the nation bound in covenant to the Creator— merits a specific version of this commanded love of the other: not the convenient love of the local Jew *qua* neighbor, but the love of Israel— taken here as an abstract notion inspiring a spiritual project that, for all sorts of reasons obvious and obscure, has manifested itself in a particular nation. The midrash is speaking in precisely this vein when it declares, not fancifully but profoundly, that ideational Israel existed even before the world was created.[12]

The love of Israel derives directly from this ideational construct relating to the pre-existence of Israel (in this regard, not unlike the Torah) before God even began to create the world.[13] Similarly, the pre-existent Torah also needed to become manifest in a particular text, the work known to us as "the" Torah but which is only the carrying-case, so to speak, of a celestial Torah far more profound than its earthly counterpart, a Torah of such infinite majesty that we can only hope to find some sparks of its other-worldly existence through the study of its literary projection into the world. Similarly, Israel—taken here as a spiritual concept—needed to find a terrestrial framework in which to exist in created reality and so self-manifested as a specific people...but it is this earlier, celestial Israel that we are called upon to love. It is for this reason that the midrash imagines that Abraham and Isaac too were called "Israel," and no less meaningfully than was Jacob.[14] Seen from this point of view, the love of Israel is not the mere love of one's neighbor, but rather the love of the *concept* of Israel that the Jewish people has borne throughout the generations in a way unrelated to the behavior of individual Jews or the moral flaws of any specific generation of Jewish people.

Taken as a corollary of the unconditional election of Israel to bear God's covenant into the world, the love of Israel must be as unconditional as it anomalous. And, indeed, this notion of unconditional obligation finds its expression in the words of many biblical prophets who, despite their endless willingness to berate specific individuals or communities for their moral failings, invariably insisted on the irreducible nature of the covenant—which exists eternally and unconditionally outside the framework of specific individuals and their ethical or ritual shortcomings. We find this idea as well, and in terms similar to the text of the introductory blessing of the *kohanim*, in the second blessing that precedes the recitation of the Shema in the morning service. This blessing proposes that the remarkable relationship of God and Israel derives from the fact that it was upon Israel that the Torah was bestowed, and this should be taken both as a sign of the infinite love of the Creator for the people Israel and also as tangible proof of their election. The Talmud reinforces this idea when it affirms that the Jewish people were only called by the name "Israel" after receiving the Torah at Sinai—that is to say, after having taken a solemn oath to adhere both to the covenant of the patriarchs and to the laws of the Torah.[15] The love of Israel thus implies the love of that which Israel bears into the world: the love of a promise, and the love of a Jewish people that exists independent of how one may or may not feel about individual Jews.

This unconditional love cannot be explained with reference to the moral qualities possessed by the nation in question, but rather solely by its role as conveyer of God's blessing into the world, as implied by the verse in the Torah that reads baldly, "You are the least of peoples" (Deuteronomy 7:7).[16] And the rabbis, too, said on many occasions that nothing really explains the election of the Jewish people other than a certain inexplicable (and unearned) capacity to receive the Torah, a capacity that is not to be equated with any particular willingness on the people's part to play that role in the history of humankind.[17] The love of Israel is therefore neither subjective nor dependent on any particular thing. It cannot be explained as anything other than a promise.

The choice made by God of this specific people to bear the divine word to the world is in this category of idea as well: a people was needed and this specific one was chosen. The rabbis of ancient times insisted on the fundamental universalism of the Torah insofar as they understood it to embody God's message to all humanity. Nor was it problematic in this regard to agree that the revelation itself—the actual text of the Torah—is particularistic insofar as it is framed as a Jewish text addressed to the Jewish people because, for those same rabbis, the Torah's text is only the visible part, so to speak, of a celestial Torah revealed *through* Israel to all the world. Indeed, this is the specific reason that the rabbis allowed themselves to go so far as to claim that the Torah was revealed at Sinai not solely in Hebrew but in seventy languages: so that all nations, imagined in antiquity to number seventy, could understand it—even if they ended up choosing not to accept the revelation as their national spiritual path.[18] The prophetic gift of the Torah to Israel can therefore not in and of itself be taken to exclude the possibility of a parallel revelation to other nations.

Similarly, the choice of Aaron's line to constitute a heritable priesthood unrelated to the personal merit of any specific *kohen* should also be seen as an arbitrary disposition of sacerdotal responsibility on a particular group of individuals—not because they particularly merited it, but because a priesthood was requisite and *someone* needed to serve in its ranks. This arbitrariness resonates with God's original choice of Abraham: he was commanded to leave his homeland against a promise of what he might yet become, but nothing in Abraham's previous life story presaged his election in any meaningful way.[19] And it is precisely this arbitrariness that lends rich meaning to the blessing offered by the *kohanim* by situating it precisely on the narrow boundary between particularism and universalism: the particularism of Jewish destiny and the universalism of God's promise to humankind. This arbitrariness may seem to be the determinative factor, both in the election of Israel to receive the Torah and in the election of the line of Aaron to bless Israel. But it is also so that these two elections are mere functions of love that, for all that it may be unconditional, is nevertheless justified by the universalist notion that the Torah is, at least in the ultimate sense, God's revelation to *all* human beings, each the equal of the other by virtue of the divine image they all bear.

If Israel merits this love, then, it is neither because of what Israel is nor because of the exceptional moral qualities the people Israel could or should have, but, exactly as in the case of Abraham, because of what Israel becomes through the agency of Torah, because of the promise Israel bears to the world. And if Israel merits the love of God, then that too is a function of what it possesses: a Torah that has the capacity to transform, to inspire becoming instead of mere being. Indeed, Israel is not—and could never be—what Israel merely *is*, but rather what it is in the continual process of *becoming*. And, at least ideally, Israel is meant to exist in a constant state of *becoming*, in permanent *lekh-l'kha* mode,[20] in a permanent march forward through the millennia toward its best self. And, indeed, the blessing of the *kohanim* is focused solely on the future; each of its verbs, usually translated in jussive mode ("*may* the Eternal bless you and guard you"), are actually simple imperfect verbs in Hebrew, a construction regularly used also to denote the simple future ("the Eternal *will* bless you and guard you"). Birkat Kohanim is thus rooted in the idea of the love of Israel precisely because the blessing is intimately linked to the idea of the Torah not as a text written once and for all time but rather as a work in progress, as a text in the process itself of becoming, as a projection of sublime divine orality that Israel is charged to bear in the world. It was not by accident that the priests of Temple times pronounced their blessing before the building that housed the Holy of Holies, in which was kept the Ark of the Covenant, itself built to be transported endlessly into the future. And it is for this reason that in today's synagogue service the *kohanim* stand before the Ark of the synagogue, which contains the Torah scrolls, when they bestow the blessing on the congregation.[21]

The concept of the love of God is thus not really separable from the concept of the love of the Torah, which in turn cannot really be thought of as meaningfully distinct from the concept of the love of God.[22] And indeed, we human beings love that which *is* nowhere as ardently or intently as we love that which *inspires* to be, which *leads* to becoming, which *suggests* by its nature the dynamic nature of human existence at its finest. For Jews, it all develops around this notion of the holiness borne into the world by Aaron and his descendants for the specific purpose of serving the people Israel in carrying out its mission to bear the word of God to the world—a national mission that itself only makes sense in universalist terms, in terms of the ability of that word to bring life to the living. Far from being a particularistic benediction suggestive solely of the self-absorbed nationalist aspirations of its pronouncers, the Priestly Blessing begs to be explained as a kind of universalistic vehicle, intended to remind the people Israel of their mission to the nations of the world. God's love of Israel only makes real sense in this universalistic context, for the specific elements in the blessing—light, grace, protection, and peace— are by their very definition gifts that would naturally be bestowed by the Creator not only to the servants commanded to bear the divine word, but also to those for whom it was meant and to whom it was sent.

For all these reasons, it seems logical to see in the Priestly Blessing the extension, or possibly even the realization, of the promise made to Abraham that he would be a blessing for *all* the families of the world. Birkat Kohanim thus brings us to the very center of the paradox that churns and roils at the core of the Jewish experience: the specificity of Israel that leads not to chauvinism but to a universalistic worldview, one which rests on a deep sense of the interconnectedness of all of God's creatures.

The Word Articulated

The Priestly Blessing must be pronounced aloud, with the priests' hands stretched out toward the congregation in a gesture that suggests both protectiveness and the desire of the *kohanim* to fill the sanctuary with the positive energy generated by their benedictory ritual. For Judaism, great potential creativity inheres not solely in the voice of God but also in the voices of human beings created in God's image. There is great power in the spoken word. God's spoken word brought into existence the world and all of humanity, of course. But human language also has the capacity to alter how things are in the world...both for those who hear the words spoken and also for those who speak them aloud.[23]

The creative power of human speech, and particularly that of the *kohen*, was highlighted in ancient times by the prophet Malachi, who wrote: "The lips of the *kohen* embody knowledge, and [for this reason] do people seek [to hear God's] *torah* from his lips. He is [sent to you as] a messenger of the Eternal One [who rules over the celestial] hosts" (2:7). This verse references an era during which *kohanim* were widely revered as sages. But even in our own time, when *kohanim* are mere conveyors of God's blessings to the world, they continue—by virtue of the liturgy they pronounce aloud—to bear knowledge into the world. This knowledge is unrelated to the learning of any specific member of the priestly caste but, as I have tried to demonstrate, by its very nature has the capacity to project the love of God, which *is* the knowledge of God, into the world.

The prophet's remark that it is possible to find the knowledge of God preserved on the lips of the *kohen* is suggestive of a different verse, one from Psalms, that says as much regarding the unadulterated word of God: "The words of the Eternal are purified speech, the spoken equivalent of silver refined seven times in a furnace [sunk] in the earth" (12:7). This word is offered to all: it flows to the world through the desert crucible in which it was first forged, through the agency of those who ever since bear it to the world, through the agency of the "voice of thin silence" referenced in the narrative of the prophet Elijah.[24] Given the wilderness setting in which the Torah was first revealed, it is hardly accidental that the Hebrew words for "wilderness" (*midbar*) and for "he speaks" (*m'dabbeir*) are homographs.[25] An ancient *midrash* teaches that the Torah was given "through" three agents: fire, water, and wilderness—for insofar as these three things are available to all for the taking or experiencing, so shall be the fate of a Torah sent to earth beneath the sign of the universal. (And this is precisely what the prophet meant to suggest when he proclaimed that all who thirst [for the knowledge of God] are welcome to drink of its waters.[26]) But the Torah is also a fourth thing that cannot be bought, which is free for all who wish to acquire and own: neither fire nor water, but love itself.

The *kohanim* do not take their audience into account, nor do they choose the blessings they offer. Instead, they speak the word of God to all who gather to hear. The blessing is not theirs to offer at will, or to withhold; it does not belong to them in any meaningful way. It is by its nature universal, in fact, precisely because it is *not* offered by its conveyors to their families or to their friends, or to others who have gained their trust or their affection, but rather to "God's people Israel." But for all that it is offered to Israel, it is not about them either: the Priestly Blessing is "about" humankind taken as a whole (as explained above).

It is not, however, sufficient for a blessing—or any word—merely to be spoken; it must also be heard. And the liturgy provides for this formally by requiring that the congregation respond to the pronouncement of each of the three verses that constitute the Priestly Blessing. And, in that context as well, the response of the blessed is rooted in love—not love for the *kohen* standing before the congregation, but rather for that which the *kohen* brings to the world. But how exactly does one hear the blessing, does one go about hearing the blessing? To this question the *midrash* too has an answer: one must become a human wilderness. The ancient text is explicit in this mysterious regard: "Any individual who fails to make of him or herself a wilderness open to all will never be able to receive the wisdom of the Torah, and it was to stress this point exactly that the Torah was offered [to Israel] in the wilderness [of Sinai]."[27] In other words, in order to hear the voice of God one must first allow oneself to become audible to one's "inner Israel." And that is why the great declaration of faith begins with the words, "Hear, O Israel…" (Deuteronomy 6:4).

The blessing (*b'rakhah*) serves as the connective link (*berekh*, literally "knee") between the spoken word and the heard word, and this connection can only work well in the context of love. I mean to reference the love of human speech in this regard, obviously, but also the love of oneself, for no one can love another without first loving oneself. (I prefer to read the famous injunction to love another "as oneself" at Leviticus 19:18 as though it ordained loving another "as one loves oneself.") The love of self of which I speak, however, is not the egocentric, narcissistic version of self-love so prevalent in modern society, but something quite different: it is the love of the potential one senses in oneself, of one's "inner Israel"—which is attained not through self-aggrandizement but through the subjugation of the overweening sense of self that interferes with, rather than enhances, the attainment of one's fullest potential. In Hebrew, this is best expressed with a kind of a word game: by re-arranging the letters that spell out the word for "I" (*ani*), one can write out the word for "nothingness" (*ayin*). And, indeed, the Talmud teaches as much when it declares, "The words of the Torah can only be maintained by those who see themselves as barely existent, as the verse in Job reads, 'Wisdom comes from nothingness.'"[28]

While it is the *kohanim* who recite the blessing, the custom is for all those present who are wearing *tallitot* to hide beneath them in a gesture intended to suggest the nullification of the self, as they receive the blessing of God—as articulated in their presence and for their benefit by *kohanim*, who are themselves *also* hidden beneath their *tallitot*. The use of the *tallit* here is key: it appears here in its various midrashic guises as the garment of light, the garment of the Torah, and the garment of humility, but also as the garment suggestive the most clearly of the pride Israel takes, or should take, in its unearned potential to acquire God's choicest blessings of light, grace, protection, and peace through the agency of a priesthood chosen expressly for that purpose.

This articulation of those blessings touches, too, on a core concept of Judaism: at the moment it is pronounced, the blessing suggests that the presence of the Divine in the world is rooted in nothing more physically real than orality itself—and the listener is thus set outside of time and personally challenged to find his or her own personal destiny in the cadences of the Priestly Blessing. By ordaining that it be written in a Torah scroll according to their rules, the Masoretes can be imagined to be suggesting that the foundational ideas of Judaism may be discerned in this short text, in its sequential rhythm of words endlessly rotating around the ineffable axis of God's most sacred name, repeated over and over. And by adding a preliminary blessing in which the blessers bless the Source of blessing, even before they offer the Blesser's blessing to the blessed in a context suggestive of the triply entwined concepts of love, Israel, and sanctity, the rabbis of old continued the biblical tradition wisely, by creating a liturgical setting for Birkat Kohanim that itself is suggestive of the great project called Israel...whereby God seeks to bring redemption rooted in love to the world.

NOTES

[1] The law regarding the layout of this passage in a Torah scroll, along with the laws governing all other anomalous passages, can be found in Maimonides' *Mishneh Torah* at Hilkhot Sefer Torah, chapter 8.

[2] Regarding the so-called Ketef Hinnom amulets, see Gabriel Barkay, Marilyn J. Lunberg, Andrew G. Vaughn, and Bruce Zuckerman, "The Amulets from Ketef Hinnom: A New Edition and Evaluation," in *Bulletin of the American Schools of Oriental Research* 334 (May 2004), pp. 41–71. The amulets were discovered by Gabriel Barkay in 1979.

[3] The biblical passage is Numbers 6:22–27. The talmudic passage is B. Sotah 37b–40b.

[4] Cf. Numbers 6:23, where the text specifically depicts God commanding Aaron and his sons to bless the Israelites. See below regarding this verse in more detail.

[5] Aaron's sons and one of his grandsons are, of course, named in Scripture. But I am thinking more specifically of the *kohanim* that would eventually take their place as the priestly caste.

[6] Abraham's uncountable progeny is referenced twice in the biblical narrative: at Genesis 13:16 and 15:5, cf. 32:13 and even 16:10, both of which passages reference Abraham's descendants as well.

[7] See, e.g., Isaiah 42:6 and 49:6.

[8] See B. Sotah 39a, where the blessing is attributed to Rabbi Eliezer ben Shamua (a disciple of Rabbi Akiva), in a lesson taught by Rabbi Zeira in the name of Rabbi Ḥisda. Cf. also M.T. Hilkhot Tefillah U-nesiat Kapayim 14:12 and S.A. Oraḥ Ḥayyim 128:11. Note, however, the comment in the Talmud that precedes the one just cited, in which Rabbi Eliezer ben Shamua attributes his exceptionally long life, at least in part, to the fact that he, a *kohen*, never in the course of all his years pronounced the Priestly Blessing without first reciting the preparatory blessing—a comment that only makes sense if this were not the universal practice it is today.

[9] Rabbi Akiva's comment may be found in the Yerushalmi at Y. Nedarim 9:4, 41c. For an example of a text that limits the injunction to those with whom one shares common values and a common Torah, see the *Sefer Mitzvot Gadol* of Rabbi Moses ben Jacob of Coucy (thirteenth century), positive commandment 9 (ed. Venice, 1547; p. 97b).

[10] See in this regard the material gathered in the *Entziklopedia Talmudit*, ed. Meir Berlin and Shlomo Yosef Zevin (Jerusalem: Hotzaat Entziklopedia Talmudit, 1947), vol. 1, col. 211, s.v. *ahavat yisrael*.

[11] Humankind created in the divine image: Genesis 9:6. The broad approach is already taken in the Mishnah, cf. Pirkei Avot 3:14.

[12] Cf. Bereishit Rabbah 1:4, ed. Theodor-Albeck (1903–1929; rpt. Jerusalem: Wahrman, 1967), p. 6.

[13] The opening passage of Bereishit Rabbah (1:1) teaches exactly that: that the Torah existed before the world was created.

[14] Bereishit Rabbah, 63:3. In the actual scriptural narrative, of course, it is Jacob alone whose name is changed to Israel; see Genesis 32:29 and 35:10.

[15] B. Ḥullin 101b.

[16] This is my own *midrash*. In context, the verse references the smallness of the Israelite population when compared to its multitudinous neighbors.

[17] Cf. B. Shabbat 88a and Avodah Zarah 2b, where Rabbi Avdimi bar Ḥama bar Ḥasa teaches that Sinai was suspended over the people's heads and allowed to dangle like a barrel of whiskey…until the people "willingly" decided to accept their role in history as the covenanted people. The precise translation of the word *k'gigit*, here translated as "like a barrel of whiskey," derives directly from Rashi's comment to B. Avodah Zarah 2b, s.v. *v'al da tivart'hun*.

[18] Cf. B. Shabbat 88b and Shemot Rabbah 5:9 and 28:6, where the multilingual nature of the revelation at Sinai is affirmed. And cf. also the material preserved at Sifrei Devarim §343, where the text imagines God traveling the world to offer the Torah to various other nations, each one of which declines the offer for one reason or another. If, at the end of the day, Judaism never became a missionary faith, it is important to note that it also never abandoned its mission to serve as an example to other nations and a source of spiritual inspiration for all humanity.

[19] I am obviously basing myself solely on the scriptural narrative. There are countless *midrashim* that attempt to speak to this issue by providing all sorts of stories about Abraham's childhood, each demonstrating some quality God's choice of Abraham specifically. But none of those midrashic tales justifies the heritable nature of the election of Abraham's seed after him as the bearers of God's covenanted presence in the world.

[20] The Hebrew words *lekh l'kha* mean "go forth" and together constitute the first of God's commands to Abraham at Genesis 12:1.

[21] Cf. the talmudic tradition preserved at B. Yoma 72a to the effect that the wooden poles, by means of which the Ark was carried forward in the wilderness, were never removed—not even when the Ark was finally brought to its permanent resting place in the Temple of Solomon. The poles thus served as the permanent reminder that both the scroll and the divine message it bears were constructed to be in constant motion forward.

[22] This progression of ideas flows from Deuteronomy 6:5–9, which verses constitute the Shema and V'ahavta paragraph, one of the Torah's best-known liturgical passages.

[23] The rabbis never tired of finding parallels between the voice of God, which created the world with ten fiats and which spoke aloud the Ten Commandments at Sinai, and the voice of humankind, as manifested in the ten "Hallelujah" psalms (Psalms 106, 111, 112, 113, 135, 146, 147, 148, 149, and 150); the voice of ten students gathered to study Torah in the *beit midrash*; the ten blessings offered by Isaac to Jacob; and even the ten blasts of the *shofar* on Rosh Hashanah (cf. B. Rosh Hashanah 32a and Megillah 21b, and *Pirkei D'rabbi Eliezer*, chap. 31). And in this regard, cf. also Pirkei Avot 5:1, where we read that the survival

of the world created with ten divine statements depends on the deeds of humankind—which to me specifically references their speech, for the words of the righteous sustain the world while the words of the wicket destroy it.

[24] Cf. 1 Kings 19:12.

[25] Both are written in Hebrew with the same four letters: *mem, dalet, bet, resh.*

[26] Bemidbar Rabbah 1:7, citing Isaiah 55:1.

[27] Bemidbar Rabbah 1:7.

[28] B. Sotah 21b, quoting Job 28:12. The opening of the original, taught in the name of Rabbi Yoḥanan, reads: *ein divrei torah mitkayy'mim ella b'mi she-meisim atzmo k'mi she-eino.*

"And I Will Bless Them": Becoming Channels for Divine Flow

Shohama Harris Wiener and David Evan Markus

How does Jewish tradition teach us to transmit blessings with maximum power and inspiration? The words of the Priestly Blessing, Birkat Kohanim, offer clues hidden inside a paradox. Birkat Kohanim begins with the instruction, "Here is how you will bless the people Israel" (Numbers 6:23), but then seems to reserve all power of blessing to God:

> God spoke to Moses, saying: "Speak to Aaron and his sons, saying: 'Here is how you will bless the people Israel; say to them: *May the Eternal bless you and keep you. May the countenance of the Eternal illuminate you and give you grace. May the countenance of the Eternal turn toward you and give you peace.* So shall you place My name on the people Israel and I [=God] will bless them.'" (Numbers 6:23–27)

What, then, is the role of the person who bestows blessing, and what does it mean to "place [God's] name," beyond merely speaking these words?[1] While Birkat Kohanim recognizes that God is the true source of blessing, tradition offers a profound and transformative role—a partnership with God—for all who convey blessing in God's name. This partnership in the transmission of blessing invites us to open ourselves as spiritual channels through which to perceive, receive, and convey the flow of divinity. Just as it was in biblical days for Aaron and his sons, today this invitation to become a channel for divine flow is vital for anyone stepping into the legacy bequeathed to us from this ancient and powerful tradition.

This essay explores this spiritual role of the bestower of blessing through the use of text and the implementation of esoteric practices, and uses the rubric of *hashpa·ah*—Jewish spiritual direction—to formulate practical guidance for spiritual growth. As we will see, the path of conveying blessing is one of cultivating profound awe, love, and transparency to the flow of divinity in and through our lives. This path renders the human bestower of blessing not a passive bystander but an indispensable participant in the flow of divine transmission—something the world especially needs now.

The Intention of Blessing: A Teaching for This Hour

Because the Priestly Blessing invokes God's name as a means to convey blessing and transformation, we begin with Ezra the Scribe, one of the Jewish tradition's most pivotal exemplars of invoking God's name. As we will see, while tradition does not record that Ezra used the Priestly Blessing to convey blessing, Ezra's explicit use of God's name illustrates the power of the name to transform people by connecting them with transcendent awe.

After the Jewish people returned to Jerusalem from Babylonian exile in the sixth century B.C.E., Ezra—a priest descended from the *kohen gadol* (High Priest) of Israel,[2] and perhaps even functioning as *kohen gadol* in his own right[3] —assembled the people to hear the public reading of the "Book of the Law of Moses" (Nehemiah 8:1). This ceremonial public reading was a collective re-dedication, another Sinai moment in which the people assembled together *k'ish ehad*, "as one person" (Nehemiah 8:1), as one collective soul—to receive Torah anew. The scene was electric: with all the people united, Ezra stood high on a makeshift pulpit of wood, and the people rose as Ezra opened the scroll. When Ezra began, "[he blessed] the Eternal, the great God, and all the people answered 'Amen! Amen!' with hands uplifted, and they bowed their heads and bowed low before God, with their faces to the ground" (Nehemiah 8:6). The moment was transformational: a physical, emotional, and spiritual scene of "holy inspiration, charged for them all with exceptional meaning and promise."[4]

What is the connection between Ezra's reading of the Torah and the modern means and method of blessing? The Talmud records that Ezra invoked the ineffable name of God with the intention of "magnifying God before the people."[5] Ezra's purpose, plainly, was to evoke a heart-opening awe that, by its nature, could not be compelled but only inspired and then freely chosen: in tradition's wisdom, everything is in God's hands except awe of God.[6] The experience of divine awe—the "wow" of limitless potentiality and generativity that we call "God"[7] —is thus a human choice, a cultivated practice, and a key purpose of spiritual life itself.

In Ezra's day, however, the people were restrained from making this choice because Babylonian exile had heightened the people's disconnection from tradition and alienation from spirit. In the words of the psalmist, exile had brought the people to weeping, sapped their ability to sing, and drained their joy (Psalm 137:1–6). Thus facing a beleaguered people in their fateful moment of return, Ezra's mission was to restore their spiritual connection and rekindle their flame of awe. Befitting the moment's importance, Ezra's means of sparking awe anew was to declaim the awesome name of God— the *sheim ha-m'forash*, the "explicit name" spelled in Hebrew with the letters *yod-hei-vav-hei*, the Tetragrammaton[8] linked to Moses' revelatory experience at the burning bush (Exodus 3:6). Tradition, however, understood the name of God to be so holy that its mere utterance was forbidden, except to the High Priest on Yom Kippur.[9] Centuries later, when the rabbis of the Talmud objected that Ezra had violated this sacred prohibition, Rav Giddel[10] replied that Ezra's act of explicitly invoking the name of God was a *hora·at sha·ah*—a "teaching of the hour," typically reserved for exigent or emergency circumstances[11]—and therefore appropriate and defensible. Given the spiritual stakes, the rabbis concluded that Ezra's ends justified the means.

Today we do not pronounce this particular name of God (the Tetragrammaton), but Birkat Kohanim still invites us to "place [it] on the people Israel." Thus, when we accept the invitation of Birkat Kohanim to invoke God's name, in a sense we are standing in Ezra's shoes. While we may not be returning from physical exile, as our ancestors were in Ezra's day, how many of us nevertheless live in states of emotional or spiritual exile? How many of us can authentically claim holiness in our lives? How many of us were reared in spiritual circumstances that were calcified, brittle, or parched? How many feel so alienated from connection to spiritual tradition that our flames of awe flicker? How many forget that we are created *b'tzelem Elohim*, "in the image of God" (Genesis 1:27), and therefore have a *nitzutz* (spark) of holiness within? In the emotional and spiritual dynamics of lived experience, are we today so different from Ezra's Israelites just returning to Jerusalem after decades in exile?

As in Ezra's day, today's spiritual stakes are high, and there is a burgeoning need to rekindle our inner flames of spirituality and divine awe—whether or not most modern Jews would use such language. Within the boundaries of Jewish tradition, many Jews of the post-Holocaust generations continue to search (or perhaps have given up the search altogether) for authentically nourishing connections of Jewish spirituality—connections that reach out into community, back in time to tradition, and inward to the realm of transcendence. Even for those of us who may not feel internally exiled or disconnected, whose flame of divine awe might yet burn brightly, there are invariably times in life—moments of celebration and gratitude, as well as moments of loss, doubt, and despair—when a blessing can sanctify experience, strengthen spiritual connection, and elevate awareness and expression of holiness. And as humanity slowly comes to grips with unprecedented ecological and sociopolitical challenges, the need for elevated spiritual attunement becomes even more palpable and dramatic.

For all of these reasons, just as Ezra's *hora·at sha·ah*—his emergency action—was to invoke God's name for the purpose of rekindling the flame of awe among the people of his day, this same purpose must be the "lesson of our own hour" for anyone who would convey blessing with meaningful effect. The intention of the bestower of blessing must be to connect—or even to re-connect—the recipient of blessing with the Source of Blessing. Connection, of course, only has the meaning and effect in real time that one experiences in real life: spiritually speaking, there is no such thing as theoretical connection, just as there is no such thing as theoretical blessing. Rather, experience itself is the kindling for the flame of spiritual nourishment. After all, experiences of holiness, while refracted through our human senses and narratives, are the fount of divine existence on the human plane. Provocatively, tradition offers that God is diminished and, in a sense, even disappears whenever the human flame of spiritual experience flickers and fades:

> "You are My witnesses, says God, that I am the Eternal One..." Explained Rabbi Shimon bar Yoḥai: "If you are My witnesses—then I am [God]...but if you are not My witnesses—then I am not, as it were, God."[12]

When we witness holiness and manifest spiritual flow in the world, we achieve in the moment what Martin Buber called an "intensification" of our spiritual reality.[13] When we intensify our spiritual reality in these ways, we experience God in our lives. Conversely, if we do not experience God, then in a very real sense, God cannot be said to exist meaningfully on the human plane.

Through this experiential lens, then, a blessing—and particularly one that invokes God's name, as does Birkat Kohanim—serves its connective purpose only to the extent that it inspires experience of holiness and awe. Achievement of this purpose must be the deep intention of anyone who conveys blessing. One who blesses must aspire to transport the blessing's recipient into a deep and authentic experience of spirit, so that both bestower and recipient of the blessing cannot help but witness the truth and flow of divinity in and through themselves in that moment. One who blesses therefore must be—and feel oneself to be—a holy connector. Far from a bystander or mere functionary, one who blesses thereby becomes a channel for God's flow in and through the world of human experience. One who blesses thus stands in the shoes of Ezra, rekindling the passion and awe that can illuminate the world.

Birkat Kohanim as Physical Portal

Of course, none of us is an Ezra. On the other hand, none of us is disqualified from aspiring to this sacred calling of becoming a holy connector on behalf of another. Whatever restrictions and disqualifications Jewish law once attached to the office of the *kohen gadol*, none of these limitations necessarily applies to one who conveys blessing in our own day. Even though Birkat Kohanim is part of the prayer leader's traditional repetition of the morning Amidah, in modern practice the *sh'li·ah tzibbur* (community prayer leader) often is not a *kohen*. Moreover, parents commonly bless their children on Friday evening with the words of Birkat Kohanim, and in some congregations, a lay Board of Directors may itself stand in place of the *kohanim* of ancient days to offer the blessing to members of the community it serves—neither of which instances involves a *kohen*.

In the context of synagogue prayer, three physical elements often accompany the ritual of Birkat Kohanim, often referred to as *dukhenen*:[14] removing shoes, raising *tallitot* (prayer shawls) overhead to conceal the face, and lifting hands.[15] The physicality of these three ritual elements of *dukhenen* can intensify the Priestly Blessing's experiential reality—not only because they evoke a scene that may seem otherworldly to modern eyes, but also because they re-actualize three pivotal moments of Jewish spirituality.

The first physical ritual of *dukhenen*, removing one's shoes, recalls Moses removing his own shoes at God's direction before the burning bush, where God proclaimed the ground to be holy (Exodus 3:5). As for Moses, so for us: Birkat Kohanim evokes the experience of divine encounter and sanctifies the ground beneath, so the *kohanim* remove their shoes before reciting the Priestly Blessing, in order to feel and draw on the earth's power.[16]

The second physical ritual, obscuring the face with prayer shawls, can be understood to symbolize that the giver of blessing stands in for God: "So shall you place My name on the people Israel and I [God] will bless them." God, however, emphatically cannot be seen: not even Moses was allowed to see God's "face" when God's "glory" passed before Moses in the cleft of a rock on Mount Sinai (Exodus 33:20).[17] God's proclamation of the thirteen attributes brought Moses to experience profound awe (Exodus 34:6–8). Critically, the Torah makes clear that God obscured Moses' physical sight at that fateful moment (Exodus 33:22–23), requiring Moses instead to use an inner capacity of vision. As for Moses, so for us: by obscuring the face in *dukhenen*, the giver of blessing invites the recipient to experience the thirteen attributes of God with inner vision and awe.[18]

The third physical ritual, the lifting of hands outstretched, recalls that Moses' brother, Aaron, the first *kohen gadol*, blessed the people with "hands uplifted" outside the Tent of Meeting that the people

Israel carried during their forty years of wandering the desert (Leviticus 9:22). At that moment of blessing, God's glory "appeared" before the people (Leviticus 9:23). The Tent of Meeting literally was the "place of indwelling," and God was understood to "dwell" in both the Tent of Meeting and amidst the people themselves (Exodus 25:8), so God could "meet" them there (Exodus 29:42). As for Aaron and the priestly line who first transmitted the Priestly Blessing, so for us: the lifting of hands during Birkat Kohanim evokes a spiritual *mishkan*—literally, a dwelling place for God—so that God can "meet" us anew.[19]

Layered with the symbolism of these physical rituals of *dukhenen*, Birkat Kohanim is no mere liturgical remnant of bygone days: it becomes a portal for one of the most profoundly symbolic experiences in Jewish collective memory. The ground becomes holy, as beneath Moses' feet at the burning bush; inner sight re-actualizes God's glory, as before Moses' obscured face at the cleft in the rock; and Aaron's priestly service, in blessing the people at the Tent of Meeting, returns for us to "meet" God. At the moment of the Priestly Blessing, all at once we kneel at the burning bush, stand at Sinai, and raise our hands in the *mishkan*. What other Jewish experience can concentrate such significance and harness such power, in a single moment?

Transcending the Physical Plane

Ritual physicality, however, is only one level of human experience. The quip that we are not only human *doings* but also human *beings* reflects the essential truth that we are far more than our physicality. Rather, in the language of Kabbalah, we can understand human experience on four levels simultaneously: doing, in the physical realm of *assiyah*; feeling, in the emotional realm of *y'tzirah*; thinking, in the intellectual realm of *b'ri·ah*; and existing, in the ineffable realm of *atzilut*. Thus, to serve as a channel for the flow of divinity—literally, to be a *k'li kodesh*, a holy vessel—is to receive and transmit in all four realms, because each is a pathway of experience and transformation. Beyond the physical plane, then, how can the emotional, intellectual, and ineffable realms shape our experience of Birkat Kohanim?

The emotional realm, the world of *y'tzirah*, focuses on the heart as a metaphor for the wellspring of feeling. Unsurprisingly, the feeling most important to prime the flow of blessing is the love of God. Says the Zohar: "When [one] recites a blessing, one should have…a good heart, and a feeling of love in [one's] heart. This is the reason it is written, 'And you shall love the Eternal your God with all your heart, and with all your soul, and with all your might.'"[20] Birkat Kohanim, then, calls the bestower to place this name of God, the ineffable Tetragrammaton, on the people with all one's heart—not by rote or with kind thoughts alone. Rather, love of God is a precondition of this most transformational blessing. Simply put: if we do not experience love of God as much as we can in the moment, then we cannot bless in God's name with powerful effect. On the holy path of blessing, what we do not feel, we cannot do.

Neither can we truly bless anyone with whom we do not feel connected in love. Tradition invites us to do all that we do in the name of love,[21] and how much more so for the conveyance of blessing. Indeed, the Zohar is emphatic that feeling love for the recipient of blessing is an emotional condition to convey Birkat Kohanim:

> We are told that a priest not beloved by the people should not take part in blessing the people. On one occasion, when a priest went up and spread forth his hands, before he completed the blessing he turned into a heap of bones. This happened to him because there was no love between him and the people….A priest who loves not the people, or whom they love not, may not pronounce the [Priestly] Blessing.[22]

It is tempting to imagine that this kind of love comes from within oneself. After all, love is a feeling, and anyone who has loved knows that feeling within: just as each heart "knows its own bitterness,"[23] each heart also knows its own joy. Of course love must be felt— or else it is not love—but the love that most primes the flow and transmission of blessing is a love that emanates from beyond us. This is true in two ways. First and most importantly, when we love, what we feel is the flow of divinity itself.[24] Second, when we love another, the highest form of love is the love that exists because of the one we love, not because of ourselves. Even the great rationalist Maimonides understood that "when you love [literally, "conjoin with another"], do not love on your own terms but rather on the terms of your beloved."[25] This kind of love is not one of willfulness, self-indulgence, or narcissism, but is rather a love rooted in altruism, surrender, and unification with the one we love.[26]

These are the felt emotions of blessing: altruism, selflessness, empathy, surrender, and unity. And these emotions offer a way to understand why the people appearing before Ezra stood together *k'ish ehad*, "as one person" (Nehemiah 8:1): because that transcendent moment's power dissolved the illusion of separateness between souls that human consciousness perceives in our ordinary lived experience. The resulting sense of emotional unification, manifesting love and awe, is precisely the flow of God between the bestower and recipient of blessing. Yehudah Aryeh Leib Alter, the S'fat Emet (1847–1905), put it this way:

> It is written: "You shall love your neighbor as yourself," which is the fundamental principle of the Torah. This explains that when one clings to the living spark within, in that place all of the people Israel are as one, and that *itself* is loving one's neighbor. This, too, is what Rashi wrote: "your neighbor" is the blessed Holy One, in whom all is one.[27]

Hence we find two emotional fuels to convey blessing to another: experiencing love of God; and, through experiencing the love of God, coming to love another in a connective way that dissolves the illusion of spiritual separateness. By loving God, and selflessly loving another in loving God, one who blesses becomes a channel linking God and the person on whom the bestower would place God's name.

While text and tradition confirm that love is the true power of blessing, we know this truth both intuitively and by experience. The blessing that most deeply touches and transforms is the blessing that is most heartfelt. The love that can radiate in a moment of blessing is palpable beyond words. The eyes may gleam, words or music can peel back layers to caress the spirit, and a touch of the hand can transmit otherworldly energy. In that moment, time can seem to slow or even stop; the room can seem weighty or filled with light; and silence can resonate like sound. The language-defying "wow" of such a moment is the experience of divine awe. The word "love," for all the depth of emotion and experience it conveys, pales compared to the reality.

By its nature, such a love cannot be intellectualized, much less realized by mere words: there is no word or concept that can adequately depict this quality of love, much less depict the limitless potentiality we call God. And, yet, often we need words and ideas to journey through our own layers of awareness, so that we can enter into the experience of divine love and awe fully and with authenticity. This level of abstraction, which we experience as the world of *b'ri·ah*, evokes constructs and symbols of the intellect but asks us to hold them gently because they are, at best, only crude approximations.

What intellectual constructs can help us understand and enter into the experience of Birkat Kohanim? As we've seen, the physical rituals of *dukhenen* evoke the burning bush, Mount Sinai, and the Tent of Meeting, three quintessential experiences of God in the Torah. These three representations, in turn, can be understood to symbolize the three Jewish festivals: Passover, in which Moses liberated Israel from

Egyptian bondage, following the instructions he received from God at the burning bush; Shavuot, the giving of Torah at Mount Sinai; and Sukkot, when tradition calls Jews to dwell in booths reminiscent of the Tent of Meeting. These are Judaism's tributes to liberation, revelation, and redemption—the three pillars of Jewish identity and relationship with God.[29] The three festivals also are Judaism's historic pilgrimage times, in which the people collectively assembled before God (Exodus 23:17) at the place of God's choosing (Deuteronomy 16:16)—later understood to be the Temple in Jerusalem. Birkat Kohanim therefore connects not only with the three festivals but also with their communal gatherings before God. The Priestly Blessing bends the arc of the Jewish year into a single point in time, unifying the people across physical and psychic space and investing the physical location of blessing with the symbolic power of the Tent of Meeting.

By symbolically connecting the three festivals and three peak experiences of the Jewish spiritual narrative, Birkat Kohanim seems to distill essential experiences of the entire Torah. This symbolism is no accident: when the Priestly Blessing invites us to place the name of God on the people as a way of blessing them, we can understand this name of God as the Torah itself. In the words of Ezra ben Solomon, a kabbalist of thirteenth-century Spain, "The five books of the Torah are the name of the blessed Holy One!"[30]

In this way, we can understand the Priestly Blessing's focus on placing God's name on the people as, in a sense, placing the entire Torah on them. To be sure, this is not a physical placing; but by evoking the burning bush, Sinai, and the Tent of Meeting, the Torah's experiences of holiness, of supreme power, and of meaning are called to mind and effectively "placed" on the people. This understanding does not denigrate the traditional sense of Torah, as conveying the Jewish narrative of identity and the laws that are Jews' historical ways of being in the world. Rather, it invites us to expand our understanding of Torah beyond the "black-letter law" of biblical command, to include also the space between the black letters, the "white space" that in mystical thought represents the infinite generativity of God. It is also this "white space"—not just the black letters of Birkat Kohanim on the Torah scroll—that is the source of the directive to bless the people with this infinite generativity. Thus, when one transmits Birkat Kohanim, one does so not only in the name of the Tetragrammaton, but also from the white space that transcends any one name of God. In the words of Naḥmanides (1194–1270):

> We possess an authentic tradition showing that the entire Torah consists of the names of God and that the words we read can be divided in a very different way, so as to form [esoteric] names....The statement in the *aggadah* to the effect that the Torah was originally written with black fire on white fire [see, e.g., Y. Shekalim 6:1, 49d] obviously confirms our opinion that the writing was continuous, without division into words—which made it possible to read it either as a sequence of esoteric names or in the traditional way as history and *mitzvot*. Thus the Torah, as given to Moses, was divided into words in such a way as to be read as divine *mitzvot*. But at the same time he also received the oral tradition, according to which it was to be read as a sequence of names.[31]

Indeed, while Rashi might have been certain that the name of God referenced in Birkat Kohanim is the Tetragrammaton, its combination of the letters *yod-hei-vav-hei* is hardly a name at all—and certainly not one that we can pronounce. This unpronounceable "name" is a stand-in for both the entire Torah and, as Marcia Prager teaches, the inherent impossibility of accurately depicting any concept of God. Precisely because no words can suffice, the Tetragrammaton refracts myriad God-names that Torah and tradition record, to approximate the breadth of our understandings and experiences of God:

Jewish wisdom teaches us an unpronounceable name to remind us that the eternal power, the source of all, is beyond our approbation. This is the "hidden" name, hidden in its very unpronounceability; hidden because we can intend it but not say it; hidden because its very nature is to point beyond itself to the ultimate mystery of existence. When we see the name, we can only pause and breathe.

The name is mysterious and unpronounceable. So how are we to speak God's name? When we really need to say something, what should we say? It is a powerful practice to hold God's name in mind and breathe. But sometimes we really do wish to communicate and with intention call out to God by a name we can speak.

The naming of God reflects the multiple facets of the crystal revealed to our people. In Jewish (as in Islamic) tradition, we call the One by many descriptive names. Jewish prayer is a rich treasury of God-names and words of praise. *Yotzeir* means to create like an artisan from what already exists. We at times call God the great *Yotzeir*, the Artisan. We also call God *Borei*, the One who creates everything out of nothingness. We call God *Ha-rahaman*, Source of Compassionate Love. *Rehem* means "womb'" and *Ha-rahaman* is the aspect of the Holy One we know as the Source of unconditional nurturance. We call God *M'kor Ha-hayyim*, Source of Life; *Ein Sof*, the Limitless, Without End; *Hei Ha-olamim*, Life Force of Time and Space; *El Elyon*, the Most High; *Ma·ayan Raz*, the Mysterious Well; *Go·eil*, Saving Power; *Atika Kaddisha*, the Ancient Holy One; *Yah*, Breath of Life; *El Ro·i*, God Who Sees Me; *Ha-Makom*, the Place of the World or the Place we go to. Sometimes we just call God *Ha-sheim*, the Name.[32]

The "name" that the Priestly Blessing invites the priests to place on the people, then, is not truly a name but rather a "treasury" of names that encompasses the rich variety of human understandings and experiences of divinity—while transcending them all. How appropriate, then, that our ancestors intended the name to evoke divine awe: after all, in modern spiritual language, the mission of channeling such a treasury is truly awesome for anyone who would convey blessing. It follows that this experience of awe must begin with the one who blesses: whether Birkat Kohanim with full *dukhenen* or a spontaneous blessing weaved in the moment, the path of blessing begins with the bestower's lived experience of love and awe. Where we who convey blessing cannot go, we cannot bring anyone else.

But how to go there—*really* go there—when concepts and intellectual understandings are so inadequate? One helpful practice for the giver of blessing is to recall precisely that, as Zalman Schachter-Shalomi observed, all theology is an "afterthought of the believer," a feeble attempt to graft language onto experiences and ideas inherently transcending language.[33] "All creedal formulations" of religion, including those of Judaism, "are at best puny attempts at speaking of the cosmic."[34] For that reason, we must hold our ideas about God loosely and allow consciousness to flow, rather than embrace any false fixity about God or holiness.

A second helpful practice is to stop and breathe the letters *yod-hei-vav-hei*. Because these letters represent sounds of breath, this practice can cultivate inner awareness and spiritual access to God as the Breath of Life flowing through us all. In this understanding, God is as close as our next breath.

A third practice is to cultivate genuine love and awe in our own lives—and thereby lower our inner resistance to the flow of divinity— with an authentic and ongoing spiritual practice of our own. Our practice may include personal prayer, meditation, or *hitbod'dut*.[35] *Hashpa·ah*, the modality of Jewish spiritual direction attuned to discerning and priming divine flow (*shefa*) in and through our lives, is an especially helpful way to experience in our lives the truth attributed to Menaḥem Mendel, the Kotzker rebbe (1787–1859):

"Where is God? Wherever we let God in."[36] By letting God into our lives in these real and experiential ways, we can prime the flow of love and awe by which truly transformative blessing can unfold organically.

A fourth helpful practice invites an exercise of projecting imagery onto the recipient of blessing. Before offering Birkat Kohanim or any other blessing, imagine the name—this time, the Tetragrammaton— literally placed on the recipient of blessing, in the way that Birkat Kohanim suggests. Arranging the Hebrew letters *yod, hei, vav, and hei* vertically along the body from the head down the torso, the letters would hint at a human form:[37]

As a tool of focusing one's intention at the moment of blessing, this image can "remind us that we are [made] in the Divine Image, and that the energies of the letters which manifest ultimate divinity also flow through us."[38] This practice, in turn, can remind that as a being created in the image of God, every recipient of blessing already bears the name of God. Thus, the true role before any conveyer of blessing is not so much to "place" the name of God, as the Priestly Blessing invites, but rather to "see" the name already there—already manifest on the body, heart, and soul of everyone whom one would bless. Like the inner vision that Moses cultivated on Mount Sinai when God proclaimed the thirteen attributes, the bestower of blessing can deploy inner vision to see divinity already inhering in whomever he or she blesses in and with God's name.

What's more, we can imagine this name as equally visible to others. What if everyone could see the *shem ha-m'forash*, the Tetragrammaton, already placed on everyone else? What if everyone could see that everyone is inherently created *b'tzelem Elohim*, in the divine image? This would hearken back to the hasidic teaching, attributed to Rabbi Naḥman of Bratslav, of the tainted grain. In this parable, the world was going mad from eating tainted wheat. A king and his prime minister decided to consume the tainted wheat, so that they would not starve, but they also decided to mark their foreheads—so that each others' marks would also remind them that they were going mad.[39] If all of us could see the divine name on everyone, all would see that we come ready-marked not for madness but for a profound sanity our world has never known. One who can see the potential of that world can transmit its transformative power in blessing.

Such a world is not beyond reach, nor is it merely potential: it exists already in the ineffable realm of *atzilut*, the world of spirit transcending duality and imperfection, the Source of Blessing in which the illusion of separateness truly melts into unity. In this realm of spirit, we need not imagine that we are connected: we truly *are*, existentially, because in *atzilut* division and disconnection do not exist. In *atzilut*, we are within the benevolent vastness of God, the infinitude of existence itself beyond any concept or image accessible to the human mind. We melt into the experience of divine love.

Centuries of Jewish mystics have observed that the Hebrew letters of the word "me," *ani* (*alef-nun-yod*), are the same as the letters of the word "nothing," *ayin* (*alef-yod-nun*), also known as *Ein Sof* ("without end"),[40] the highest kabbalistic rendition of the divine Infinite from which all creation flows.[41] In wisdom attributed to the Maggid of Mezritch (1710–1772), successor of the Baal Shem Tov, "all beings return to the divine Nothingness (*Ayin*) through the process of *d'veikut*," cleaving to God with all one's heart and soul.[42] By this spiritual cleaving, the Maggid taught, one draws divine inflow (*shefa*) through oneself into the world.[43] Others understand spiritual return to God not as cleaving to God but rather as immersing oneself so totally in God that one achieves *bittul ha-yeish* (the diffusion of one's independent selfhood into the Divine), so that one's personal *ani* merges into the infinite *Ayin*.[44] Whether we understand this spiritual experience as cleaving to God or diffusing into God, when we temporarily surrender our individual "I" to the Infinite divine *Ayin* in this way, we approach the realm of *atzilut*, from which flows the greatest power to transmit blessing. In the language of spiritual cleaving, Rabbi Levi Yitzhak of Berditchev (1740–1810) taught: "The blessed Holy One constantly causes the flow of holiness (*mashpi·a tamid shefa*), so all worlds flow from [i.e., have their source in] *Ayin*." In turn, one can harness the fullest power of blessing "when one cleaves with all one's power to *Ayin*."[45]

These mystical understandings offer a profound approach to Birkat Kohanim, by reading God's subsequent reference to *ani* ("and *I* will bless them") as the *Ayin* of God's benevolent infinitude. When a bestower of blessing temporarily suspends the illusion of spiritual separateness and cleaves to (or diffuses into) God, that is how one can "place [God's] name on the people Israel and [then *Ayin*] will bless them" (Numbers 6:27). A giver of blessing who experiences this suspension of spiritual boundaries can become a vessel for holy Oneness, and the *Ayin* that is God's constant flow of holiness can permeate that Oneness into lived reality.

To be sure, because the world of *atzilut* defies precise language, any description ultimately will miss the point—or, worse, obscure the point. Anyone who has ever experienced transcendence knows that words fail to describe the experience. No words can fully describe experiences that envelop us so completely that we temporarily surrender our individuality and emerge touched and changed. These experiences invite countless words of explanation, but ultimately they leave us wordless: they are the stuff of awe, the realm of *atzilut*. It is this realm of the inexplicable— the wordless surrender to "wow"—to which anyone aspiring to bless in God's name must become open so the power of transformation emanating from that realm can flow through.

This way of bestowing Birkat Kohanim models how we all can become conveyers of blessing. By connecting deeply and experientially to both love of God and love of another, we can become vessels to transmit the love and awe that are the power of every blessing. In the deepest sense, love and awe *are* the blessings we place as the name of God in the exquisite moment of blessing, when the Infinite that is God and the "I" that is each of us become one. In the merit of our legacy of Birkat Kohanim, may each of us become vessels to transmit the name of God in this way—and thereby become true partners with the Holy One of Blessing.

NOTES

[1] In the most literal sense, one who speaks the words of Birkat Kohanim, or any blessing, does so as God's physical representative and thereby serves as God's "symbolic exemplar." See generally Jack Bloom, *Rabbi as Symbolic Exemplar: By the Power Invested in Me* (Binghamton, NY: Haworth, 2002).

[2] See generally Ezra 7:1.

[3] See, e.g., Reuven Chaim Klein, "Was Ezra a High Priest?" in *Jewish Bible Quarterly* 41:3 (2013), pp. 182–184; cf. also M. Parah 4:1.

[4] Eliezer Berkovits, *Not in Heaven: The Nature and Function of Halakha* (New York: KTAV 1983), p. 69.

[5] B. Yoma 69b.

[6] B. Megillah 25a.

[7] See, e.g., Gershom Scholem, "The Meaning of Torah in Jewish Mysticism," in *On the Kabbalah and Its Symbolism* (New York: Schocken, 1965), p. 40.

[8] See Rashi to Numbers 6:27, s.v. *v'samu et sh'mi*.

[9] B. Yoma 39b.

[10] Rav Giddel was a talmudic sage of the late third century C.E. It is especially noteworthy that he figures prominently in the rabbinic response to Ezra invoking of the name of God. Rav Giddel taught laws of *t'vilah* (ritual bathing) at the gates of bathhouses where women assembled, an apparent breach of modesty; when asked about this seemingly unusual practice, Rav Giddel replied that he was unafraid because his passion did not control him. See B. Berakhot 20a. Even this task-oriented Rav Giddel insisted that it was not just appropriate but also necessary for Ezra to invoke God's name, ostensibly to arouse passion and awe.

[11] B. Yoma 69b. Halakhically speaking, *hora·at sha·ah* is best understood as a judicial principle of limited focus, a so-called "emergency principle" that may suspend a legal norm temporarily given the great pressure of a time-limited circumstance. See, e.g., Alan J. Yuter, "*Hora'at Sha'ah*: The Emergency Principle in Jewish Law and a Contemporary Application," in *Jewish Political Studies Review* 13:3–4 (Fall 2001), pp. 2–3. In perhaps its most classical rendition, *hora·at sha·ah* may seek "to bring people at large back to the Jewish faith," even to the extent of nullifying a positive *mitzvah* or violating a negative *mitzvah* for that purpose. See Maimonides, M.T. Hilkhot Mamrim 2:4. By design, therefore, *hora·at sha·ah* should be invoked sparingly, lest this exception swallow whatever halakhic rule might be suspended in its service; cf. M.T. Hilkhot Mamrim 2:8. Beyond legal formalism, however, *hora·at sha·ah* operates as an energetic principle by which to discern a holistic trajectory for "paradigm shifting" social, legal, and spiritual developments based on pressing "needs of the hour" with sweeping transformational potential. See Zalman Schachter-Shalomi and Daniel Siegel,

Integral Halachah: Transcending and Including (Victoria, B.C.: Trafford, 2007), p. 29. If bringing people back to faith and spiritual attunement may justify a suspension of even Torah law within the four corners of *halakhah*, then *a fortiori* that goal must rivet and motivate the heartfelt intention of spiritual leaders who would convey blessing in tradition's name.

[12] *Pesikta D'rav Kahana*, ed. Bernard Mandelbaum (1962; rpt. New York: Jewish Theological Seminary, 1987), pp. 40a–b, quoting Isaiah 43:10.

[13] Martin Buber, *On Judaism* (New York: Schocken, 1967), p. 84.

[14] The Yiddish word for conveying Birkat Kohanim, *dukhenen* derives from the Hebrew noun *dukhan,* the cultic "platform" where priests stood in Temple times. See, e.g., B. Shabbat 118a.

[15] See generally Ismar Elbogen, *Jewish Liturgy: A Comprehensive History*, trans. Raymond P. Scheindlin (Philadelphia: Jewish Publication Society 1993), p. 62; Sandor S. Feldman, "The Blessing of the Kohenites," in *The Psychodynamics of American Jewish Life*, ed. Norman Kiell (New York: Twayne, 1967), pp. 403–430.

[16] This practice of "barefoot blessing" derives from Rabbi Yoḥanan ben Zakkai in one of the earliest strata of post-biblical Jewish law and custom; see B. Sotah 40a.

[17] To be sure, God spoke to Moses "face to face, as one speaks to a friend" (Exodus 33:11), and "there never again arose a prophet in Israel like Moses, whom God knew face to face" (Deuteronomy 34:10). Likewise, God spoke to Moses "mouth to mouth" rather than by parable or dream (Numbers 12:8). While these verses depict an intimacy between God and Moses unparalleled in Jewish textual tradition, the verses depict God—and not Moses—as the One who speaks and knows "face to face" and "mouth to mouth." Far from passive in his relationship with God, Moses also spoke directly to God—a practice we can emulate in *hitbod'dut*, as described below—but textually not even Moses could see God's "face."

[18] In this spirit, Rabbi Akiva banned the people from looking at the priests during Birkat Kohanim—hence the modern practice of obscuring the giver of blessing's face with a *tallit*. See Elbogen, *Jewish Liturgy*, p. 63, and cf. B. Ḥagigah 16a.

[19] The Torah records that God instructed Moses: *v'asu li mikdash v'shakhanti b'tokham*, "They shall make me a sanctuary that I may dwell among them" (Exodus 25:8). This verse emphasizes that God would dwell not only within the physical structure of the sanctuary but also among the people—and even *b'tokham*, "within them." Even so, the Tent of Meeting was the "place of meeting" between God and the people (Exodus 29:42), which begs the question of why any physical place should be necessary if God "dwells among" or "dwells within" the people. While answers to this timeless question are beyond the scope of this essay, we can understand the physicality of the *dukhenen* rituals, and especially the outstretching of hands, as evocative of the ancient priestly service in the *mishkan*, which served to evoke the indwelling of the Divine Presence that our ancestors experienced and narrated in such physical terms.

[20] Zohar III 117a, quoting Deuteronomy 6:5.

[21] See, e.g., Shohama H. Wiener, "Love is the Answer: A New Paradigm," in *Lifecycles: Jewish Women on Biblical Themes in Contemporary Life*, eds. Debra Orenstein and Jane Rachel Litman (Woodstock, VT: Jewish Lights Publishing, 1997), vol. 2, p. 312, citing Sifrei Devarim §32 on Deuteronomy 6:5.

[22] Zohar III 147b.

[23] Proverbs 14:10.

[24] If this axiom is not self-evident, the numerical value of *yod-hei-vav-hei*, the Tetragrammaton, is twenty-six, equal to the numerical value for *eḥad* ("one") and *ahavah* ("love"), each of which is thirteen. The essence of God is unity in love.

[25] Maimonides, Commentary on Pirkei Avot 1:6.

[26] This is not to diminish the emotional and psychological importance of healthy boundaries. A selfless love that unifies in a manner befitting holiness is not possible in a context of co-dependence, abuse, or other damaging behavior.

[27] *S'fat Emet, drash* for Purim 1873 (authors' translation), quoting Sifra *K'doshim* 3:12 and Leviticus 19:18.

[28] See *S'fat Emet* 106:8 ("The Feast of Booths is the [symbolic] representation of the *mishkan*"); see also Amos 9:11.

[29] Adapted from Franz Rosenzweig, *The Star of Redemption*, trans. William W. Hallo (New York: Holt, Rinehart and Winston, 1971), part 2.

[30] Quoted in Scholem, "The Meaning of Torah," p. 39, n. 2. Similarly, in Scholem's understanding: "Torah is interpreted as a mystical unity, whose primary purpose is not to convey a specific meaning but rather to express the immensity of God's power, which is concentrated in [God's] 'name.' To say that the Torah is a name does not mean that it is a name that might be pronounced as such, nor has it anything to do with any rational conception of the social function of a name. The meaning is, rather, that in the Torah God expressed transcendent Being, or at least that part or aspect of [God's] Being that can be revealed to Creation and through Creation....For [this] instrument which brought the world into being is far more than a mere instrument since...Torah is the concentrated power of God['s] Self, as expressed in [God's] name" (ibid., p.40).

[31] Naḥmanides, "Introduction to Commentary on the Torah," reprinted in Scholem, "The Meaning of Torah," p. 38.

[32] Marcia Prager, *The Path of Blessing: Experiencing the Energy and Abundance of the Divine* (Woodstock, VT: Jewish Lights, 1988), pp. 99–100 (transliterations adapted).

[33] Zalman Schachter-Shalomi, "Deep Ecumenism" (a 1998 manuscript in private circulation), p. 9.

[34] Ibid, p. 13.

[35] *Hitbod'dut* is a practice of personal, spontaneous, and direct oral communication with God popularized by Rabbi Naḥman of Bratslav. For modern guidance in *hitbod'dut* practices, see e.g. Howard Cohen, "Spiritual Development in Nature: Methods of Individual and Group *Hashpa'ah*," in *Seeking and Soaring: Jewish*

Approaches to Spiritual Guidance and Development, eds. Goldie Milgram and Shohama Harris Wiener (2d ed.; New Rochelle, NY: Reclaiming Judaism Press, 2014), pp. 74–77; and Yitzhak Buxbaum, *Jewish Spiritual Practices* (Northvale, NJ: Jason Aronson, 1990), pp. 610–615.

[36] *The Sayings of Menahem Mendel of Kotsk,* ed. Simcha Raz and trans. Edward Levin (Northvale, NJ: Jason Aronson, 1995), p. 10.

[37] Image reprinted with permission from Deborah Kerdeman and Lawrence Kushner, *The Invisible Chariot: An Introduction to Kabbalah and Jewish Spirituality* (Denver: Alternatives in Religious Education, 1986).

[38] Marcia Prager, *A Siddur for Erev Shabbat* (Philadelphia: Pnai Or, 2009), p. ii.

[39] Cf., e.g., Howard Schwartz, *Reimagining the Bible: The Storytelling of the Rabbis* (New York: Oxford University Press, 1988), p. 171.

[40] The words *ayin* and *ein* are homographs in Hebrew.

[41] See, e.g., Gershom Scholem, *Major Trends in Jewish Mysticism* (1941; rpt. New York: Schocken Books, 1995), p. 218; Zohar I 23a.

[42] Joseph Ben-Shlomo, "Gershom Scholem on Pantheism in the Kabbalah," in, *Gershom Scholem: The Man and His Work,* ed. Paul Mendes-Flohr (Albany, NY: State University of New York Press, 1994), p. 68.

[43] Ibid.

[44] See Zohar II 42b.

[45] *Sefer K'dushat Levi,* ed. S. Berger (Tel Aviv: Mechon Hadrat Ḥein, 2004), vol. 2, p. 152 (authors' translation), citing B. Rosh Hashanah 10b.

I Have Dreamed a Dream...

Howard Avruhm Addison

Sovereign of the Universe, I am Yours as are my dreams. I have dreamed a dream and know not what it is. Whether I have dreamed of myself, or my companions have dreamed of me, or I have dreamed of others—if they be good dreams, confirm and reinforce them like the dreams of Joseph; if they require remedy, heal them, as the waters of Marah were healed by our teacher, Moses, as Miriam was healed of her leprosy, Naaman of his leprosy, Hezekiah of his sickness, and the waters of Jericho by Elisha. As You turned the curse of the wicked Balaam into a blessing, so turn all my dreams into something good for me.[1]

Truth be told, I was twenty-one before I ever witnessed the *kohanim* (priests) ascend the *bimah* to ritually bless the congregation. Raised in a community where those of priestly descent didn't *dukhen*,[2] I recall being totally intrigued. However, I also remember looking at the Birnbaum prayerbook,[3] which instructed us to murmur the above-cited prayer, and wondering: how is this meant to work? Was the experience of standing completely enfolded in *tallitot* or otherwise shielding our eyes as the light of the Divine Presence, *or ha-sh'khinah*, purportedly streamed through the outstretched priests' fingers meant to induce a dream-like state? But even if that were so, then what was this ceremony's connection to my personal dreams? How was it possibly going to advance the good ones and transform the bad? And, most basic of all: whatever does the "healing of dreams" mean, anyway?

More than four decades have passed since my initial encounter with this curious prayer. As I've grown more interested in dreams, I find myself being drawn back to its words, and the customs and interpretations that surround it. Yet, I can't help but wonder: what wisdom and healing power might still inhere in this ancient entreaty? On an even broader level, what relevance might our tradition's views of dreams and dreaming hold for us who live in this modern, psycho-scientific age? And what does any of this have to do with Birkat Kohanim?

Judaism and Dreams: On Being of Two Minds

Arguably, the word that best summarizes Judaism's orientation toward dreams was chosen by Monford Harris as the title for the penultimate chapter of his *Studies in Jewish Dream Interpretation*:[4] "ambivalence." Depending on who is doing the counting, dreams are mentioned as many as thirty-three times in the Hebrew Bible, with nine such instances occurring in Genesis alone. However, the various texts of Scripture are hardly unequivocal in their judgment of dreams or their value. The prophet Joel, speaking in God's name, declared: "And it will come about after this, that I will pour out My spirit on all humankind and your sons and daughters will prophesy; your old men will dream dreams and your young men will see visions" (2:28). Conversely, Kohelet warns: "For through the multitude of dreams and vanities, there are many words; but one should revere [only] God" (5:6). Deuteronomy seems divided against itself over the reliability of dreamers and visions, dithering over how to determine if their communications are of God or derived from presumption or malevolent forces—to the extent of wondering whether even the fulfillment of their messages is a mark of validity.[6]

The classical texts of Rabbinic Judaism also speak with a split voice. Rabbi Meir, a second-century sage from the Land of Israel, found dreams inconsequential, stating that "dreams neither help nor harm,"[7] while the third-century Babylonian teacher, Rav Judah, said in the name of (his teacher) Rav: "There are three things for which one should pray: good rulers, good years, and good dreams...as it is written, 'You make me dream and thereby cause me to live.'"[8] The Talmud's compendium on dream interpretation[9] first indicates that a pertinent interpretation need be specific to the dreamer and his or her dream, and then offers what seems to be an authoritative list of dream images and their meanings!

Post-talmudic Judaism's valuation of dreams waxes and wanes. Classic mystical texts—including the twelfth-century German *Sefer Ḥasidim* ("The Book of the Pious"), as well as *Sefer Ha-zohar* ("The Book of Splendor"), which first appeared in thirteenth-century Spain—contain ample references to dreams. During that same era in France, Rabbi Jacob of Marvège employed dream questions to decide some matters of Jewish law, as recounted in his *She'eilot U-t'shuvot Min Ha-shamayim* ("Inquiries and Responsa from Heaven").[10] In sixteenth-century Italy, Rabbi Solomon Almoli composed a dream manual entitled *Pitron Ha-halomot* (literally, "The Interpretation of Dreams"). However, many authorities then and later most likely shared Maimonides' perspective that dreams are solely products of the imagination.[11]

Our modern period reflects a similar dichotomy. The literature of Hasidism, beginning with the lessons taught by its founding teacher, Rabbi Israel Baal Shem Tov (1698–1760), is replete with tales of visions and dreams. Monford Harris describes both Iraqi and American Yiddish dream texts written in the early twentieth century.[12] Students of the late North African kabbalist Madame Colette Aboulker-Muscat (1909–2003), including Catherine Shainberg of New York, continue to teach and/or practice versions of Jewish dream interpretation that they learned from her in Jerusalem.[13] However, most contemporary rabbis, and the vast majority of modern Jewry (save some in the Hasidic and Sephardic communities), reflect a modern scientific bias that prefers Western therapeutic modes to traditional forms of counsel that are deemed "old worldly," unreliable, and outmoded. In disproportionate numbers, today's Jews will discuss their dreams with psychotherapists—while the possibility of addressing them in Jewish contexts has been largely foreclosed.

When We Sleep: The Process of Dreaming

For more than a century, great advances have been made in our understanding of dreams. Sigmund Freud's *The Interpretation of Dreams*, published in 1900, marked a breakthrough in the study of how the unconscious manifests itself through our dreams. Freud's theory of dreams as wish fulfillment,[14] Carl Jung's insight into the compensatory and complementary roles dreams play in the integrative growth of the self,[15] and Fritz Perls's observation that each character in a dream represents projected aspects of the dreamer,[16] have all furthered our understanding and interpreting of dreams. Advances in neuroscience have even made it possible to locate which parts of the brain go "off line" and which continue to function when we sleep, which helps explain the associative, nonlinear, symbolic, and even surreal quality of our dreams.[17]

If we are to understand the primary intent underlying the "Sovereign of the Universe" prayer (found at the beginning of this essay) and its connection to Birkat Kohanim, we will need a sense of the cultural setting in which it arose—a setting far different from our own. In the introductory lines of *Dreamers, Scribes, and Priests,* Frances Flannery-Dailey reminds us:

> Ancient Mediterranean and Near Eastern peoples regarded dreams quite differently than do those of us in Post-Freudian, modern society. Whereas we tend to view dreams as unreal, interior phenomena, ancient peoples believed that some dreams were genuine visits from the deity or their divine

representatives. . . .Modern dreamers tend to hold that the value
of dreams lies in their ability to yield information about the
dreamers' past or present psychology; ancient peoples believed
that dreams impart knowledge of the future or knowledge of
events apart from the interior life of the dreamer.[18]

Today, most of us use the words "I had a dream" to connote the
inner physical and psychological processes that occur while we are
asleep. The ancients, who viewed dreams as visitations from other
dimensions, would "see," be "met," or be "visited" by their dreams.[19]
"Pleasant" or "evil" dreams were understood to reflect the dreamer's
psychological status. "Message" dreams, which directly conveyed
God's word (like Jacob's ladder dream[20]), and "symbol" dreams (akin
to Joseph's dreams and those he interpreted for Pharaoh's cup-
bearer and baker, and later for Pharaoh himself[21]) were of far greater
import. These had ramifications for the health and fortunes of both
individuals and nations.

The understanding of dreams put forward in the literature of
Rabbinic Judaism is based, in part, on the belief that the spirit of
prophecy had departed from Israel during the early Second Temple
period.[22] While some sages claimed that what one sees in dreams is
only suggested by the dreamer's own thoughts,[23] others maintained
that even during this post-prophetic era, when we lack bona fide
prophets to clearly speak God's word, God still communicates with
us through dreams.[24] As the talmudic master Rabba said, "Though
the blessed Holy One declared, 'I will surely hide My face on that
day,' God also said, 'I shall speak with him in a dream.'"[25] Sleep may
be considered an incomplete or sixtieth part of death, but dreams are
a sixtieth part of prophecy.[26]

Perhaps the most quoted talmudic dictum about dreams is
attributed to the Babylonian sage Rav Ḥisda (d. 320 C.E.): "A dream
left uninterpreted is like a letter left unread."[27] This statement implies

that, like their predecessors in the ancient Near East, there were many sages who considered dreams to be visitations from another dimension. They relate tales of individuals visited by departed biblical figures, who may symbolize a certain value or even impart a message.[28] Twice the Talmud refers to a dispenser of supernatural information called the "master of the dream" (ba·al ha-ḥalom), a variant of the title "master of dreams," which Joseph's brothers pejoratively applied to him.[29] Harris ascribes little importance to this figure,[30] who is rarely mentioned in Jewish lore and whose messages the Talmud twice tells the dreamer to ignore, even though the ba·al ha-ḥalom appeared in the dream. It is interesting to note that in another rabbinic text, the instructions of the ba·al ha-ḥalom led to the freeing of a female Jewish captive by her Greek captor,[31] and that the Zohar later identifies the archangel Gabriel as the ba·al ha-ḥalom.[32]

While the sixteenth-century dream interpreter Solomon Almoli basically maintained the sages' view that dreams are visitations from heaven,[33] the Zohar sets forth a complementary understanding according to which the soul actually leaves the body during the dreaming process and ascends to heaven, where it learns of future events and receives warnings of various sorts:

> For when one sleeps, the soul leaves and soars aloft. God then reveals to the soul...future events or things that correspond to one's own thoughts, so as to serve as a warning. For no revelation comes when the body is in full vigor [i.e., awake and moving][34] but an angel communicates things to the soul, and the soul transmits them; dreams, then, originate on high when souls leave the bodies, each one taking its own route.[35]

This view is reflected in the traditional prayer recited upon waking, Modeh Ani, which thanks God for faithfully and compassionately restoring our souls to us each morning of our lives.[36] Examples of both motifs—both dreams as visitations and dreams as the ascent of the soul—can be found throughout kabbalistic and hasidic lore.[37]

To Heal Troubling Dreams

Because most ancients and medievals believed that dreams originated in other-worldly dimensions, the need to find a proper response to disturbing night visions took on special importance. Texts from as far back as ancient Assyria and Babylonia describe various petitions offered and rites employed to ameliorate the potential impact of "evil" dreams. Examples of such prayers include the following:

> Make pleasant my dream [when I am on my] nocturnal couch. May the dream I shall see [this night] be good. May the dream I shall see be reliable; transform [O gods] the dreams I shall see into pleasant ones.

Some devotees even turned to burying figurines under their bedroom floors inscribed with phrases like, "Get out, O evil [caused] by dreams; come in, O pleasantness [caused] by dreams."[38]

It is against this backdrop that we can better understand the dream amelioration rituals that are later found in the Talmud. While many sages believed that dreams are a sixtieth part of prophecy, they were concerned about the portents and the sources of dreams. Does a disturbing image foretell harm? Is it a warning or a call to repentance? Or is it a veiled symbol of good tidings?[39] Can one even rely on the veracity of a dream message, or has it been sent by demonic forces to mislead the dreamer?[40] To avoid any potentially negative consequences, the Talmud prescribes three alternative amelioration rituals, all subsumed under the Hebrew rubric *hatavat ha-ḥalom*, literally to "make better" or "enhance" (the implications of) our dreams.

Through a "dream fast," one who experienced a troubling dream could do penance in hope of averting any portended harm. Considered effective against bad dreams (as is "fire, which consumes fibers"), some authorities even permitted the dreamer an otherwise forbidden fast on Shabbat, provided the dream had occurred the night before.[41] A primary goal of this fast, as well as the other ceremonies described below, is to move the dreamer to repent, so that God will mercifully forgive and "sweeten" the outcome of the troubling dream.

A second rite entails gathering three friends[42] together immediately after the morning service on the day following a troubling dream.[43] All four participants recognize but never openly speak of the convener's disturbing dream. Instead, the dreamer begins by stating seven times that his (or possibly her) dream was good, which the friends affirm seven times.[44] Antiphonally they recite a total of three sets of three biblical verses: the first containing derivations of the word "to reverse or transform,"[45] the second set based on verses including variations of the verb "to redeem,"[46] and the third all containing the word for well-being and peace.[47] The ceremony concludes with the recitation of several biblical passages, each begun by the dreamer and concluded by the friends.[48] As the dreamer then contributes to *tzedakah*, the friends recite words now familiar to us from the High Holy Day Musaf: "Repentance, prayer, and charity avert the harshness of the decree" and bless the dreamer, saying, "peace be to you, us and to all Israel. Amen."

As might be evident from the two rituals described above, the dreamer never asks to have his (or her) dreams stop, or even to have them interpreted. Instead, these rites are intended to "sweeten" or transform the dreams. The healing power of this dynamic will become clearer still, as we now explore of the entreaty "Sovereign of the Universe, I have dreamed a dream."[49]

"Sovereign of the Universe"

The Priestly Blessing, as prescribed in Numbers 6:24–26, was originally offered daily following the morning sacrifices in the Temple. Now incorporated into the prayer service, it is still recited by the *kohanim* present each morning in Jerusalem; other communities throughout Israel recite it only on Shabbat and festival days. Outside the Land of Israel, the most prevalent custom is for the *kohanim* only to invoke the threefold blessing during the repetition of the Musaf Amidah on all major Holy Days (first and last days of Passover and the first days of Sukkot, as well as on Shavuot, Rosh Hashanah, and Yom Kippur, Shemini Atzeret) except Simḥat Torah, when it is recited during the Shaḥarit Amidah.

When Birkat Kohanim was recited regularly, all the dismayed dreamer had to do was attend worship the next morning and recite "Sovereign of the Universe" as the *kohanim* blessed the community. However, as the opportunities to hear Birkat Kohanim decreased, several procedural questions arose. Should the dreamer only recite "Sovereign of the Universe" if he or she had a disturbing dream the night before the holy day, or can it cover all disturbing dreams one has experienced since the previous festival? If one recites it on the first day of a festival and has no troubling dream the following night, should it be recited again on the second day, or would that violate the proscription against taking God's name in vain? In those locales where Birkat Kohanim is recited on Shabbat, is everyone allowed to say "Sovereign of the Universe," or is it—like the "dream fast"—permitted only to those who had disturbing dreams the night before? When should the recitation of the "Sovereign of the Universe" prayer begin and end? And what happens if it seems the worshipper is unable to complete the entire prayer before the *kohanim* finish their blessing?[50]

The practice today in congregations that recite "Sovereign of the Universe" is for everyone present to say it on each festival day.[51] The first day's recitation covers all disturbing dreams since the last festival. Since the prayer asks God to heal dreams others have had about you, it also can be recited on the second day; after all, who knows who might have dreamed of you the night before, even if you yourself had no disturbing dream then? In Israel, where Birkat Kohanim is recited on Shabbat, the custom is for "Sovereign of the Universe" to be recited solely by those troubled by their Friday night dreams, similar to the restriction cited above covering a "dream fast"; this is a moot point for those who reside outside of Israel.

To assist in deciphering the meaning of the prayer, it might be useful to understand exactly how this dramatic rite proceeds *in situ*. The cantor and the kohanim antiphonally recite the first two words of the blessing, *y'varekh'kha Adonai* ("May the Eternal bless you"). The *kohanim* then chant a melody as the congregants recite the text of "Sovereign of the Universe," and then conclude with the third word of the first blessing, *v'yishm'rekha* ("and guard you"). The community then responds, *amen*. The cantor and *kohanim* then antiphonally recite the next four words of blessing, *ya·eir Adonai panav eilekha* ("May the Eternal's face shine upon you"). The *kohanim* again chant a melody while the congregants repeat the text of "Sovereign of the Universe," and they then conclude with the fifth and final word of the second blessing, *vi-ḥunneka* ("and be gracious unto you"). The community again responds with an amen. The cantor and *kohanim* then antiphonally recite the first six words of final blessing, *yissa Adonai panav eilekha v'yaseim l'kha* ("May the Eternal's face be turned toward you [connoting divine favor] and grant you…"), chant the melody, and conclude with the final word, *shalom* ("peace") as the community responds with a final amen. While the *kohanim* privately recite their own concluding prayer, the congregation offers a different entreaty: "You who are majestic on high and who abides in might, You are peace and Your name is peace. May it be Your will to bestow peace on us."[52]

Underlying both the recitation of the "Sovereign of the Universe" prayer and the aforementioned "gathering of three friends" ceremony is the talmudic principle according to which "all dreams follow the mouth [i.e., their stated interpretation].[53] Tractate Berakhot even recounts the misadventures of an unscrupulous dream interpreter, one Bar Hedya, whose pronouncements would determine whether identical dreams would be fulfilled for good or for ill, based on whether or not the dreamers paid him his fee.[54] On a practical level, the notion that dreams "mean" whatever their interpreters claim they mean might indicate that the dreamer is more likely to focus on those aspects of the dream highlighted by the interpreter, while remaining insensitive to other elements in the dream. However, I believe this notion is rooted more firmly in Judaism's beliefs about the power of words in general. Genesis 1 depicts a God who speaks the world into existence. A great deal of Jewish superstitious practice is based on name magic and the recombination of the letters of various Hebrew words (including equating their numeric value with those of other phrases, all of which are subsumed under the general rubric of *gematria*). A popular incantation used even today by magicians, "Abracadabra," is actually an anglicized version of an ancient Aramaic phrase meaning, "I shall create through speaking."[55]

Neither when reciting "Sovereign of the Universe," nor through the ritual of "gathering three friends" is the dreamer looking for verbal interpretations. Even to admit out loud the belief that one's dream images were evil might trigger harmful consequences, as indicated by the talmudic warning not to "open your mouth to Satan"—intended to warn against inadvertently allowing one's words to serve as portals for demonic forces.[56] Through the recitation of Birkat Kohanim and its attendant prayer, or by the dreamer and the three friends repeatedly affirming that the dream was good, and through the calls during both rituals for transformation, release, fortification, healing, and peace, the dreamer finds assurance that the troubling images of his or her dream might ultimately bode well for the dreamer.

Through its fifteen Hebrew words, Birkat Kohanim invokes God's blessing, protection, illumination, grace, favor, and peace. When recited by the *kohanim*, God's presence is understood to be directly manifest amidst the congregation gathered in the sanctuary. It is particularly within this flow of blessing, and the sense of the immediacy of the Divine evoked by Birkat Kohanim, that the potentially harmful portends of our dreams can best and most thoroughly be transformed for good.

One analogy used to describe this ceremony's widely perceived and intense power to heal dreams was offered by the seventeenth-century Galician commentator, Rabbi Avraham Hayyim Schor.[57] It derives from a principle associated with the Torah's dietary laws, known to halakhic cognoscenti as the *bateil b'shishim* rule. The words *bateil b'shishim* literally mean "it is annulled through sixty [parts]," and the principle can best be explained by example: if, for example, milk were inadvertently to drip into a vat of meat soup, the soup would be rendered non-kosher—unless the soup's original volume was at least sixty times greater than the spilled milk. If, however, this proportion is met or exceeded, then the milk is deemed nullified and the soup is considered kosher. When the *kohanim* bless the people, the radiant Divine Presence—itself acknowledged in our texts as the source of prophecy—is believed to flood the sanctuary. Its infinite volume is more than sufficient to annul a bad dream, imagined literally to constitute a sixtieth part of prophecy,[59] even if that dream emanated from demonic forces. It has even been noted that if one adds up the number of letters that constitute the fifteen Hebrew words of Birkat Kohanim, the total is sixty![60]

Given its long history, reciting "Sovereign of the Universe" during Birkat Kohanim must have proved reassuring and cleansing for our forebears. However, the question remains whether its recitation—or participation in any of the other traditional dream amelioration rites—might so impact us today.

Dreams and Their Meanings: Then and Now

Flannery-Dailey was definitely correct: our contemporary understanding of dreams is far different from that of the pre-moderns.[61] However, the more I study the classical Jewish texts that address dreams, the more foreshadowing I see of principles that we moderns often claim to have discovered during the twentieth and twenty-first centuries. To be sure, the observations scattered throughout tradition are often formulated in mythopoeic language and clearly were not derived through scientific study. Indeed, save in the work of Almoli and a few others, they were not presented in any systematic fashion at all. Contrary to talmudic claims that all dreams contain an admixture of nonsense,[62] we are now coming to understand that potentially every aspect of a dream can be meaningful. It certainly would be unwarranted to claim that all elements of Freud's or Jung's theories of dreams can be found in rabbinic or kabbalistic literature; however, there is certainly wisdom in these classical sources that we should not discount—as some of them presage, by centuries, the findings of modern psychology and even neurology.[63]

Carl Jung claimed that imagery and symbol are in and of themselves the language of dreams, a fact now borne out by the current findings of neurobiology.[64] In the twelfth century, the aforementioned *Sefer Ḥasidim* already observed that "the symbolic imagery of dreams may be compared to sign language. When travelling in a foreign country, one will meet people whose language one does not understand. They will communicate through sign language, much like we communicate with the deaf. Yet the wise can discern what is being shown in the dream, why it is shown through symbols, and for what the symbols stand."[65]

Centuries ago, Rabbi Zeira claimed: "One who goes seven days without a dream is called *ra* ['unfortunate' or 'bad'], since Scripture says, 'One shall abide satisfied and shall not be visited by misfortune (*ra*).'—Read not *savei·a* (satisfied) but *sheva* (seven). What it means is this: one sees [all sorts of things in a dream], but does not remember what has been seen."[66]

We now know that all human beings (as well as other living creatures) dream during REM sleep, as well during other times in the sleep cycle, even if those dreams are not remembered upon waking.[67] Rabbi Zeira might well be right that one who cannot recall even one dream per week is "unfortunate" because this lack represents a serious disconnect from one's unconscious, thus from a vital source of new insight and a path toward personal integration. That person might also be deemed "bad" because disconnection from one's dreams insulates one from their warnings—and so we might thus be more susceptible to acting out harmful impulses unconsciously, or to failing to see dangers that can result from not heeding a dream's warning to moderate or rebalance our behavior.[68] As the Zohar recounts: "Rabbi Ḥiyya and Rabbi Yosi used to study with Rabbi Simeon. Rabbi Ḥiyya once put to him the following question: 'We have learned that a dream left uninterpreted is like a letter left unopened. Does this mean that the dream comes true without the dreamer being conscious of it, or that it remains unfulfilled?' Rabbi Simeon answered: 'The dream comes true, but without the dreamer being aware of it.'"[69]

Rabbi Banaah taught that "there were twenty-four dream interpreters in Jerusalem. Once I dreamed a dream and I went round to all of them and they all gave different interpretations, and all were fulfilled, thus confirming that which is said: 'All dreams follow the mouth.'"[70] At first glance, this claim might seem overblown, if not fully preposterous. Yet we now know that a single dream can resonate on multiple levels, including different layers of personal meaning and import for one's immediate community and the greater society. The dreams may even manifest telepathic and non-temporal qualities.[71] Even though rabbinic literature does use the number twenty-four as a formulaic expression when it means "many,"[72] it is quite possible that each interpreter correctly highlighted a different aspect of Rabbi Banaah's dream. However, lest we think that dream interpretation is a free-for-all, the talmudic passage above continues: "Is this notion scriptural? Yes it is, as stated by Rabbi Eleazar: 'Whence do we know that all dreams follow the mouth? Because it says, *and it came to pass, as he [Joseph] interpreted to us [Pharaoh's cup-bearer and baker], so it was*. Rava said: 'This is only if the interpretation corresponds to the content of the dream: for Scripture says, *to each man according to his dream he did interpret*.'"[73]

It is now considered a sine qua non that any legitimate dream interpretation must not go too far afield into chains of associations or universal symbols, but instead must remain faithful to the elements of the dream and the dreamer's experience. Ultimately, the dreamer is the authority on the meaning of his or her dream and it is the dreamer, therefore, who must validate any interpretation with his or her "aha!" assent.[74] As early as the twelfth century, the author of *Sefer Hasidim* stated that "if an interpretation fits the elements of the dream and the dreamer is satisfied with that interpretation, it is an indication that this is indeed what the dreamer has been shown."[75]

"Sovereign of the Universe" Revisited

In my opinion, the same prescient wisdom manifest in the texts cited above inheres in the words of the "Sovereign of the Universe" prayer that is recited during Birkat Kohanim. The Polish talmudic scholar and legist Rabbi Joshua Falk (1555–1614) notes that nowhere within this dream amelioration prayer do the petitioners ask that their troubling dreams stop.[76] Then, going further, reflecting talmudic wisdom and anticipating the observations of contemporary psychology, Falk indicates that having troubling dreams is preferable to having no dreams at all. This is why "Sovereign of the Universe" cites Moses sweetening the bitter waters at Marah:[77] had Moses instead prayed that the bitter waters disappear, the Israelites would have been left in an even worse state, with the possibility of no water to drink. Thus, the examples of healing cited by this dream prayer demonstrate the purpose and power found in the transformation of harmful conditions. While not intentionally desired, these can strengthen the distressed and those who know them in ways unavailable to those who have not had to overcome affliction. For example, Miriam's healing from leprosy strengthened Israel's resolve to avoid harmful speech,[78] and Naaman's healing by the prophet Elisha led to the exaltation of the true God in the eyes of the ancient pagan nobility.[79]

The aforementioned Rabbi Avraham Ḥayyim Schor highlighted a homeopathic element present in the examples of remedy cited in "Sovereign of the Universe."[80] In several instances, the stated means of healing seem counterintuitive to what one might normally think to be an appropriate cure. Moses cast a tree, bark and all, into the waters of Marah and Elisha poured salt into the contaminated waters of Jericho[81]—and both of these acts normally would render water undrinkable. And Hezekiah's ulcer was healed by applying a poultice of figs, which ordinarily would have exacerbated the boil.[82] This insight resonates with what we now know about disturbing dreams: the more terrifying the dreams, the less one really wishes to revisit them. However counterintuitive it may seem, it is by confronting those disturbing images—sometimes even by engaging them in an imaginary dialogue—that we find the potential to discover that they are not in fact harbingers of ill, but rather are symbols of help or needed warning.[83]

My interest in dreams has led me to study aspects of dream interpretation and to train as a dream group leader.[84] Once, a dreamer reported to me that she was completely overworked yet feared letting go of one of her jobs for financial reasons. One night she dreamed that she and a friend were sitting in the anteroom of a lawyer's office.

Through a partition window, they saw three large, shadowy figures enter an inner room. Shots rang out and the two women dropped, cowering, to the floor. I asked her to contemplatively re-imagine the dream scene and simply ask the figures, "Who are you?" Upon doing so, the figures replied, "We're bail bondsmen and we've come to rescue you." When asked about the shooting they answered, "Did you think you were going to leave here without some blood being spilled?"

This re-imagining and further engaging with the elements of a dream is but one example of a Jungian contemplative process known as Active Imagination.[85] Its practice might offer us a modern twist on the concept of "sweetening" or "transforming the dream," a contemporary analogue to throwing tree bark or salt into water. The dreamer's imaginary dialogue, described above, uncovered a hopeful message at the core of what she had first experienced with fright. She realized that she could change her work life, but not without some cost to her and disappointment by those at work who had come to depend on her. And since dreams are notorious for expressing their meaning through non-literal symbols and wordplay, the term "bail bondsmen" reminded her that her late father had left her some valuable treasury bonds that could help "bail" her out of her stressful work situation.[86] Thus, her dream was transformed from terror into an intimation of potential blessing—just as "Sovereign of the Universe" hints can happen by noting that God did not eliminate but rather transformed Balaam's words from curses into blessing.

Monford Harris observed that, with the exception of Yom Kippur, all of the occasions when we recite "Sovereign of the Universe" occur during multi-day festivals.[87] This insight casts a special light on our understanding of the relationship between Birkat Kohanim and dream amelioration. As a participant in the recurring ritual drama of Birkat Kohanim during these holidays, the dreamer could again and again feel enveloped by its uniquely transformative sense of the holy. Combined with the concurrent repetition of "Sovereign of the

Universe" amid sacred community over the course of these days, the
dreamer could find both inspiration and a safe therapeutic setting
in which to process his or her disturbing dream. During this period
the dreamer could revisit the dream, re-examine it, and possibly
reengage with its images, recognizing where amends to others might
be needed and discerning what guidance was being offered to shape
future behavior and action. By the end of the festival, infused with
the spirit of the Priestly Blessing and the hopes that "Sovereign of
the Universe" convey, the dreamer could feel forgiven, renewed, and
encouraged upon returning to everyday life.

Healing and Wholeness

Jeremy Taylor, a foremost expert in Dream Studies, is fond of saying,
"All dreams come in the service of healing and wholeness…and invite
you to new understandings."[88] The words and practices associated
with "Sovereign of the Universe" seem structured to lead the troubled
worshipper to just such realizations. Its phrases impel us to admit that
we don't know the meaning of our dreams and remind us that, like
Joseph's dreams, their ultimate purpose might only be revealed over
time.[89] Its examples point us to the healing potential nestled amid
even frightening dream images. This unfolding prayerful process,
repeated amid the compelling ritual drama of Birkat Kohanim, can
inspire us to revisit and explore previously unrecognized aspects of
our dreams and our lives, buoying us with the promise that both can
be transformed for our good.

The current version of "Sovereign of the Universe" offers an
addendum to the words found in the Talmud.[90] At the end of the
prayer, we add: "May [God] protect me, be gracious to me, and find
favor in me. Amen." These three requests invoke the blessings found
respectively in each of the three lines of Birkat Kohanim. It expresses

a hope as relevant today as it was when "Sovereign of the Universe" was first composed. Through that divine sense of safety, grace, and favor so movingly promised by Birkat Kohanim, may we find healing messages amid even our most troubling dreams, thus transforming them and our lives for good. Amen.

NOTES

[1] B. Berakhot 55b, attributed to one of three late talmudic figures, Amemar, Mar Zutra, or Rav Ashi.

[2] Literally "to ascend a platform," dukhening is a Yiddish-derived term in widespread use in Jewish American English to denote the rite in which the *kohanim* bless the community with Birkat Kohanim.

[3] Philip Birnbaum, *Daily Prayer Book: Ha-Siddur Ha-Shalem* (New York: Hebrew Publishing Company, 1949), pp. 627–630.

[4] Monford Harris, *Studies in Jewish Dream Interpretation* (Northvale, NJ: Jason Aronson, 1994), p. 107.

[5] This renders the Hebrew word *hevel*, the author's regular term for "impermanence."

[6] Compare, e.g., Deuteronomy 13:2–6 to Deuteronomy 18:15–22.

[7] B. Horayot 13b.

[8] B. Berakhot 55a, citing Isaiah 38:16.

[9] Found at B. Berakhot 55b–57b and frequently cited in this essay.

[10] A full examination of dream incubation, a practice that extends back to Greece and the ancient Near East, is beyond the scope of this essay. Treatments of this practice in antiquity can be found throughout Frances Flannery-Dailey's *Dreamers, Scribes, and Priests: Jewish Dreams in the Hellenistic and Roman Eras* (Leiden: Brill, 2004) and in Shaul Bar, *A Letter That Has Not Been Read: Dreams in the Hebrew Bible*, trans. Lenn J. Schramm (Cincinnati: Hebrew Union College Press, 2001), pp. 223–232. Discussions of later Jewish practices of dream incubation, divination, and the posing of dream questions can be found in Joshua Trachtenberg, *Jewish Magic and Superstition* (New York: Atheneum, 1970), pp. 230–248 and in Joel Covitz, *Visions in the Night* (Toronto: Inner City Books, 2000) pp. 76–82.

[11] *Guide for the Perplexed* II 36–37.

[12] Harris, *Studies*, chaps. 4 and 5.

[13] Collette Aboulker-Muscat, *Alone With the One* (New York: ACMI Press, 1995) and Catherine Shainberg, *Kabbalah and the Power of Dreaming* (Rochester, VT: Inner Traditions, 2005).

[14] Sigmund Freud, *The Interpretation of Dream*, trans. A. A. Brill (New York: Macmillan, 1913), chap. 3, pp. 103–112.

[15] Carl Jung, "The Practical Use of Dream Analysis" (1934), excerpted in *The Essential Jung*, ed. Anthony Storr (Princeton, NJ: Princeton University Press, 1983), pp. 168–189.

[16] Fredrick (Fritz) Perls (d. 1970) was a founder of Gestalt Therapy.

[17] For a full description of this research complete with diagrams, see Robert Hoss's excellent website, www.dreamscience.org.

[18] Frances Flannery-Dailey, *Dreamers, Scribes, and Priests*, p. 1.

[19] Ibid.

[20] Genesis 28:10–22.

[21] Genesis 37:5–11; 40:4–22, and 41:1–43.

[22] B. Sotah 48b, Sanhedrin 11a, and Yoma 9b.

[23] B. Berakhot 55b.

[24] B. Ḥagigah 5b.

[25] Ibid., citing Deuteronomy 31:18 and Numbers 12:6.

[26] Bereishit Rabbah 17:5, cf. B. Berakhot 57b.

[27] B. Berakhot 55a.

[28] Representative instances can be found in B. Berakhot 56b, Sanhedrin 102b, and *Avot D'rabbi Natan*, chap. 40 (regarding which, see Judah Goldin's translation in his *The Fathers According to Rabbi Nathan* [New York: Schocken Books, 1974], p. 167).

[29] At B. Berakhot 10b and Sanhedrin 30a; for the biblical usage, see Genesis 37:18.

[30] Harris, *Studies*, pp. 12–14.

[31] *Avot D'rabbi Natan*, chap. 17. (Goldin's translation is in his *Fathers*, p. 89.)

[32] Zohar I 183a–b.

[33] Solomon Almoli, *Pitron Ḥalomot*, gate 1, as translated by Joel Covitz in his *Visions in the Night*, pp. 88–92. Almoli's categorization of dreams is of particular interest. Relegating "psychological status dreams" to the realm of the imagination, which spins visions from the dreamer's daily thoughts, Almoli then describes: (1) "prophetic" dreams with their direct message from God; (2) "ordinary" dreams instilled by the *ba·al ha-ḥalomot*, which are a variant of prophecy still vouchsafed to Israel; and (3) "magical" dreams, which are self-induced by the dark arts of sorcerers and are to be repudiated.

[34] Interestingly enough, current neurobiology has discovered that the aspect of our brain structure which controls the generation of motor commands, the primary motor cortex, is inactive when we sleep. See Robert Hoss, "The Dreaming Brain," section 3.1, available online at www.dreamscience.org/idx_science_of_dreaming.htm.

[35] Zohar I 183a–b.

[36] The Modeh Ani appears in almost every comprehensive prayerbook, cf., e.g., Siddur Sim Shalom (New York: The Rabbinical Assembly, 1994), p. 1.

[37] Prime examples of a visitation dream and an ascent vision can be found respectively in the *Sefer Ha-ḥezyonot* of Rabbi Ḥayyim Vital (1543–1620), III:9, and in the *Tzava·at Ha-Rivash* (The Ethical Will of the Baal Shem Tov). Translations of both texts can be found in Louis Jacobs, *Jewish Mystical Testimonies* (New York: Schocken Books, 1977), pp. 127–128 and 149–153.

[38] These examples come from A. Leo Oppenheim's essay, "The Interpretation of Dreams in the Ancient Near East, With a Translation of an Assyrian Dream-Book," in *Transactions of the American Philosophical Society,* New Series 46:3

(1956), p. 230.

[39] B. Berakhot 57b: "Our rabbis taught: [If one dreams of] a corpse in the house, it is a sign of peace in the house."

[40] B. Berakhot 55b.

[41] B. Shabbat 11a.

[42] Here the Talmud already prescribes a condition that modern dream work considers axiomatic: one should only share dreams with those whom the dreamer considers emotionally safe. The Zohar further cautions: "And Joseph dreamed a dream, which he told to his brothers and they hated him the more....From this we learn that a person should not tell one's dream save to a friend, otherwise the listener may pervert the significance of the dream" (I 183b).

[43] The primary source of this rite is B. Berakhot 55b. The entire ritual as summarized here, including post-talmudic additions, is detailed in Harris, *Studies*, pp. 98–102, which he cites from Seligmann Baer's *Seder Avodat Yisrael* (1868; rpt. Berlin: Schocken, 1936), pp. 578–579.

[44] Harris, *Studies*, suggests that the three friends might constitute a *beit din*, a religious court, which can be composed of three lay people for small civil matters.

[45] That is, words based on the Hebrew root *hei-pei-kaf*; the verses are Psalm 30:12, Jeremiah 30:13, and Deuteronomy 30:6.

[46] That is, words based on the Hebrew root *pei-dalet-hei*; the verses are Psalm 40:19, Isaiah 30:10, and 1 Samuel 14:45.

[47] That is, *shalom*; the verses are Isaiah 57:19, 1 Chronicles 12:19, and 1 Samuel 25:6.

[48] The respective passages begin with Psalm 121, followed by Numbers 6:22–26, Psalm 16:11, and Kohelet 9:7.

[49] The full text can be found at the opening of this essay. In many Hebrew texts this prayer is referred to the by the first word of the prayer, *ribbon*.

[50] For a full discussion of these issues, see *Sefer Eliyahu Rabbah* (the Vilna Gaon's commentary on the *Shulḥan Arukh*) to S.A. *Oraḥ Ḥayyim* 130:1.

[51] Jonathan Sacks, *The Koren Sacks Siddur* (Jerusalem: Koren Publishing, 2009), pp. 832–837.

[52] B. Berakhot 55b. Originally this passage was recited only if one could not finish "Sovereign of the Universe" before the *kohanim* concluded the benediction.

[53] B. Berakhot 55b.

[54] B. Berakhot 56a.

[55] Trachtenberg, *Magic*, chap. 7.

[56] B. Berakhot 19a.

[57] *Sefer Torat Ḥayyim* on B. Bava Kamma 55a (New York: Ḥayyim Zimmerman Publishing, 5707 [1946/1947]), p. 12a.

[58] Cf., e.g., 1 Samuel 10:6 or 16:13.

[59] Bereishit Rabbah 17:5 and B. Berakhot 57b.

[60] *Sefer Torat Ḥayyim* on B. Bava Kamma 55a, p. 12a.

[61] Flannery-Dailey, *Dreamers, Scribes, and Priests*, p. 1. See discussion above,

under "When We Sleep: The Process of Dreaming."

[62] B. Berakhot 55a.

[63] For anticipation of Jung's concepts of the collective unconscious. see *Avot D'rabbi Natan*, chap. 31, and B. Niddah 30b; for Jung's anima and animus, cf. Zohar III 43a; for Jung's concept of projection, see B. Kiddushin 70a.

[64] The aspects of our brain structure responsible for spatial imagery, pictographs, and emotional processing, particularly in the right-brain hemisphere, remain active as we sleep; those associated with logic, planning, inhibition, and episodic memory, especially in the brain's left hemisphere, are blocked. For a full treatment see Robert Hoss, *Dream Language* (Ashland, OR: Innersource, 2005), chap. 3.

[65] *Sefer Ḥasidim*, §606, based on the translation of Rabbi A. Y. Finkel in his *Sefer Chasidim: The Book of the Pious* (Northvale, NJ: Jason Aronson In, 1996), p. 341.

[66] B. Berakhot 55b, quoting Proverbs 19:23. This homily is based on a play on the words *savei·a* and *sheva*, both of which contain the same consonants and would thus appear identical to each other in an unvocalized text.

[67] REM (Rapid Eye Movement) is one of two states that alternate during the natural cycle of brain activity when we sleep. (The other is called NREM, or non-REM.) REM sleep is the state most associated with dreaming. See Robert Hoss, "The Science of Dreaming," section 1, available online at www.dreamscience.org/idx_science_of_dreaming.htm.

[68] See Carl Jung, *Memories, Dreams, and Reflections*, ed. Aniela Jaffe, trans. Richard and Clara Winston (New York: Random House, 1961), concerning a mountaineer who ignored his dreams in which he envisioned stepping out into space. Jung, who tried unsuccessfully to get this patient to heed this dream warning, later learned that he had fallen to his death while mountain climbing.

[69] Zohar I 183a–b. Carl Jung cites two instances of the consequences paid by those insensitive to the warnings of their dreams in his *Man and His Symbols* (New York: Dell, 1968), p. 34.

[70] B. Berakhot 55b. Rabbi Banaah was citing a well-known apothegm.

[71] For a full and accessible treatment of each of these types of dreams based on forty years of study, see Jeremy Taylor, *The Wisdom of Your Dreams* (New York: Tarcher, 2009).

[72] Eikhah Rabbah 1:2.

[73] B. Berakhot 55b, citing Genesis 40:22 and 41:13.

[74] See Jeremy Taylor's "Basic Dream Work Toolkit," online at www.jeremytaylor.com.

[75] *Sefer Ḥasidim*, §605, as translated by Finkel, p. 341.

[76] *P'rishah* commentary on S. A. Oraḥ Ḥayyim 130.

[77] The story is found in Exodus 15:23–26.

[78] Numbers 12:1–15. On the midrashic connection between leprosy and slander, see B. Shabbat 97a.

[79] 2 Kings 5.

[80] *Sefer Torat Ḥayyim* on B. Bava Kamma 55a.

[81] 2 Kings 2:19–22.

[82] 2 Kings 20:7 and Isaiah 38:21.

[83] Louis Savary, Patricia H. Berne, and Stephon Kaplan Williams, *Dreams and Spiritual Growth* (Mahwah, NJ: Paulist Press, 1984), pp. 58–63.

[84] On the nature and dynamics of dream groups, see Robert Haden, Jr., *Unopened Letters from God* (Hendersonville, NC: Haden Institute Publishing, 2010), Appendix B; and Jeremy Taylor, "Dreamwork," at www.jeremytaylor.org.

[85] See Robert Johnson, *Inner Work* (New York: HarperCollins, 1986), section III, pp. 135–222.

[86] In his *Interpretation of Dreams*, Freud notes that ancient Near Eastern dream books had recognized the prevalence of punning and the non-literal nature of dreams millennia ago. The Talmud, at B. Berakhot 56b–57a, is replete with examples of such wordplay, including the following: "Our rabbis taught: If one sees a reed (*kaneh*) in a dream, one may hope for wisdom, for it says: Get (*k'neih*) wisdom" (Proverbs 4:5).

[87] Harris, *Studies*, pp. 104–105.

[88] "Basic Dream Work Toolkit," online at www.jeremytaylor.com.

[89] B. Berakhot 55b points out that it took Joseph twenty-two years to appreciate fully the implications of his youthful dreams.

[90] Jonathan Sacks, *The Koren Sacks Siddur* (Jerusalem: Koren Publishing, 2009), pp. 832–833.

Following God's Lure Through the Priestly Blessing

Michael Knopf

Most Jews have likely heard or recited the so-called "Priestly Blessing" at some point in their lives. The prayer leader chants it at the close of his or her repetition of the Amidah, the collection of blessings forming the core of traditional Jewish worship services. Clergy commonly recite it at life-cycle celebrations: circumcisions, baby namings, *b'nei mitzvah*, and weddings. Many parents intone this blessing to their children each Friday evening (humbly, a practice worthy of all parents' consideration). Few blessings or prayers in the Jewish tradition share this status and role.

The ubiquity of this blessing is doubly amazing considering its ancient pedigree. Extra-biblical sources confirm that the Priestly Blessing is one of the Jewish tradition's oldest texts. Archaeologists digging near Jerusalem at Ketef Hinnom discovered pieces of silver foil, likely made in the late seventh century B.C.E., inscribed with the blessing's words—making them the oldest piece of biblical text uncovered to date.[1]

At the same time, the meaning of the Blessing's particulars is enigmatic,[2] and its apparent underlying theological premise—that the right cluster of words and phrases, uttered by the right people at the right time, will persuade a(n impassible, omniscient, and omnipotent) deity to change the trajectory of a person or a nation's life—is suspect in our time.[3] Fortunately, there is another, more satisfying, way of understanding this ancient prayer.

Currently, I am influenced by an approach to comprehending our reality known as Process Thought. Originally developed in the early twentieth century by the British philosopher Alfred North Whitehead, Process Thought argues that God is neither supernatural nor coercive. God cannot violate the laws of nature or force a desired outcome. God only has persuasive power. In each moment, we are met with any number of choices. Only some options will lead toward greater "love, justice, experience, and compassion."[4] According to Process thinkers, those options are God's "lure." They represent God's attempt to invite or persuade us to choose the best possible option held out before us in each moment. Seen through this lens, one of the most important roles religion plays is teaching us to recognize and follow the divine lure when we encounter it.

Prayer, then, becomes about centering "ourselves with God at the core,"[5] rather than attempting to convince a supernatural power to break the rules of cosmos. Praying opens our eyes to God's lure and inspires us to follow it. Praying on behalf of others in their presence invites those others to engage in that same process of centering, vision, and inspiration.

Seen through this lens, the Priestly Blessing is fundamentally about aligning with God's will and enhancing the power of God's lure in our lives. To achieve this end, the Priestly Blessing asserts that, while its words are to be uttered by the priests, God is its author.[6] Thus the Blessing is, in effect, a concrete expression of the divine lure. Its words embody what God wants for us; they reflect a set of choices God hopes we will make. True, the choices are phrased as though they are gifts God might bestow as an act of supernatural power and grace. Upon deeper examination, however, we will discover that they are actually gifts we can (only) attain through our own deeds.

Moreover, the Priestly Blessing outlines these choices in a successive, interlocking series, indicating that these choices, and the actions they lead to, build upon and reinforce each other. One cannot reach the next step in the blessing without having accomplished the preceding step, and later progress can be undermined if the recipient shirks a prerequisite. This structure evokes the Process insight that with each successive act of following God's lure, we increase our ability to discern it in the future and enhance its persuasive power over our actions. It also echoes the rabbinic teaching that "performance of a commandment leads to another commandment, and a sin leads to another sin, since the reward for performing a commandment is another commandment, and the reward for a sin is another sin" (Pirkei Avot 4:2).

The Priestly Blessing offers a challenge to follow God's lure. It outlines how following that lure enables a perpetually increasing ability to discern and make godly choices. And it shows how this process offers a path to better lives and a better world.

"May the Eternal Bless You": Prosperity

The first step in the process is blessing, meaning material prosperity and physical health. That is the view of Rashi, who teaches that "blessing" in this context refers to one's property becoming bountiful. He bases his interpretation on the Bible's use of the verb *bet-resh-kaf*, where it almost always refers to bounty, health, and material prosperity. Thus, when God tells Abraham, "I will bless you," the narrative goes on to specify that the meaning of the blessing is twofold: "I will make of you a great nation" and "I will make your name great" (Genesis 12:2). In Deuteronomy, to "be blessed" (7:14) means to be given "abounding prosperity in the issue of your womb, the offspring of your cattle, and the produce of your soil" (28:11). It further means to be free from all sickness, to be victorious over enemies (7:13–16), and to have plentiful food, nice houses, and riches (8:12).

It makes perfect sense for the Priestly Blessing to begin here. First, it is hard for a person to care about any other value if he or she is struggling to survive. This view is reminiscent of the ancient lesson of Rabbi Eleazar ben Azariah as cited in Pirkei Avot: "If there is no flour, there is no Torah" (3:17). But more pointedly, if the goal of the Priestly Blessing is to place a person on the path to discerning and following God's lure, prosperity is the easiest and best place to start. It is a godly choice in the sense that, if we understand God as the source of all life, then the most basic urging of the divine lure must be to live, and to live as well as one possibly can. This truth is evidenced by the fact that the command to live—to make those choices that facilitate our own physical and material well-being—is central to and prevalent in the Torah and the later Jewish tradition. Deuteronomy 30:19, for example, instructs us to "choose life." Later sages, such as Maimonides, argue that Judaism's primary objective is human flourishing, that all the Torah aims at is our working toward "the welfare of the soul and the welfare of the body." Far from other religious systems that celebrate a life of austerity, self-denial, and the renouncement of worldly pleasures, the Jewish tradition affirms that God invites us to live the best, healthiest, most successful, wealthiest lives possible. Moreover, the Priestly Blessing begins with health and prosperity because the pursuit of our own well-being is more or less instinctive to most of us.[8] It is an aspect of God's lure that most have little trouble following.

Because God does not have coercive power or control over outcomes, God cannot ensure that wealth goes to the righteous and poverty to the sinful. However, the Priestly Blessing holds out the assertion that God invites us to strive for success and greatness. We are urged to courageously reach for the highest possible heights, with God rooting for our success and doing everything possible to help us attain it.

"And Protect You": Protection of and from Prosperity

Protection naturally follows blessing. We cannot truly flourish without insulation from that which threatens us. Thus, God invites us to protect ourselves from that which would rob us of our blessings. Reflecting this value, the Jewish legal tradition obligates and empowers us to take care of ourselves, to take the necessary steps to stay healthy and avoid that which harms the body.[9] Thus, the Priestly Blessing asserts that the next step in discerning and following the divine lure is to make those choices that enable us to protect our lives and defend our assets. As Rashi teaches, "What good is a great gift"—namely, the wealth that God invites us to secure for ourselves—"if bandits come and take it from you?"

But a lure that leads to greater love, justice, and compassion will not only invite us to protect ourselves; it also leads us to recognize the crucial limits to defending our own wealth. As much as "protection" in the Priestly Blessing refers to the protection of our own well-being, then, it also must mean protection *from* our wealth, at least in a spiritual and moral sense. Wealth, though not inherently bad, can be morally toxic.

Wealthy people, for example, tend to give proportionally less to charity than poor people.[10] Moreover, when wealthy people do give to charity, they tend to disproportionately give to institutions that serve their interests and needs—like universities, private schools, symphonies, and museums—rather than to those that serve the less fortunate.[11] Underscoring these facts is the recent finding that the wealthy are slower to embrace compassion.[12]

One reason for this phenomenon is that, in the process of trying to protect their wealth, many cordon themselves off from disadvantaged people and places. When separated from need, we can become ignorant of and indifferent to the desperation of others.[13] Conversely, the more we see suffering, the more likely we are to try to alleviate it. This is evidenced by the fact that wealthy people who live primarily among other wealthy people are less generous than wealthy people who live in more heterogeneous communities.[14]

A powerful talmudic passage illustrates this insight, telling of Elijah regularly going to see a pious man, but refusing to visit when the pious man built a fortified wall around his home.[15] Why did Elijah object to the fortified wall? According to Rashi, the wall prevented those inside the enclosure from hearing the voices of poor people who might be crying out for help outside the enclosure. By taking steps to protect his wealth, the pious man had closed himself off from the ability to hear those in need.

The Torah emphatically warns of the spiritual dangers of prosperity, because of wealth's propensity to close us off from need: "When you have eaten your fill, and have built fine houses to live in, and your herds and flocks have multiplied, and your silver and gold have increased, and everything you own has prospered—beware, lest your heart grow haughty and you forget the Eternal your God who freed you from the land of Egypt" (Deuteronomy 8:12–14). Wealth makes us apt to forget God. God's defining characteristic, we are reminded here, is liberating the enslaved. A few verses later, the Deuteronomist adds to that definition, noting that God, above all else, fights for "the orphan and the widow; befriending and providing the stranger with food and clothing" (10:18). Forgetting God, then, is biblical shorthand for forgetting our obligations to champion the disadvantaged. Contemporary talmudist Aryeh Cohen puts this imperative in stark terms:

> The experience of the Israelites in Egypt is consecrated in law as the experience of God hearing the cries of oppression. The law obligates us to choose to be like God—hearing the stranger, the widow, the orphan, the marginal and unprotected members of society—and at the same time to choose not to be like Pharaoh by ignoring the stranger, the widow, the orphan, the marginal and unprotected members of society.[16]

Serving the God of the Exodus is ultimately the responsibility to "befriend the stranger, for you were strangers in the land of Egypt" (Deuteronomy 10:19). The Priestly Blessing thus challenges us to see God luring us not only to protect our prosperity but also to protect ourselves from it.

"May the Eternal Shine God's Face Upon You": Pleasing God

The centrality of protecting ourselves from the nefarious aspects of wealth builds to the next piece of the Priestly Blessing, the next crucial stage in the process of recognizing and enhancing the power of God's lure in our lives. "May the Eternal shine God's face upon you" is an idiom and should not be understood literally. According to Jacob Milgrom, the expression is best understood in light of its "semantic opposite, the hiding of God's face," indicating God's anger.[17] It is thus best understood to mean, "May God be pleased with you." This is likely what Rashi meant when he interpreted the phrase as "God will show you a smiling face, a glowing [or: happy] face." Biblically speaking, God hides God's face—that is to say, God is angry or displeased—most commonly when people violate the covenant. For example, in Deuteronomy 31:16–21 we find:

> The Eternal said to Moses: You are soon to lie with your ancestors. This people will thereupon go astray after the alien gods in their midst, in the land that they are about to enter; they will forsake Me and break My covenant that I made with them. Then My anger will flare up against them, and I will abandon them and hide My countenance from them. They shall be ready prey; and many evils and troubles shall befall them. And they shall say on that day, "Surely it is because our God is not in our midst that these evils have befallen us." Yet I will keep My countenance hidden on that day, because of all the evil they have done in turning to other gods.

Recall that, according to Deuteronomy 8, we are most likely to turn from God as a consequence of our prospering in the Land of Israel. Furthermore, recall that we defined turning from God as shirking our obligations to tend to the needs of the poor. The equation implied by the Priestly Blessing thus comes into focus: God's being pleased with us depends on our loyally heeding God's call in our lives, and we heed God's call—at least in large part—by helping the most disadvantaged in our society. In other words, striving for social justice secures the blessing of God being pleased with us. This imperative evokes Rabbi Ḥanina ben Dosa's teaching that "all who please people, God is pleased with them; and all who do not please people, God is not pleased with them" (Pirkei Avot 3:10).

Pleasing God is about more than our psychological drive to gratify an authority figure. Similarly, it is about more than our obligation to "love the Eternal your God with all your heart" (Deuteronomy 6:5), which would seem to include being altruistically devoted to God's happiness, expecting nothing in return. There is in fact a *quid pro quo* implied here. Note that, according to the Deuteronomy text above, God's being pleased with us is directly connected to God's presence in our world and God's physical protection of us. The hiding of God's face due to God's anger will make us "ready prey" for "many evils and troubles." This passage has frequently been interpreted to mean that suffering is divine punishment for the sin of betrayal, that God withholds God's protection when God feels we are not deserving of it. The theological problems with that interpretation, especially after the horrors of Auschwitz, are too many to enumerate here.

But there is at least one other way to understand what Deuteronomy is describing: if we, as individuals and as a collective, fulfill our covenantal responsibilities; if we care wholeheartedly for the least advantaged, elevate the dignity of all human beings, fashion communities of justice and righteousness, and strive toward peace; if, ultimately, we advance an agenda of oneness, of the fundamental unity of all that is—then God, the personification, source, and ultimate expression of that oneness, will be present in our world. And, in such a world, we will have no need for supernatural protection from an external power, for we will have already built a world in which there is only godliness and only goodness, a world in which there is no evil or trouble.

The call for God's face to shine on us is, in this sense, a challenge to make God more present in our lives and world. It is about discerning God's lure, making those choices that will enable us to thrive, but also those that prevent us from becoming hard-hearted and that enable us to support the thriving of others. It is about habituating ourselves to make the choices to follow the lure and thereby making godly action instinctive and reflexive in our lives.

"And Be Gracious to You": Keeping God Close

Since the successive components of the Priestly Blessing intertwine and build upon each other, the presence of God alluded to with "May the Eternal shine God's face upon you" leads inexorably to the next part of the blessing, where a better translation might be, "May the Eternal be close by you." This interpretation follows Rabbi Ḥiyya the Great, who uses a bit of creative philology to connect the word *vi-ḥunneka*, from the root *ḥet-nun-nun*, to the related but distinct root *ḥet-nun-hei*, meaning to camp or to dwell—thus understanding the verse to be saying, "May Eternal dwell close to you."[18]

Remember that, according to Deuteronomy 31, God's pleasure in us leads to God's palpable presence in the world. We interpreted that concept to mean that fulfilling our covenantal responsibilities, advancing goodness, justice, and peace, enhances the godliness manifest in our world. God—the ultimate expression of the oneness of all creation—dwells with us, to borrow a phrase from Rabbi Menaḥem Mendel of Kotzk, only if "we let God in"[19]—a notion that itself evokes God's words in Exodus, "I will dwell among you when you make a holy space for Me" (25:8). In other words, the Priestly Blessing assures the recipient that, if one pursues the program outlined in the first three stages of the blessing, one will have created not only a more just and peaceful world, but also a world in which godliness is more present.

However, living in such a world is of little value if it is unsustainable. After all, what good is having a more godly world if it only stays that way for a brief moment before devolving back into lawlessness, injustice, and suffering? Fortunately, we human beings are creatures of conditioning and habit. Over time, our actions crystallize into habits, which become instincts, which become almost like innate parts of who we are. How we accustom ourselves to act is how we will be likely to act in the future, and every action one takes defines the options one will have to act in every consequent situation.

Moreover, we are heavily influenced by our culture and environment. Living in an environment where dignity, compassion, justice, and peace are the norm increase the likelihood that we will live our lives in consonance with those values, that those values will be native to our personalities. Thus, the blessing of God's closeness, understood in the way we have outlined, is also the blessing of godliness becoming a natural part of us through our regularly performing acts of godliness.

At first blush, this may appear to be a radical departure from the plain meaning of the Priestly Blessing; but from a certain point of view, closeness is very much in line with the concept of graciousness. According to Milgrom, graciousness means mercy: "God will not judge Israel according to its sins but will deal kindly with it as [God's] free gift."[20] Many biblical passages support this interpretation, the most notable of which is Exodus 34:6, where gracious is used as a synonym for compassion: "The Eternal! The Eternal! A compassionate and gracious God..."

Compassion, it must be pointed out, is directly related to proximity. Evolutionary psychology insightfully points out that the best predictor of a compassionate response is propinquity, especially in the filial relationship:

[It's] relatively rare for human beings to use blood revenge against their own kin....[Harsh] revenge against a blood relative, insofar as it actually reduces the relative's fitness, reduces the avenger's fitness as well. Like it or not, your sister Tracy and your cousin Tommy are carrying around some of your genes...so if you remove your genes from the gene pool, you're removing some of their's as well.... Therefore, a proneness to forgive our blood relatives probably evolved because people who had such a trait were able to avoid shooting themselves in the foot (or the genes?) by reducing the fitness of their blood relatives....[A] big part of why we're inclined to forgive our friends, neighbors, and associates today is probably because forgiveness enabled our ancestors to develop and maintain the cooperative alliances that they needed to thrive in large groups.[21]

Praying for God's graciousness, then, is at its core an expression of hope that God will be close to us; that, like a relative, God will see us as part of God, and that we will see God as part of us. Again, we are drawn back to understanding this piece of the Priestly Blessing as the challenge to make godliness a natural part of us—which we do, in large part, by regularly acting in godly ways.

"May the Eternal Lift God's Face Up To You": God's Favor

The Priestly Blessing nurtures a self-reinforcing cycle, fitting for a passage whose structure of three, then five, then seven words, featuring interlocking language, resembles, in a way, a spiral or loop.[22] If the Blessing's recipient upholds his or her covenantal responsibilities, the world will be infused with more godliness. A more godly world will invite more godly action, which will lead to God having a more secure presence, and so on. It is therefore not surprising that the next piece of the Blessing would continue this cycle.

As was the case with the shining of God's face, lifting up God's face is idiomatic. Elsewhere in the Bible, "lifting the face" means to see someone favorably and give that person preferential treatment. Especially common is one lifting up one's face in response to someone who does something good for you—that is, bribery. Hence, when Lot asks to flee to a nearby town during the destruction of Sodom, God's angel replies, "Very well, I will also lift up my face to you [i.e., grant you this favor] and I will not annihilate the town of which you have spoken" (Genesis 19:21). The angel presumably grants the request because of Lot's hospitality during the latter's sojourn in Sodom. Similarly, Jacob reasons that, if he showers his vengeful brother with gifts, "he will lift up my face" (Genesis 32:21)— that is, perhaps Esau will show Jacob favor in return.

Notably, one character in the Bible does not lift up the face in this way: God. According to Deuteronomy 10:17–19, "[God] does not lift up God's face [i.e., God shows no favor] and takes no bribe, but does justice for the fatherless and the widow, and befriends the stranger, providing them with food and clothing. You too must befriend the stranger, for you were strangers in the land of Egypt." This notion of God seems to contradict the Priestly Blessing, if it is understood through the lens of the dominant theology. If God does not show favor, if God's blessings cannot be bought, then what good would it do to pray for God to show us favor? Also, even if one were to argue that the favor for which the Priestly Blessing asks is simply for God to be swayed by and to reward our good behavior, we would still face the theological problem that God frequently seems not to reward good behavior or punish bad behavior, that righteous people suffer and wicked people flourish. Moreover, there seems to be a contradiction embedded within this very passage. How can God show no favor and simultaneously do justice for and befriend the disadvantaged?

But remember: when we ask in this prayer for God's blessings to come to us, we are not asking for gold stars or cash rewards. We are not asking for health, long life, and prosperity to be gifted to us from heaven, though the Priestly Blessing encourages us to seek those gifts for ourselves. Rather, we are praying that our godly work yields godly results, that we succeed in fashioning lives and building a world in which godliness is manifest. Thus, what we mean by asking that God show us favor is that our work on God's behalf be effective in bringing God closer to our world. And let one's heart not grow faint in the belief that God categorically rejects that kind of favoritism, for we know that God does indeed favor the weak and marginalized; and if we, like God, fight for justice and human dignity, we will, as a result, receive God's favor by virtue of there being more godliness present in our world. When we defend the cause of the downtrodden, God's presence is made more manifest in our world. When we do not, God's presence flees the world. There is no middle ground. The cycle thus continues: we pray that we engage in more godly behavior, which will lead to God being more present in the world, which will, in turn, urge more godly behavior.

"And Grant You Peace": It Ends, and Begins, with Peace

It is fitting, then, that the Priestly Blessing should conclude with *shalom*. *Shalom*, usually translated as "peace," means two things, which are in some ways connected and in some ways distinct: it means an absence of violence, and it also refers to wholeness, completion, or fulfillment. The goal of our following God's lure, of striving to live lives of justice and righteousness, of mending fractured lives and a fractured world, and of making the world a more suitable dwelling for the Divine is *shalom*—completed, harmonized, and perfected lives, and a completed, harmonized, and perfected world. Ultimately, the Priestly Blessing challenges us to fashion lives, communities, and a world of *shalom*.

This ending, in a sense, turns the Blessing's incremental structure into something more cyclical. In a sense, the ending is also the beginning. Peace is the goal, but it is also, in many important ways, the prerequisite. It is hard to flourish without first enjoying peace. Insofar as peace means a cessation of hostilities and an expansion of justice, those who live in areas of the world brutalized by war, injustice, and corruption know that the promise of prosperity is impossible for most outside a context of social justice and peace. Conversely, those fortunate enough to live in peaceful, prosperous countries governed by the rule of law owe their blessings, in large part, to the tranquility of their societies.

Moreover, *shalom* is also an internal quality, a sense of harmony and contentment in one's life. A person who has true inner *shalom* will need fewer material blessings than someone who has no internal sense of satisfaction, and so constantly has to seek external trappings of prosperity. As Ben Zoma teaches in the Mishnah, "Who is wealthy? The one who is happy with one's portion" (Pirkei Avot 4:1). Thus, the Priestly Blessing teaches us that the only way to truly fulfill its godly challenges is first to cultivate peace in our lives and in our world. This means that we must work to make our societies more just and to bring an end to the violence that plagues our communities and planet. And it means also that we are invited to be personally balanced, contented, and grateful; to make ourselves spiritually, psychologically, and emotionally whole. Hence Rabbi Shimon ben Ḥalafta's teaching in the Mishnah (perhaps not coincidentally, the very last teaching in the whole of the Mishnah, as if to underscore its importance), "The blessed Holy One found no vessel that could hold blessing for Israel except for peace" (Uktzin 3:12).

Ironically, the result of this inner and outer work will be a peace that would negate our need for doing all the other work the Priestly Blessing invites us to do! Indeed, the power of the Blessing is that it has built-in obsolescence. Blessed lives and a blessed world are not a result of divine grace, but rather the product of human action, of the extent to which we acknowledge and follow God's lure. Only we, following God's invitation, can make peace in our lives and peace in our world. God cannot do it *for* us. God needs our partnership.

Ultimately, this understanding of the Priestly Blessing makes sense of the context in which the Torah places it. It is a blessing the priests give because, according to tradition, the priests embody *shalom*. The sage Hillel famously taught that the defining trait of Aaron, the High Priest to whom the command in Numbers to recite the Priestly Blessing is addressed, is that he was a lover of peace and a pursuer of peace (Pirkei Avot 1:12). The Blessing, then, is an imperative for its recipients to themselves become lovers of peace and pursuers of peace.

The way to do that, according to the Jewish tradition, is to study, practice, and live a life of Torah: "Rabbi Eleazar said in the name of Rabbi Hanina, 'Students of the sages increase peace in the world.'"[23] The Priestly Blessing, then, is not a wish-list of the things we hope for God to give, but is rather an invitation to engage in a program of following God's lure, of working toward a better, more just, more peaceful world through Torah.

The Priestly Blessing embodies a challenge to discern God's call and make godly choices, offering a process for building to better lives and a better world. When we hear this blessing recited over us, let it move us to live lives of Torah, lives of peace and peacemaking, and lives dedicated to bringing God to the world. And when we recite it over our children, let it move them to become the "builders" of a repaired world.[24]

NOTES

[1] Stephen Caesar, "The Blessing of the Silver Scrolls," in *Associates for Biblical Research* (January 6, 2010), available online at www.biblearchaeology.org. And see also the essays elsewhere in this volume by Jonathan Sacks, Avram I. Reisner, Aubrey Glazer, Yeshaya Dalsace, and Michael Graetz, who also discuss the Ketef Hinnom find.

[2] As Jacob Milgrom writes, "a satisfactory explanation of the occurrence of the Priestly Benediction in its present setting has yet to be found" (*The JPS Torah Commentary: Numbers* [Philadelphia: Jewish Publication Society, 1989], p. 51).

[3] See Bradley Shavit Artson, *God of Becoming and Relationship: The Dynamic Nature of Process Theology* (Woodstock, VT: Jewish Lights Publishing and The Rabbinical Assembly, 2013), p. 123.

[4] Ibid., p. 125.

[5] Ibid.

[6] Numbers 6:22–23.

[7] *Guide for the Perplexed* III 28, where Maimonides further explains "body" to mean "the betterment of society achieved by establishing rules of justice, warding off injustice, inculcating good moral qualities and eradicating bad ones, and abolishing reciprocal wrongdoing, in addition to maintaining the health of one's personal physical body," and soul to mean "beliefs, opinions, and mind."

[8] Hans Jonas, "The Burden and Blessing of Mortality," in *Mortality and Morality: The Search for the Good After Auschwitz*, ed. Lawrence Vogel (Evanston, IL: Northwestern University Press, 1996), p. 91.

[9] M.T. Hilkhot Dei·ot 4:1.

[10] Judith Warner, "The Charitable Giving Divide," in *The New York Times* (August 22, 2010), available online at www.nytimes.com.

[11] Yasmin Anwar, "Lower Classes Quicker to Show Compassion in the Face of Suffering," in *UC Berkley News Center* (December 19, 2011), available online at newscenter.berkeley.edu.

[12] Ibid.

[13] Ibid.

[14] Ken Stern, "Why the Rich Don't Give to Charity," in *The Atlantic* (March 20, 2013), available online at www.theatlantic.com.

[15] B. Bava Batra 7b.

[16] Rabbi Aryeh Cohen, "Shabbat Parashat Ekev: The Spiritual Challenge of Wealth" (July 31, 2010), available online at ziegler.aju.edu.

[17] Milgrom, *The JPS Torah Commentary: Numbers*, pp. 51–52.

[18] Bemidbar Rabbah 11:6. Cf. the reference to this text by Baḥya ben Asher ibn Halawa (called Rabbeinu Baḥya), in his commentary to Numbers 6:25.

[19] Martin Buber, *Tales of the Hasidim: Later Masters*, trans. Olga Marx (New York: Schocken Books, 1947), p. 277.

[20] Milgrom, p. 52.

[21] Michael E. McCullough, *Beyond Revenge: The Evolution of the Forgiveness Instinct* (San Francisco: Jossey-Bass, 2008), pp. 89–90.

[22] Milgrom puts it thus: "The structure of the formula is simple, and in its simplicity lies its strength. The threefold blessing is a rising crescendo of 3, 5, and 7 words, respectively. The number of consonants are respectively 15, 20, and 25. The increased progression is also evidenced in the number of words (15, 20, 25), of stressed syllables or meter (3, 5, 7) and of total syllables (12, 14, 16). The first and last cola of the poem are exactly the same length (7 syllables), and they form an envelope about the poem that summarizes its essence: "The Lord bless you / and grant you peace…" (p. 51).

[23] B. Berakhot 64a.

[24] Ibid.

Why Pray?

Alon C. Ferency

So I'm with my father, my grandfather, and my brother, sitting in the bench seats—women were upstairs. Five or six guys get up on the bimah, the stage, facing the congregation. They get their tallits over their heads, and they start this chanting....And my father said to me, "Don't look." So everyone's got their eyes covered with their hands or their tallit down over their faces....And I hear this strange sound coming from them. They're not singers, they were shouters. And dissonant....It was all discordant...it was chilling. I thought, "Something major is happening here." So I peeked. And I saw them with their hands stuck out from beneath the tallit like this....Wow. Something really got hold of me. I had no idea what was going on, but the sound of it and the look of it was magical.

—Leonard Nimoy[1]

Generally, people pray (or don't) with one of two assumptions: (1) prayer is magic, or (2) prayer is meaningless. Advocates of the former believe that speaking to God will change the speaker's fate, whereas advocates of the latter believe that speaking to God has no effect, and that it would be better to save one's breath and not speak at all. This is a false dichotomy. Prayer is meaningful, but not magical. Prayer may appear to be a request for material change, but its true spiritual effect is much more subtle and profound. It is neither prescriptive nor descriptive, but aspirational. We seek divine energy to help us transform our own lives. We imagine that we are changing God, when in fact we are changing ourselves, if we are so lucky. We bless ourselves to become our best selves.

I might further offer that the Priestly Blessing (Birkat Kohanim), appearing out of an early strand of Jewish experience in the Torah, is a signal prayer—one that may serve as a paradigm for other prayers. Through better understanding the text and context of its words—*the Eternal bless you and keep you; the Eternal light up the divine face for you in grace; the Eternal lift up the divine face to you and bestow peace unto you*—we may learn why we pray at all.[2]

First, let us address a false premise, that some believe lies at the heart of prayer: that our actions, above all our prayers, affect the inner life of God. Roughly, one might call this "theurgy," a belief that the goal of ritual is to evoke a response from the divine realm. Such a theurgic supposition is the principle behind saying Kaddish for a parent in the months after his or her death. By offering praise to God, our sages imagined that recitation of Kaddish might force God's hand, as it were, and make God judge the deceased more mercifully. In so doing, we might ensure the ascent of their spirit to heaven. To be sure, it's a premise that many assume to be behind all prayer: somehow, our words will change God's mind, as it were, and thereby change our fate. In prayer, we are seeking God's intercession to change the future.

Admittedly, this was a piece of our sages' thinking about prayer. For example, Rabbi Eleazar said: "Why are the prayers of the righteous compared to a pitchfork? To teach you that just as the pitchfork turns the grains from place to place in the barn, so the prayers of the righteous turn the mind of the blessed Holy One, from the side of sternness to that of mercy."[4] Even though we may be far removed from the agricultural times of Rabbi Eleazar, we can still grasp this marvelous image. A pitchfork is useful, powerful, even dangerous; so too are our prayers. Rabbi Eleazar is not saying that the pitchfork politely asks the grain to move itself; rather, it picks it up and hurls it across the granary. In that case, prayer is not a gentle request that God change God's mind;

it is electroshock therapy. It is inspiring to imagine that our prayers are powerful enough to change God's mind—turn it over, even—from a cruel fate to a more appealing outcome. It makes me want to pray more, which I suspect to be Rabbi Eleazar's true intention. It is a fine image, but a dangerous idea. Theologically, if God listens to and "obeys" some requests, why does God say no to equally valid demands? For example, why should God respond to a prayer for a good grade, but not for remission from leukemia? Furthermore, how much should my words matter to God? Who could have that kind of power? It's a Pandora's box of theological problems.

Why, then, ought we to pray?

Let me begin my answer by way of a story. In our community of Knoxville, Tennessee, services on the first night of Rosh Hashanah are sparsely attended, and then generally by persons who do not set foot in the synagogue at any other time. These are people dipping a toe in the waters of Jewish life. So I have taken it upon myself to lead these services alone, in a simple, improvisational fashion. Weather permitting, we move a few dozen chairs into our modest, pleasant courtyard. Early on in the one-hour service, I like to pair up the attendees with someone they have not met before, and ask them to interview each other briefly, with the intention of offering each other a blessing for the coming year; then, they exchange simple blessings. I think it is a wonderful moment of strangers attending to one another. "I really liked that," someone invariably tells me afterward, "but it felt too Christian."

Allow me to address that perception, as it is a passion of mine to reclaim for Judaism theology and practice that has been deemed "too Christian." Indeed, there is precedent within Jewish tradition for exchanging blessings. For example, consider the following verse from the Book of Psalms: "May the one who enters be blessed in the name of the Eternal; we bless you from the house of the Eternal" (118:26). Or the following exchange found in the Book of Ruth, one of our foundational stories that intertwines conversion, social justice, and messianism: "Boaz came from Bethlehem, and said to the reapers, 'May the Eternal be with you.' And they answered him, 'May the Eternal bless you'" (2:4).[5] These blessings were reciprocal, not unlike the aesthetic and theological context of the Priestly Blessing.

Therefore, through the Priestly Blessing, we may discover anew why we pray. What do we hope to achieve with the words *the Eternal bless you and keep you; the Eternal light up the divine face for you in grace; the Eternal lift up the divine face to you and bestow peace unto you*? What might be the priests' intent when they recite this blessing, now or in ancient times? Is it either meaningless, simply a trite greeting; or magical, a way of forcing God to grant the blessings that the priests recite? Let's assume that it is not a bland nostrum, offered in the way that you might say "How are you?" to which I reply, "Fine, thanks." Prayer must have some meaning, else why would people do it? Then, is it magic? Might the priests force God's hand, and make God treat us well? Is their prayer a sort of decree, couched in a request—a public pitchfork, as it were?

In a different teaching, Rabbi Ukba explains that the priests conclude their ritual by saying "Ruler of the Universe, we have performed what You decreed upon us; now You fulfill for us what You promised."[6] This too appears to a compelling instruction, yet one rooted in the worst kind of hubris. First of all, it suggests a wholly transactional understanding of prayer: we do what God wants (i.e., we obey the *mitzvot*) and so must God do what we ask (in prayer). That is certainly not a healthy understanding of prayer; at the very least, it makes our relationship with God less intimate. Hopefully, our relationship with the Divine is not so mercenary. Moreover, if we have this power over God, to invoke a blessing and compel a response, then it is not really "prayer" at all, but an order for shoes. If prayer is not a metaphysical zappos.com—neither theurgy nor magic—then how is it meaningful?

With this essay, I hope to shift the inquiry from causes to effects: what is the effect of prayer? Join me in re-framing prayer not as a matter of humans soliciting clemency from God's decrees. This outmoded framework places the pray-er[7] either in the position of sycophant or petulant child. If the intellectually honest and mature goal of prayer is not—at least, not mainly—to change God's mind or to reform God's plan, then what is its goal? Why pray, and why pray in a community? How might it move us or motivate us? In this, it seems that the Priestly Blessing *is* an excellent test case, which may in turn elucidate prayer generally.

Foremost, the Priestly Blessing can have transformative, even radical, effects on a community. Namely, it is by nature a blessing by the community, to the community, of the community—which is a fancy way to say that via Birkat Kohanim, we ourselves bless ourselves from ourselves. Primarily, the Priestly Blessing is a sacred moment to foster unity within community, which effect may ideally spread beyond the time of its recitation. In fact, the grammar of the blessing should be understood in this way. It is *the Eternal bless you and keep you*, with "you" in the singular, not the plural. Shlomo Leib of Łęczna (d. 1843) notes that the blessing is writ singular to indicate that "the essential truth of the blessing is unity...[so that the recipients may feel like] one person with one heart."[8] We recite or hear the blessing only when in community, and we only receive it as one, literally. Maybe the threefold Priestly Blessing is a reminder of our capacity when we are together, and our incapacity when apart. As Kohelet says, in a poetic parallel, "The three-ply cord is not easily broken" (4:12). Just as Kohelet notes that persons and things are greater than the sum of their parts, so too the parts of the Priestly Blesssing, as well as the community that receives blessing, are greater in sum than apart. Another salutary effect of the Priestly Blessing is to instill in us a sense of awe. The priests remove their shoes before offering the blessing, in a distant echo of Moses' commission: "Remove the sandals from your feet, for the place where you stand is holy ground"

(Exodus 3:5).[9] It is a call for all communities and community members to recognize their sanctity.

Since it is a blessing by the community, to the community, of the community, a major effect of the Priestly Blessing is fellowship. In this way, it is not so far removed from certain practices of early Christianity. Like blessing, another religious precept that we ceded too hastily to our Christian neighbors (although, in truth, it is "ours" as much as it is "theirs") is *commensality*, the practice of eating in a social group. A common anthropological observation of Jesus' early ministry is that he practiced radical commensality. Commensality, or table-fellowship, indicates that Jesus broke bread with persons of high and low status alike. His cohort included dissolute women, lepers, and other ritually unclean members of society without distinction, a radical break from the social hierarchy of his era. Allow me to suggest that the Priestly Blessing is an invitation to commensality. ("How is it any sort of commensality," you must quickly retort, "if it is a blessing offered by one class—socially elevated priests—to everyone else?!") Perhaps the commensality of the Priestly Blessing is not as radical as Jesus' version, yet it is a moment of equality, when everyone receives blessing together.

It is more egalitarian than it appears at first blush.[10] Consider a tension in the enactment of the practice itself: recipients of the blessing are instructed to lower their eyes yet be face to face with the priests.[11] (Well, which is it?) The posture of giver and receiver is already indeterminate; which figure is dominant, and which submissive? This poses a tension between received notions of priestly spiritual superiority, on the one hand, and a growing sense that the priests are themselves simply *representations* of God amid the community, on the other hand. Moreover, in order for the Priestly Blessing to shape harmonious community, it is effective only insofar as the priests are *representatives* of that community which they bless. They are proxies of the community, just as their vestments are made or paid for by the community.[12] In other words, they are only special because a community deems them so. Their election to the priestly caste appears almost incidental, or even accidental. They are neither gods nor kings, but selected arbitrarily by birth.

Next, the Priestly Blessing continues to challenge our notions about the effects of prayer. As I suggested above, there is a problematic assumption at the heart of prayer: that our words will affect God, which may in turn transform the physical world. Instead, it appears that the priests' work is actually threefold: to invite God's favor, to channel divine blessing, and to serve as a vessel for prayer. At no point, however, need this effect a change in the physical world. God does not grant wishes, which would be a travesty to a religious worldview. (Why does God grant your wishes but not mine? For that matter, why does it appear that God favorably answers the prayers of scoundrels, while many prayers of the righteous appear to go unheeded?) Prayer is not magic. This is underlined by the fact that the nature of the blessing is intentionally vague. We may call down, and perhaps orient God's blessing potential, but the blessing is God's to choose. The exact form of the blessing must depend on the needs, says Naftali Tzvi Yehudah Berlin,[13] indicating that an individual may ask for a blessing, but only God determines the ultimate result of the blessing bestowed. This is another way of saying, as the K'tav Sofeir remarks, that "God knows what is good for you."[14]

In the same way, the ritual of blessing and curse in Deuteronomy 27 does not expect that God will come down to reward or punish, but it is invoked to demand a fair world—something to which God and humans aspire together. The Priestly Blessing works the same way: it entails neither demands nor expectations, but rather hope and faith. In their work, the priests seek to draw down God's favor. Prayer is not a bland endorsement of the status quo, nor an irascible demand for divine intervention. Prayer gives us agency and latitude to become better. We ask more of God, and in effect, we ask more from ourselves.

To better understand this sensibility, consider the relation between the Shekhinah and creation. The Shekhinah is the immanent presence of God, considered to be the most accessible aspect of the Godhead, which is conceptualized in feminine terms in mystical contexts. How does "She" act in the world? A typical verb used in conjunction with the Shekhinah is *l'hashrot*, which means approximately "to suffuse." The Shekhinah suffuses creation like fresh-bought guavas left out in a basket will suffuse the air in a kitchen, just as God's presence inhabits the world "like a cloud that brings spring rain."[15] Accordingly, the verb *l'hashrot* suggests that we may observe God's presence as it suffuses our lives, yet we cannot force it to do so. This might be akin to becoming more alert to the scent of a loved one's cologne as it lingers in a room once that person steps away. What we seek are traces of the Divine Presence, and training in attending to those. Perhaps, what is really accomplished in prayer is making oneself more aware of the coming of spring rain.[16] Or perhaps it means becoming attuned to the better angels of our nature, which are all about us; in the language of the psalmist, "for [God] shall give the angels charge over you, to keep you in all your ways" (Psalm 91:11).

Conversely, one might describe the Priestly Blessing as directing God's presence outward among ourselves. This ritual calls on God to help us be our best selves for each other by channeling a perceived blessing from person to person. Priests conduct blessing throughout the body politic, as the circulatory system conducts antibodies throughout a child's body after he or she receives the measles vaccine. This is best illustrated in the Talmud,[17] where the question arises of how to conduct the Priestly Blessing if all congregants present are priests. We read there: "Adda said in the name of Rabbi Simlai: 'They all ascend to the platform.'" If all the priests in the community are up on the dais, whom are they blessing? Are they blessing each other? Do priests need a Priestly Blessing? "Rabbi Zera answered: '[They pronounce the blessing for the benefit of] their brethren [working] in the fields.'" It is as though God's energies are flowing into the priests, and becoming redirected outward to the fields, outside the synagogue. (To help visualize the scene, picture the climactic ritual of *Raiders of the Lost Ark*, before faces melt.) In this, the priests are, at best, conduits. I know of several congregants who follow this image to a logical conclusion: they offer their children the Sabbath Priestly Blessing in absentia. One congregant turns and raises his hands toward his married children in the Midwest, and another uses Skype and voicemail to channel blessing to his son in Israel, including "tailored wishes for the upcoming week."[18]

Furthermore, it is possible that the metaphor of a priest as a conduit for blessing is not the most accurate one. It may be more precise to call the priest a vessel, or better yet, a capacitor: he receives, stores, and discharges God's energies. Our tradition is very clear on the priests' lack of agency: "There should be no saying: 'My strength and the force of my hands,'"[19] the Torah and the sages caution. Our tradition dictates clearly that the priests are specifically *not* to think of themselves as the originators of the blessing. The priests' work is to impress the divine stamp on the people–although in many ways, the priest is superfluous to the equation. God can relate to us in any way God sees fit, and God does.

> In God's goodness, God wishes to bless God's people through [pure] servants....Were God to desire it, God might decree the blessing and [there would be] no need for the Priestly Blessing...[likewise,] God's blessed hand is open to any who ask, being fit and ready to receive goodness.[20]

Why, then, have human intercessors at all? Perhaps God is glorified through the priests; the majesty of the ceremony is awe-inspiring. "Through those near to me I show Myself holy; and gain glory before all people."[21]

The most amusing reason offered for why God asks humans to serve as intermediaries is this: we are more charitable than God. "Why should the priests bless if God will surely assent?" asks the hasidic rebbe Asher of Karlin. "Rather, God who sees secrets might not have such charity as a human who is not omniscient."[22] Perhaps the human component of the ritual tempers God's judgment. Frankly, I find this comment amusing. In my experience, human judgments are usually much more severe and caustic than God's. Simply on the basis of my own self-evaluation, I imagine that God's is much more charitable. Nevertheless, Karlin's perception may foster human relations, as we will see. At the end of the day, I believe that the most likely reason for human intermediaries at all is effectively to call the meeting to order. They get the ball rolling, so to speak, by suggesting that God bless humankind. The rules-of-procedure are these: someone offers a motion, and God accepts the motion. "The priests bless Israel," says the Talmud, "and the blessed Holy One approves their effort and blesses the people accordingly."[23]

If such is the form of the blessing, what then is its content? That is: what are we offering each other through the blessings? Aware that prayer is not wish-fulfillment, that priests are first-among-equals selected in an arbitrary fashion to be the capacitors of God's grace, I may suggest that the Priestly Blessing is designed to inculcate certain personal and communal values. This ritual has the germ of transformation within it. Nonetheless, the Priestly Blessing seems very materialistic. Superficially at least, the first of the blessings, *the Eternal bless you and keep you*, appears to offer prosperity on tap. Citing the midrash, Rashi notes that the blessing is an offering "that your possessions shall be blessed."[24] Other commentators likewise understand this as a blessing for increased wealth and assets, as well as protection from thieves. Material prosperity is a fine thing, and within a certain cosmology, not beyond God's power to provide, but it is also a bit tawdry to ask of God. Is "gimme!" the most important thing we want to ask of God? It also seems an absurd conclusion: are we really hoping that our goods will increase? Although it would be nice—marvelous, even—if our chattel could reproduce like cattle,[26] we don't live in such a world. I am reminded of the scene after the bank run in *It's a Wonderful Life*, when George says, "A toast to Papa Dollar and to Mama Dollar, and if you want the old Building and Loan to stay in business, you better have a family real quick."[27]

Rashi's second comment on the verse, however, gives an honest indication of what we might actually expect from a Priestly Blessing. Regarding the latter phrase, *and keep you*, Rashi explains: "that no thieves shall attack you and steal your money. For when one gives one's servant a gift, one cannot protect it from all other people, so if robbers come and take it, what benefit has [the servant] from this gift? As for the blessed Holy One, however, God is the One who [both] gives and protects."[28] What a wonderful analogy that teaches that God, unlike humankind, can both offer a gift and protect that gift. But it does not have to be a material gift. The gift may be a surety, in the financial and psychological senses. What God offers through the vessel of the priests is not a loan guarantee, but rather confidence, trust, and faith. Such a blessing might be aptly summarized by Leviticus 26:9: "I will look with favor upon you, and make you fertile and multiply you, and I will maintain My covenant with you." This is an essential part of God's nature: the ability to offer, give, and protect with no expectation of return. Some sages call this a *matnat ḥinam*, a free gift,[29] the essence of God's heritage (*naḥalah*) for us.

It would even seem that God's blessing must transcend the material. Already in the time of the prophet Malachi (c. fifth century B.C.E.), the sense of physical sacrifice was diminished, and the prophet cast doubt upon the efficacy of ritual.[30] It is not, he might have said, to bring about *God's* favor, but rather to open *our* hearts to a generous spirit. Perhaps the oral and aural experience of the Priestly Blessing might inspire us to become more giving and forgiving. This is the prosperity offered through the Priestly Blessing: it inspires us to offer each other gifts through a wellspring of our own generosity. Again, I am not referring to possessions, nor glibly suggesting that the Priestly Blessing become an occasion for gift-giving. Prosperity is nothing without presence; we are to offer each other joyful spirits. Rabbi Hezekiah ben Manoah, the thirteenth-century French commentator, suggests as much in his commentary to the Priestly Blessing.[31] Perhaps the sole outcome of the blessing, he suggests, is that God be nice to you, make you successful, and cheer you up. The priest or recipient might infer that this is a pretty ideal formulation for human interactions, too: be kind, help each other out, and try to make others happy.

Another tantalizing potential is that the blessing might begin to re-orient our priorities. To me, this seems to be the impetus of most religious experience: giving voice to an alternate source and set of values. (For example, Western culture prizes the individual, and individual rights; Judaism valorizes the community, and communal responsibilities.) In the case of the Priestly Blessing, perhaps the first phrase draws our awareness to the principle that the best things in life are free—or, that the best things in life are not even things. Maybe the point is not to ask for endlessly more remuneration, wealth, assets, or even protection and providence over what we already possess, but rather to strive for awareness of our own great good fortune. Furthermore, by offering blessings of prosperity amid community, we may become less possessive of our own goods and welfare. As we wish prosperity for others, might we be more willing to give from what we have? If God can be so generous, why can we not be as generous to ourselves? And, by noting our own charitable impulses at a given moment, we may become more tolerant of who we are. Moshe Alshekh concurs, by suggesting that the first blessing is, in fact, a reminder for each person to be *samei·ah b'helko*, satisfied with one's portion in life.[32]

Recently, I had the great honor to bury a woman of 101 years of age, Yetta Burnett. She was truly *s'meiḥah b'ḥelkah*, content and happy with her portion in life. In preparation for her funeral, her son worried that there would not be enough to say about his mother: she lived a quiet life, and many of the people who knew her best were long since departed. But his fears were unfounded. It is not that her life was too simple to celebrate; it is that the lesson of her life, to all of us, is this: a simple life and a quiet death are among the best of lives one can hope for, perhaps the best. Yetta was an uncomplaining, unassuming, and kind lady, deeply devoted to her husband, her children, and her extended family. Her life was neither big nor flashy, but it taught an important lesson to us: what really matters is neither your resume nor your achievements, but being a decent person, a *mensch*, without making a big fuss about it. Like Yetta's example, the Priestly Blessing invites us to grow in this generosity of spirit.

What, then, is the meaning of the second sentence of the blessing, the prayer that *the Eternal light up the divine face for you in grace*? Should the recipient understand it—as has been normative practice— as a reference to of God's luminous and numinous face, and thus as an expression intended to denote God's favor?[33] Some authors in this volume posit that in ancient Israel, there was indeed a mystic, ecstatic experience of seeing God's radiance.[34] It is stirring to conceive of our ancestors having a sensory interaction with the Divine, but I doubt that most Jews could reach that today, and I fear that failure to achieve such ecstasies might dishearten some. I humbly offer that the essence of this verse is instead suggested by the psalmist: "There are many who say, 'Who will show us good?' God, lift up the light of Your countenance upon us" (Psalm 4:7). The light of God's countenance *is* the essence of God's goodness. In the centerpiece of the Priestly Blessing, we are reminded to emulate God—in effect, to become mirrors of God's gentle light. Blessing each other with reference to God's face is a way of inculcating mercy and kindness toward our fellow. To do so, it behooves us to ask what the aforementioned grace might entail as a personality trait. Among other things, interpersonal grace is a "quality of being liked by others"[35]—that is, being pleasant. Being liked by others is often contingent upon making them feel liked, loved, or at least appreciated. In my experience, nothing garners friendship more than giving someone your attention. That is the crux of this blessing: to extend God's grace toward another by extending ourselves.

I might suggest that it is for this reason that the Priestly Blessing is offered *b'ahavah*, with love. Moving backwards in order to move forward, let us consider the blessing that the priests say before pronouncing the Priestly Blessing: Blessed are You, Adonai our God, Ruler of the universe, who has sanctified us with Aaron's holiness, and commanded us to bless the people Israel with love (*b'ahavah*). Joy is a crucial component of that love.[36] In fact, the mystical tradition emphasizes the element of joyous fellowship (*ahavat yisrael*). The Zohar suggests that "any priest who does not have love for the congregation or for whom the congregation has no love, may not raise his hands to bless the congregation."[37] You may smile at this injunction, thinking, "Who might dare to accuse a co-religionist of being unloving or unlovable?!" Yet, it happens…and I doubt that my congregation is the only one that has had this experience. When I arrived at my pulpit, I noticed that the Priestly Blessing was not recited on major holidays.[38] I was excited to reinstate the tradition of festival *dukhenen*. As the community rabbi, and as a *kohen* no less, I felt it well within my purview to lead this wonderful practice. At first, the community was enchanted, or so it appeared to me. ("Wow! They must really like the Priestly Blessing, and find it quite moving," I thought. "They'll really appreciate me.") Some time later, I learned the rest of the story. Years before my arrival, it *had* been the synagogue's practice to offer the Priestly Blessing. A problem presented itself, however, when there was enmity between a priest (not the rabbi, that time!) and another congregant. Since it is impossible to bless others without being moved by a feeling of love, and certainly not when the priest is an "enemy,"[39] the practice of having the priests recite Birkat Kohanim was quietly allowed to fall into disuse.

Perhaps this is only as it should be. The Priestly Blessing ought to make us more godlike, or at least more aware of God. Consequently, it is not entirely unfair to suspend the Priestly Blessing when there is enmity, and persons are incapable of reaching out to others. On the other hand, one might imagine that the act of blessing another may thaw the chill in one's heart. Rabbi Naftali Tzvi Yehudah Berlin notes that "according to the person's virtues, the expression of the face changes."[40] By saying the blessing or by receiving it, and by ruminating on God's grace, might we not become more kindly disposed toward others? A hoped-for effect of the Priestly Blessing might be the development of comity within community. This echoes the same logic of Asher Karlin (above), who believed human judgment to be more generous than divine judgment. Consider also the following source:

> The priests bless Israel so that they themselves be suffused with love and great *affection* and be vessels [that] retain blessing. Hence, "the One who chooses the people Israel with love" [a reference to the morning liturgy]—if there is love among them, then the choice is faithful [and] upheld, for they are a vessel [capable] of retaining blessing.[41]

In the foregoing, it appears that the success of the blessing is contingent upon love, both by the blessers and by the blessed. Levi Yitzhak of Berditchev underscores this sentiment, suggesting that this contains the sense of great dearness, even glory.[42] The word he uses to gloss *ahavah* ("love") is *hibbah* (rendered here by "affection"), which has connotations of fondness, and also of debt.[43] *Hibbah* suggests a tenderness we owe to our fellow creatures. Thus, it might be understandable that one who has alienated oneself from another person is in default of such *hibbah*, and therefore incapable of either bestowing or receiving blessing until the debt is repaid.

So, is the point of the Priestly Blessing to teach us how to be friends to our fellows? Partly, yes. A chain of teachers, claiming authority from Rashi, suggest that *b'ahavah*, the condition in which the Priestly Blessing is offered (and apparently also received), is the opposite of *b'hippazon*, the condition in which we left Egypt—namely, in a rush. Instead of hurriedly, we do it with intention and whole heart.[44] This is the selfsame reason for which outside of the Land of Israel, the Priestly Blessing is only offered on holidays: we await seasons of joy and contentment.

A personal aside: in my youth, I was a child of Greater Boston, always doing and achieving—a classic "Type A" personality. For the first years of my tenure in Tennessee, a frequent complaint was that I always "rushed off." I had to learn to linger, a venerable Southern tradition. As I groped toward this technique, I learned that it really does enhance relationships. Having one's feet firmly planted where you are is a great foundation for a warm conversation. That is what this blessing intends: give your time to another person, and your heart will follow. Compassion, surely, is a cornerstone of love. Through the Priestly Blessing we learn to express God's grace, and send it out in generosity, compassion, and gratitude.

Whence gratitude? The Talmud says that *avodah v'hoda·ah hadda milta hi*, it is reasonable to regard service and thanksgiving as one.[45] Serving someone else can make us more grateful for our own accomplishments. This seems to be the message behind the final step of Alcoholics Anonymous: to help others. By reaching out to help others, addicts are reminded of their own sobriety. Similarly, as we serve others by standing to bless them, or even allowing them to bless us, might we not be made aware of our own gifts, challenges, and blessings? As in the Erev Rosh Hashanah experience I described above, blessing others can engender joy. Such gratitude can also make us both humble and grateful, to recognize, like Jacob, that "I am too small for all the kindnesses You did for me" (Genesis 32:11). In the moment of the Priestly Blessing, one may not feel worthy to bless another Jew, nor worthy of blessing. In fact, even rabbis and priests do not truly merit their task. At some level, we are all frauds!

Fortunately, that is all right. We are each, all of us, too small for the kindnesses God bestows, and that is as it should be. Baruch Halevi Epstein (1860–1941), a great Lithuanian rabbi, felt the same ambivalence, albeit in a different circumstance. When called upon to preach, this saintly rabbi said: "I know of myself that I am not worthy…but even though I am not worthy, if my friends ask me to rise and teach, I rise."[46] The Priestly Blessing is there to demonstrate that at some point, any of us (even by dint of birth) may be called upon to rise, lead, and bless others. So: stand up with trust in others' faith in you, and you may be pleasantly surprised by the way in which their faith transforms you. So much of the Priestly Blessing is about recognizing God's face, light, and glory, and bathing in the reflected light. God's grace is piqued, as it were, when God sees us. Wouldn't that be a great thing for us to acknowledge as we bless and are blessed?

The conclusion of the tripartite Priestly Blessing is this: *May the Eternal lift up the divine face to you and bestow peace (shalom) unto you.* This blessing is echoed by the psalmist: "May the Eternal grant strength to God's people; may the Eternal bless God's people with *shalom.*" (Psalm 29:11). What, then, is *shalom*, and why might we wish to receive it or bestow it upon others? *Shalom* is most commonly translated as "peace,"[47] but that is not exactly what it means. For instance, after a recent suicide of a troubled teen, many of the young man's acquaintances in our community said, "He's at peace now; at least he's not suffering anymore." To which, I rebuked the community at the boy's memorial: "Death is not the same as peace!" Although we may say colloquially and liturgically that one "rests in peace" in the grave,[48] I assert that death is not *shalom*—one cannot possess *shalom* without measures of health, friendship, and welfare.[49] Like peace, *shalom* is ineffable and intangible, but it implies, at the very least, fullness. As such, I would call it "wholeness," "welfare," or best yet, "harmony." On the other hand, *shalom* is what civil libertarians might call a negative freedom—that is, "freedom from." *Shalom* is freedom from disasters, freedom from ills, and freedom from want. We bless each other through *shalom* as a manner of expressing our desire to be free from fury and rage, whether God's or our own.[50]

Aware that peace/*shalom* may only come in when we are free from fear and loneliness, and can only arise in a community where the ill and the traumatized are tended to, we see that the conclusion of the Priestly Blessing may serve as an admonition to build more loving and just communities. This is a blessing to fill each other with mutual love and admiration, tolerance and appreciation. Envision a community that takes the mandate of *shalom* seriously, in all of its aspects! It would be a place of home and healing. For *shalom* is, truly, the greatest of God's gifts. It is not merely "peace," but the pinnacle and completion of God's creation:

> Rabbi Simeon son of Ḥalafta said: The blessed Holy One found no vessel that could contain blessing for Israel save that of peace, as it is written, "The Eternal grants strength unto God's people; the Eternal blesses God's people with peace" (Psalm 29:11).[51]

In conclusion, let us return to the question of why this blessing is offered at all. Obviously, if God wished to bless anyone, God could do so directly. That might be common sense. All of us who give or receive the Priestly Blessing know this in some way. Have no fear; our sages understood the same problem, as the following midrash makes clear:

> Master of Worlds, You tell priests to bless us, yet we only need *Your* blessings, to be blessed by *Your* mouth…[Hence] the blessed Holy One said to them, "Although I have told the priests to bless you, I stand amid them and bless you."

That is why the priests spread their fingers, to show that the blessed Holy One is behind them.[52]

It is as though the priests are a stained-glass window through which we perceive God's holy emanation. They may color the light through their words and timbres, but the light is ours to use as we desire.

The Priestly Blessing is neither about human intervention nor about affecting God. It is about humbly trying to realize our greatest selves through an ordained system of blessing. Moreover, there is a virtuous cycle in place: blessing begets blessing. As we bless, we too are blessed, and we become God's proxies. Rabbi Joshua son of Levi is reported to have said, "Every priest who pronounces the benediction is himself blessed, but if he does not pronounce it he is not blessed; as it is said: 'I will bless those who bless you.'"[53] We call upon God to bless us, but in fact *we* are the ones who bring blessing. By aspiring to God's protection, grace, and completion, we give our best selves to each other, and thus manifest God's love in this world. That is the meaning of prayer.

NOTES

[1] Quoted by Elissa Goldstein in "Leonard Nimoy on the Jewish Story Behind the Vulcan Salute" (February 25, 2014), available online at www.jewcy.com.

[2] This is my own translation of the Priestly Blessing, as found in Numbers 6:24–26. All translations of ancient sources (both biblical and rabbinic) in this essay are my own.

[3] B. Shabbat 119b.

[4] B. Sukkah 14a.

[5] I am told that many Sephardic communities use these same words to exchange greetings with those called forward for *aliyot* to the Torah.

[6] B. Sotah 39a–b.

[7] There has never been a satisfactory nominal form in English for the one-who-prays.

[8] Rabbi Shlomo Leib of Łęczna, as cited in *Itturei Torah*, ed. Aaron Jacob Greenberg (Tel Aviv: Yavneh Publishing House, 1996), vol. 5, p. 44. The Jewish pronunciation of Łęczna was Lantshina.

[9] Cf. also Joshua 5:15.

[10] For more on the question of Birkat Kohanim and an egalitarian worldview, see the essay of Daniel Greyber elsewhere in this volume.

[11] See Rambam, M.T. Hilkhot Tefillah U-nesiat Kapayim 14:13.

[12] See Exodus 35:19.

[13] See his *Ha·ameik Davar* commentary to Numbers 6:26 (Jerusalem: Yeshivat Volozhin, 1999), vol. 6, p. 64.

[14] Rabbi Abraham Samuel Benjamin Sofer (1815–1871), *K'tav Sofeir al Ha-torah* to Numbers 6:23 (ed. Bratislava, 1873), p. 198b.

[15] Proverbs 16:15.

[16] Jeremiah 17:5–8: "Thus says the Eternal, 'Cursed be the one who trusts in humans, and makes flesh his arm, and whose heart departs from the Eternal. For such a person shall be like the juniper tree in the desert, and shall not see when good comes; but shall inhabit the parched places in the wilderness, in a salt land and not inhabited. Blessed is the one who trusts in the Eternal, and whose hope is the Eternal. For such a person shall be like a tree planted by the waters, that spreads out its roots by the river, and shall not see when heat comes, but its leaf shall be green; and shall not be anxious in the year of drought, nor shall it cease from yielding fruit."

[17] B. Sotah 38b.

[18] Barry P. Allen, private correspondence, February 23, 2014.

[19] *Itturei Torah*, vol. 5, p. 40 (citing Deuteronomy 8:17), referencing the *Akeidah* and citing a passage also cited in the *Sefer V'dibbarta Bam* of Nisim Ohayon (B'nei Brak: N. Ohayon, 5763[2002/2003], p. 33.

[20] *Sefer Ha-ḥinnukh* (attributed to Aaron HaLevi of Barcelona), *mitzvah* 378 (Jerusalem: Shai Lamorah Publishing, 2002), vol. 2, p. 505.

[21] Leviticus 10:3.

[22] *Itturei Torah*, vol. 5, p. 45, citing Rabbi Asher of Karlin (1802–1872).

[23] B. Ḥullin 49a.

[24] Rashi to Numbers 6:24, based on *Tanḥuma Naso* §10 and Sifrei Bemidbar §40.

[25] Ibn Ezra to Numbers 6:24; Seforno to Numbers 6:25.

[26] And perhaps that is what Rashi intended, speaking to an agrarian society.

[27] Frances Goodrich, Albert Hackett, Frank Capra, and Jo Swerling, *It's a Wonderful Life* (New York: St. Martin's Press, 1986), p. 81.

[28] Rashi to Numbers 6:24, s.v. *v'yishm'rekha*.

[29] *Itturei Torah*, Numbers 6:25.

[30] Malachi 1:8–10, but see too in this regard also all the earlier sources cited by Jacob Chinitz in his essay, "Were the Prophets Opposed to Sacrifice?" in *Jewish Bible Quarterly* 36:2 (April 2008), pp. 73–80, available online at http://jbq.jewishbible.org.

[31] *Ḥizkuni* to Numbers 6:26.

[32] *Itturei Torah*, pp. 43–44, citing the *Torat Moshe* of Rabbi Moshe Alshekh (1508–1593).

[33] Here, I understand the normative understanding to be that put forth by Rashi (Numbers 6:25): "May [God] show you a pleasant, radiant countenance...May [God] grant you favor." See *Tanḥuma Naso* §10; Sifrei Bemidbar §41.

[34] For more extended discussion on this notion, see the essays by Martin S. Cohen and Admiel Kosman elsewhere in this volume.

[35] Avie Gold, *Bircas Kohanim* (Brooklyn: Mesorah Productions, 1981), p. 76.

[36] Ibid., p. 37.

[37] Zohar III 147b, as cited in ibid., p. 62.

[38] This is the most common practice in traditional diaspora communities.

[39] Gold, *Bircas Kohanim*, p. 63.

[40] *Ha·ameik Davar* to Numbers 6:26, vol. 6, p. 65.

[41] *Ta·ammei Ha-manhig* to Numbers 6:23, citing the *Torah Ḥayyim*, in the *Itturei Torah*, vol. 5, p. 43, my emphasis.

[42] Cf. his *Kedushat Levi*: "This is the sense of great dearness, and glory (*hibbah g'dolah v'tiferet*)," in *Nitzutzei Zohar*, cited in the *Itturei Torah* to Numbers 6:23, vol. 5, pp. 42–43.

[43] Alternately, I might choose to gloss *hibbah* with the Spanish word *cariño*, a common greeting at the end of letters that suggests both fondness and longing—unless the Internet and email have changed epistolary mores.

[44] As cited in *Nitzutzei Zohar*, in *Itturei Torah* to Numbers 6:23, vol. 5, pp. 42–43; likewise, Rashi to Numbers 6:23, wherein *b'ahavah* is set in opposition to *b'hippazon*, indicating intent and whole-heartedness.

[45] B. Megillah 18a.

[46] Rabbi Baruch Halevi Epstein to Numbers 6:23, cited in *Itturei Torah*, vol. 5, p. 41; a similar discourse is found in his *Torah Temimah* to Numbers (Israel: "Torah" Institute, 2005) , vol. 4, p. 108.

[47] No, it means neither "hello" nor "goodbye"—it is simply used as a greeting in

these contexts! Instead of the wan "hi" and "bye" of American culture, traditional Jews bless each other with peace, both upon encountering one other and departing the company of another.

[48] Cf., for example, the line *v'yanu·ah/v'tanu·ah b'shalom al mishkavo/mishakavah* ("may the deceased rest in peace in his or her resting place"), found in the El Malei prayer recited in memory of loved ones at funerals and on *yahrzeits*.

[49] Jacob Milgrom, *The JPS Torah Commentary: Numbers* (Philadelphia: Jewish Publication Society, 1990), p. 52.

[50] Rashi to Numbers 6:26.

[51] M. Uktzin 3:12.

[52] Bemidbar Rabbah 11:2.

[53] B. Sotah 38b.

special acknowledgement to

Nora Frydman

Translation
Grant peace everywhere goodness and blessing,
Grace, lovingkindness and mercy to us and unto all Israel

Transliteration
Sim shalom tovah u-v'rakhah
ḥein va-ḥesed v'raḥamim aleinu ve-al kol Yisrael amekha

שִׂים שָׁלוֹם*

שִׂים שָׁלוֹם טוֹבָה וּבְרָכָה
חֵן וָחֶסֶד וְרַחֲמִים עָלֵינוּ וְעַל כָּל יִשְׂרָאֵל עַמֶּךְ

---

* **Sim Shalom** (Hebrew: שִׂים שָׁלוֹם; "Grant Peace") is a blessing that is recited near the end of formal Jewish prayer services. The precise form of the blessing varies depending on the service and the precise denomination along the Jewish spectrum.

www.BlechTapes.com

a focused YouTube channel

Benjamin Blech Exegesis

on 10-theme Mesorah Matrix

sequence of 12 twenty-minute tapes:

intro + 10 themes + outro

www.UnifyingScienceSpirituality.com

About the Contributors

Howard Avruhm Addison, Ph.D., serves as an Assistant Professor for Instruction at Temple University, where he teaches in the Intellectual Heritage Program. Trained in Dream Group Leadership by North Carolina's Haden Institute, he directs the Graduate Theological Foundation's Doctor of Ministry Program in Jewish Spirituality. Rabbi Addison was one of the founders of the Lev Shomea Jewish Spiritual Direction Training Institute and is the author of *The Enneagram and Kabbalah* (Jewish Lights, 1998) and co-editor of *Jewish Spiritual Direction* (Jewish Lights, 2006).

Michael J. Broyde is a law professor at Emory University, and the Projects Directors of the Center for the Study of Law and Religion at Emory. Rabbi Broyde served for many years in diverse religious capacities as well, from being the rabbi of the Young Israel in Atlanta to being a member of the Beth Din of America to serving as the head of the Atlanta Torah Mitzion Kollel.

Reuven P. Bulka, C.M., has been the rabbi of Congregation Machzikei Hadas in Ottawa, Ontario, Canada, since 1967. He chairs the Trillium Gift of Life Network in the Ministry of Health and Long Term Care, responsible for organ and tissue donation and transplantation in all of Ontario. The author of more than thirty books, Rabbi Bulka is a member of the Order of Canada, Canada's highest civilian honor.

Shalom Carmy teaches Jewish Studies and Philosophy at Yeshiva University and also serves as editor-in-chief of *Tradition*.

Aryeh Cohen is Professor of Rabbinic Literature at American Jewish University in Los Angeles. He serves on the Board of Clergy and Laity United for Economic Justice (CLUE), and

T'ruah: The Rabbinic Call for Human Rights. His latest article for the *Journal of Jewish Ethics* is "'The Foremost Amongst the Divine Attributes Is to Hate the Vulgar Power of Violence': Aharon Shmuel Tamares and Recovering Nonviolence for Jewish Ethics." Rabbi Dr. Cohen's latest book is *Justice in the City: An Argument from the Sources of Rabbinic Judaism* (Academic Studies Press). He blogs at Justice in the City (www.justice-in-the-city.com).

Martin S. Cohen is the rabbi of the Shelter Rock Jewish Center in Roslyn, New York, and one of the senior editors of the Mesorah Matrix series. He is the author of *The Boy on the Door on the Ox* (Aviv Press, 2008), *Our Haven and our Strength: The Book of Psalms* (Aviv Press, 2004), and four novels. Rabbi Dr. Cohen served as senior editor of *The Observant Life*, published in 2012 by the Rabbinical Assembly, and his translation and commentary on the Torah are forthcoming.

Yeshaya Dalsace is the rabbi of Dor Va-dor, the Massorti Community of East Paris.

Elliot N. Dorff is Rector and Distinguished Service Professor of Philosophy at American Jewish University and Visiting Professor at UCLA School of Law. Rabbi Dorff chairs the Conservative Movement's Committee on Jewish Law and Standards, and he is a past president of the Society of Jewish Ethics, the Academy of Jewish Philosophy, the Jewish Law Association, the Academy of Judaic, Christian, and Islamic Studies, and Jewish Family Service of Los Angeles. Of the twelve books and over 200 articles he has written on Jewish thought, law, and ethics, his writings most germane to the essay printed in this volume are his book *Knowing God: Jewish Journeys to the Unknowable*

(Jason Aaronson, 1992),and the theological commentaries to the ten volumes of *My People's Prayerbook* (Jewish Lights, 1997-2007), edited by Lawrence Hoffman.

Alon C. Ferency is the rabbi of Heska Amuna Synagogue in Knoxville, Tennessee, and the rabbi-in-residence at Bonnaroo Music and Arts Festival. He is a contributor to *Conservative Judaism quarterly* and *Sh'ma*, and has forthcoming work in books on liturgy, and the connections between physicality and spirituality. His sermons are available on iTunes.

Aubrey L. Glazer is the senior rabbi at Congregation Beth Sholom in San Francisco. Rabbi Dr. Glazer is the author of *Mystical Vertigo: Kabbalistic Hebrew Poetry Dancing Cross the Divide* (Academic Studies Press, 2013), *A New Physiognomy of Jewish Thinking: Critical Theory After Adorno as Applied to Jewish Thought* (Continuum, 2011), and *Contemporary Hebrew Mystical Poetry: How It Redeems Jewish Thinking* (Edwin Mellen Press, 2009).

Mark Goldfeder is Senior Lecturer at Emory University School of Law and the Spruill Family Senior Fellow at the Center for the Study of Law and Religion.

Michael Graetz worked as assistant to the editor-in-chief of Encyclo-pedia Judaica, and wrote articles on modern Jewish thought for the Encyclopedia. He is rabbi emeritus of Magen Avraham congregation in Omer, a suburb of Beer Sheva, and was one of the founders of the Masorti Movement and the Schechter Rabbinical school in Israel.

Daniel Greyber is rabbi at Beth El Synagogue in Durham, North Carolina, author of *Faith Unravels: A Rabbi's Struggle with Grief and God*, (Resource Publications, 2013) and recently served as Team USA Rabbi at the 19th World Maccabiah Games in Israel. Formerly a Jerusalem Fellow at the Mandel Leadership Institute, faculty member at the Ziegler School of Rabbinic Studies in Los Angeles, and the Executive Director of Camp Ramah in California, Rabbi Greyber's articles have been featured in a wide range of Jewish publications.

Robert A. Harris is associate professor of Bible at The Jewish Theological Seminary, teaching courses in biblical literature and medieval Jewish biblical exegesis. An expert in the history of medieval biblical exegesis, Rabbi Harris's dissertation was titled "The Literary Hermeneutic of Rabbi Eliezer of Beaugency." In 2004, Dr. Harris published a book in the Brown Judaic Studies series, *Discerning Parallelism: A Study in Northern French Medieval Jewish Biblical Exegesis* (Brown Judaic Series, 2004). In addition, he has published many articles and reviews in both American and Israeli journals.

James Jacobson-Maisels is the founder of Or HaLev: A Center for Jewish Spirituality and Meditation (http://orhalev.org/). Rabbi Dr. Jacobson-Maisels teaches at Haifa University, the Pardes Institute of Jewish Studies, the Institute for Jewish Spirituality, Yeshivat Hadar, and in a variety of settings in Israel and around the world.

Michael Knopf is the rabbi of Temple Beth-El in Richmond, Virginia and a fellow of CLAL's Rabbis Without Borders. Named by *The Jewish Daily Forward* as one of "America's Most Inspiring Rabbis," he has published in several anthologies and is a regular contributor to *Haaretz* and *Huffington Post*.

Admiel Kosman, a renowned poet, is Professor for Jewish Studies at Potsdam University as well as the academic director of Geiger College, a training school for liberal rabbis, in Berlin. The author of several books and many articles in the field of talmudic research, and of collections of Hebrew verse, he also writes a regular column for *Haaretz* in which he interprets traditional stories in a postmodern light. His latest academic book is *Gender and Dialogue in the Rabbinic Prism* (Walter de Gruyter, 2012), and his most recent collection of poetry is *Approaching You in English: Selected Poems* (Zephyr Press, 2011).

David Evan Markus is co-chair of ALEPH: Alliance for Jewish Rene-wal; co-rabbi of Temple Beth-El of City Island (New York City); and serves as spiritual direction faculty and adjunct rabbinics faculty for the ALEPH Ordination Program. A fellow of CLAL's Rabbis Without Borders, he has presented at NewCAJE, OHALAH (rabbinical association for Jewish Renewal), Limmud and Routes; he blogs regularly for My Jewish Learning, and publishes widely on liturgy, rabbinic education, spiritual direction and the innovation space. In secular life, he presides as judicial officer in New York Supreme Court, and is among the few U.S. government officials simultaneously to serve in an active rabbinic pulpit.

David Mescheloff, retired university lecturer and community rabbi, teaches and writes on Jewish Law and Thought. A co-founder of "The Israeli Rabbis' Forum," he wrote a "Marital Agreement to Mediate," a "Completion of the Haggadah," a "Driver's Prayer," and more.

Nehemia Polen is Professor of Jewish Thought at Boston's Hebrew College. He is the author of *The Holy Fire: The Teachings of Rabbi Kalonymus Shapira, the Rebbe of the Warsaw Ghetto* (Jason Aronson, 1994), and is a contributing commentator to *My People's Prayer Book* (Jewish Lights, 1997-2007). His book *The Rebbe's Daughter* (Jewish Publication Society, 2002), was awarded a National Jewish Book Award. His essay "Hasidic *Derashah* As Illuminated Exegesis" has just been published in *The Value of the Particular: Lessons from Judaism and the Modern Jewish Experience: Festschrift for Steven T. Katz on the Occasion of his Seventieth Birthday*, edited by Michael Zank and Ingrid Anderson (Brill, 2015).

Avram Israel Reisner is rabbi emeritus of Congregation Chevrei Tzedek in Baltimore, Maryland, and an Adjunct Professor at Towson University and St. Mary's Ecumenical Institute. He is a member of longstanding on the Conservative Movement's Committee of Jewish Law and Standards.

Jonathan Sacks is a rabbi, philosopher, and author of twenty-seven books. He is currently the Ingeborg and Ira Rennert Global Distinguished Professor of Judaic Thought at New York University, the Kressel and Ephrat Family University Professor of Jewish Thought at Yeshiva University, and Professor of Law, Ethics and the Bible at King's College London. Rabbi Sacks served as Chief Rabbi of the United Hebrew Congregations of the Commonwealth between September 1991 and September 2013. He was awarded the Jerusalem Prize in 1995 for his contribution to diaspora Jewish life and The Ladislaus Laszt Ecumenical and Social Concern Award from Ben Gurion University in Israel in 2011. He was knighted by Her Majesty The Queen in 2005 and made a Life Peer, taking his seat in the House of Lords in October 2009.

Shohama Harris Wiener serves as Rosh Hashpa'ah (Head of Spiritual Direction) for ALEPH: Alliance for Jewish Renewal and its Ordination Program; co-rabbi of Temple Beth-El of City Island (New York City); Founding Director of HASHPA'AH (ALEPH's training program in spiritual direction); and President Emerita of the Academy for Jewish Religion. In these positions her focus has been on bringing Jewish spirituality into seminary education as well as to the wider public. Her most recent books include co-editing *Seeking and Soaring* (Reclaiming Judaism Press, 2004), *Jewish Approaches to Spiritual Guidance and Development*, and *The Wisdom of Reb Zalman* (forthcoming from Reclaiming Judaism Press).

MESORAH MATRIX

10-BOOK SERIES
150+ Essayists

dimensions of

Spirituality & Kedushah

THE SPARK OF THE INFINITE DIVINE

Mesorah Matrix
Series

David Birnbaum

Editor-in-Chief

10-theme

10-volume

Sanctification — 2015

Tikkun Olam — 2015

Birkat Kohanim — 2016

Kaddish — 2016

Modeh Ani — 2017

Havdalah — 2017

Search for Meaning — 2018

U-Vacharta Ba-Chayim — 2018

Ehyeh Asher Ehyeh — 2019

U'shamru — 2019

200+ original essays

jewish thought & spirituality

150+ global thought leaders

a decade-long unified endeavor

LIGHTS OF CREATION & TRANSCENDENCE
David Birnbaum / Mesorah Matrix Series

MESORAH MATRIX

10-BOOK SERIES
150+ Essayists

Sanctification

Tikkun Olam

Birkat Kohanim

The Kaddish

Modeh Ani

Havdalah

Search for Meaning

U-VACHARTA BA-CHAYIM

Ehyeh asher Ehyeh

V'Shamru

THE SPARK OF THE INFINITE DIVINE

Mesorah Matrix Series

Sanctification ("Kedushah")

Tikkun Olam ("Repair the World")

Birkat Kohanim (The Priestly Blessings: a contemporary take)

The Kaddish (specifically, The Mourner's Praise of God)

Modeh Ani (The solo daily morning prayer of Gratitude)

Havdalah (separating Holy from Secular: Sabbath > secular)

Search for Meaning (pegging-off of Viktor Frankl's classic)

U-VACHARTA BA-CHAYIM (The 613th precept-Choose Life)

Ehyeh asher Ehyeh ("I Will Be That Which I Will Be" – at the Burning Bush)

V'Shamru (The Sabbath)

21st CENTURY PUBLISHING

David.Birnbaum.NY@gmail.com

www.NewParadigmMatrix.com

MESORAH
MATRIX
VOLUME 1

David Birnbaum / Mesorah Matrix Series
LIGHTS OF CREATION & TRANSCENDENCE

Sanctification

Editors

David
Birnbaum & **Blech**
Benjamin

LEAD ESSAY: **Jonathan Sacks**

New Paradigm Matrix™

EXPLORING HIGHER DIMENSIONS

MESORAH MATRIX
VOLUME 2

TIKKUN OLAM

JUDAISM, HUMANISM & TRANSCENDENCE

David Birnbaum / Mesorah Matrix Series
LIGHTS OF CREATION & TRANSCENDENCE

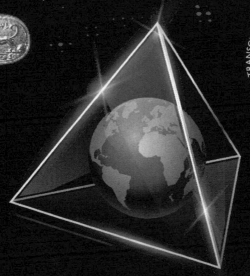

Editors

David
Birnbaum &

Martin S.
Cohen

Associate Editor: **Saul J. Berman**

New Paradigm Matrix™

EXPLORING HIGHER DIMENSIONS

VOLUME 3

BIRKAT KOHANIM

David Birnbaum | Mesorah Matrix Series

LIGHTS OF CREATION & TRANSCENDENCE

EXPLORING HIGHER DIMENSIONS

Editors

David
Birnbaum & Cohen
Martin S.

Associate Editor: **Saul J. Berman**

New Paradigm Matrix

VOLUME 4

KADDISH

LIGHTS OF CREATION & TRANSCENDENCE / Mesorah Matrix Series / David Birnbaum

Editors

David
Birnbaum &
Martin S.
Cohen

Associate Editor: **Saul J. Berman**

New Paradigm Matrix™

EXPLORING HIGHER DIMENSIONS

LIGHTS OF CREATION & TRANSCENDENCE

David Birnbaum / Mesorah Matrix Series

Modeh Ani

THE TRANSCENDENT PRAYER OF GRATITUDE

Editors

David
Birnbaum & Martin S. Cohen

Associate Editor: **Saul J. Berman**

New Paradigm Matrix

EXPLORING HIGHER DIMENSIONS

MESORAH MATRIX
VOLUME 6

LIGHTS OF CREATION & TRANSCENDENCE
David Birnbaum Mesorah Matrix Series

HAVDALAH

Editors

David
Birnbaum & Cohen
Martin S.

Associate Editor: **Saul J. Berman**

EXPLORING HIGHER DIMENSIONS

New Paradigm Matrix™

MESORAH
MATRIX
VOLUME 7

LIGHTS OF CREATION & TRANSCENDENCE
David Birnbaum / Mesorah Matrix Series

SEARCH FOR MEANING

Editors

David
Birnbaum & Martin S.
Cohen

Associate Editor: **Saul J. Berman**

New Paradigm Matrix™

EXPLORING HIGHER DIMENSIONS

MESORAH
MATRIX
VOLUME 8

David Birnbaum / Mesorah Matrix Series
LIGHTS OF CREATION & TRANSCENDENCE

U-VACHARTA BA-CHAYIM

Editors

David
Birnbaum & Cohen
Martin S.

New Paradigm Matrix™

EXPLORING HIGHER DIMENSIONS

MESORAH MATRIX
VOLUME 9

LIGHTS OF CREATION & TRANSCENDENCE / Mesorah Matrix Series

David Birnbaum

Ehyeh asher Ehyeh

Editors

David
Birnbaum & Martin S.
Cohen

New Paradigm Matrix™

EXPLORING HIGHER DIMENSIONS

VOLUME 10

U'shamru

Editors

David
Birnbaum & Cohen
Martin S.

New Paradigm Matrix™

ESSAYISTS

Avivah Zornberg
Author

London, UK

David Ellenson
HUC-JIR

New York, NY

Saul Berman
Y.U. / Stern

New York, NY

Jonathan Sacks
United Hebrew
Congregations
London, UK

James Kugel
Bar Ilan University

Ramat Gan, Israel

Shalom Carmy
Yeshiva University,
Tradition Magazine
New York, NY

Rachel Barenblat
Bayit

Williamstown, MA

Rachel Friedman
Lamdeinu

New York, NY

W. Zeev Harvey
The Hebrew University of Jerusalem
Jerusalem

Rachel Adelman
Hebrew College

Newton Centre, MA

Shlomo Riskin
Ohr Torah Stone
Colleges
Efrat, Israel

Mark Goldfeder
Emory University

Atlanta, GA

Hillel Goldberg
Intermountain
Jewish News
Denver, CO

Lawrence
Schiffman
NYU
New York, NY

Alan Cooper
Jewish Theological
Seminary
New York, NY

Yonatan Feintuch
Bar Ilan University

Tel Aviv, Israel

Jacob Schacter
Yeshiva University

New York, NY

Aryeh Cohen
American Jewish
University
Los Angeles, CA

Avram Reisner
Chevrei Tzedek
Congregation
Baltimore, MD

Elliot Dorff
American Jewish
University
Los Angeles, CA

Michael Graetz
Congregation Eshel
Avraham
Omer, Israel

Steven Kepnes
Colgate University

Hamilton, NY

Reuven Bulka
Congregation
Machzikei Hadas
Ottawa, Canada

Adena Berkowitz
Kol Ha-neshamah

New York, NY

Alan Mittleman
Jewish Theological
Seminary
New York, NY

Tzvi Sinensky
Rosh Beit Midrash

Lower Merion, PA

Bradley Artson
American Jewish
University
Los Angeles, CA

Jill Jacobs
T'ruah: The Rabbinic
Call for Human Rights
New York, NY

Michael Broyde
Emory University

Atlanta, GA

Noam Zion
Hartman Institute

Jerusalem

Sid Schwarz
CLAL

New York, NY

Rahel Berkovits
Pardes Institute

Jerusalem

Howard Addison
Temple University

Philadelphia, PA

Robert Harris
Jewish Theological
Seminary
New York, NY

Samuel Lebens
Rutgers University

New Brunswick, NJ

Richard Hidary
Congregation
Shearith Israel
New York, NY

Jonathan Schorsch
Universität Potsdam
Potsdam
Germany

Eliezer Shore
Hebrew University
of Jerusalem
Jerusalem

Roberta Kwall
DePaul University
Law School
Chicago, IL

Alon Ferency
Heska Amuna
Synagogue
Knoxville, TN

Aubrey Glazer
Congregation Beth
Shalom
San Francisco, CA

Rebecca W. Sirbu
Rabbis Without
Borders, CLAL
New York, NY

Geoffrey Claussen
Elon University

Elon, NC

Jeremy Gordon
New London
Synagogue
London, U.K.

Shoshana Klein
Poupko
Ahavath Torah
Englewood, NJ

Michael
Wasserman
The New Shul
Scottsdale, AZ

Daniel Greyber
Beth El Synagogue

Durham, NC

Gail Labovitz
American Jewish
University
Los Angeles, CA

James Jacobson-Maisels
Or HaLev, Center for Jew-
ish Spirituality & Meditation
New York, NY

Yeshaya Dalsace
Dor Vador Com-
munaute Massorti
Paris, France

Kari Tuling
Congregation
Kol Haverim
Glastonbury, CT

Karyn Kedar
B'nai Jehoshua
Beth Elohim
Deerfield, IL

Nina Cardin
Rabbinical
Assembly
New York, NY

Aryeh Klapper
Center for Modern
Torah Leadership
Sharon, MA

Jonathan Wittenberg
New North London
Synagogue
London, UK

Michael Knopf
Temple Beth-El

Richmond, VA

Rivon Krygier
Congregation
Adath Shalom
Paris

Elie Spitz
Congregation
B'nai Israel
Tustin, CA

Ira Bedzow
Aspen Center for
Social Values
Aspen, CO

Yitzchak Blau
RCA

Jerusalem

Alfred Cohen
YU High School

New York, NY

Elliot Cosgrove
Park Avenue
Synagogue
New York, NY

Yehonatan
Chipman
Hitzei Yehonatan
Israel

David Flatto
Penn State Law

University Park, PA

Shohama H. Wiener
Temple Beth-El

City Island, NY

David Evan Markus
Temple Beth-El

City Island, NY

Nathaniel Helfgot
Yeshivat Chovevei
Torah
New York, NY

Cass Fisher
University of South
Florida
Tampa, FL

Admiel Kosman
Postdam University

Germany

Simcha Krauss
Eretz Hatzvi

Jerusalem

Melanie Landau
Monash University

Australia

Vernon Kurtz
North Suburban
Synagogue Beth-El
Highland Park, IL

Rolando Matalon
B'nai Jeshurun

New York, NY

Shmuly Yanklowitz
Valley Beit Midrash
President & Dean
Scottsdale, AZ

Peter Knobel
Beth Emet

Evanston, IL

Harvey Meirovich
Zacharias Frankel
College
Berlin, Germany

Aryeh Frimer
Bar-Ilan University

Ramat Gan

Martin Lockshin
York University

Ontario, Canada

Shai Cherry
Shaar Hamayim

Del Mar, CA

David Shatz
Yeshiva University

New York, NY

Jeremy Rosen
Persian Jewish
Center
New York, NY

David Greenstein
Congregation
Shomrei Emunah
Montclair, NJ

Avraham Walfish
Herzog College and
Michala Jerusalem
Tekoa, Israel

David Mescheloff
RCA

Israel

Barbara Thiede
UNC Charlotte

Concord, NC

Lawrence Troster
GreenFaith

Highland Park, NJ

Ruth Walfish
Herzog College and
Michala Jerusalem
Tekoa, Israel

Lenn Goodman
Vanderbilt
University
Nashville, TN

Dan Ornstein
Ohav Shalom

Albany, NY

Dena Freundlich
Ma'ayanot AMIT

Jerusalem

Elaine Goodfriend
California State
University
Northridge, CA

Berel Dov Lerner
Western Galilee
College, Herzl Inst
Northern Israel

Orna Triguboff
Neshama Life
Organisation
Sydney, Australia

Nehemia Polen
Hebrew College

Newton Centre, MA

Mark Greenspan
Oceanside Jewish
Center
Oceanside, NY

Richard Claman
Zeramim Journal

New York, NY

Avi Olitzky
Beth El Synagogue

St. Louis Park, MN

Michelle J. Levine
Stern College for Women
Yeshiva University
New York, NY

Yehuda Gellman
Ben-Gurion
University
Negev, Israel

Herbert Bronstein
Lake Forest
College,
Lake Forest, IL

Avraham Feder
Beit Knesset
Moreshet Yisrael
Jerusalem

Elyse Goldstein
City Shul

Ontario, Canada

Kerry M. Olitzky
Big Tent Judaism

New York, NY

Dalia Marx
Hebrew Union
College
Jerusalem

Jason Rubenstein
Mechon Hadar

New York, NY

Herbert Yoskowitz
Adat Shalom
Synagogue
Farmington Hills, MI

Mark Sameth
Pleasantville Com-
munity Synagogue
Westchester, NY

Catharine Clark
Congregation
Or Shalom
London, Ontario

Jacob Adler
Temple Shalom of
Northwest Arkansas
Fayetteville, AR

Jonathan Jacobs
John Jay College,
CUNY
New York, NY

David Kunin
Beth Shalom
Synagogue
Edmonton, AB

Michael Marmur
Hebrew Union
College
Jerusalem

Mordechai Luria
Institute for Jewish
Ideas & Ideals
New York, NY

Noah Farkas
Valley Beth Shalom

Encino, CA

Alex Maged
Yeshiva University

New York, NY

Hayyim Angel
Yeshiva University

New York, NY

Elie Kaunfer
Mechon Hadar

New York, NY

Alex Sztuden
The Herzl Institute

Jerusalem

David Golinkin
Schechter Institute
of Jewish Studies
Jerusalem

Mark Washofsky
Hebrew Union
College
Cincinnati, OH

Edwin C. Goldberg
Temple Sholom of
Chicago
Chicago, IL

Baruch Frydman-Kohl
Beth Tzedec
Congregation
Toronto, Canada

Ora Horn Prouser
Academy for
Jewish Religion
Yonkers, NY

Howard Wettstein
University of
California
Riverside, CA

Zvi Grumet
Yeshivat Eretz
Hatzvi
Jerusalem

Erica Brown
The Jewish
Federation
Rockville, MD

Meesh Hammer-Kossoy
Pardes Institute
of Jewish Studies
Jerusalem

Michael J. Cook
Hebrew Union
College
Cincinnati, OH

James Diamond
University of
Waterloo
Ontario, Canada

Shira Weiss
Ben Gurion
University
Beer Sheba, Israel

Gidon Rothstein

Bronx, NY

Ariel Mayse
Stanford University
Stanford,
California

Dr. Elyssa Wortzman
Mindful art-based
spiritual education
San Francisco

Ellen LeVee
Spertus Institute

Chicago, IL

Kim Treiger-Bar-Am
Tel Aviv

Israel

David Maayan
Boston College

Newton, MA

Senior Editors

Benjamin Blech
Yeshiva University

New York, NY

Martin S. Cohen
Shelter Rock,
Jewish Center
Roslyn, NY

21st CENTURY PUBLISHING

David.Birnbaum.NY@gmail.com

www.NewParadigmMatrix.com

Sanctification

'Sanctification'
from Essay by Chief Rabbi Lord Jonathan Sacks

... And there is the priestly task of kedushah, sanctifying
life by honouring the sacred ontology, the deep moral
structure of the universe, through the life of the 613
commands, a life of discipline and self-restraint, honesty
and integrity, respect and love, the code set out in the
chapter of the Torah that opens with the momentous
words, "Be holy for I, the Lord your God, am holy." Other
cultures and faiths drew inspiration from its wisdom and
prophetic traditions, but kedushah remained a specific
Jewish imperative that made us different. Even so, it
contains a message for the world, which Jews bear witness
to whenever and wherever they remain faithful to it.
Our vocation remains, to be mamlechet cohanim vegoi
kadosh, "a kingdom of priests and a holy nation."
- The Ethic of Holiness, August 2012

to view series updated authors list,

see www.MesorahMatrix.com

Mesorah Matrix Series

Editors

David Birnbaum

Martin S. Cohen

Benjamin Blech

Editor

- born in Zurich in 1933, is an Orthodox rabbi who now lives in New York City.

Rabbi Blech has been a Professor of Talmud at Yeshiva University since 1966, and was the Rabbi of Young Israel of Oceanside for 37 years. In addition to his work in the rabbinate, Rabbi Blech has written many books on Judaism and the Jewish people and speaks on Jewish topics to communities around the world.

Benjamin Blech
Yeshiva University,
"Understanding
Judaism"

Education

Rabbi Blech received a Bachelor of Arts degree from Yeshiva University, a Master of Arts degree in psychology from Columbia University, and rabbinic ordination from the Rabbi Isaac Elchanan Theological Seminary.

Milestones

Rabbi Blech is the author of twelve highly acclaimed and best selling books, with combined sales of close to half a million copies, including three as part of the highly popular Idiot's Guide series. His book, *Understanding Judaism*: The Basics of Deed and Creed, was chosen by the Union of Orthodox Jewish Congregations as "the single best book on Judaism in our generation".

Wikipedia online, http://en.wikipedia.org/wiki/Benjamin_Blech (accessed November 8, 2012)

Martin S. Cohen

Martin S. Cohen

Martin S. Cohen has been a Senior Editor of the inter-denominational Mesorah Matrix series since 2012.

From 2000-2014, he served as Chairman of the Publications Committee of the quarterly journal *Conservative Judaism*, which was under the joint auspices of the JTS (Jewish Theological Seminary) and the RA (Rabbinical Assembly) during that span.

Rabbi Cohen also served as the senior editor of *The Observant Life*, a compendium of Jewish law, custom published by the Rabbinical Assembly in 2012.

Martin's weekly blog can be viewed at www.TheRuminativeRabbi. blogspot.com. He serves as rabbi of the Shelter Rock Jewish Center in Roslyn, New York.

Rabbi Cohen was educated at the City University of New York and at Jewish Theological Seminary of America, where he was ordained a rabbi and received his Ph.D. in Ancient Judaism. He is the recipient of fellowships at the Hebrew University (Jerusalem) in 1983 and Harvard University in 1993.

Martin Cohen has taught at Hunter College, the Jewish Theological Seminary of America, the Institute for Jewish Studies of the University of Heidelberg, as well as at the University of British Columbia and the Vancouver School of Theology.

His published works include *The Boy on the Door on the Ox* (2008) and *Our Haven and Our Strength: A Translation and Commentary on the Book of Psalms* (2004).

Rabbi Cohen is currently writing a translation and commentary on the Torah and the Five Megillot.

Saul Berman
Mesorah Editor

Saul Berman
Yeshiva University,
Stern College

Saul J. Berman is one of the world's leading Jewish intellects.

He is an American Jewish scholar and Modern Orthodox rabbinic.

Rabbi Berman was ordained at Yeshiva University, from which he also received his B.A. and his M.H.L. He completed a degree in law, a J.D., at New York University, and an M.A. in Political Sciesnce at the University of California, Berkeley, where he studied with David Daube. He spent two years studying mishpat ivri in Israel at Hebrew University of Jerusalem and at Tel Aviv University. He did advanced studies in Jewish Law at Hebrew University and Tel Aviv University Law Schools. Since 1971 Rabbi Berman serves as Associate Professor of Jewish Studies at Stern College for Women of Yeshiva University. Rabbi Berman was Rabbi of Congregation Beth Israel of Berkeley CA (1963-1969), Young Israel of Brookline, MA (1969-1971) and of Lincoln Square Synagogue in Manhattan (1984-1990.) Since 1990 he has served as an Adjunct Professor at Columbia University School of Law, where he teaches a seminar in Jewish Law. Aside his academic appointments, from 1997 until 2006.

Rabbi Berman is a contributor to the *Encyclopedia Judaica* and is the author of numerous articles which have been published in journals such as *Tradition, Judaism, Journal of Jewish Studies, Dinei Yisrael*, and others.

Rabbi Berman was the founder and director of the Edah organization for the promotion of Modern Orthodoxy. Edah was ultimately absorbed into Yeshivat Chovevei Torah.

He is married to Shellee Berman; they have four children and seven grandchildren.

Wikipedia online, http://en.wikipedia.org/wiki/Saul_Berman (accessed February 15, 2013) +
The Tikvah Center for Law & Jewish Civilization online, http://www.nyutikvah.org/fellows/
saul_berman.html (accessed February 15, 2013)

Shalom Carmy
Contributing Editor

Shalom Carmy is an Orthodox rabbi teaching Jewish Studies and philosophy atYeshiva University, where he is Chair of Bible and Jewish Philosophy at Yeshiva College. He is an affiliated scholar at Cardozo Law School of Yeshiva University. He is also Editor of Tradition, an Orthodox theological journal.

Shalom Carmy
Yeshiva University,
Tradition Magazine

A Brooklyn native, he is a prominent Modern Orthodox theologian, historian, and philosopher. He received his B.A. in 1969 and M.S. from Yeshiva University, and received his rabbinic ordination from its affiliated Rabbi Isaac Elchanan Theological Seminary, studying under Rabbis Aharon Lichtenstein and Joseph Soloveitchik. He has edited some of R. Soloveitchik's work for publication. Carmy has written many articles on Biblical theology, Jewish thought, Orthodoxy in the 20th century, and the role of liberal arts in Torah education. He edited "*Modern Scholarship in the Study of Torah*: Contributions and Limitations" (ISBN 1-56821-450-2), "*Jewish Perspectives on the Experience of Suffering*", as well as several other works. He writes a regular personal column in *Tradition*, and contributes regularly on Jewish and general subjects to *First Things* and other journals. In addition to his exegetical and analytic work, Carmy's theological contribution is distinguished by preoccupation with the way religious doctrine and practice express themselves in the life of the individual.

David Birnbaum

Saul Berman

Benjamin Blech

Martin S. Cohen

Shalom Carmy

Mesorah Matrix
SENIOR EDITORIAL BOARD

- **David Birnbaum**
  Editor-in-Chief
  author, Summa Metaphysica series

- **Martin S. Cohen**
  Senior Editor
  former editor, Conservative Judaism quarterly

- **Benjamin Blech**
  Senior Editor
  author, academic, scholar & lecturer

- **Saul Berman**
  Senior Editor
  author, academic, scholar & lecturer

- **Shalom Carmy**
  Contributing Editor
  editor, Tradition Magazine

LIGHTS OF CREATION & TRANSCENDENCE

David Birnbaum

Mesorah Matrix Series

March 2018

www.MesorahMatrix.com

www.NewParadigmMatrix.com

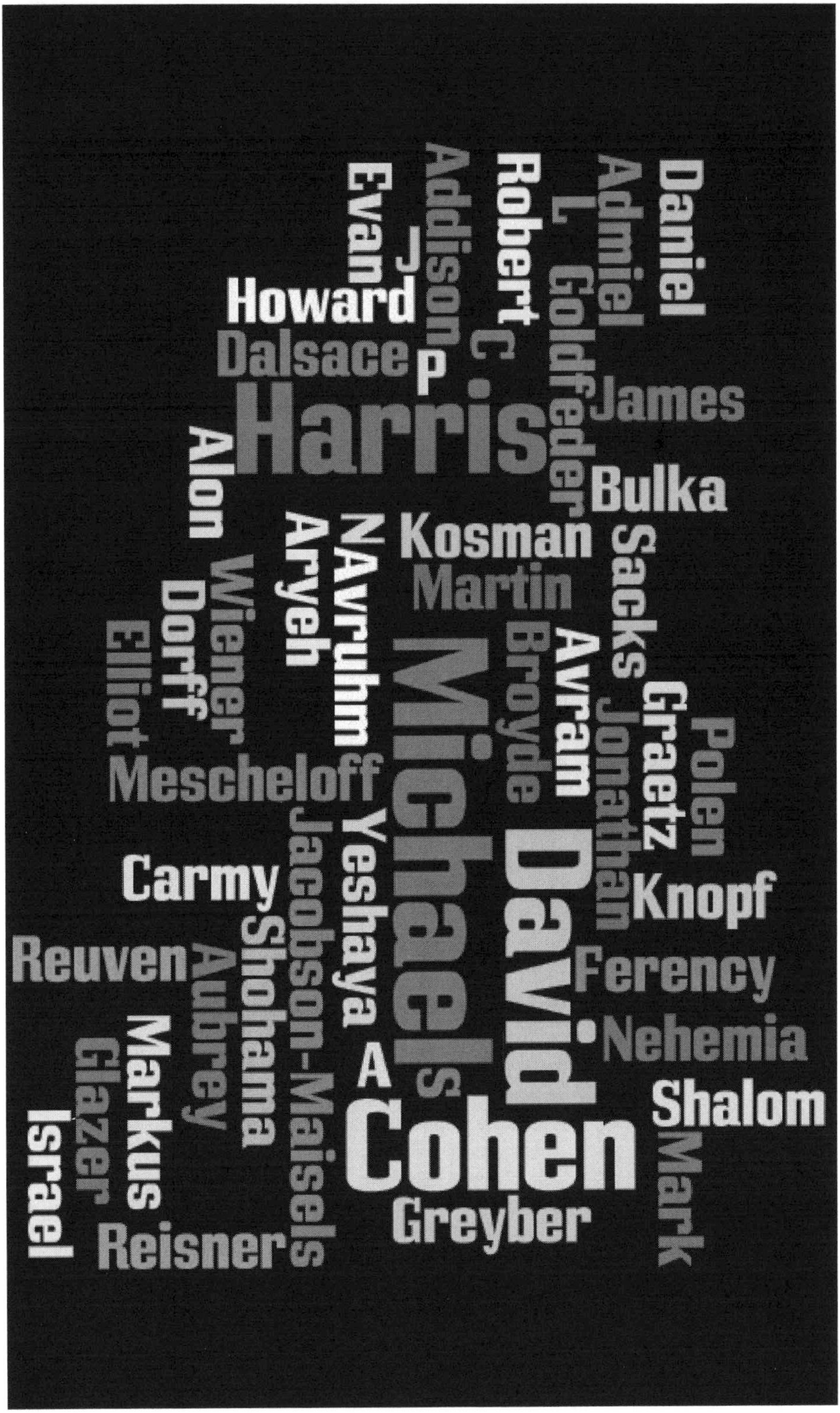

Daniel
Admiel
L
Goldfeder
Robert
C
Addison
P
J
Evan
Howard
Dalsace
Harris
James
Bulka
Alon
Kosman
Martin
Sacks
N
Avruhm
Aryeh
Wiener
Dorff
Elliot
Broyde
Avram
Jonathan
Graetz
Polen
Michael
Mescheloff
Yeshaya
Jacobson-Maisels
Carmy
David
Knopf
Reuven
Aubrey
Shohama
Ferency
Nehemia
Markus
Glazer
Israel
A
S
Cohen
Shalom
Mark
Greyber
Reisner

For the mountains shall erode

and the hills indeed collapse,

but My grace towards you shall never waver.

- Isaiah 54:10

כִּי הֶהָרִים יָמוּשׁוּ

וְהַגְּבָעוֹת תְּמוּטֶינָה

וְחַסְדִּי מֵאִתֵּךְ לֹא יָמוּשׁ

יְשַׁעְיָהוּ 54:10 -

21st CENTURY PUBLISHING

David Birnbaum
Editor-in-Chief

New Paradigm Matrix
att: David Birnbaum
Tower 49
12 E 49th St.
11th Floor
New York, NY 10017

David.Birnbaum.NY@gmail.com

$16.00 / book

Birkat Kohanim

ISBN: 978-0-9961995-1-3

Made in the USA
Monee, IL
30 August 2022

12918961R00300